MUSEUM BARBERINI

POTSDAM

Gerhard Richter
Abstraction

A publication series by the Museum Barberini
Edited by
Ortrud Westheider and Michael Philipp

Exhibition
Dietmar Elger
Ortrud Westheider
with Valerie Hortolani

With contributions by
Janice Bretz
Hubertus Butin
Dietmar Elger
Valerie Hortolani
Matthias Krüger
Kerstin Küster
Ortrud Westheider
Armin Zweite

PRESTEL Munich · London · New York

Lenders to the exhibition

Museum Frieder Burda, Baden-Baden
The "M" Art Foundation, Belgium
Block Collection, Berlin
Staatliche Museen zu Berlin, Nationalgalerie
Kunsthalle Bremen – Der Kunstverein in Bremen
Gerhard Richter Archive, Staatliche Kunstsammlungen Dresden
Museum Küppersmühle für Moderne Kunst, Duisburg
Stedelijk van Abbemuseum, Eindhoven
Kunsthalle Emden – Stiftung Henri und Eske Nannen und Schenkung Otto van de Loo
Olbricht Collection, Essen
Hamburger Kunsthalle
Sprengel Museum Hannover
Stefan Asbrand-Eickhoff, Hesse
Gion Collection, Japan
Kunstmuseen Krefeld
Würth Collection, Künzelsau
Collezione Prada, Milan
Städtische Galerie im Lenbachhaus und Kunstbau, Munich
Neues Museum. Staatliches Museum für Kunst und Design, Nuremberg
Vanmoerkerke Collection, Ostend
Fundação de Serralves, Museu de Arte Contemporânea, Porto
Museum Wiesbaden
Migros Museum für Gegenwartskunst, Zurich
Anthony d'Offay

as well as private collections which do not wish to be named

Foreword

Gerhard Richter's work has already been honored in major retrospectives. In 2002, the Museum of Modern Art in New York devoted a solo show to the artist. In 2011, Tate Modern in London, the Neue Nationalgalerie in Berlin, and the Centre Pompidou in Paris mounted an exhibition that took a wide-ranging view of Richter's life work, as encapsulated in its title, *Panorama*. Our exhibition, *Gerhard Richter: Abstraction*, also traces a broad arc from the 1960s to more recent works that have not yet been seen in public. Unlike the retrospectives, however, the exhibition at the Museum Barberini concentrates upon a theme crucial to Richter's painting: abstraction.

In the 1960s, "abstraction" was a word which often triggered negative emotions in both East and West Germany. In East Germany, where Richter began studying at the Dresden Academy of Fine Arts in 1951, abstract art was attacked as an elitist, aloof, and Western style. In West Germany, where Richter continued his studies at the Düsseldorf Art Academy from 1961 onward, abstraction was already regarded as conservative, because new art was being created using new forms of expression, and painting seemed obsolete. Richter seized upon the unpopular abstract style to reexamine the possibilities of painting. It also allowed him to draw connections to the modernist tradition denounced by the Nazis, and gave him the opportunity to shape a sustainable way of painting. *Gerhard Richter: Abstraction* shows his development from the black-and-white Photo paintings and Color Charts to the Detail paintings, the Gray paintings, the Inpaintings, and the Abstract paintings, as Richter often titled his works from the late 1970s onward.

Abstraction is Richter's method, because it takes him out of visible reality and creates a new kind of reality that can be discovered through art. In 2016, the year before the Museum Barberini opened, the Hasso Plattner Foundation acquired the 1986 Abstract painting *A B, Quiet* [612-4] (cat. 63), which prompted us to propose an exhibition on the theme of abstraction to the artist himself. To our great delight, Richter agreed, and supported the exhibition with numerous loans of his own works, some of which have never been seen before. He also carefully considered the concept for our exhibition and contributed his own ideas. This exploration took place during a time when he was intently focused on preparing his exhibition at New York's Metropolitan Museum of Art in 2019. Together with Dietmar Elger, director of the Gerhard Richter Archive at the Staatliche Kunstsammlungen Dresden and cocurator of the exhibition in Potsdam, I would like to thank the artist for his generosity.

The exhibition catalog draws on a public symposium that took place on March 5, 2018, at the Museum Barberini. I join with Michael Philipp, the chief curator at the Museum Barberini and coeditor of Museum Barberini's publications, in thanking all of the authors for their latest research on Richter's abstract works, which can be read in this book. We would also like to express our gratitude to Valerie Hortolani, curator at the Museum Barberini, for editing the texts and supporting the curators in realizing the exhibition. In doing so, she worked closely with Konstanze Ell of Atelier Richter and Kerstin Küster of the Gerhard Richter Archive, and we are indebted to them both for their support.

We are grateful to Dietmar Elger and the Gerhard Richter Archive for arranging the loan of many rarely exhibited works from over twenty private collections. We are pleased that, in only its second year of existence, the Museum Barberini enjoys these collectors' trust. Our thanks also go to our colleagues at museums in Germany and abroad who have agreed to lend their works.

Abstraction runs like a golden thread through Richter's painting. As volatile and diverse as his changes from one phase to the next may have seemed to some of his contemporaries, Richter's work has nonetheless resolutely furthered and transformed abstraction. We hope that our visitors will enjoy tracing this resolute development across more than five decades in Gerhard Richter's oeuvre.

Ortrud Westheider
Director, Museum Barberini

Translated from the German by Allison Moseley

Across Art History: Gerhard Richter and Abstraction

Ortrud Westheider

Gerhard Richter paints abstract pictures. To this day. In the 1970s he began a series known as the Abstract paintings, and he has been working on it ever since. Yet his exploration of abstract art is not limited to this series alone, and nor did it begin with it. Instead, the relationship between abstraction and realism has left its mark on Richter's entire oeuvre. His work deals with abstraction as a method of painting, and is therefore deeply rooted in art history. Richter reflects upon the liberating ideas of modernism and contrasts them critically with the idealism of a "universal language" of abstraction. This universalism influenced the understanding of art in West Germany when Richter left the German Democratic Republic for the Federal Republic of Germany in 1961. There, new art had begun to respond to a Germany ideologically divided between socialist realism and informalism by "departing from the picture"[1] and turning its back on painting. Richter, too, played with these ideas and cofounded a group of artists who called their movement "capitalist realism" and tested new forms of expression through their actions.[2]

Painting Systems

Number one in his catalogue raisonné, however, is a painting titled *Table* [1] (1962, fig. 1). A year after he left the GDR, the painter confronted a depiction of an everyday object with a nonrepresentational swirl of color. The shift from one system to another was carried out in a two-stage process. First, he created a realistic image of an object found in every household. The table is a place of togetherness, from family meals to banquets. People talk, study, write, compose poetry, and also do practical work at tables. In its universality, the object Richter chose is in no way secondary to the painterly gesture he added to it. In the West it was considered an ideologeme for artistic freedom.

In West Germany from the late 1950s onward, abstract art had established a sense of exclusivity through European informalism and American abstract expressionism, which made it difficult or even impossible to connect to the work of the older generation of new objectivity painters before the Nazi era.[3] Mass murder, persecution, and the questioning of individualism had shaken the foundations of humanism that had nurtured modernist abstract art and its idealistic model of antimaterialism. Existentialism was a philosophy much admired by artists, and it centered on the individual.

In this context, after the end of World War II, the most important reinterpretation of abstraction in art history took place in Western Europe and America: Vasily Kandinsky's idealistic pursuit of the grand gesture became the spontaneous self-expression of the individual artist. Jackson Pollock's action paintings (fig. p. 61), for example, demonstrated pure subjectivity, and once again the painterly gesture embodied the presence of the painter/creator. After the failure of the great ideologies, artists overwhelmed viewers with nonhierarchically organized large-scale works and challenged them to form their own opinions. Whereas East German artists sought suitable visual motifs and artistic methods to explore the theme of social progress as a collective experience within the socialist order of the GDR, individualism in the West was literalized and identified with abstraction.[4] Karl Otto Götz, Richter's teacher at the Düsseldorf Art Academy, represented this generation of artists (fig. 2). Richter had seen and photographed Götz's work, as well as paintings by Pollock and other American abstract artists at the II. documenta in Kassel in 1959. Back in Dresden, he tried out the informalist style for himself.[5]

Yet Richter's kind of abstract art should not be equated with an uncritical affirmation of the Western ideologeme. In the GDR he had become familiar with the aims of socialist realism through his studies at the Dresden Academy of Fine Arts, and through the formalism debate[6] he had been exposed to the defamation of abstract art as a decadent expression of the capitalist bourgeoisie. After leaving the GDR, though, he encountered the emphasis on abstraction in West Germany, as well as the protests of a younger generation of artists who were critical of this fixation.

In Düsseldorf, Richter attended the fluxus actions by Joseph Beuys and Nam June Paik. They gave art a new twist, added new methods of expression and media, and expanded the concept of art. Richter, however, sought opportunities beyond the polarity of figurative and abstract art. Looking back, he observed: "I was looking for a third way in which Eastern realism and Western modernism would be resolved into one redeeming construct."[7] In this context, the painting *Table* [1] should not be regarded as a way of replacing the realist system with abstraction. The object is not painted over with a painterly gesture intended to obliterate it and depart from the path of realism in favor of abstraction. Richter's third way initially opened up in the Photo paintings. Realistically capturing/citing a found, mass-produced object gave him neutrality. This was how he was able to grasp realism (in the sense of

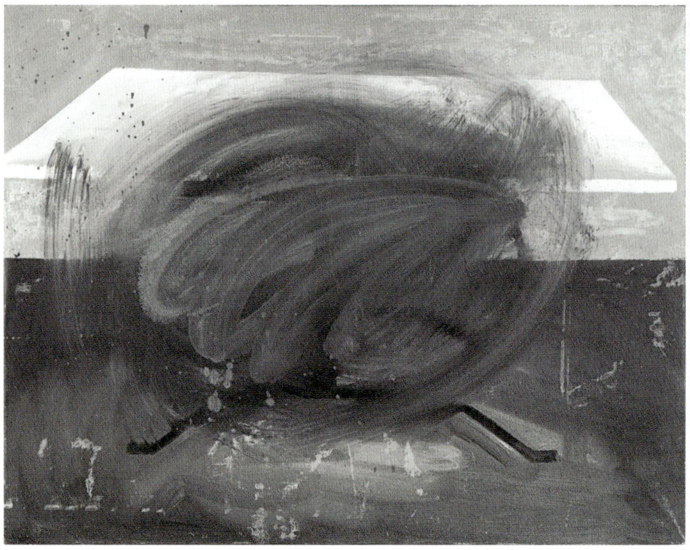

1 Gerhard Richter: *Table* [1], 1962
Oil on canvas, 90 × 113 cm
Harvard Art Museums/
Busch-Reisinger Museum, Cambridge, MA,
on loan from a private collection

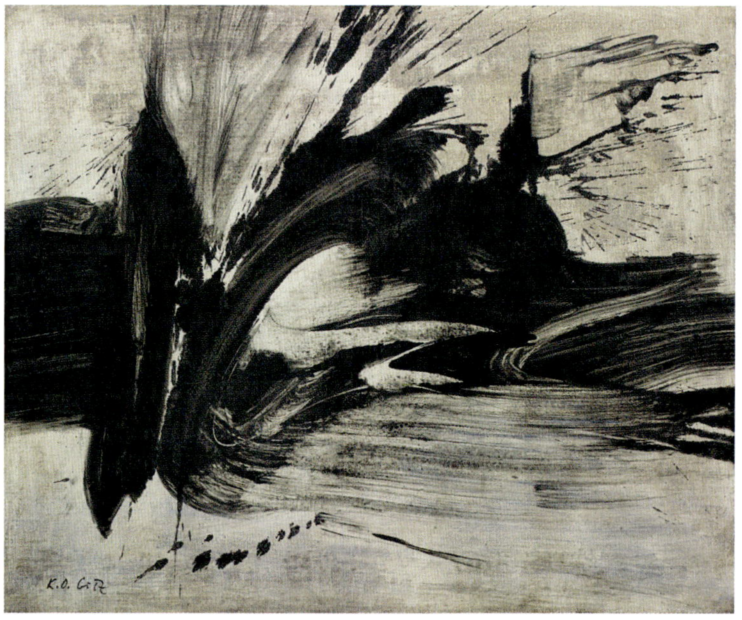

2 Karl Otto Götz: *Mymel*, 1960
Mixed technique on canvas, 100 × 120 cm
Saarlandmuseum Saarbrücken

the German pop art he propagated)[8] while at the same time separating abstraction from its ideological function in the conflict between East and West Germany. For Richter, however, the most important thing about this third way was that his Photo paintings made it possible for him to carry on painting.[9]

From the early 1960s onward, Richter went through a variety of very diverse phases. In the 1980s, critics were still reacting with skepticism to new stages of his oeuvre, accusing him of randomness.[10] This essay investigates how Richter—in clinging to painting and continuing the search for a third way between realism and nonobjectivity—continually worked to convey the realism of the illusory, while citing and updating modernism.[11] This text is divided into two parts. In the first, two contemporary depictions of the history of abstract art form a context for Richter's artistic references. The second analyzes Richter's citations of avant-garde artists such as Marcel Duchamp, Alexander Rodchenko, and Piet Mondrian, interpreting the development of his style as an act of critical commentary.

Abstraction: The Sources

In the 1960s, several art historians began writing about the antecedents of abstract art. They did not primarily consider modernism a break with the traditions of realist art. Rather, they traced the abstract tendencies of art all the way back to antiquity. Richter's works stem from his examination of these sources.

Heinrich Lützeler's book *Abstrakte Malerei* is marked by the immediate postwar situation in which he—a professor of art history and dean of the faculty at the University of Bonn—committed himself to the recovery of academic life after the end of the Nazi era. Even though it was not published until 1961, his book reflects the situation of abstract and nonobjective art during its process of rehabilitation after having been outlawed under the Nazis. Lützeler described abstract art as a European phenomenon that found resonance in America. He identified Japan and Japanese calligraphy as the most important sources of inspiration.[12] Lützeler began his history of the development of abstract art with Paul Cézanne. In his explanation of the concept, though, he equated abstract art with nonrepresentational art. This was not a self-evident assertion, since the first definition of abstraction is simply *abs-trahere*, drawing or moving away from the object. Lützeler was however writing from a background influenced by Christianity and Paul Klee's notion of an "expanded creation,"[13] and so he targeted the nonobjective, suggesting the term "concrete art" for it.[14] At the same time he elucidated numerous "abstract features" in representational art from the early Christian era onward[15] and presented a first collection of influential philosophical source texts, beginning with Plato's allegory of the cave.

On his search for a path between realism and nonrepresentational art, Gerhard Richter addressed himself to some of the central references in artistic discourse since antiquity. The curtain motif comprises a first group of works in Richter's oeuvre that is not based on photographs (cat. 1, 2).[16] In these paintings the artist adhered to photographic, documentary-style black, white, and gray.[17] The motif itself can be traced back to Pliny the Elder, who, in his *Naturalis historia* (circa 77 CE), reports the argument between the painters Zeuxis and Parrhasius about the authenticity of art. According to Pliny, Parrhasius had painted a curtain in such a deceptively realistic way that his opponent allegedly demanded that the curtain be pushed aside, so that he could study the painting.[18] Richter's painting is a detail of a curtain. He cites the motif showing the bottom hem of the curtain. His concern is not to replicate the illusion that Pliny had discussed; instead, it seems as if he is folding the canvas. As the body of the painting itself began to be treated as an object in the 1950s, this was a practice that could be found in the works of Düsseldorf's ZERO artists, such as Günther Uecker and Herbert Zangs. Still, Richter's study of the curtain motif and his reference to painting's ubiquitous tradition of playing with cloth folds remain firmly within the medium of painting.[19]

In 1964, Otto Stelzer published his book *Die Vorgeschichte der abstrakten Kunst*. Unlike Lützeler, Stelzer traced the sources of abstraction against the backdrop of informalist art.[20] Stelzer had been a professor at the Hamburg University of Fine Arts since 1955. He was interested in the role of chance and in liberating the painting from signature brushwork. Stelzer's agenda excluded geometrical abstraction. He also equated abstraction with nonobjective art. Stelzer's book was influential because it did not regard the history of modern art as a break with tradition, but traced abstract strategies in painting and literature back to the eighteenth century. Even though Richter did not read the book, he would have encountered Stelzer's ideas, because they were generally discussed among artists and at art schools.

Stelzer pursued the question of whether there is such a thing as art without form, and expanded his field of investigation beyond the nonobjective to the formless.[21] In his disquisition on this question he added Leonardo da Vinci's traditional rejection of the landscape study to the history of abstract art. One need only throw a sponge at the wall and, with a little imagination, turn the impression it makes into a landscape of sorts. He also cited Leonardo's recommendation that artists should study rough, stained walls in order to discover faces or landscapes in them. Clouds, too, provided opportunities to observe the *trasmutazione di forme*, the constant transformation of nature, and to find parallels in art.[22]

Richter, who has spoken vaguely about the beauty of Leonardo's work in interviews,[23] has reacted to Leonardo's recommendations repeatedly and in many different ways over time. He began his series of Cloud paintings in 1967, continuing to work on them until the early 1970s. Whereas the pioneers of cloud painting in the eighteenth and nineteenth centuries—artists such as Alexander Cozens, William Turner, and Pierre-Auguste Renoir—translated Leonardo's advice into a form of blot painting, which culminated in straightforward formlessness, Richter followed a middle way via photography, as evidenced by the many photographic sources in his *Atlas*. Even though some of these paintings seem like a consequential further development of his monochromatic Gray paintings (cat. 25, 26), the photos in the *Atlas* show that Richter did not, for instance, lighten the gray surfaces with freehand brushwork because he observed passing, ephemeral manifestations in the sky. Richter acted counter to Leonardo's advice and the modern adaptations executed by the nineteenth-century cloud painters. Following his work with the photographic source, he moved on to a motif that inspires formlessness in a mimetic, realistic style, thus tying one of abstract art's most powerful and enduring leitmotifs to photorealist painting.[24] The results are so reminiscent of romantic art that Richter's Cloud paintings are never linked to the German pop that Richter advocated in the 1960s, although they do in fact belong in this category.

Richter also employed informalist pictorial structures in photographically enlarged views of his own paintings. He blew up and zoomed in on the paint itself as a material, in order to reproduce it in a larger format as in the painting *Detail (Makart)* [288] (cat. 29).[25] Here, the formlessness of the paint becomes equivalent to constantly changing cloud forms. Since it can give shape to everything, the potentiality of paint is thematized. Yet just as he did with the group of Cloud paintings, Richter interposes photography, a medium that fixes the moment. In doing so, he distances himself from any sort of emphasis ascribed to the processes of informalist art—the kinds of emphases found in Stelzer's reception of Leonardo and in his reading of Jean Paul's ideas about the correspondences between the very large and distant and the very small and nearby: for example, when wagon tracks on clay roads are described as high mountains.[26]

Richter's interest in Leonardo's theory of association can be traced into the 1990s. One cannot help seeing things in his Abstract paintings.[27] The title of his squeegeed painting *Wall* [808] (cat. 70), which was not based on a photograph, alludes to the renaissance painter's practice of associating spots on a wall with objects and landscapes. In this painting, Richter moved the squeegee in parallel, vertical stripes, one after the next, across the surface of the canvas, blending the last color, a brilliant carmine red, with the dark ground. This results in a texture similar to wood. Removing the paint creates a kind of motif: Like the curtain and the wall, the wall made out of wooden slats is tied to the phenomenon of optical illusions in art discourse.[28]

As early as 1965, Richter had referred to the trompe-l'oeil tradition (fig. 4) in a group of paintings called *Turned Sheets* (fig. 3), the theme of which is the gaze that underlies the painting.[29] In Richter's paintings, one white sheet of paper lies underneath another. He is concerned only with turning over various layers and making them visible. He has also been examining the theme of layering since the 1990s in his Photo Overpaintings (cat. 56–61). Within the series, there is one work that is again identified as a *Wall* (fig. 5). The photo is of a perfect, white garden wall. The paint is slapped on top in vertical blocks—walls of paint that obstruct the view, leaving only few gaps that allow the viewer to see through. Even in a small format, Richter achieves monumentalism. He presents paint as both raw material and a powerful texture.

In the subtitle of the 1964 painting *Curtain (Morandi)* [58] (private collection, New York), Richter renders homage to the Italian painter. This is one of his rare explicit references to other artists. It takes on added significance in light of Richter's study of the sources of abstraction, because Giorgio Morandi represents a position between abstraction and realism. Even before he left the GDR, Richter

3 Gerhard Richter: *Turned Sheet* [70-1], 1965
Oil on canvas, 24 × 18 cm
Private collection, Düsseldorf

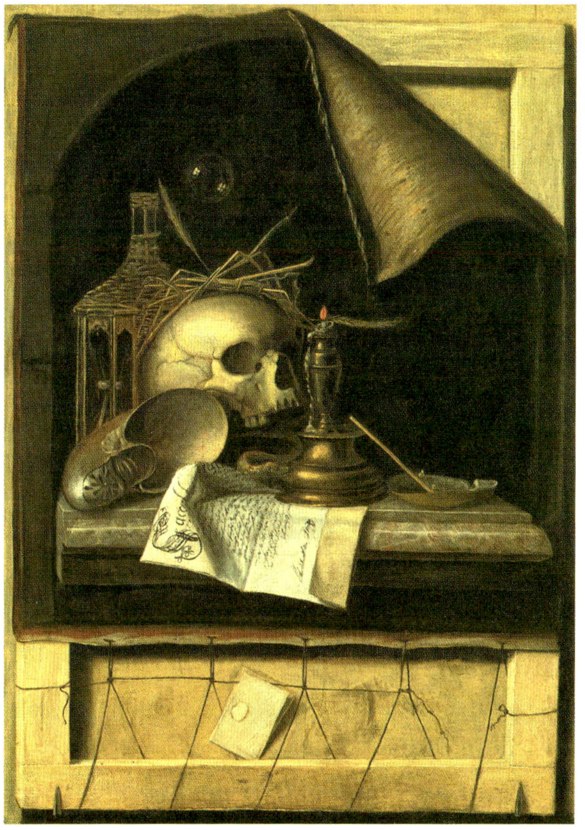

4 Cornelis Gijsbrechts: *Vanitas*, circa 1680
Oil on canvas, 89 × 62 cm
Private collection

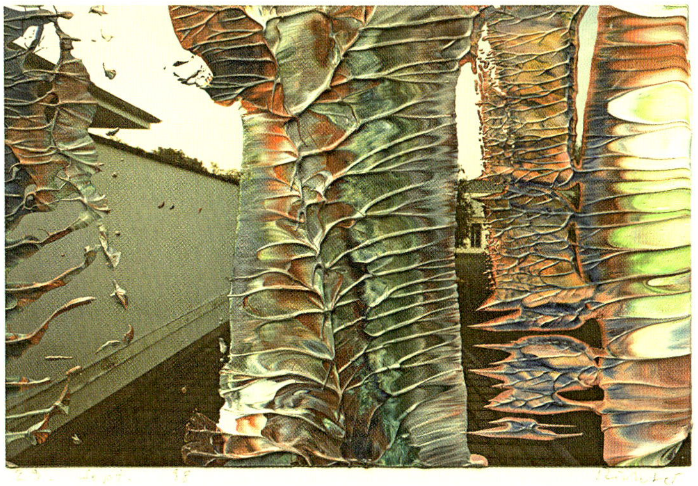

5 Gerhard Richter: *Sept. 29, 98 (Wall)*, 1998
Oil on color photograph, 9.8 × 14.5 cm
Munich Re Art Collection, Munich

had painted still lifes inspired by Morandi. He had seen works by the Italian painter (fig. 6) at the II. documenta in Kassel in 1959. Morandi's still lifes are variations on diverse constellations of solid figures: jars and bottles whose color scheme is concentrated upon very few colors. This resulted in works with stripped-down colors and forms that explore the themes of surface and volume. Realism and abstraction balance each other, and this is what made Morandi so attractive to Richter in his search for a third way. In 1965, Richter produced several sculptures made of PVC or cardboard tubes painted in oils (fig. 7), which are reminiscent of Morandi's reduced volumes. As was the case with the Curtain paintings, Richter painted the tubes in black, white, and various grays, creating an illusion that doubles the actual volume.

Richter used grisaille for motifs such as corrugated metal, tubes, doors, and, since 1968, windows (cat. 4), alluding here to the *paragone* between painting and sculpture that rose to prominence in artist treatises during the latter half of the fifteenth century. Richter's exploration of the comparisons between these media probably goes back to his days as a student at the Dresden Academy of Fine Arts, where he was taught mural painting. Among the works he completed in the GDR is a wall mural for the Dresden Hygiene Museum. Ever since then, the interplay with architecture has been one of his themes.[30] In Düsseldorf, Richter continued to paint curtains and windows, iconic motifs that point to the medium itself. Since the Renaissance, the window has represented the most effective metaphor for painting. The reduction to black and white, which is very close to architecture, and the framing that relates to the surface of the painting, brought him shortly afterward to create the first of his glass objects (fig. 8, cat. 79).

Richter was referring to painting's art historical foundations at a time when the genre was generally suspected of conveying a bourgeois, reactionary concept of art. Arte povera, minimal art, and performance and video art saw artists in both Europe and America setting off in new directions. By contrast, Richter legitimized painting by studying its foundations. This alone, however, does not explain his art. Through this exploration, his paintings take on an objectivity that robs realism of its deceptiveness and abstract art of its emotion. It fluctuates independently between media. Richter's third way took his work far beyond his Photo paintings.

Links to Modernism: Duchamp, Rodchenko, Mondrian

In summer 1965, Gerhard Richter attended the exhibition *Marcel Duchamp: Ready-mades, Objects, Collages, Sculptures* (Marcel Duchamp. Ready-mades, Objekte, Collagen, Skulpturen) at the Museum Haus Lange in Krefeld. Duchamp's utilization of the objet trouvé imbued the Rhineland art scene with the impetus to develop artworks referring to the exhibition space. Richter also took inspiration from the exhibition, returning with ideas for an installation with four panes of glass (fig. 8). Yet unlike many of his artist friends, Richter again brought his exploration of Duchamp back to painting.

In this first glass object, Richter followed the early twentieth-century avant-garde tradition, which regarded glassy transparency as the ideal realization of the utopia of the spiritual in art.[31] Surfaces seem to dematerialize in glass. Still, glass was an austere material and not an illusion. Glass released the painter from having to decide upon a color. After reducing his colors to black, white, and gray, this was the next logical step. It raised the question of whether this experiment would lead the painter permanently to sculpture in its current form, the installation. Richter, however, continued to contemplate the possibilities for expanding painting. At the same time the anti-form movement, represented by Robert Morris (and his hanging felt sculptures) and Richard Serra (with his lead splashings), used the medium of sculpture to track the morphology of the unformed, which opposed geometrical abstraction.[32] Yet in parallel with his work with glass, Richter found a way to employ the cloud motif to channel elements of traditional landscape painting into the discourse about formlessness.

In 1966, he began his series of Color Chart paintings (cat. 13–20). Twenty years later, Richter recalled, "when I painted my first color charts in 1966, that had more to do with Pop Art. They were copies of paint sample cards, and what was effective about them was that they were directed against the efforts of the Neo-Constructivists, Albers and the rest."[33] Richter's reference to Duchamp, therefore, took him back to the medium of painting. With the help of the color cards he found, he was able, however, to separate himself from the continuity of geometrical abstraction promulgated by Josef Albers, and grounded his own kind of abstraction on new terrain (see the essay by Hubertus Butin, pp. 34–45).

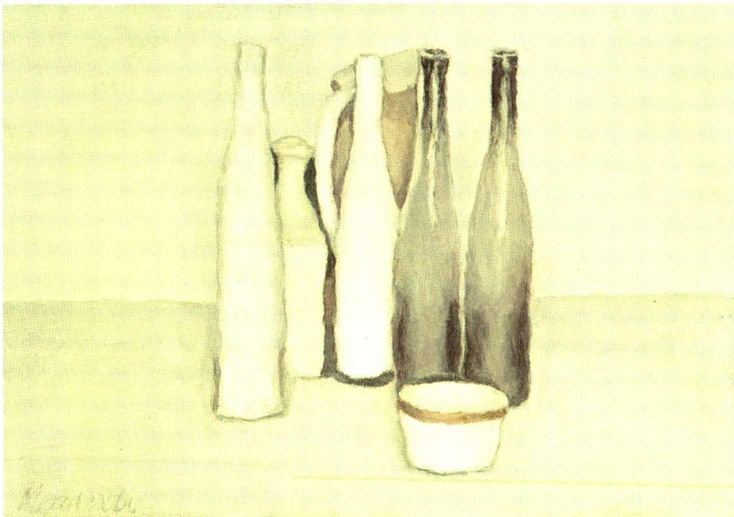

6 Giorgio Morandi: *Still Life*, 1956
Oil on canvas, 30 × 44 cm
Private collection

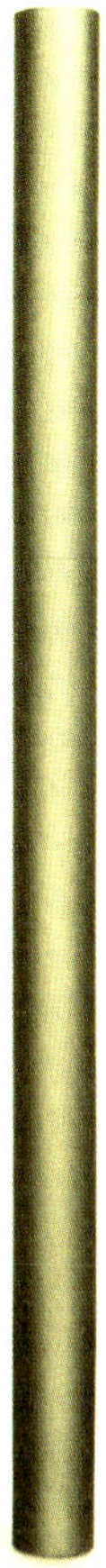

7 Gerhard Richter: *Tube* [59-c], 1965
Oil on cardboard tube, 202.5 × 12 × 12 cm
Private collection

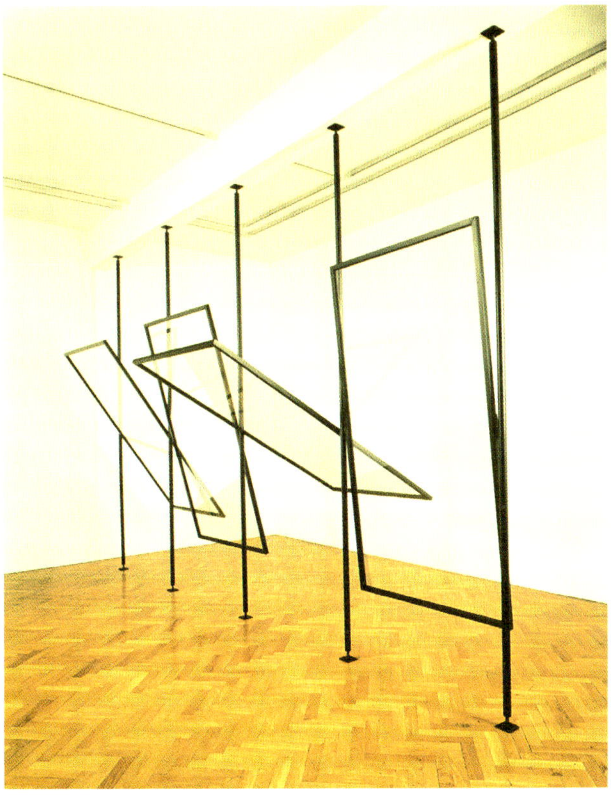

8 Gerhard Richter: *4 Panes of Glass* [160], 1967
Four glass panes in steel frames, each 190 × 100 cm
Herbert Collection, Ghent

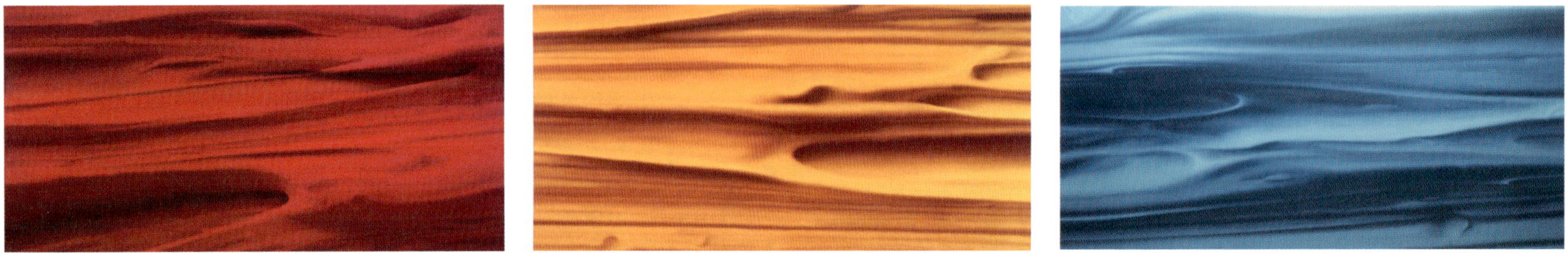

9 Gerhard Richter: *Red—Yellow—Blue* [345-1 to 345-3], 1973
Oil on canvas, each 300 × 600 cm
BMW Collection, Munich

10 Alexander Rodchenko:
Pure Color Red, *Pure Color Yellow*, and *Pure Color Blue*, 1921
Oil on canvas, each 62.5 × 52.7 cm
Rodchenko/Stepanova Collection, Moscow

While Richter used opaque colors to create a flat, non-relational type of painting in his Color Charts, in the Inpaintings, which were completed in parallel to the Gray paintings, he returned to modulating the material, and hence to the characteristic style of painting and its representations of the artist individual (cat. 21–24). In the neutral Gray paintings (cat. 25–27), the brushwork takes center stage, while the series of gray Mirrors took the opposite approach (cat. 75). This juxtaposition of different modes of painting recalls the dispute between advocates of surfaces that have the glazed, smooth, cohesive style of photography, and the impasto style that broke the academic rules of scumble in the nineteenth century. Jean-Léon Gérôme represents one side of the debate, and Vincent van Gogh the other.[34] In its freehanded, gestural application of paint, Van Gogh's painting exposes the traces of the individual.

In the Inpaintings (cat. 21–24), Richter worked the still-damp paint into the canvas with a broad brush, blending it evenly across the entire surface of the painting, at times coming close to monochromatic painting.[35] Beginning with the Inpaintings, he repeatedly explored the primary colors of red, yellow, and blue. For the BMW building in Munich in 1973, he produced three works of monumental size, measuring three by six meters each, in the style of the Detail paintings (fig. 9).[36] This preoccupation with primary colors goes back to the origins of monochromatic painting, which had been linked to discussions about the end of painting as early as the 1920s, and which became current again in the 1960s, when reservations about painting arose.

The Russian constructivist Alexander Rodchenko produced the first monochromatic paintings in art history. In 1921, he created three monochromatic panels in the primary colors, *Pure Color Red*, *Pure Color Yellow*, and *Pure Color Blue* (fig. 10). At the first presentation of these paintings in September 1921 at the *5 × 5 = 25* exhibition in Moscow, he said, "In this show I have proclaimed the three primary colors for the first time in art."[37] Looking back, he wrote in 1939: "I reduced painting to its logical conclusion and exhibited three canvases: red, blue, and yellow. I affirmed: it's all over. Basic colors. Every plane is a plane and there is to be no representation."[38] Alfred H. Barr, the founding director of the Museum of Modern Art in New York, described the three panels with the three primary colors as the end of painting in his 1929 lecture, "The Death of Painting: The Triumph of the Artist." Later critics joined him in his interpretation.[39] Only Benjamin H. D. Buchloh and Peter Weibel saw a quality in the analytical character of the panels that went beyond a farewell to painting. Buchloh summarized Rodchenko's application of scientific methods to painting as the model for a new kind of aesthetic practice; Weibel wrote that the three canvases had triggered a crisis of representationalism and set up a "culture of becoming."[40]

In January 1919, Rodchenko joined Asskranov, a circle of radical artistic innovators who had split off from the supremacists.[41] The exhibition *5 × 5 = 25* two years later was also related to their ideas—not, however, for the purpose of proclaiming the end of painting, but to present painting based on facture as object.[42] The three primary colors were supposed to formulate a concept for a new beginning. Monochromy, or "pure color," provided building blocks for future development: "Objectlessness in painting surprises you because painting precedes life and is not, as is thought, isolated from it. Objectlessness simply foresees the future," wrote Rodchenko in 1921.[43]

Abstraction: Universalism

Rodchenko's conviction that abstraction preceded the depiction of reality chimes with Richter's concept of abstract art. Discussing the paintings he showed at the documenta 7 in 1982, Richter said, "When we describe a process, or make out an invoice, or photograph a tree, we create models; without them we would know nothing of reality and would be animals. Abstract pictures are fictive models, because they make visible a reality that we can neither see nor describe, but whose existence we can postulate."[44]

In 1998, Richter painted the Abstract painting *Rhombus* [851-1] (fig. 11), citing the shape Piet Mondrian used in his paintings (fig. 12). Mondrian borrowed it from the traditional emblematic panels that ornament Dutch churches. In different contexts, the same geometric form is imbued with various different meanings. In churches, the panels commemorate the dead, but for Mondrian they illustrated theosophical ideas. Black grid lines seem to radiate into the space beyond the limited field of the painting. They sharpen the viewer's awareness of the cosmic connections within the space. In contrast, the picture field remains closed in Richter's piece. It features the primary colors of red, yellow, and blue—also significant for Mondrian's abstract work—in layers. The red dominates, but yellow and blue effect a fundamental influence on the appearance of the red. The red appears to be pulsing, held back by the blue, and fueled by the yellow, while the vertical shape becomes a counterpart to the viewer's vertical position. Whereas in his rectangular formats, Richter uses the squeegee primarily vertically in order to establish this relationship with the viewer, here, it is the rhombus form that takes on this task. The paint extends both vertically and horizontally—yet another homage to Mondrian. In Richter's work it has lost its ideological direction.

A motif runs through Richter's exploration of art theory, artistic references, and avant-garde painting. Richter claims that his Abstract paintings have a kind of universalism that is different from the "global language" of abstraction that the documenta founders Arnold Bode and Werner Haftmann celebrated as the language of the Western world after World War II.[45] Richter's universalism is not trying to convince anyone. For him, painting is legitimate because it precedes reality.

Translated from the German by Allison Moseley

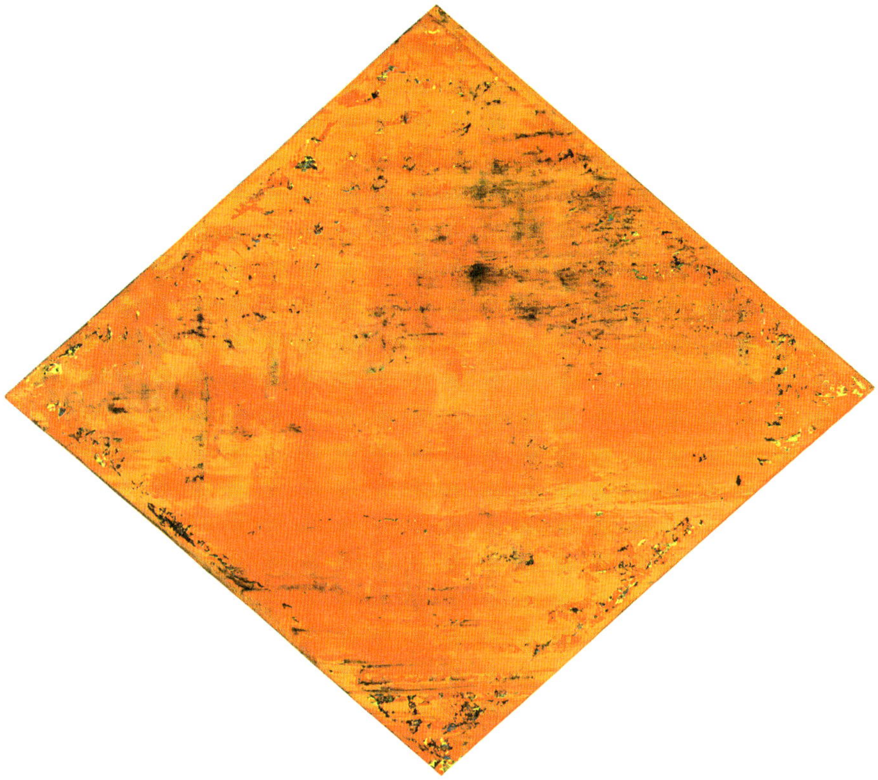

11 Gerhard Richter: *Abstract Painting, Rhombus* [851-1], 1998
Oil on canvas, 229 × 256 cm
The Museum of Fine Arts, Houston

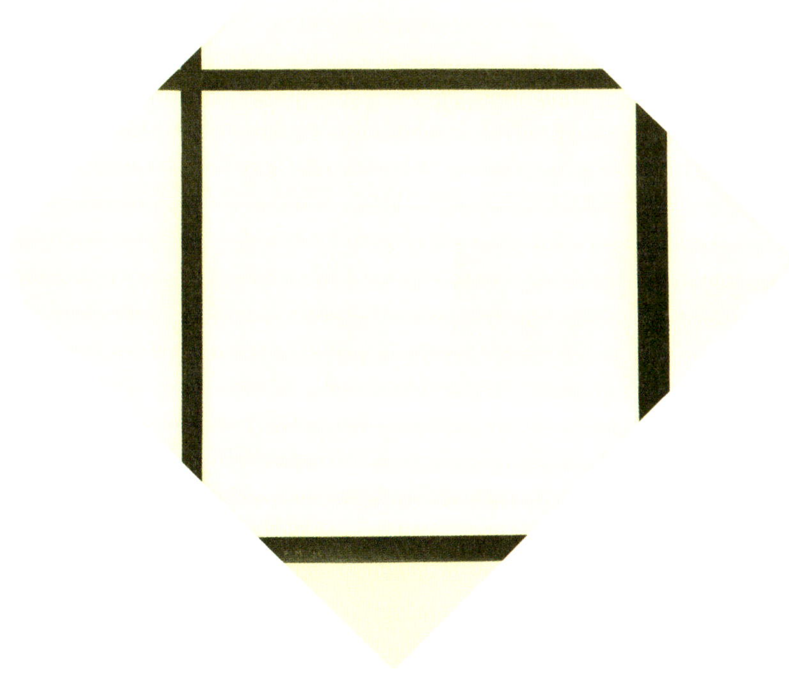

12 Piet Mondrian: *Tableau I: Rhombus with Four Lines and Gray,* 1926
Oil on canvas, 117.2 × 115.6 cm
The Museum of Modern Art, New York, bequest of Katherine S. Dreier

[1] See Laszlo Glozer, "Ausstieg aus dem Bild. Wiederkehr der Außenwelt," in *Westkunst: Zeitgenössische Kunst seit 1939*, Museen der Stadt Köln (Cologne: Dumont, 1981), 234–83, here 236. Exhibition catalog.

[2] From May 11 to 26, 1963, the exhibition *Kuttner, Lueg, Polke, Richter* took place in an empty storefront in Düsseldorf. Richter described the project as the "first exhibition of German pop art," and coined the term "capitalist realism." In October of the same year, Richter and Konrad Lueg organized a show with "demonstrations" in a furniture store in central Düsseldorf. A happening called *Living with Pop—A Demonstration of Capitalist Realism* took place, in which the artists appeared as living sculptures. See Amy Dickson, "Chronology," in London 2011, 281–94, here 283–4.

[3] See Martin Warnke, "Von der Gegenständlichkeit und der Ausbreitung der Abstrakten," in *Die fünfziger Jahre. Beiträge zu Politik und Kultur*, ed. Dieter Bänsch (Tübingen: Gunter Narr Verlag, 1985), 209–22.

[4] See Serge Guilbaut, *How New York Stole the Idea of Modern Art: Abstract Expressionism, Freedom and the Cold War* (Chicago, IL: University of Chicago Press, 1985).

[5] See New York 2002, 23.

[6] Richter recalled his encounter with abstract expressionism at the II. documenta in 1959: "The sheer brazenness of it! That really fascinates me and impressed me. I might almost say that those paintings were the real reason why I left the GDR. I realized that there was something wrong with my whole way of thinking." Richter 2009, "Interview with Benjamin H. D. Buchloh" (1986), 163–87, here 163.

[7] Elger 2009a, 22. In an interview with Benjamin H. D. Buchloh, Richter also used the concept in a negative way: "But that is what I mean. I lived my life with a group of people who laid claim to a moral aspiration, who wanted to bridge a gap, who were looking for a middle way between capitalism and socialism, a so-called Third Path. And so the way we thought, and what we wanted for our own art, was all about compromise. In this there was nothing radical—to use a more appropriate synonym for 'brazen'—and it wasn't genuine, either, but full of false deference." Richter 1986 (see note 6), 164. For more on Richter's artistic search beyond the polarity of the abstract and the figurative, see Camille Morineau, "Das Blow-up, Primärfarben und Verdopplungen," in London 2011, 123–36; Astrid Honold, "Blur in Motion. Die Verwischung als vermittelnde Bewegung im Werk von Gerhard Richter," master's thesis, Freie Universität Berlin, 2015.

[8] The January 1963 issue of *Art International* magazine introduced Richter and his friends to American pop art. Richter and Lueg drove to Paris, where they presented themselves to galleries as German pop artists. They saw works by Roy Lichtenstein at the Ileana Sonnabend Gallery.

[9] "When I copied the first photos, I had the feeling for the first time that I was doing something special and, above all, something of my own. In the jargon of the day, it was 'radical.' And those who saw it suddenly had no argument except for the one that it was unacceptable to ignore the rules and copy a photo." Elger 2009a, 46.

[10] See Walter Grasskamp, *Der lange Marsch durch die Illusionen. Über Kunst und Politik* (Munich: C. H. Beck, 1995).

[11] In *Übersicht* (1998), Richter located his place in art history in a diagram. See Stefan Gronert, "Art History as Art: A Survey," in Mehring et al., 2010, 125–44, here 136–41.

[12] See Heinrich Lützeler, *Abstrakte Malerei. Bedeutung und Grenze* (Gütersloh: Sigbert Mohn Verlag, 1961), 11.

[13] Ibid., 175.

[14] Ibid., 12.

[15] Ibid., 161.

[16] See Christoph Schreier, "Befragung der Sphinx," in Bonn 2017, 17–24, here 18.

[17] See Michael Diers, "Grauwerte. Farbe als Argument und Dokument," in *Who's Afraid of. Zum Stand der Farbforschung*, eds. Anne Hoormann and Karl Schawelka (Weimar: University Verlag, 1998), 276–301.

[18] "In a contest between Zeuxis and Parrhasius, Zeuxis produced so successful a representation of grapes that birds flew up to the stage buildings where it was hung. Then Parrhasius produced such a successful trompe-l'oeil of a curtain that Zeuxis, puffed up with pride at the judgment of the birds, asked that the curtain be drawn aside and the picture revealed. When he realized his mistake, with an unaffected modesty he conceded the prize, saying that whereas he had deceived birds, Parrhasius had deceived him, an artist." Gaius Plinius Secundus (Pliny the Elder), *Natural History: A Selection*, trans. John F. Healy (London et al.: Penguin, 1991), 330.

[19] See also *Hinter dem Vorhang. Verhüllung und Enthüllung seit der Renaissance. Von Tizian bis Christo* (Düsseldorf: Museum Kunstpalast, 2016). Exhibition catalog.

[20] Otto Stelzer, *Die Vorgeschichte der abstrakten Kunst. Denkmodelle und Vor-Bilder* (Munich: R. Piper, 1964).

[21] See ibid., 23.

[22] See ibid., 179.

[23] Gerhard Richter, "Interview with Christiane Vielhaber" (1986), in Richter 2009, 189–92, here 191.

[24] For more on cloud paintings and their role in the antecedents of abstract art, see *Wolkenbilder. Die Erfindung des Himmels*, Bucerius Kunst Forum (Hamburg: Hirmer, 2004). Exhibition catalog.

[25] See Morineau 2011 (see note 7), esp. 124. Here, Morineau argues for an interpretation that is not based solely upon the polarities of abstraction and figuration, and emphasizes that Richter views the difference between his figurative paintings and his abstract ones as merely external.

[26] See Stelzer 1964 (see note 20), 89.

[27] See also Morineau 2011 (see note 7), 124.

[28] The motif of the wooden wall upon which apparently affixed objects seem close enough to touch is one of the most important motifs in trompe-l'oeil painting. See *Täuschend echt. Illusion und Wirklichkeit in der Kunst*, Bucerius Kunst Forum (Hamburg: Hirmer, 2010). Exhibition catalog.

[29] See Hubertus Butin, "Blattecke," in ibid., 180.

[30] The *Atlas* contains drawings of architecture. Richter produced many designs for imaginary spaces by providing painted additions to photographs of clouds.

[31] Bruno Taut founded the Glass Chain artist group in 1919. Most of its members were architects. In their correspondence they developed a vision for an architecture of the future.

[32] See Monika Wagner, *Sack und Asche. Materialgeschichten aus der Hamburger Kunsthalle* (Hamburg: Kunsthalle, 1997), 28–37.

[33] Richter 1986 (see note 6), here 169.

[34] See Bernd Busch, *Belichtete Welt. Eine Wahrnehmungsgeschichte der Fotografie* (Munich: C. Hanser, 1989), 288; Matthias Krüger, *Das Relief der Farbe. Pastose Malerei in der französischen Kunstkritik 1850–1890* (Munich: Deutscher Kunstverlag, 2007), 215.

[35] See Ina Hildebrandt, *Monochromie. Gerhard Richter und das letzte Bild* (Munich: GRIN, 2014).

[36] See Friedel 2011.

[37] *5 × 5 = 25* (Moscow: Rodchenko/Stepanova Collection, 1921), typescript, n.p. Exhibition catalog.

[38] Alexander Rodchenko, "Working with Mayakovsky," 1939, manuscript, quoted in *From Painting to Design: Russian Constructivist Art of the Twenties*, Galerie Gmurzynska (Cologne: The Galerie, 1981), 190–91. Exhibition catalog. Quoted here from "The Death of Painting," accessed April 27, 2018, www.moma.org/interactives/exhibitions/1998/rodchenko/texts/death_of_painting.html.

[39] See Gail Harrison Roman, "Art after the Last Picture: Rodchenko," in *Art in America* 68 (1980), 120–31; Thierry de Duve, "Who is Afraid of Red, Yellow and Blue," in *Artforum* 22, no. 1 (1983), 30–37, 41–52; *Rot, Gelb, Blau. Die Primärfarben in der Kunst des 20. Jahrhunderts*, Kunstmuseum St. Gallen (Stuttgart: Hatje, 1988), exhibition catalog; Johannes Meinhardt, *Ende der Malerei und Malerei nach dem Ende der Malerei* (Ostfildern: Hatje-Cantz, 1997).

[40] Benjamin H. D. Buchloh, "The Primary Colors for the Second Time: A Paradigm Repetition of the Neo-Avant-Garde," in *October* 37 (1986), 41–52; Peter Weibel, "Von der Verabsolutierung der Farbe zur Selbstauflösung der Malerei," in *Nach der Destruktion des ästhetischen Scheins. Van Gogh, Malewitsch, Duchamp*, ed. Hans Matthäus Bachmayer et al. (Munich: K. Boer, 1992), 151–66, here 164.

[41] See Margarita Tupitsyn, "Being-in-Production: The Constructivist Code," in *Rodchenko & Popova: Defining Constructivism*, Tate Modern (London: Tate Publishing, 2009), 13–20, here 15. Exhibition catalog.

[42] Lyubov Popova, who also participated in the show, was interested in this concretion. She submitted five sketches under a single title, *Attempts at Pictorial Force Constructions* as a "series of preliminary attempts at concrete, materialized constructions," as she wrote in the catalog. See Cologne 1981 (see note 38), 65. She and Alexander Vesnin were in charge of the painting department at the Vkhutemas school.

[43] Alexander Rodchenko, "Alles ist Experiment" (1921), in Rodchenko, *Alles ist Experiment. Der Künstler-Ingenieur*, ed. Pierre Gallissaire (Hamburg: Nautilus, 1993), 47–48.

[44] Gerhard Richter, "Text for catalogue of documenta 7" (1982), in Richter 2009, 121.

[45] See Werner Haftmann, *Malerei im 20. Jahrhundert. Eine Entwicklungsgeschichte*, 2 vols. (Munich: Prestel, 1954).

Abstraction and Semblance in Gerhard Richter's Oeuvre

Dietmar Elger

Abstract is something everyday for me, as natural as walking or breathing.[1]
Gerhard Richter, 1999

Over a period spanning more than five decades, Gerhard Richter has tested out various stylistic elements in his work. From the mid-1960s onward, the gray Photo paintings based on photographs from magazines and family albums were followed by a rapid succession of concrete illusions of light and shadow formations, Color Charts, references to informalist paintings, romanticized landscapes, Inpaintings in red, blue, and yellow, in greens and grays, as well as the monochromatic Gray paintings. Since 1976, multicolored, gestural Abstract paintings have dominated his oeuvre, and he has continued to develop their individual manifestations of different formal vocabularies and color textures. By 1999, Richter had gained the following insight from the origins of his Abstract paintings: "For example, I am incapable of producing a picture similar to picture X, which I painted a year before."[2] More recently, he introduced two new concepts into his body of work: the mostly small-format Reverse-Glass paintings in 2008, and the monumental computer-generated Strips, which can be up to ten meters wide, in 2011.

Earlier critics therefore accused Richter of having a chameleon-like attitude to change, even though they also recognized the sense of unity amid the diversity of his work.[3] Richter himself has always emphasized the conceptual consistency of his paintings, and in 1991, he underscored methodical identity as uniting all of his alterations in style. "On the other hand, I do perceive an unchangeable basic attitude, a constant concern that runs through all my works like a style."[4] It is even the case, continued Richter, that all of his paintings are distinguished by an identical characteristic that makes it easier to identify all of his works as his than when examining the works of many other artists.[5]

This is also true of the relationship between representational motifs and abstract pictorial inventions. Since 1976, Richter has often interrupted work on his Abstract paintings in order to turn to small groups or individual figural paintings. The Candle paintings and Skulls of 1982–83 were followed by romanticized landscapes, portraits, and the occasional still life. Yet, figuration and abstraction are not opposites. Rather, they complement each other; they are, so to speak, two sides of the same coin. Many of the paintings even borrow stylistic characteristics from one another. Some of the motifs come so close to this boundary that the line separating them is no longer recognizable. In Richter's Photo Overpaintings, this interplay between two modes of depiction (photographic illusion and painterly abstraction) practically becomes the theme of this group of works (cat. 56–61). It also maintains a similarly striking presence in a few other paintings, like the Abstract paintings of 1984, work number 551. The small-format *Abstract Paintings* [551-1 to 551-3 and 551-8] (fig. 1, cat. 42–45) imitate the formula employed by Richter in the landscapes he was producing during the same period, recreating their structure sketchily and with rough brush strokes. This becomes particularly clear when comparing the *Abstract Painting* [551-2] (fig. 1, cat. 43) with the figurative landscape *Wiesental* [572-4] from 1985 (fig. 2).

The continued elucidation of the theme of abstraction will, therefore, mainly concentrate on one side of the coin: So-called abstract paintings have formed part of the artist's oeuvre since 1964. It was not until twelve years later that Richter began working on the group known as the Abstract paintings, their capitalized name defining them as an independent group. Due to their complex, contradictory structures of form and color, they are decidedly different from his earlier abstract works. To date, the Abstract paintings are the largest group of works in his entire oeuvre. After Richter titled the first of them *Construction* [389] (1979, cat. 30), he later decided to call them all Abstract paintings. He thus expressly separated these paintings from wholly nonrepresentational paintings, attributing to his abstract motifs a figural aspect of which the paintings seem to be an abstraction. This relationship has always been very important to Richter, and he does justice to it in different ways in the Abstract paintings dating from 1976 onward, as well as in all of his other and earlier abstractions. In an interview with Ulrich Wilmes in 2008, he identified the following basic condition for all of his abstract paintings: "Paintings always depict something that they are not. We even read into abstract paintings, examining them to find out <u>what</u> is being shown. If it were just about color, after all, that would be boring."[6]

Abstraction and Representationalism

From the start, Richter stressed that abstraction and recognizable, specific motifs in his work were not opposites, and that one did not necessarily exclude the other. Around 1962, he made a series of paintings based on photographs. Richter destroyed some of them later, but included others in his numbered catalogue raisonné. Occupying the first position and thus indicating the strategic beginning of his oeuvre is the painting *Table* [1] from 1962 (fig. 3). His index contains only two other paintings from that year: the (later destroyed) portrait *Hitler* [3] and *Folding Dryer* [4].

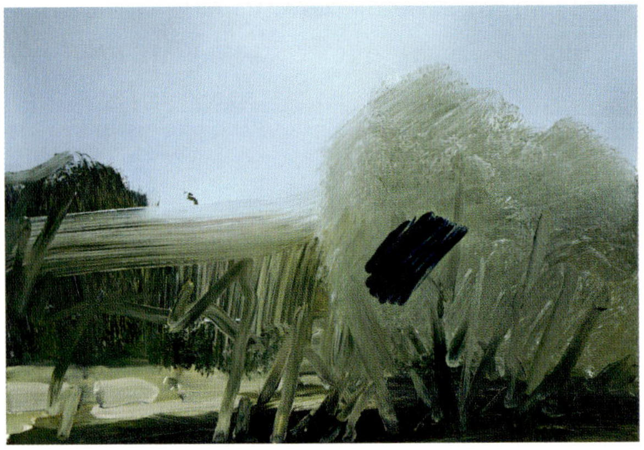

1 Gerhard Richter: *Abstract Painting* [551-2], 1984
Oil on canvas, 43 × 60 cm
Private collection, Switzerland (cat. 43)

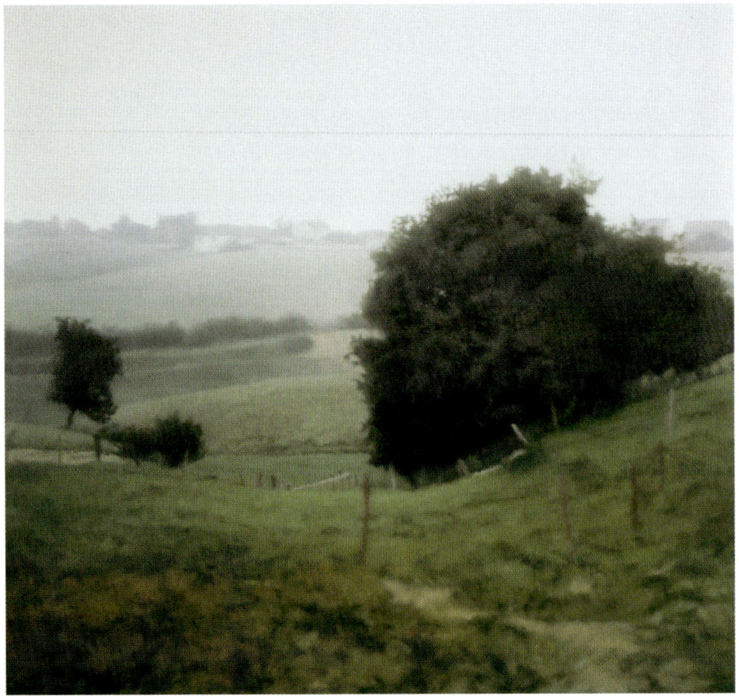

2 Gerhard Richter: *Wiesental* [572-4], 1985
Oil on canvas, 90.5 × 94.9 cm
The Museum of Modern Art, New York.
Blanchette Rockefeller, Betsy Babcock, and
Mrs. Elizabeth Bliss Parkinson Funds, 1985

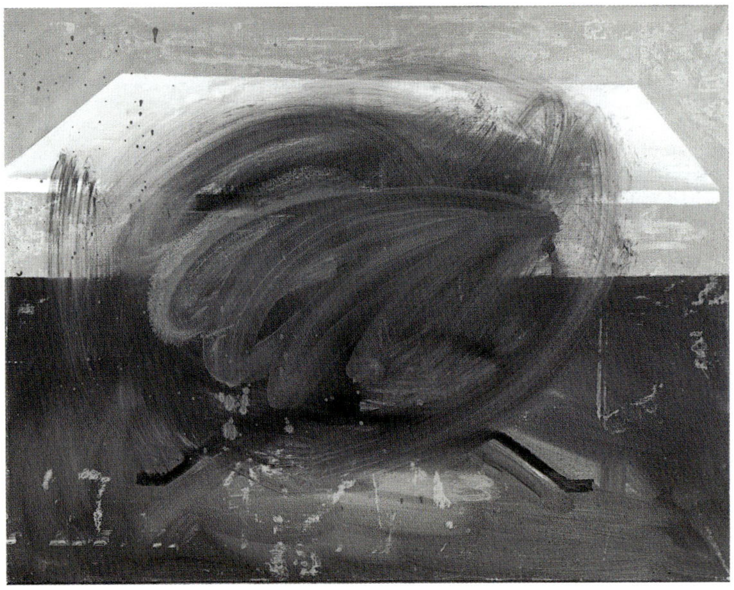

3 Gerhard Richter: *Table* [1], 1962
Oil on canvas, 90 × 113 cm
Harvard Art Museums/
Busch-Reisinger Museum, Cambridge, MA.
On loan from a private collection

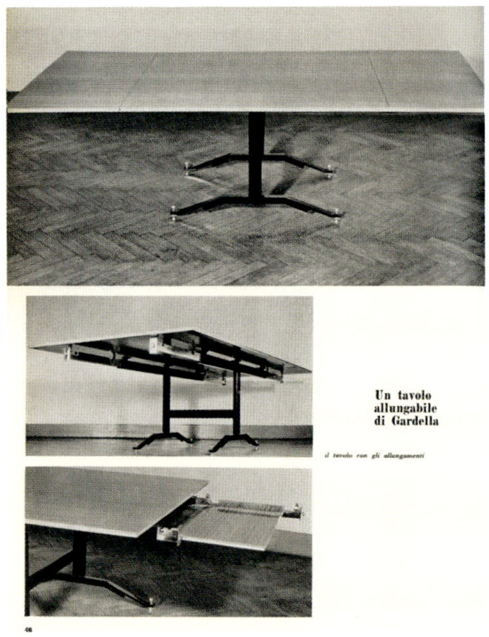

4 Source material for *Table* [1], 1962,
originally published in *domus* 329
(August 1956), 46

Table [1] is painted in oil on untreated canvas, measures 90 × 113 cm, and is both a transitional painting as well as one that signals a new beginning (see the essay by Armin Zweite, pp. 46–57). Richter borrowed his motif from the August 1956 issue of the Italian architecture and design magazine *domus* (fig. 4). In a second step, Richter's powerful, circular painting gesture partially erases the illusionary image of a piece of modernist furniture executed in gray tones. In 1991, he recalled the process of making the painting: "I painted it, but was dissatisfied with the result and pasted parts of it over with newspaper. [...] I was dissatisfied because there was too much paint on the canvas and became less happy with it, so I overpainted it. Then suddenly it acquired a quality which appealed to me and I felt it should be left that way, without knowing why."[7]

Table [1] is also one of Richter's key works because the eruptive, gestural inpainting does not obliterate, replace, or negate the figural motif. Instead, both modes of pictorializing—illusionary representation and autonomous, abstract form—remain equally legible. Here, this leads to the phenomenon that can be seen to this day in many of Richter's abstract paintings, as well as in some of his representational works: The only partially identifiable object is perceived as a geometrical, abstract form, while conversely the circular, abstract, textured color gains illusionary qualities.

Even though Richter put *Table* [1] at the beginning of his index of works, the concept of dialogue between the figural and abstract modes of painting can be traced back further than that. In 1960, when he was still in Dresden, he executed a drawing that was unusual for him at the time: *Untitled (Is That a Country ...)* (fig. 5). Here, Richter dripped thinned black ink onto the paper and allowed it to run slowly, so that it formed a random, spotted field. Afterward, he outlined the edges of this shapeless form in pen and ink. Below the drawing, he included a scale that suggests it is a depiction of a cartographic landscape covering an area of more than 30,000 kilometers. Richter added a compass rose to the upper edge of the drawing, noting the cardinal directions. This gives the abstract structure, which viewers might perceive as something resembling a Rorschach test, a nearly precise, landscape-like topography, in which the ink spots form mountains, lakes, rivers, and islands. Richter himself added a text to this "map," on the paper itself, beginning with the phrases: "Is that a country—a country. Its dimensions are unimaginable, its forests innumerable, its lakes as large as continents; the peaks of its mountains tower up into the sky, and there are caves that go all the way to Hell. What kind of a country is it."[8]

Three years earlier, Richter had made a series of thirty-one monotypes (cat. 47), in which he had used a rubber brayer to apply black printer's ink in horizontal stripes. He added small black figures to some of the motifs, lending the abstract black structures a sense of proportion and a resemblance to a landscape. In other pieces, the title of this group of works, *Elbe*, was enough to awaken in the viewer the idea that the horizontal bands of color suggested the river and its banks beneath a dark night sky. In 1971, Richter deployed the identical process of changing the perception of dimensions in the 200 × 300 cm *Large Teyde Landscape (With Two Figures)* [284] (fig. 6). This landscape is based on a photograph of a clod of dirt tossed up alongside a path, which he took while on vacation on Tenerife. Back in the studio, Richter projected this detail onto a large canvas, painted it in oil, then softly inpainted it, so that the two vertical brushstrokes suggested two hikers in a panoramic landscape.[9]

Each representation of reality is, at the same time, an abstraction of its model in nature, even when it is not always in the form of an illusionistic construction of representation, as is the case with the two examples mentioned, *Elbe* and *Large Teyde Landscape (With Two Figures)* [284]. Richter repeatedly referred to this experience in interviews and statements: "Painting as appearance—this has nothing to do with the 'world of appearances' and ideas like that. I mean to say that I know no painting that is not illusionistic—just like photography."[10] Richter has always attributed an aspect of representationalism to all of his abstract paintings, and in so doing, underscored the necessity of discovering in them a motif from nature or a memory that can be depicted. In 2008, referring to the Abstract paintings, he categorically stated: "As we do with every other image, every view, we examine it for resemblances to things and circumstances that we're familiar with and remember. And, of course, there are countless spots in completely nonrepresentational paintings that remind us of something, that resemble something. These partial similarities, however, never look like a *normal* figure or something. So they're showing a different world, an artificial one, and that's why I think it's so useful when we take these abstract—meaning indecipherable—views in the same way that we take literal depictions, like a photo, which depicts a real object."[11]

Richter follows this principle when he gives titles to some of the Abstract paintings he has made since 1976, whose details spark suggestions of objects, such as the 1983 work *Pyramid* [522-2] (cat. 38) or the 1994 work *Wall* [808] (cat. 70). Others are named after people or places, such as *Elger* [564-1] (private collection, Stuttgart) from 1981 or *Athens* [573-3] (FRAC Nord-Pas de Calais, Dunkerque), produced four years later. In contrast, titles of artworks such as *A B, Quiet* [612-4] and *Position* [660] from 1986 and 1988 respectively (cat. 63, 65) are more open-ended and therefore less pictorial, although they are in no way random or coincidental. They express more of an atmosphere or an impression.

The fundamental relation to a model from nature that Richter has postulated for all of his Abstract paintings from 1976 onward is crucial. Here, he refers to the artistic tradition of imagining the frame of a painting as the frame of a window. The frame that encloses the picture imitates the frame of a window, which permits only a limited view of nature. Ever since Leon Battista Alberti (1404–1472), this notion of nature as a model has been an ideal of art theory that painters strove to achieve, abandoned only with the advent of cubist modernism. Richter's idea is also different. His concept focuses on the depiction of a random, limited section of reality seen through a window frame. He does not necessarily regard this kind of detail as representing an ideal image of nature. Yet its detail, complexity, and randomness could be seen to contain a truth and a rightness which Richter draws on as the model for his paintings,[12] and which can do more justice to the notion of our current reality than can all of the traditional theories about the aesthetics of art. In a statement for the documenta 7 catalog in 1982, Richter described his abstract works as "fictive models, because they make visible a reality that we can neither see nor describe, but whose existence we can postulate" (see the essay by Ortrud Westheider, pp. 8–21).[13]

In 1964, Richter used the seminal painting *Table* [1] from 1962 (fig. 3) to guide two virtually diametrically opposed concepts of painting toward abstraction. That was the year in which he first had the sense that he had exhausted the possibilities of his figurative, gray Photo paintings. He was thus confronted with the question of how to create a painting without using photographic source materials. Out of this challenge first arose the Curtain paintings, and two years later, the first Color Chart paintings (see the essay by Hubertus Butin, pp. 34–45). Both groups of works originate in the visual iconography of American pop art. Initially, the curtains had simply been backgrounds for Richter's commissioned paintings based on passport photos (fig. 7). Now, he isolated this detail, elevating it to a theme in and of itself. At the same time, he reduced the curtain motif to the depiction of abstract interplays of light and shadow, borrowing from op art, which was popular in the mid-1960s. The process of abstraction in his 1964 work *Curtain* [58-1] (cat. 1) already alluded to an illusionary texture of light and darkness. In the subsequent year's *Curtain III (Light)* [56] (cat. 2), Richter took this process of abstraction further. In the 1967 work *Large Curtain* [163-1] (fig. 8), only the literal title refers to the origin of the motif. At the same time, Richter developed related groups of works, including the 1967 paintings *Corrugated Iron* [162] (Collezione Prada, Milan) and *Grid* [166] (cat. 5), and the *Shadow Picture* [209-8] (cat. 4) from the subsequent year. All of the paintings deal with the theme of light and shadows, and their primary theme is the illusionistic qualities of painting.

Abstraction and Photography

The *Shadow Picture* [209-8] of 1968 shows a light grid structure surrounded by a painted frame lit from the upper left, casting a precise shadow onto an illusionary back wall. This double illusion of picture and pictorial depiction is the main theme of the piece. In a statement from this period, Richter expressly emphasized the transference of illusion to his abstract paintings: "Somewhere along the line it no longer satisfied me to paint photographs; I took the stylistic devices of photographs—accuracy, blurring, illusoriness—and made doors, curtains, and pipes with them."[14] Richter often underscored the abstract painting's relationship to the photograph. He not only transferred the characteristics of photography, especially its illusionism, to his abstract paintings, he even saw both mediums as equals: "[I]f I disregard the assumption that a photograph is a piece of paper exposed to light, then I am practicing photography by other means: I'm not producing paintings that remind you of a photograph but producing photographs. And, seen in this way, those of my paintings that have no photographic source (the abstracts, etc.) are also photographs."[15] Richter had emphasized this equation of abstract painting and photography, based on the transference of one medium to the other, in an interview as early as

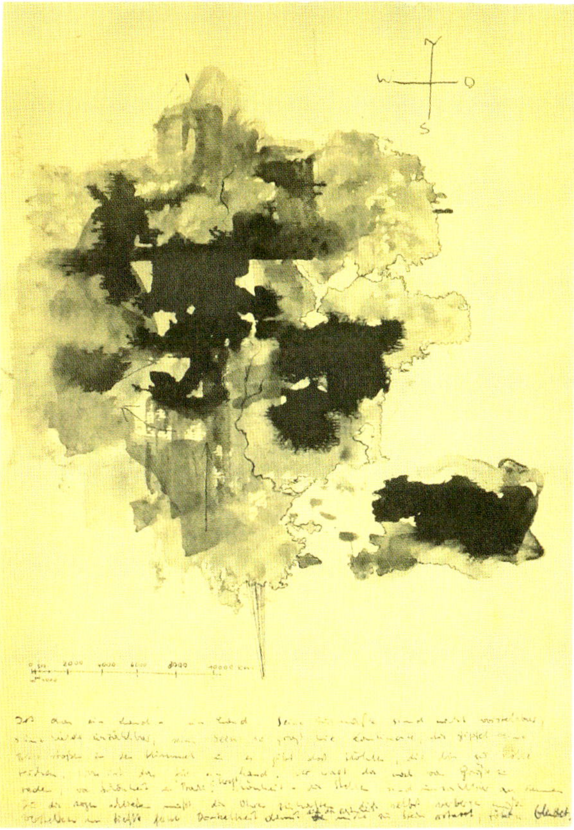

5 Gerhard Richter: *Untitled (Is That a Country...)*, 1960
India ink on paper, 34.3 × 23.7 cm
Gerhard Richter Archive,
Staatliche Kunstsammlungen Dresden

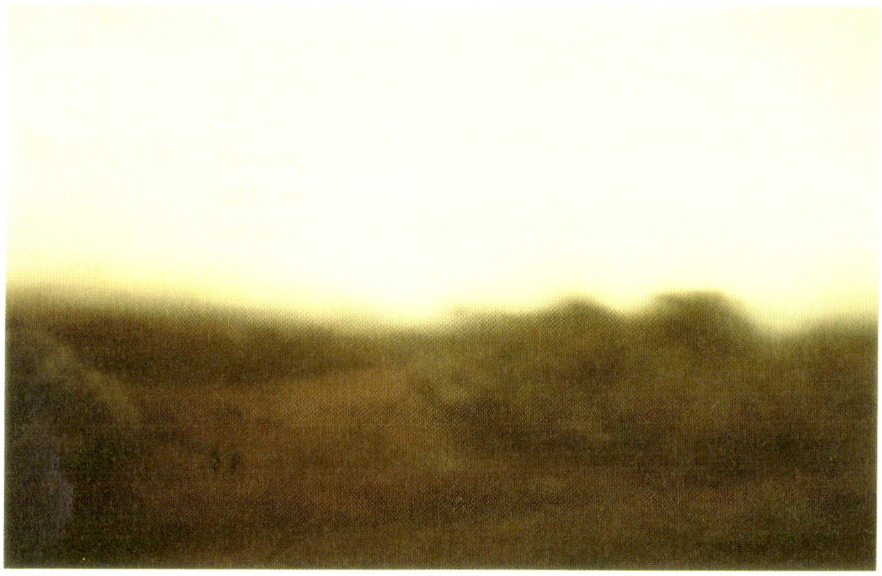

6 Gerhard Richter: *Large Teyde Landscape (With Two Figures)* [284], 1971
Oil on canvas, 200 × 300 cm
Crex Collection, Zurich

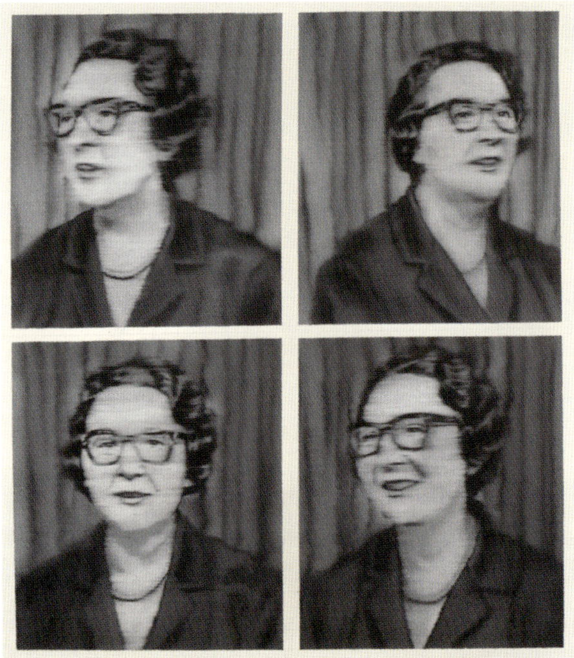

7 Gerhard Richter: *Portrait of Dr. Knobloch* [41], 1964
Oil on canvas, 100 × 90 cm
Gerhard Richter Archive,
Staatliche Kunstsammlungen Dresden

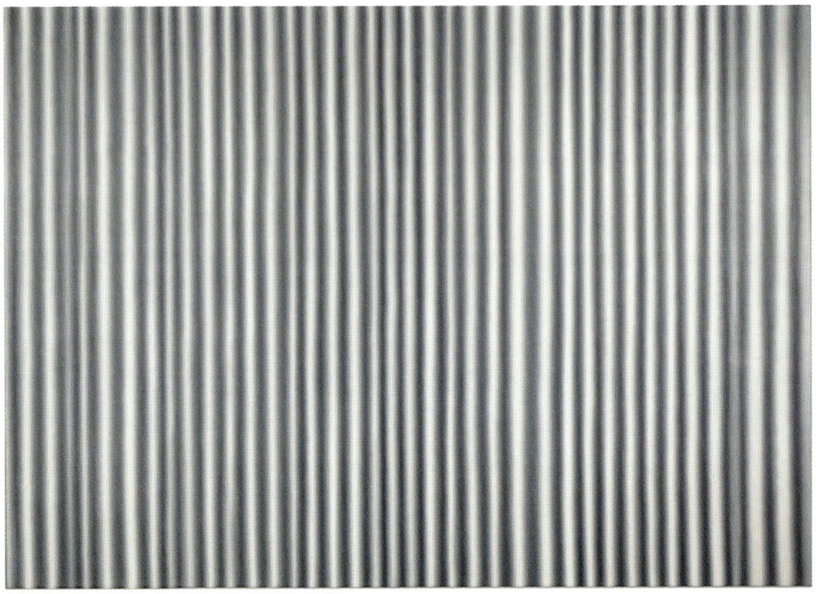

8 Gerhard Richter: *Large Curtain* [163-1], 1967
Oil on canvas, 200 × 280 cm
Städel Museum, Frankfurt am Main

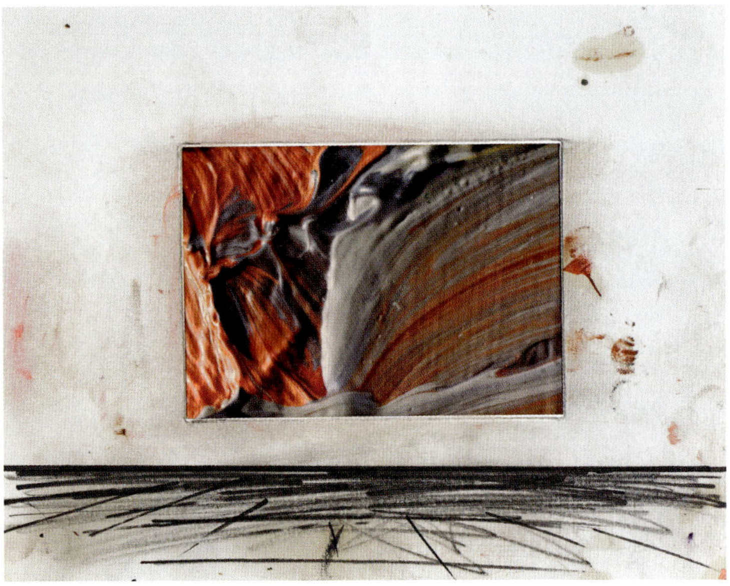

9 Gerhard Richter: *Atlas* (detail) [Plate 95], 1970
Städtische Galerie im Lenbachhaus und Kunstbau,
Munich (see cat. 28)

1972, and it has remained true of his painting to this day. Illusion—Richter also talks about illusion as his life's theme[16]—means having a partial similarity to things, spaces, forms, circumstances, and ideas that viewers believe they are familiar with or remember. Richter regards this experience as a process of recognition that is necessary for viewers, if abstract paintings are not to be considered "merely color."[17] With this statement, the artist reaffirmed his claim that all of his abstract works have an inherent relationship to the world of objects, even when they visualize nothingness, like the monochromatic Gray paintings from the 1970s.[18]

An extensive group of monochromatic Gray paintings (cat. 25–27) was produced between 1969 and 1976. Richter mixed black and white with blue or brown to make various hues of gray, and applied it evenly over the entire surface of the canvas with a brush, roller, or spatula. Some of these works have a closed structure, while others reveal an active style of brushwork or impasto blobs of paint. The Gray paintings appear to have dark and sealed surfaces, and it is these paintings that Richter describes as "the most rigorously illusionistic of all."[19] In a letter from 1975, he overrode this apparent contradiction to emphasize the Gray paintings' similarities to photographs. "Its inconspicuousness gives it the capacity to mediate, to make visible, in a positively illusionistic way, like a photograph. It has the capacity that no other color has, to make 'nothing' visible."[20] In 1978, Richter confirmed these contradictory characteristics of the Gray paintings to his interviewers in the following anecdote: "In Venice there is an international exhibition with a theme: Reality and Abstraction, in two separate pavilions. I sent two identical large monochrome gray paintings and they put one in the Realist pavilion and one in the Abstract pavilion [...] and I agreed."[21]

Abstraction and Illusion

From 1970 to 1971 and again between 1977 and 1980, Richter executed two groups of works that deal with the challenges of illusionism or semblance in the abstract, using a method that was the direct opposite of the method he used for the Gray paintings. These works are also different from the earlier Curtain, Grid, Tube, and Shadow paintings. The paintings produced in the 1970s are more complex, and their theme is illusion within the context of interplay between painting and photography. All of the examples, among them the 1970 work *Detail (Red-Blue)* [273] and *Detail (Makart)* [288] from 1971 (cat. 28, 29), and the *Abstract Paintings* [421, 426] from 1977 and 1978 (cat. 31, 32), are large format, as a consequence of a joint methodical process. Here, the method of the blow-up is an essential part of making these works. A small photographic detail of an original photograph is the source for each of the works, which Richter enlarged onto a canvas of over four square meters.

The aforementioned *Large Teyde Landscape (With Two Figures)* [284] (1971, fig. 6) may have been the inspiration for the first of these Detail paintings. The process, at least, is the same in both cases. For the Details, Richter took many close-up photographs of small sections—each one to two square centimeters—of his palette.[22] The details mounted on plates 89 to 105 in the *Atlas* feature the results of this process, in which the material qualities of the paint still remain visible (fig. 9). It was not until Richter projected the original onto the large canvas and painted a realistic reproduction of it, blurring it softly, that the motif dissolved into an illusionary, indeterminate, colorful vortex. "In the enlarged paintings," as he wrote in a letter in 1980, "the excerpts [become] the abstract semblance of indeterminate 'beauty.'"[23]

The results confront viewers with depictions of colors and textures that are unfamiliar in the narrow spectrum of our natural perception. So we begin searching the paintings for familiar details and resemblances, and are probably reminded of a microcosm or macrocosm.[24] In 1982, Richter assessed this process of recognition as follows: "the unknown simultaneously alarms us and fills us with hope, and so we accept the pictures as a possible way to make the inexplicable more explicable, or at all events more accessible."[25] The year before he returned to the group of works in 1977, establishing an even more ingenious interplay between painting and photography in his body of work, he produced *Construction* [389] (cat. 30), a painting that took on a similar landmark position for the ensuing Abstract paintings as had *Table* [1], produced fourteen years earlier, for the polarity of representationalism and abstraction in his work.

After the Gray paintings, Richter started work on the Abstract paintings in summer 1976 with a thunderbolt. Without any preparation—no drawings, no smaller paintings—he created *Construction* [389] (cat. 30) on a canvas measuring 250 × 300 cm. The complicatedly structured, multicolored, abstract composition certainly does justice to its title. Here, Richter laid out numerous precisely contoured bars and bands, running toward several imaginary vanishing points. In this way, the geometric structures and shapes penetrate and overlap each other, so that there is no unified space on the surface and its illusionism is permanently broken. The austere, practically didactic Grid and Shadow paintings from the latter half of the 1960s are simpler models for the complicated, abstract *Construction* [389].

After this first Abstract painting, Richter needed to take a detour via photography to produce a less constructed, yet more painterly kind of abstract illusionism. Because he was initially not successful at transferring a painterly gesture to canvases on the scale of *Construction*, he created many small, abstract sketches in oil. He later selected and photographed some of these sketches, and then transferred their motifs in oil to large canvases in an illusionistic way. In this process, he also drew on the Detail paintings from 1971. But his concept is different, more complex; it recalls Richter's practice since 1966 of translating his own works into another medium, in order to give them new, intensified meaning. In a letter to Benjamin H. D. Buchloh in 1979, Richter described this process of transforming media: "Over the past two years, I have rendered the oil studies mentioned above (as experiments with no particular plan, style, ideology, construction or expression, but at the same time not executed blindly or automatically or determined by mere coincidence) as large-sized 'pictures' that replace the reality of the painted studies with their appearance."[26]

The *Abstract Painting* [421] (cat. 31) from 1977, which measures 250 × 200 cm, came into being based on one of the first sketches in oil, the smaller *Abstract Painting* [398-2] from the previous year, measuring only 26 by 23 cm (fig. 11). Richter executed another *Abstract Painting* [436] (cat. 32) in 1978, using a watercolor as his source material (fig. 12). At first, he found these sources were too much like "raw material."[27] Only gradually did he realize that their painterly characteristics made them completely valid paintings, and he stopped describing them with the more limiting word "sketches." In a 2009 interview, Richter explained that "paintings always depict something that they are not."[28] Applying this to his so-called "soft abstracts" (1977–1980), it means that they refer to the reality of their models, which are themselves already Abstract paintings. In 1981, with works such as *Abstract Painting* [479-1] (cat. 34), Richter succeeded in producing his first large-format, gestural abstract paintings, some of which were executed in impasto. From then on, they were as spontaneous, contradictory, and yet deliberate as only his small sketches in oil had been previously.

At the same time as the "soft abstracts," Richter created the photographic work *128 Photographs of a Painting* [441] in 1978, which he also turned into the small artist's edition *128 Details from a Picture (Halifax 1978) II* in 1998 (cat. 46). For this piece, he took 128 black-and-white close-ups of his *Abstract Painting (Halifax)* [432-5] (figs. pp. 54, 232), made in the same year. He shot the unstretched canvas under changing light conditions, positioning the camera at various angles to and distances from the painting (fig. 10). In doing so, he fragmented the painting in a near-cubist manner and anonymized it. Due to the extreme close-up angle of the photos and the use of black and white, the motifs can no longer be identified as details of a painting's surface. Viewers discover a different reality in the photographs than the one shown in the painting.[29] The arrangement, made up of eight sheets of paper, each with sixteen individual photographs, looks like a view of a strange, bare landscape reconstructed out of 128 details, again balanced between microcosm and macrocosm, as seen in the Detail paintings from 1971 and the "soft abstracts" made during this period. Richter described the associative impact of the *128 Photographs of a Painting* [441] in an interview: "The details themselves weren't that interesting; rather, it was the fact that I could see them as landscapes, as if they were views of a strange planet that you walk on or fly over."[30]

The Strips made from 2011 onward draw on another, earlier Abstract painting in a different way. Richter created all of the Strips using the 1990 *Abstract Painting* [724-4] (cat. 67), which is distinguished by its many small elements of color, and was therefore particularly suited to be the source material for conceiving the Strips. The Strips are digital prints on paper mounted on aluminum Dibond behind plexiglass. Their horizontal stripe motifs are derived from the color structure of the *Abstract Painting* [724-4], although even intense observation does not make this relationship conclusive.

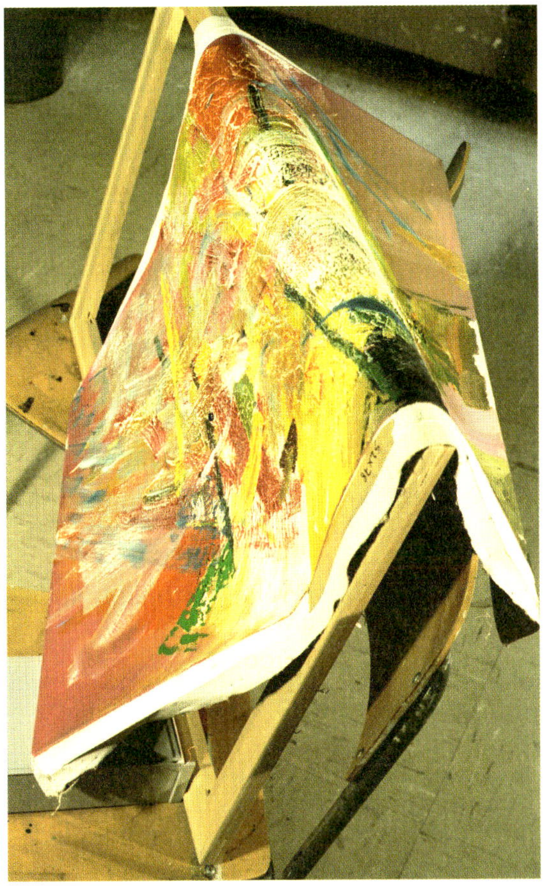

10 The canvas of Richter's *Abstract Painting (Halifax)* [432-5], 1978 (fig. p. 54), taken off its stretcher frame

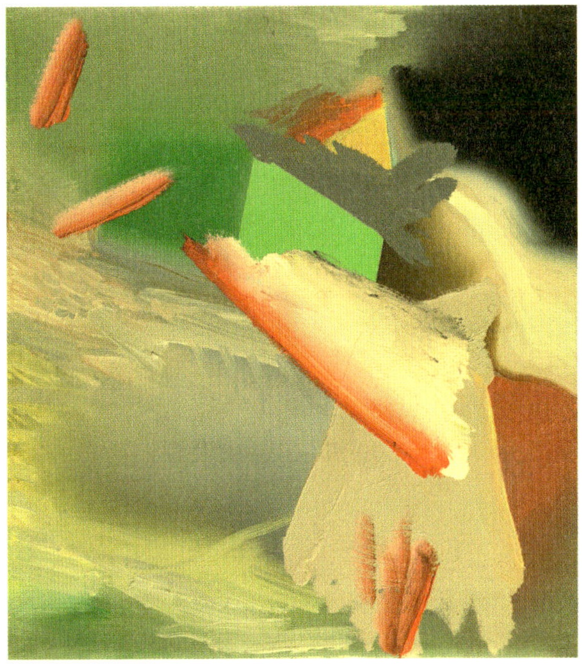

11 Gerhard Richter: *Abstract Painting* [398-2], 1976
Oil on canvas, 26 × 23 cm
Private collection, Amsterdam (see cat. 31)

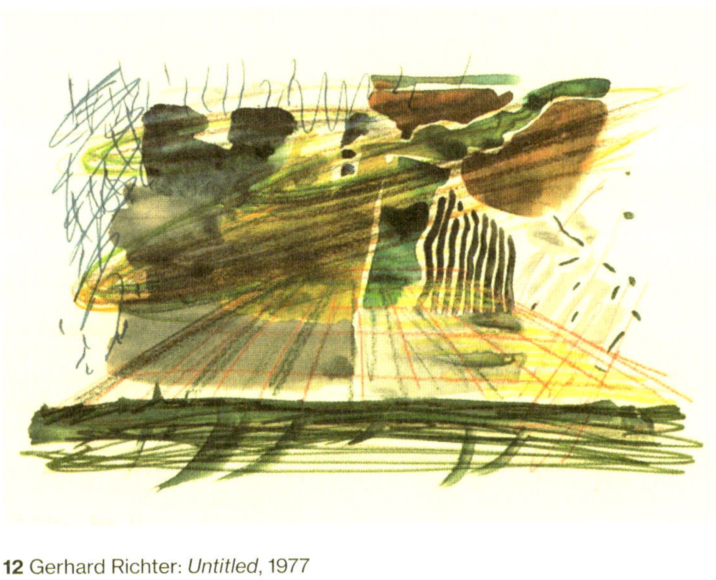

12 Gerhard Richter: *Untitled*, 1977
Watercolor, crayon, marker, and pencil on paper, 21 × 29.7 cm
Private collection (see cat. 32)

The Strips are the result of a complicated work process involving a computer program which deconstructed the surface of the *Abstract Painting* [724-4] and fragmented it into 4,096 vertical strips (see the chapter “Transparent and Reflected: Mirrors, Glass, and Strips,” pp. 194–207). Each of these sections—only 0.08 mm wide—were stretched lengthwise through mirroring and dissected into short, vertical pieces. Then Richter reassembled the printed strips and printed them using an inkjet process. The results, such as the monumental, ten-meter-wide *Strip* [930-4] from 2013 (cat. 78), are a combination of the seemingly random strips, found in a predetermined process, and Richter's orderly design. The artist has always considered this method of inventing images through chance and manipulation as a windfall for his work: “I'm always dealing with chance in my paintings, anyway, and I like to get gifts. I have the feeling that these pictures are gifted to me.”[31] Even the tiniest of details in the Strips were already contained in the *Abstract Painting* [724-4] from 1990, even if the viewer cannot identify one single section of the painting in the Strips. Thus, from 2011 onward, the *Abstract Painting* [724-4] from 1990 became the original picture, as well as the reality, to which each individual example from the Strips group of works refers.

“Abstract pictures are fictive models, because they make visible a reality that we can neither see nor describe, but whose existence we can postulate,” asserted Richter in 1982 in his statement for the documenta 7 catalog.[32] In all of his abstract paintings from the 1960s onward, he creates a model for the relationship of abstract art to its source materials in the figural world, which no longer strives to achieve the traditional idealized image of an aesthetic, harmonious composition. Instead, all of Richter's abstract paintings reveal a sense of incompleteness, as if they were all details; their colors and shapes organize themselves without any sort of hierarchy on the picture's surface, and much room is left for chance in the creative process. In this respect, his abstract paintings—especially those made after 1976—represent a fictional, yet very contemporary and democratic model of the complex, fragmented, and contradictory reality.

Translated from the German by Allison Moseley

[1] Gerhard Richter, "Conversation with Paolo Vagheggi" (1999), in Richter 2009, 347–48, here 347.
[2] Quoted in Dieter Schwarz, "About Watercolors and Related Things: Gerhard Richter in conversation with Dieter Schwarz, Cologne, June 26, 1999," in Winterthur 1999, 17–27, here 25.
[3] See Elger 2009b, 167.
[4] Gerhard Richter, "Interview with Jonas Storsve" (1991), in Richter 2009, 271–76, here 274.
[5] Ibid.
[6] Gerhard Richter, "Abstrakte Bilder müssen eine Richtigkeit haben. Gerhard Richter im Gespräch mit Ulrich Wilmes," in Wilmes 2009, 45–55, here 49.
[7] Gerhard Richter, "Comments on Some Works" (1991), in Richter 2009, 259–70, here 259.
[8] Gerhard Richter, written on the drawing *Untitled (Is That a Country ...)*, 1960, Gerhard Richter Archive, Staatliche Kunstsammlungen Dresden, see fig. 5.
[9] The same principles are followed in *Evening Landscape (With Figure)* [260] (Hannover: Sprengel Museum, 1970).
[10] Gerhard Richter, "Interview with Amine Haase" (1977), in Richter 2009, 96–98, here 97. See also Gerhard Richter, "Interview with Irmeline Lebeer" (1973), in ibid., 72–83, here 72: "For me, there's no difference between a landscape and an abstract painting. The term 'realism,' to my mind, has no meaning."
[11] Richter 2009 (see note 6), 49.
[12] See Gerhard Richter, "Interview with Christiane Vielhaber" (1986), in Richter 2009, 189–92, here 192.
[13] Gerhard Richter, "Text for catalog of documenta 7" (1982), in ibid., 121.
[14] Gerhard Richter, "Statement" (1967), in ibid., 47–48.
[15] Gerhard Richter, "Interview with Rolf Schön" (1972), in ibid., 59–61, here 60.
[16] See Gerhard Richter, "Notes" (1989) in ibid., 212–16, here 215: "Illusion—or rather appearance, semblance—is the theme of my life."
[17] Richter 2009 (see note 6), 49.
[18] See Gerhard Richter, "From a Letter to Edy de Wilde" (February 23, 1975), in Richter 2009, 91–92.
[19] Richter 1977 (see note 10), 97.
[20] Richter 1975 (see note 18), 92.
[21] Gerhard Richter, "Interview with Bruce Ferguson and Jeffrey Spalding" (1978), in ibid., 106–12, here 111. Here, Richter refers to the exhibition *Dalla natura all'arte, dall'arte alla natura* at the 1978 Venice Biennial. Both pieces measure 250 × 200 cm; one is the 1973 painting *Gray* [349-2] (Staatliche Museen zu Berlin, Nationalgalerie) and another is an unidentified Gray painting from 1974.
[22] See Gerhard Richter, "Letter to Birgit Pelzer" (March 25, 1980), in ibid., 115–16, here 115.
[23] Ibid.
[24] With the four-part series of paintings titled *Silicate* [885-1 to 885-4] (2003, Kunstsammlung Nordrhein-Westfalen, Düsseldorf) and pieces such as *Abstract Painting (Silicate)* [880-4] (2002, Artist Room Collection, Tate, London, and National Galleries of Scotland, Edinburgh) and *Abstract Painting (Skin)* [887-2 and 887-3] (2004, Artist Room Collection, Tate, London, and National Galleries of Scotland, Edinburgh), Richter went back to sources of motifs from the molecular and atomic area, which are only visible through electron microscopes.
[25] Richter 1982 (see note 13), 121.
[26] Gerhard Richter, "Letter to Benjamin H. D. Buchloh" (August 30, 1979), in ibid., 113–15, here 114.
[27] Gerhard Richter, "Answers to Questions from Marlies Grüterich" (September 2, 1977), in ibid., 94–95, here 95.
[28] Richter 2009 (see note 6), 49.
[29] In terms of method, Richter's work is similar to the photographic work *Élevage de poussière* (1920) by Man Ray and Marcel Duchamp (see the chapter "Nature and Materials: Abstract Landscapes," pp. 146–67).
[30] Hans Ulrich Obrist, "Interview mit Gerhard Richter," in Obrist/Schwarz 2013, 55.
[31] Ibid., 112–13.
[32] Richter 1982 (see note 13), 121.

Grids and Readymades: Gerhard Richter's Color Chart Paintings in the 1960s and 1970s

Hubertus Butin

Both paintings have similar-sounding titles, both are dedicated to the color yellow, and yet the two works could scarcely be more different. Ernst Wilhelm Nay's oil painting from 1958 is called *With Diverse Yellows*, while Gerhard Richter's lacquer painting from 1966 is titled *Six Yellows* [141] (figs. 1, 2). Nay was one of the most influential and successful painters from the Federal Republic of Germany during the West German economic miracle of the 1950s; during that decade, his work was even exhibited a number of times in New York. The so-called *Disk Paintings* he created from 1954 onward, with their rhythmic structures and modulations of color, are particularly well-known.[1] The painting *With Diverse Yellows* is an abstract composition consisting primarily of lemon yellow, dark yellow, and ocher. In the same year that Nay produced this work, he referred to his painting with mystifying pathos as "a universal sensation [...] that contains a new definition of the religious, a transcendence *turned to face the world*."[2] With exaggerated self-confidence, he mentioned his name in the same breath as Kazimir Malevich and Vasily Kandinsky, even though his art did not come close to the radicalness of the avant-garde of the 1910s and the 1920s and its art historical significance. Today Nay's paintings seem for the most part—the critical tone is deliberate here—innocuously decorative. Friedrich Wolfram Heubach, who edited the pioneering artists' journal *Interfunktionen* in Cologne from 1968 to 1973, retrospectively described the intellectual climate in the Federal Republic of Germany in the 1950s in scathing terms: "Only if one keeps in mind the degree to which the politics and culture of the time were dominated by a convoluted existentialism castrated by Christianity [...] and a [...] terror of the positive, of 'authenticity' and 'depth'—in short, by a mentality that was repulsed by anything concrete and critical as 'unspiritual'—only then will one be able to appreciate how radical happenings, the Fluxus movement, the situationists, and even the early pop artists were."[3]

Because of its very different pictorial conception, Richter's *Six Yellows* seems like a natural foil to Nay's *With Diverse Yellows*. Although both works are about color, both in their titles and in their formal aesthetics, Richter relies on a different understanding of pictoriality. In the following analysis, the significance and historical context of this understanding will be examined.

Paint as Readymade

In October 1963, Marcel Duchamp formulated a provocative thesis in an interview, which ran counter to the traditional concept of color as having an expressive or symbolic meaning: "A tube of paint that an artist uses is not made by the artist; it is made by the manufacturer that makes paints. So the painter really is making a Ready-made [sic] when he paints with a manufactured object that is called paints."[4] Two years earlier in a lecture at the Museum of Modern Art in New York, Duchamp had already emphasized that all paintings produced with tubes of paint were "readymades aided."[5] These statements seem exaggerated, especially since it is not the paintings themselves but really only the tubes used that could be termed readymades in the sense of a preexisting industrial product. And yet the idea of paint as readymade is one of the paradigmatic ideas of twentieth-century art.[6] It represents an especially radical way of making color independent and autonomous, in that it no longer appears in an abstract painting on a canvas, but is instead presented as pure material in the form of pigments and tubes, cans, or half pans of paint.[7] In the 1950s and 1960s, this artistic practice can be found in the work of artists including Man Ray, Yves Klein, Robert Rauschenberg, Jasper Johns, and Giulio Paolini.[8] In a 1969 work titled *Paint Cup* (Wilhelm-Hack-Museum, Ludwigshafen am Rhein), Richter, too, presented paint as pure material in its direct and unpainterly thingness and self-referential intrinsic value. The object consists of a porcelain cup filled with gray oil paint and a mixing stick.[9]

In addition to this object-like variant of the absolutizing of paint, there is also a pictorial variant, whose art historical tradition is even more relevant for Richter's work. It is based on the standard printed or painted sample cards paint stores offer customers showing their selection of available paints. Probably the first artwork in which industrially produced sample cards appear as a motif is Marcel Duchamp's 1918 oil painting *Tu m'* (Yale University Art Gallery, New Haven, Connecticut). This highly complex work shows, among other things, a foreshortened view of a seemingly endless series of superimposed rhombuses in various colors.[10] According to Duchamp's gallerist Arturo Schwarz, they were copies of paint samples from an oil paint catalog.[11] Robert Rauschenberg had seen this work in the 1953 exhibition *Dada 1916–1923* at the Sidney Janis Gallery in New York and this was probably the source of inspiration for the work that he would go on to create. Whereas Duchamp still painted his paint sample cards illusionistically, Rauschenberg used actual samples in 1955. For Rauschenberg's

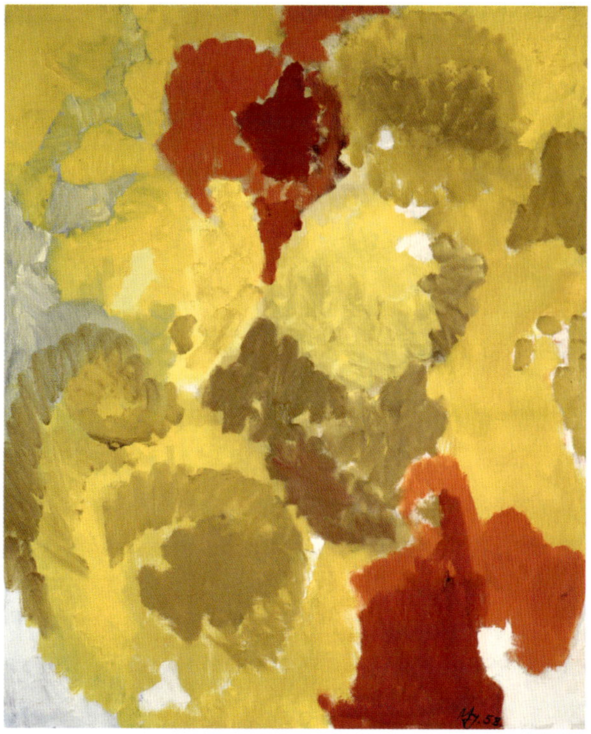

1 Ernst Wilhelm Nay: *With Diverse Yellows*, 1958
Oil on canvas, 100 × 81 cm
Private collection

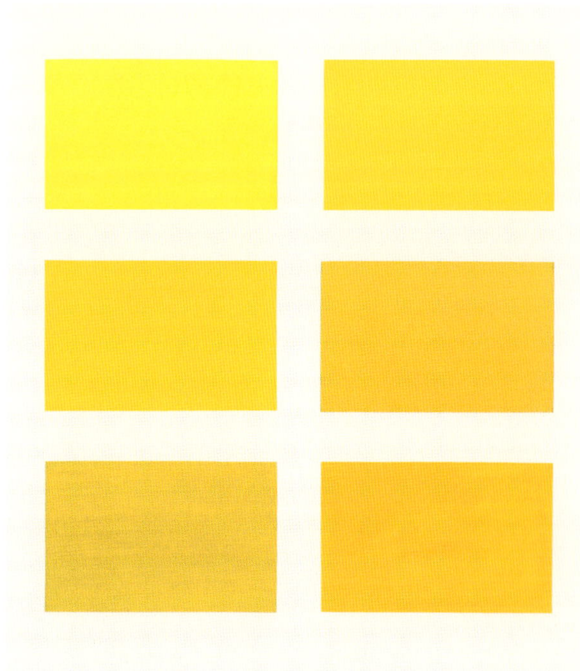

2 Gerhard Richter: *Six Yellows* [141], 1966
Lacquer on canvas, 200 × 170 cm
Museum Frieder Burda, Baden-Baden

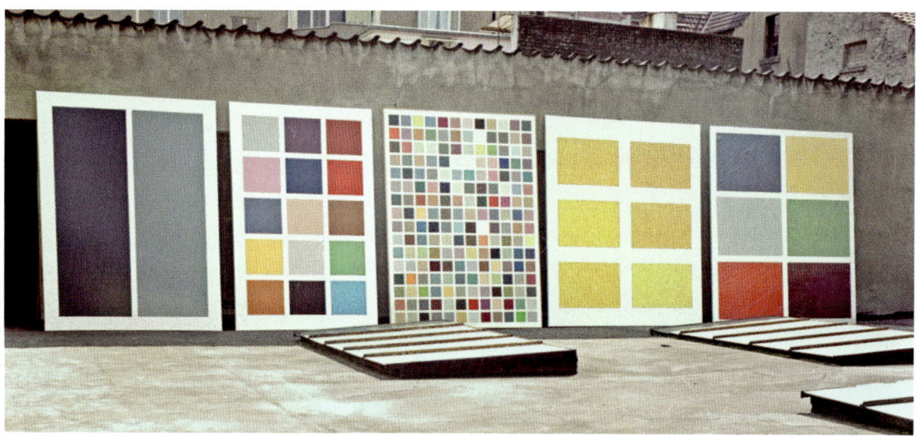

3 Color Chart paintings on the roof of Richter's studio
at Fürstenwall 204 in Düsseldorf, 1966

large-format combine painting *Rebus* (private collection, permanent loan to the Museum of Modern Art, New York), the artist made a collage from more than one hundred small monochrome strips of paint from a book of paint samples he had purchased in a store, arranging them in a horizontal row in the center of the canvas.[12] On the upper edge of each sample, the two holes that had been used to bind the strips together are visible. The paint samples are clearly recognizable in the painting as industrial paint samples and hence as readymades. They are not, however, an element that essentially determines the painting, since the artist also glued pieces of fabric, comic strips, posters, drawings, photographs, and printed matter onto the three-part canvas, which he then reworked with brushstrokes and dashes of paint. By contrast, in 1962 the Italian artist Giulio Paolini used such paint samples as the sole and dominant motif in his work *Untitled* (private collection).[13] Using small metal staples, he fastened twenty-five monochrome cardboard cards of various colors to a transparent plastic film stretched over a wooden frame. By presenting the colors as models, this work comes across as a rigorous analysis of the principles of artistic practice.

Paint Sample Cards as Pictorial Models

In 1966, the paint sample cards displayed at Sonnen-Herzog, a hardware store in Düsseldorf, caught Richter's attention. He was immediately fascinated by these functional motifs that in no way pointed to an artist's subject.[14] That same year, the artist made his first serial Color Chart paintings (fig. 3), modeled on sample cards produced by the German company Ducolux. He produced eighteen works on canvas and one on a wood panel, all of which present large monochrome color surfaces in a square or horizontal rectangular form similar to paint sample cards (see the chapter "Chance and Concept: Color Charts," pp. 88–103). The colors arranged in the series do not touch but are rather separated by white borders, so that every color has a generous open space around it, and there is little or no interaction with the adjacent colors. Each painting has two, three, six, eight, nine, ten, twelve, fifteen, or eighteen areas of color, with just two with more (100 and 192 respectively) (cat. 13–15). The titles either indicate the number of colors—for example, *Nine Colors*—or else simply read *Color Chart*. Richter's first painting of this series, *192 Colors* [136] (cat. 13), was executed in oil paint, while all the others were painted with industrial lacquer paints manufactured by Ducolux. The artist chose the latter painting material because it creates a smooth, glossy surface that does not reveal an individual brushwork style, thus making the paintings seem emphatically impersonal.

In the spirit of pop art, Richter elevated his banal and mass-produced hardware store models and made them worthy of artistic representation. These paintings reference both the presentation of paints as readymades and the oblong planar form and model-like, anticompositional appearance of paint sample cards. The artist did not, however, copy the sample cards exactly, but rather distributed the colors "completely arbitrarily," as he himself explained in 2015.[15] Nevertheless, or precisely for that reason, the structure of his Color Chart paintings does indeed resemble that of actual paint sample cards, as a comparison makes clear.

If one looks at a Ducolux sample card from 1963 (fig. 4), it is striking that only the yellow, blue, and red shades form groups, while the other colors do not follow any systematic order. For example, dark brown is followed by a bright green and dark green by a brilliant red, which makes no sense from a color theory perspective. A continuous sequence of colors is not at all necessary from the manufacturer's perspective, since such a card is merely supposed to depict a color collection aimed at specific market needs and hence represents particular fashions and trends. That is why the front of the old Ducolux card is described as containing "The fashionable shades of the season." Richter's lacquer painting *Ten Colors* [135-1] (fig. 5, 1966) also avoids presenting an aesthetically normative arrangement of colors: In addition to an intense red, there are four shades of gray, two pastel green and two brown shades, and turquoise.

Even the one hundred colors of the more complex work *Ten Large Color Charts* [144] from the same year form only partial color families, each with a common basic shade.[16] The system is repeatedly disregarded, in the same way one sees on real paint sample cards. This ten-part work is a particularly clear example of Richter's occasional desire to demonstratively indicate the sources he used. Whereas the paintings are now hung flat against the wall in their current location at the Kunstsammlung Nordrhein-Westfalen in Düsseldorf, the artist had exhibited them on stands and placed side by side like an unfolded leporello in the group exhibition *Demonstrative 67*, held in the DuMont publishing house in Cologne in 1967 (fig. 6). This was a direct allusion to the form of an unfolded paint sample card.

In 1966, he also painted the lacquer painting *Fifteen Colors* [138] (fig. 7), which features five rows of three squares of color in a serial grid structure. Back in 1963, the American pop artist Jim Dine had produced a very similar painting (fig. 8). It uses almost the same structure and concept as Richter's *Fifteen Colors*, but Dine placed his title on the canvas in large letters beneath the color squares: *A Color Chart*. By doing so he was referring unmistakably, but also all too didactically, to the painting's source. Richter was not familiar with Dine's painting when he produced his own work.[17] Four plates in Richter's *Atlas*—his ongoing collection of photographs, collages, and sketches—show designs for Color Chart paintings that have labels next to or below individual planes of color in the form of the names and product numbers of paints.[18] When executing the paintings, however, the artist chose not to include such technical details or even to adopt the terms "color chart" or "paint sample chart."

Richter began his Color Chart paintings in 1966, the same year Blinky Palermo was working on his first fabric picture, which has the laconic title *Red-Pink* (Sattler Collection, Munich).[19] The two artists had met in 1963 when studying at the Düsseldorf Art Academy and became close friends. Palermo had Richter's then-wife, Ema, horizontally or vertically sew together two or three monochrome lengths of fabric (of cotton, linen, or nettle cloth) for his pictures. He then spanned the fabric on stretcher bars. The fabric and its color—that is, the medium and its colored surface—are one in such works, since the color was not applied by the artist but was already a component of the industrially produced fabrics. The identity of color and material again makes the color seem like a readymade, which may have reinforced Richter's own views, especially since the artists were close and frequently exchanged ideas.

Strategic Arbitrariness versus Traditional Color Theories

Richter was so fascinated by commercial color samples not merely because he could use them to make paints seem like readymades, but also because such sample cards represented the exact opposite of traditional artistic color systems. The latter always establish a hierarchical and normative order, of the sort familiar to us, for example, from the color spectra of the rainbow or from optical prisms. Famous classical color systems from the history of art and science include, for example, the color wheel of the natural scientist Isaac Newton (1704), the color sphere of the Romantic artist Philipp Otto Runge (1810), the artistically influential color wheel of the chemist Michel-Eugène Chevreul (1839), and the unfolded color sphere of the Bauhaus master Johannes Itten (1921). These color theories and their depictions are based on a continuous color spectrum whose gradations of color range from red, orange, and yellow to green, blue, and violet.

Richter finds the artists who refer to such color systems or who have used them to develop their own theories suspect. As he expressed in an interview in 1986, he sees his Color Chart paintings in clear contrast to the works of Josef Albers, for example. One can cite Albers's famous series of paintings and prints *Homage to the Square* as an example of work that is entirely in the Bauhaus tradition. Between 1949 and 1976—that is, including the period in which Richter was working on his Color Chart paintings—Albers, then working in the United States, produced numerous works under this title that can be regarded as classic examples of a systematic analysis of the interaction between colors. His 1962 series of screen prints on paper titled *Homage to the Square* consists of ten uniformly sized sheets, each of which presents three or four nested squares of different colors.[20] Driven by a didactic impetus, Albers showed that colors are a highly relative artistic means due to their optical interaction, i.e. the mutual influence of neighboring colors. A single color can take on a number of different appearances and effects when placed next to various other colors. The series thus systematically reflects on issues of the aesthetics of the image and its reception. Richter found such works, as he put it, "too arty-crafty and too decorative."[21] Subjective sensations and the psychological and perceptual effects of color had no place in Richter's art in the 1960s and 1970s. He presents the colors as readymades without any expressive value or any symbolism. As a result, Richter's Color Chart paintings are outside the tradition of geometric-constructive art of the sort familiar from the works of Bauhaus or Swiss concrete artists, for example.

Richter negated everything with which color is normally associated in the history of art. That becomes clear from the terminology employed, since one can speak of color in his Color Chart

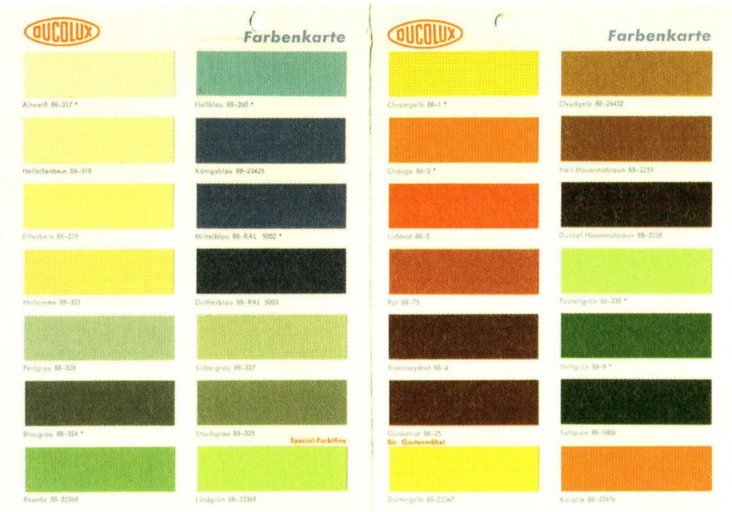

4 Ducolux paint sample card, 1963, private collection

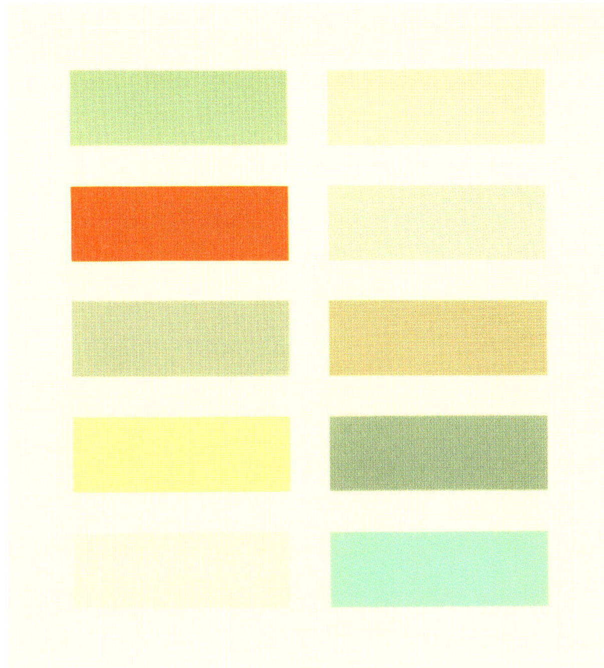

5 Gerhard Richter: *Ten Colors* [135-1], 1966
Lacquer on canvas, 135 × 120 cm
Minskoff Collection, New York

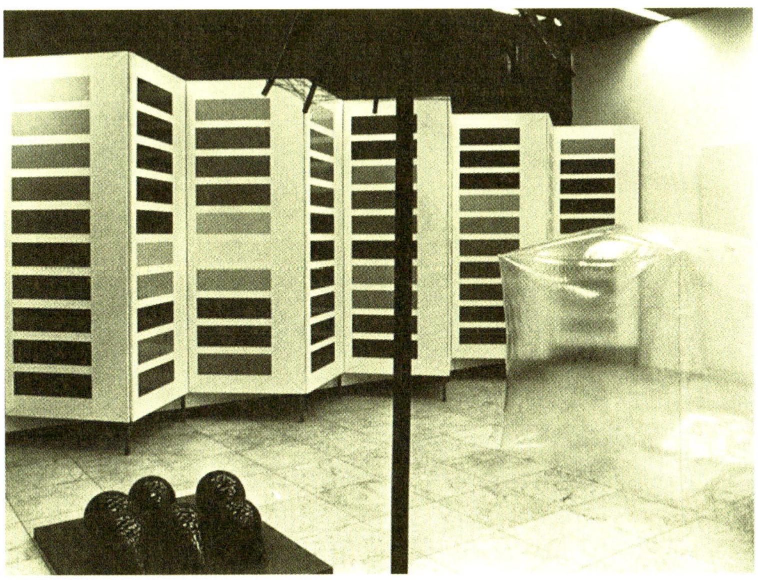

6 Richter's *Ten Large Color Charts* [144], 1966,
in the group exhibition *Demonstrative 67*, held at the
DuMont publishing house offices in Cologne, 1967

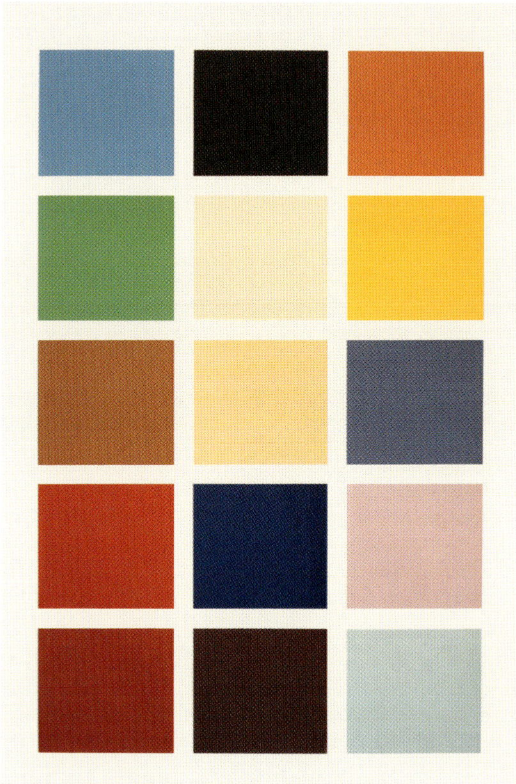

7 Gerhard Richter: *Fifteen Colors* [138], 1966
Lacquer on canvas, 200 × 130 cm
Collection of Robert M. Kaye

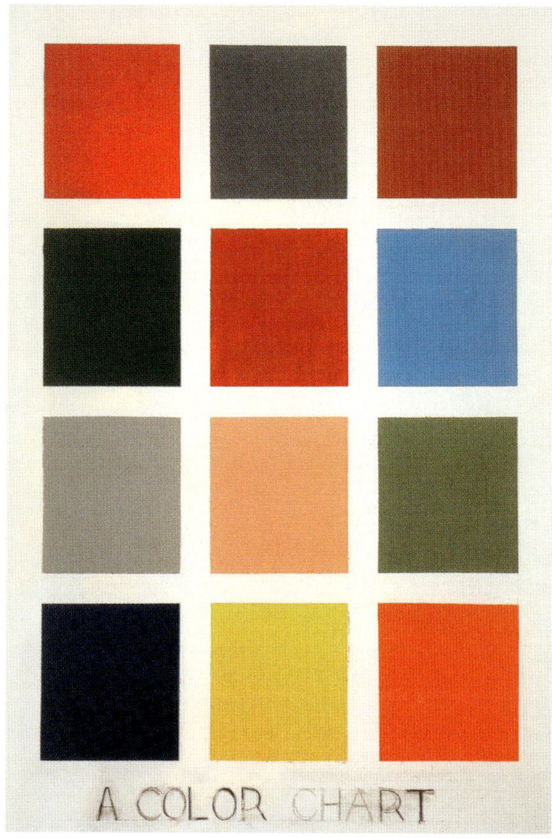

8 Jim Dine: *A Color Chart*, 1963
Oil on canvas, 184 × 122 cm
Private collection, New York

paintings, but no longer of coloration. The term "coloration" refers to the overall color impression of a painting, which is achieved by employing a uniform color design throughout a work. The idea of coloration has been a key aesthetic category in painting since the sixteenth century—an ideal of painterly appearance that, over the course of time and up to the present day, has been granted sometimes more, sometimes less significance.[22] Richter rejects coloration because he does not create a compositional context with the color samples in their pure materiality. This is because the arbitrary distribution of the colors cannot produce a composition based on contrasts. Instead, it results in something that can only be called, quite objectively, structure.

Chance as a Concept for Constituting the Image

After an interruption of several years, Richter again took up the theme of the Color Chart paintings in 1971, though he fundamentally modified the concept. That year he produced four lacquer paintings with 180 colors each and another twenty with nine colors each, as well as a screen print. The 1971 work *180 Colors* [300-1] (fig. 9) was the first work no longer based on the model of paint sample cards, but rather on a strictly conceptual strategy. From the primary colors yellow, red, and blue, the artist mixed 180 different shades and determined their arrangement by a chance procedure, namely by drawing slips of paper with numbers on them from a bucket. Richter thus employed chance as a central concept for constituting the image. When he told his then-printer Tünn Konerding that not he but his artist friend Blinky Palermo had picked the color numbers for a particular painting, Konerding remarked: "You can tell."[23] It is bizarre and also absurd to think that a chance procedure generated by drawing lots could lead to an individual style recognizable in the painting—in this case, that of Palermo. It was nevertheless for this reason that Richter subsequently preferred to handle the process of drawing lots himself.

The introduction of chance into the artistic process has a long, albeit highly varied history. Without going into it in detail here, it should at least be mentioned briefly that the specific practice of drawing lots as a way of determining the structure of a work of art was also used in the work of Marcel Duchamp in the early twentieth century. His work *Erratum Musical* is a score for three parts that was composed in 1913 in the following way: Duchamp and his two sisters drew small slips of paper from a hat, one after the other, each of which had a single musical note written on it.[24] Duchamp wrote the notes for each voice on a sheet of staff paper in the order they were drawn, so that both the sequence of the notes and the harmony of the three parts were a product of chance. Richter too determined his pictorial elements by lot, excluding any subjectivity, resulting in a deliberately organized chaos in the sense of a state of extreme disorder. Drawing lots as a random generating device—like the earlier arbitrary distribution of colors in the 1966 Color Chart paintings—necessarily rules out any order based on gradations in a color spectrum or intentional compositional contrasts. Whereas the rectangles are highly ordered as a result of the grid, the distribution of colors is highly disordered. Richter's Color Chart paintings are a classic example of an artistic language without a hierarchy of color.

In 1973 and 1974, Richter added a further twenty-five lacquer paintings, each with between four and 4,096 shades, to the twenty-five works he had produced in 1971 (cat. 16–18, fig. p. 231). The work *4096 Colors* [359] (1974, private collection, London), is the most complex of the Color Chart paintings. That same year the artist applied the structural principle of his paintings to the medium of the print. He produced the offset print *1260 Colors* and the similar print series *Color Fields: Six Arrangements of 1260 Colors*. Each of the six offset prints contains 1,260 colors in the form of small rectangles arranged next to and beneath one another, and each print features a different distribution of the colors (fig. 10). When establishing the concept for this series of prints, Richter made a drawing on cardboard with pencil and black marker (fig. 11). This sheet is of remarkable art historical significance, since it reveals how the artist developed his concept. The drawing shows the boxes without colors; instead, each has a three-digit number that the artist wrote within the planar forms. The printer later converted the number noted by Richter into a color, as in the following example: The number 258 indicates two parts red and five parts blue plus eight parts yellow, resulting in a bright olive green. Several boxes contain a V rather than a number, which is a printing term for *Vollton* (solid color), which is to say, this color should be printed at one hundred percent.

The sequence of numbers and the resulting colors were drawn by lots for all the boxes of the first of the six prints, with Richter pulling numbered slips of paper from a bucket. He thus once again employed chance as a central principle for constituting the image. The sequences of numbers obtained in this way were retained for the other five sheets but, following the artist's instructions, the printer applied the numbers to different colors. As a result, the number 258 no longer yielded a bright olive green but, in the next print, a subdued bluish-violet. Each of the six sheets in the series thus features a different distribution of colors.

Serial Grid Structures as Ordering Principle

In addition to the concept of chance introduced by the choosing of lots described above, the principle of serialism is the second fundamental category that characterizes Richter's six-part *Color Fields* series and all the other Color Chart paintings of the 1970s. In the 1960s and 1970s in particular, working in series was a central artistic method in pop art, minimalism, and conceptual art, as well as in the geometric constructive art of the period. Serialism as an artistic concept and form of design is always based on the principle of repeating identical or at least similar elements. The American artist Mel Bochner, whose exhibitions and publications explicitly called attention to the serial method, expressed this fundamental principle in 1967: "Serial order is a method, not a style."[25] For Bochner, the use of serial principles is not a stylistic phenomenon that conforms to a certain aesthetic, but is instead the manifestation of a specific artistic approach. In place of intuitive or even expressive works, Bochner argues in the spirit of conceptual art for a systematic method that is characteristic of a predetermined concept.

That is also true of Richter's 1970s Color Chart paintings. These works feature a strict pictorial organization based on a serial and symmetrical principle of ordering. For example, in the lacquer painting *1024 Colors* [351] (1973) (cat. 16), 1,024 colored squares are distributed across the entire pictorial surface, resulting in an allover structure.[26] The rectangular arrangement of the color fields and the spaces between them establish a regular grid structure. The term "composition" seems inappropriate here, since all the elements relate to one another in an egalitarian relationship without any compositional hierarchy; that is to say, the boxes in general are not just uniform but also equal in value. In 1978, the American art historian Rosalind E. Krauss characterized the pictorial structure of the grid as "an emblem of modernity,"[27] since it can be viewed as a paradigmatic pictorial form of the twentieth century.

The principle of pictorial grid structures was developed both by Piet Mondrian (fig. p. 19) and Josef Albers, and by Man Ray and Hans Arp in the 1910s and 1920s. In the 1950s, it was adopted by Ellsworth Kelly.[28] Richter then further developed the grid in the 1960s and 1970s and connected it to the idea of paint as readymade (see the chapter "Structures and Illusions: Abstract Works in the 1960s," pp. 70–87). The latter idea, however, applies only to Richter's 1966 Color Chart paintings, since the more intricate and complex these paintings became in the 1970s, the less they recalled actual sample cards. The colors became autonomous as purely self-referential pictorial elements. This is particularly true of the paintings that have a very large number of colors, such as the aforementioned lacquer painting *4096 Colors*.

By fundamentally reflecting on the possibilities of contemporary painting and printing, Richter found in his Color Chart paintings a motif and a form of artistic production that is—with an eye to the contemporaneous movements of pop art, minimalism, and conceptual art—of course grounded in its historical context. Yet Richter explored the possibilities of such an art in a specific way and developed radical pictorial forms by bringing together several fundamental aspects: first, the idea of paint as readymade by using color sample cards as models for paintings; second, the concept of chance as a principle for constituting the image; third, the associated rejection of traditional color theories; fourth, the use of strictly serial and anticompositional grid structures; and, fifth, the related substantial elimination of subjective categories. Despite or precisely because of this turn away from traditional forms of pictorial invention, the Color Chart paintings have an art historically important place within Richter's extremely diverse oeuvre. Their site-specific apex was doubtless Gerhard Richter's *Cologne Cathedral Window* [900], which can surely be described as his most popular work (fig. 12).[29]

Translated from the German by Steven Lindberg

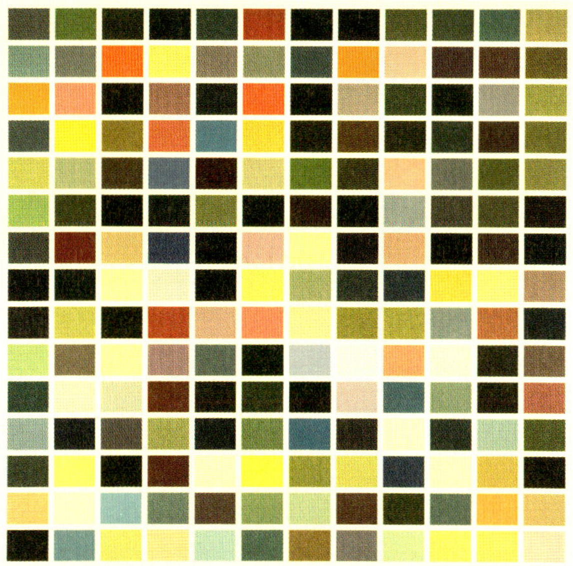

9 Gerhard Richter: *180 Colors* [300-1], 1971
Lacquer on canvas, 200 × 200 cm
Private collection, New York

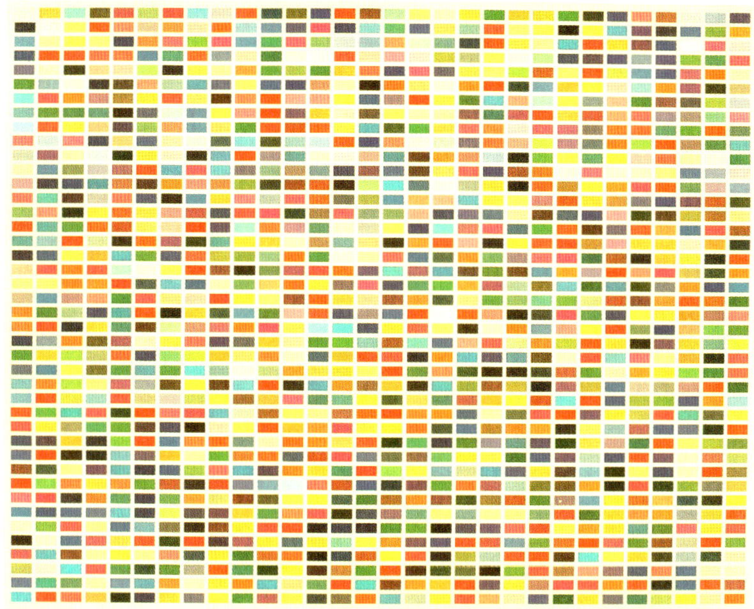

10 Gerhard Richter: *Color Fields: Six Arrangements of 1260 Colors (Red-Yellow-Blue)* [Edition 51, sheet a], 1974
Offset print on cardboard, 64.4 × 79.2 cm
Private collection

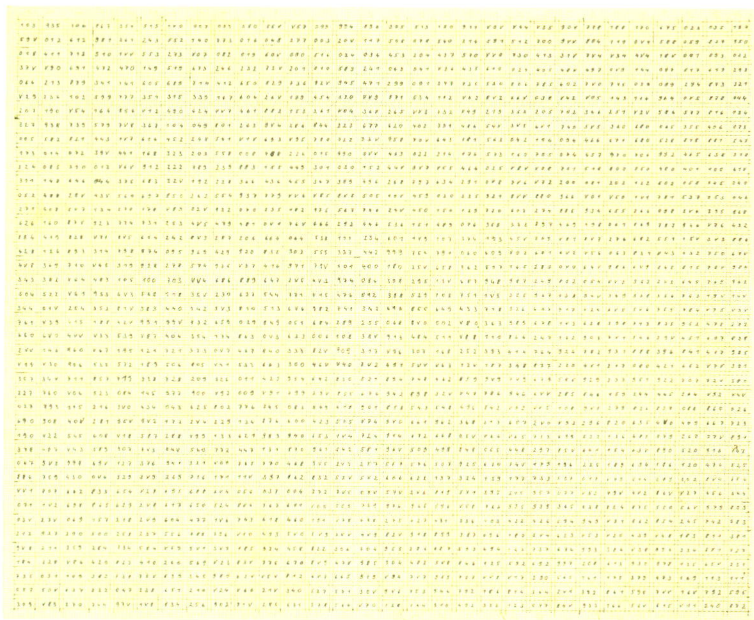

11 Gerhard Richter: Conceptual sketch for *Color Fields: Six Arrangements of 1260 Colors*, 1974
Marker and pencil on cardboard, 65.5 × 80 cm
Collection of Thomas Olbricht, Essen

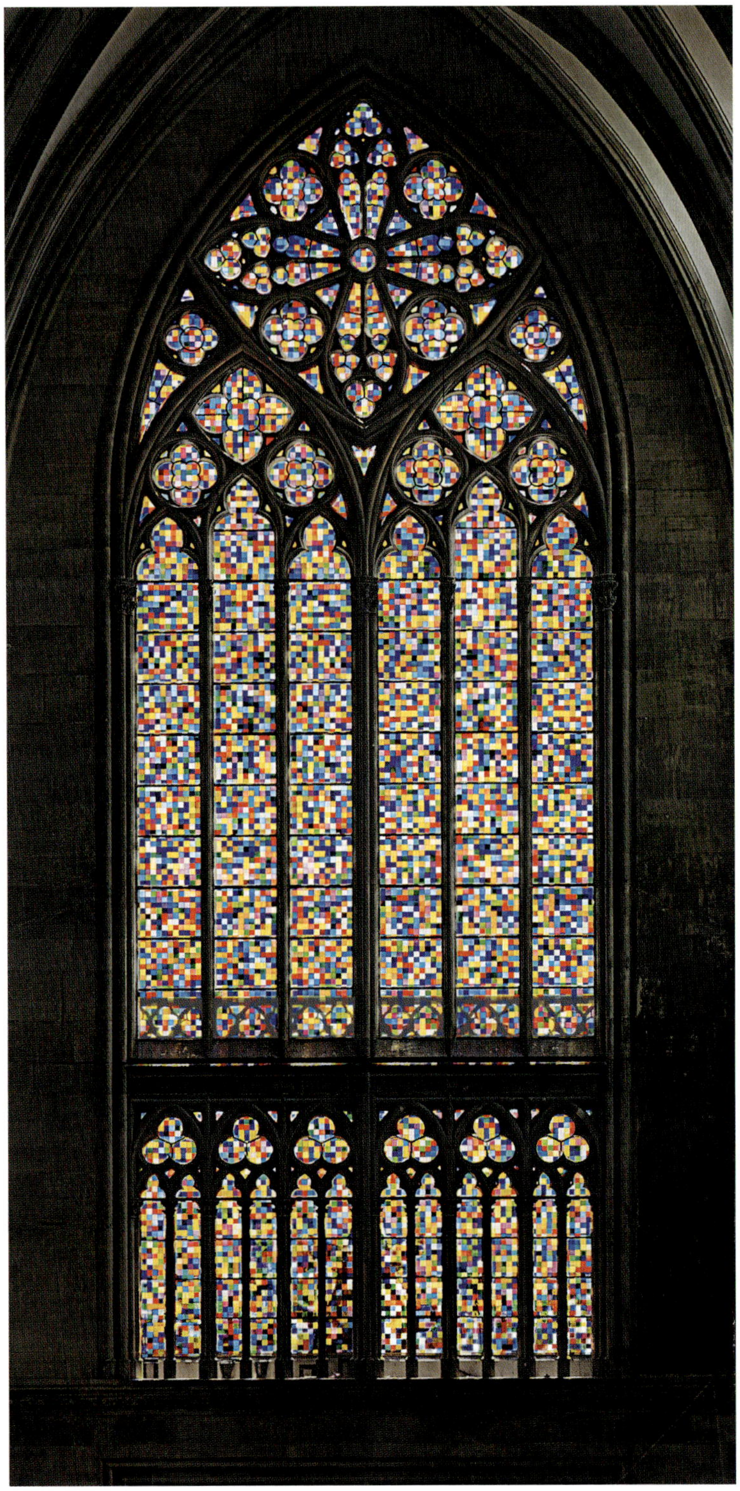

12 Gerhard Richter: *Cologne Cathedral Window* [900], 2007
Antique glass, handblown, 2,300 × 900 cm
Cologne Cathedral

[1] Aurel Scheibler, *Ernst Wilhelm Nay. Werkverzeichnis der Ölgemälde*, vol. 2: *1952–1968* (Cologne: DuMont, 1990), 64–237.

[2] *E. W. Nay. Lesebuch. Selbstzeugnisse und Schriften 1931–1968*, rev. Magdalene Claesges (Cologne: DuMont, 2002), 186–87.

[3] Friedrich Wolfram Heubach, "Die Kunst der 60er Jahre," in *Die 60er Jahre: Kölns Weg zur Kunstmetropole; Vom Happening zum Kunstmarkt* (Cologne: Kölnischer Kunstverein, 1986), 112–16, here 114. Exhibition catalog.

[4] Marcel Duchamp in Francis Roberts, "'I Propose to Strain the Laws of Physics': Interview with Marcel Duchamp," *Art News* 67, no. 8 (December 1968): 46–47 and 62–64, here 47.

[5] Marcel Duchamp's lecture was first published under the title "Apropos of Readymades," *Art and Artists* 1, no. 4 (July 1966): 47.

[6] See, for example, *Color Chart: Reinventing Color, 1950 to Today*, ed. Ann Temkin (New York: Museum of Modern Art, 2008). Exhibition catalog.

[7] The idea of paint as readymade had already been suggested by Vincent van Gogh. Although color certainly still had an expressive, representational function in his work, he seems to have understood industrially produced paint as material that could be employed directly when he wrote of his depictions of nature: "I squeezed roots and trunks in from the tube"; Vincent van Gogh to Theo van Gogh, September 3, 1882, in *The Letters of Vincent van Gogh*, ed. Ronald de Leeuw, trans. Arnold Pomerans (London: Penguin, 2003), 195.

[8] Hubertus Butin, "Gerhard Richter's Editions and the Discourses of Images," Butin et al. 2014, 11–107, here 32–34.

[9] Illustrated in ibid., 33.

[10] Arturo Schwarz, *The Complete Works of Marcel Duchamp*, third edition, two volumes (New York: Delano Greenidge, 1997), 1:225, figs. in ibid., 2:439 and 658.

[11] Illustrated in ibid., 1:225.

[12] Illustrated in *Robert Rauschenberg: A Retrospective*, ed. Walter Hopps and Susan Davidson (New York: Solomon R. Guggenheim Museum, 1997), 117. Exhibition catalog.

[13] Illustrated in *Giulio Paolini: Von heute bis gestern / Da oggi a ieri*, ed. Peter Weibel (Ostfildern: Neue Galerie im Landesmuseum Joanneum, 1998), 195. Exhibition catalog.

[14] The British paint manufacturer Craig & Rose had begun producing similar paint sample cards around 1910. Illustrated in Patrick Baty, *The Anatomy of Colour: The Story of Heritage Paints and Pigments* (London: Thames & Hudson, 2017), 206.

[15] Gerhard Richter to Hubertus Butin, email, June 15, 2015.

[16] Illustrated in Elger 2011–2017, 1:299.

[17] In 2015, the British artist Damien Hirst transformed the 1963 Ducolux color chart (fig. 4) into three large-format lacquer paintings and thus produced a kind of painted readymade; illustrated in *Colori: Emotions of Color in Art* (Rivoli: Castello di Rivoli, Museo d'Arte Contemporanea and Turin: Galleria Civica d'Arte Moderna e Contemporanea, 2017), 243. Exhibition catalog.

[18] Illustrated in Richter 2015a, plates 275, 276, 279, 280.

[19] Illustrated in *Palermo: Werkverzeichnis*, vol. 1, *Bilder und Objekte*, ed. Thordis Moeller (Bonn: Kunstmuseum Bonn, 1995), cat. no. 49. Exhibition catalog.

[20] Illustrated in Brenda Danilowitz, *The Prints of Josef Albers: A Catalogue Raisonné, 1915–1976*, second edition (Manchester, VT: Hudson Hills Press, 2010), 96–98.

[21] Gerhard Richter in "Interview with Benjamin H. D. Buchloh" (1986), in Richter 2009, 170.

[22] Christoph Wagner, "'Kolorit' und 'Farbe' als Kategorien der Ästhetikgeschichte," in *Farben in Kunst- und Geisteswissenschaften*, ed. Jakob Steinbrenner, Christoph Wagner, and Oliver Jehle (Regensburg: Schnell & Steiner, 2011), 94–121.

[23] Gerhard Richter, in Corinna Belz, *Gerhard Richter: Das Kölner Domfenster*, documentary film, Germany, 2008.

[24] Illustrated in Schwarz, *The Complete Works of Marcel Duchamp* (see note 10), 1:329, 572.

[25] Mel Bochner, "The Serial Attitude," *Artforum* 6, no. 4 (December 1967): 28–33, here 28.

[26] Illustrated in Elger, ed., *Gerhard Richter* (see note 16), 2:567.

[27] Rosalind E. Krauss, "Grids, You Say," in *Grids: Format and Image in 20th Century Art* (New York: Pace Gallery and Akron, OH: Akron Art Institute, 1978), n.p. Exhibition catalog.

[28] For a comparison with works by these artists, see Butin, "Gerhard Richter's Editions and the Discourses of Images" (see note 8), 36–39.

[29] Hubertus Butin, "Gerhard Richter's Window for Cologne Cathedral," in *Gerhard Richter, Zufall: Das Kölner Domfenster und 4900 Farben / The Cologne Cathedral Window, and 4900 Colours* (Cologne: Verlag Kölner Dom; König, 2007), 117–24.

“In Painting Thinking is Painting”: The Primacy of Form in Gerhard Richter’s Art

Armin Zweite

When Gerhard Richter began developing an index of his works in 1969, the first work he entered went by the succinct title of *Table* [1] (figs. pp. 10, 24). He painted it in Düsseldorf in 1962. It seems a surprising choice to begin a retrospective catalogue raisonné, in that this work was not so much a promising prelude as a mark of failure, deletion, and escape. The artist had based his painting on a reproduction in the August 1956 issue of the Italian architecture and design magazine *domus* (fig. p. 24).[1] The photograph shows a pull-out table by Ignazio Gardella, one of Italy's leading architects at the time.[2] Rather than simply copying this emblem of Italian modernism, Richter substantially altered the proportions of the object itself and its relationship to the space, transforming its volatile elegance into sterling sobriety. His subsequent efforts at correction misfired, so Richter tried to erase the composition with a few vigorous rubs.

What remained in the middle of the picture was a large oval patch with a dynamic internal structure that became a fulcrum between the upper and lower halves. Moreover, there seems to be an off-white shape, truncated by perspective, hovering in the upper, paler section, and this is reflected in the center of the lower section by a smaller matt blob with blurred contours, held in place by two blackish diagonal lines. It is clear from the original photograph that the diagonals are the slender legs of the table, while the flat corpus floating above is the table top. The segregation of the pictorial components and their symmetric arrangement demonstrate that, despite the vehement act of obliteration, an essential feature of the original layout has been preserved: the equilibrium. Bits of paper, stains, and other irregularities in various areas of the painting do little to alter the carefully distributed weight of the composition, which has resisted the energetic attempt to conceal it—a characteristic also highlighted by the essentially elliptical figure at the center created by the rubbing-out.

Prospectively, *Table* [1] illustrates the two poles in Richter's art: on the one hand, his efforts to depict reality with the aid of photographs, and on the other, his eagerness to emancipate the painter's tools and adopt abstract methods.[3] Both bring their impact to bear here: the calculated, formally defined, balanced, realistic side, and the gestural, free, spontaneous, random side. These two intentions figure together in the work without being played off against each other.[4] This depiction marked a watershed moment in the artist's creative work.[5] There are already indications here of those strategies toward obliteration, abstention, negation, and concealment that would later feature in Richter's abstractions (see the essay by Dietmar Elger, pp. 22–33).[6]

He exhibited the painting in summer 1964 in his first solo show at the Munich gallery Friedrich & Dahlem. Five years on, the work was reproduced in his first major exhibition catalog.[7] He had evidently discovered a special quality in his destructive act—even if he was not yet quite sure what exactly it was, as he observed thirty years later.[8] His priority, after all, lay with making rather than with thinking.

The example briefly presented here suggests that in the process of painting, the act of making—which in this specific instance entailed deleting, destroying, and reforming—is not understood merely as exercising primacy over the act of thinking, but that this making, which is undeniably spontaneous, is actually supposed to replace reflection. If that is indeed the case, Richter was latching onto an idea which had already been formulated in the late nineteenth century, although its impact was not fully felt until the twentieth. Back then, a focus on the production process had prompted artists to start stepping back from techniques driven by reception- and content-based aesthetics—as formulated by, for example, Immanuel Kant and Georg Wilhelm Friedrich Hegel—and hence from assumptions which had long helped to define aesthetic discourse right up until the early twentieth century. While for Kant, fine art is "a way of presenting that is purposive on its own and that furthers, even though without a purpose, the culture of our mental powers to [facilitate] social communication," and hence "whose standard is the reflective power of judgment, rather than sensation proper,"[9] for Hegel art was realized within the ideal of "an individual configuration of reality destined essentially to embody and reveal the Idea."[10] While Kant determined that pleasure in art and beauty was disinterested and called for a mood of "quiet contemplation," Hegel saw fine art as long since overlaid by thoughts and reflections, so that in its "highest vocation" it could only be appreciated as a thing of the past. For Hegel, then, the aesthetic present of art was its past. If for Kant, the value of the work of art was engendered by the mental state of the viewer, for Hegel, it manifested in its significance.

It was Konrad Fiedler (1841–1895) who, in a series of writings, set out a completely different view of the nature of art, and of painting in particular, which seems to have found its way into Richter's practice and into the ideas accompanying this process. Fiedler was born into a family of Jewish industrialists, and after graduating in law he worked briefly as an articled clerk in Leipzig before embarking on an itinerant life as an art critic. His friendships with Anselm Feuerbach, Hans von Marées, and Adolf von Hildebrand played a significant role in the formulation of his theoretical ideas. According to the art historian Gottfried Boehm, who must be credited with Fiedler's rediscovery in recent years, he challenged the view that art was peripheral to life, supporting instead "the program of an art that provides not only incidental ornament for the fruits of scientific cognition, but a legitimate type of cognition of its own."[11] By comparing some of Richter's comments with passages by Fiedler, and pausing to describe a few examples of the artist's work, this essay seeks to cast light on some substantive links between them, without however questioning the independence of the artist's views.

Distinguishing Practice from Theory

The works Richter painted in Düsseldorf in the early 1960s—just after he left the GDR—are heterogeneous in both theme and style. At the same time, he was reflecting upon the criteria applied to evaluating art. In 1962, in a letter to the sculptor Wieland Förster in East Berlin, he commented on his situation and on the credibility of what he was doing: "things only have a certain quality—in relation to the environment. Even existence is only possible in relation to the environment. Which is almost to say that I can't live in Dresden and keep Picasso, Moore, Pollock in the cupboard. It's a torment and draining to live between two things. Unless one had a different profession that included reflecting on and comprehending the world, art, the divided world, or one that permitted reflection, left space for reflection (like woodcutter, cowherd, toilet attendant). But painting can't be thought about and comprehended. In painting thinking is painting (without even the slightest verbal thought), i.e. responding with a color to the previous one, with a shape to the current one."[12]

This passage not only describes how torn Richter had felt in Dresden at the height of the so-called formalism debate, but also reveals how he viewed the artistic process. He had been obliged to keep all the things that interested and inspired him locked away inside, to keep them secret, suppress them, because they were at odds with official art doctrine in the GDR. This schizophrenia might have been bearable when tackling more trivial tasks, but not when engaged in something as existential as art. But for an artist who wished to devote himself entirely to his art, there could be no division between thought and action. Richter would frequently repeat this insight in later years. In his notes of 1962, he formulated it thus: "Painting has nothing to do with thinking, because in painting thinking is painting."[13]

What Richter is expressing here was to remain crucial to all his artistic output,[14] even if he added and modified the sentiment in decisive ways. The first striking aspect is that he separates painterly practice—the craft of working on a canvas with brush and paint—from all theoretical conceptualizing. This does not rule out theorizing before starting on the practical work, but the theoretical element plays no decisive role in the implementation of the painting because—as Richter can be understood to be suggesting—artistic imaginings first start to evolve in the physical process of painting and can only be reflected upon and analyzed after the event. In a note in 1962, Richter jotted down: "Thinking is language—record-keeping—and has to take place before and after."[15] Reflecting on objectives and possible results can be done, in Richter's view, before beginning an artistic activity or when the painting process is over, but during the activity itself all such contemplations are switched off or relegated to the background. Richter's comment "in painting thinking is painting" is a way of saying that the artist—to quote Konrad Fiedler—"possesses reality in a far more undistorted form in his sensory imaginings than in the system of words and concepts."[16]

Throughout his entire oeuvre, Richter has maintained an interest in how a motif is visualized and how this is achieved in practice. Either the subject is presented to the viewer in blurred form, as in *Sailors* [126] (fig. 1) of 1966, or else only the contours can be made out, as in *Drinking Woman* [196-1] of 1968 (fig. 2) or *Christmas Market* [198] from the same year (cat. 6). In the landscapes of the late 1960s, this interplay became a defining trait, like in the painting *Vintage* [195] of 1968 (fig. 3), which differs in only minimal ways from *Color Streaks* [192-2] (fig. 4), another work from the same year. The alternation between identifiable—even if in most cases diffusely rendered—subjects and representations that dispense with any reference at all to a motif is a defining principle of Richter's entire body of work, but from the late 1960s the group of works that can be labelled nonrepresentational acquired increasing weight. Richter was lauded at that time for his near-realist works based on photographs, whereas the Abstract paintings initially met with a reserved response.

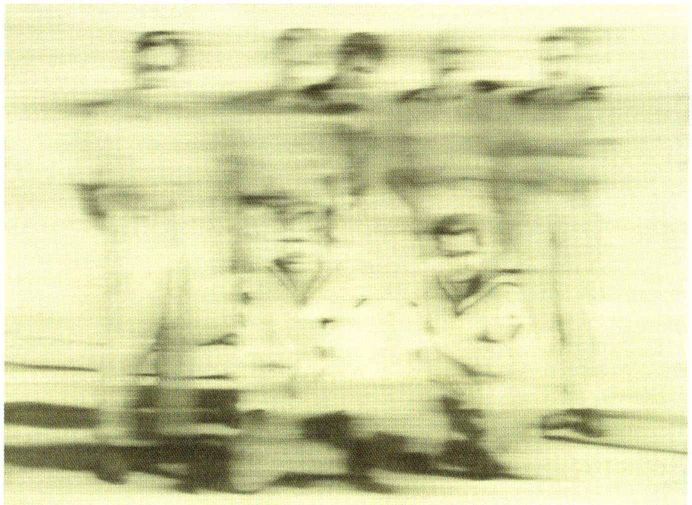

1 Gerhard Richter: *Sailors* [126], 1966
Oil on canvas, 150 × 200 cm
Private collection, US

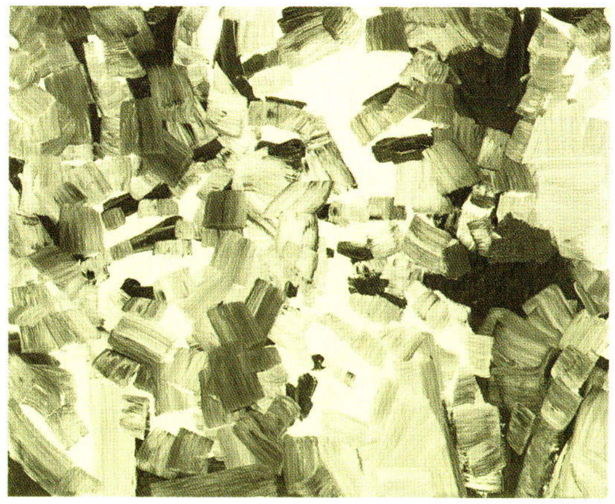

2 Gerhard Richter: *Drinking Woman* [196-1], 1968
Oil on canvas, 95 × 115 cm
Private collection, Austria

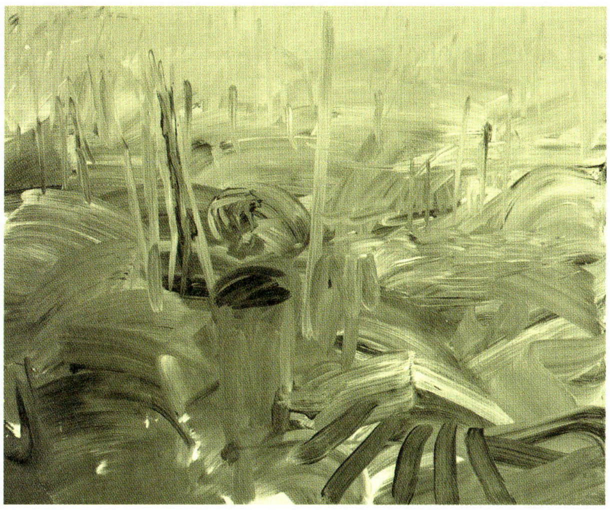

3 Gerhard Richter: *Vintage* [195], 1968
Oil on canvas, 95 × 115 cm
Private collection

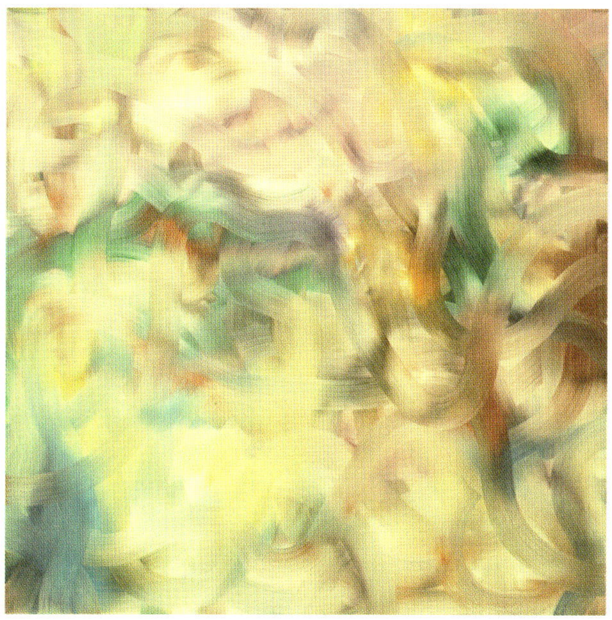

4 Gerhard Richter: *Color Streaks* [192-2], 1968
Oil on canvas, 200 × 200 cm
Private collection

His motto "in painting thinking is painting" testifies to an affinity between Richter and a tradition and practice in art theory described seventy-five years earlier by Konrad Fiedler in the context of a production-based aesthetic: "The artist, of all people, will be aware that the higher development of his mental, artistic life begins only at the moment when his imaginary urge sets the external organs of his body in motion, when the activity of his eye and brain is joined by the activity of his hand." It is artistic practice, according to Fiedler, that unlocks the door to mental development, for the artist begins "only then [...] [to enter] the path which he then climbs from darkness and limitation to growing clarity and freedom. All his talent, all his genius unfolds only in this externally perceivable action through which is realized not the depiction but the genesis of the artistic mindscape."[17]

Richter was similarly conscious of this genesis of the artistic mindscape and its link to a physical act when he noted in 1962: "The idea that art copies nature is a fatal misconception." Besides, Richter went on, it "makes no sense to expect or claim to 'make the invisible visible,' the unknown known, or the unthinkable thinkable."[18] In Richter's opinion, the artist is depicting nothing real or imaginary in his painting, be it a landscape, a still life, a portrait, or a figurative scene. He does not visualize or illustrate what he perceives or imagines; rather, a picture develops and becomes concrete through the practical use of brushes and paints. Richter thus distances himself from approaches which are born of an aesthetic founded on reception or content. This can be observed in his works of the early 1970s, like *Detail* [291] of 1971 (fig. 5). Plate 89 of his *Atlas* reproduces nine photographic details of paint samples, each approximately 13 × 18 cm (fig. 6). The photo on the top left was the basis for the later monumental painting measuring 250 × 375 cm, which rotates the original by 180 degrees.

Richter's statement "in painting thinking is painting" reveals that he judges the artistic value of a work exclusively on its visible design and form. In 1972, he commented on the issue of how his painting related to reality: "I can make no statement about reality clearer than my own relationship to reality; and this has a great deal to do with imprecision, uncertainty, transience, incompleteness, or whatever. But this doesn't explain the pictures. At best, it explains what led to their being painted. Pictures are something different, you see; for instance, they are never blurred. What we regard as blurring is imprecision, and that means that they are different from the object represented."[19] Richter is concerned here to make clear that painting does not copy or imitate reality, but that art lends visuality to another reality, an independent reality, accomplished above all in the way the work acquires form.

In sum, this position again reveals similarities with the neo-Kantian theories of Konrad Fiedler, who had close links with the artists Hans von Marées and Adolf von Hildebrand. Fiedler wrote that the accomplishment of a painting lay in "isolating the visuality of a thing in such a way that the conception of an object to which visuality attaches disappears entirely, and the latter becomes an independent form of being."[20] This visuality is in itself separate, detached from the object and its tangibility.[21] However, the independent construct known as a work of art or painting requires "a substance that is itself visible, the processing of which permits the making of the visuality construct."[22] Processing forces this substance—oil on canvas, say—"to deny itself" because it "only serves the purpose of expressing such a non-substantial construct as the form of the things themselves as they present themselves to the sense of sight."[23]

When Fiedler writes that "the content of the work of art [is] [...] nothing but the forming itself,"[24] Richter could well apply the statement to his own creative activity. This idea is reflected in works such as his Inpaintings (cat. 21–24), and in many others. In these instances, art is not imitating reality, nor transforming it, but producing it by combining primary colors into an impenetrable mixture that depicts nothing but this mixture, the result of slurry fabrication, in which the substance, i.e. the paint, is "forced to deny itself." "For art," says Fiedler, "is nothing but one of the means by which humans acquire reality."[25] Rather than being, there is constant becoming and passing away. "It seems to us," writes Fiedler, "that we have lost the grip afforded by the assumption of a given reality, be it independent of ourselves or dependent on ourselves, and we find ourselves reliant with all our consciousness of reality on an event which happens not outside us but in and through us."[26] Richter also registers this lack of a firm hold when he repeatedly applies terms like "lack of focus, uncertainty, volatility, partiality" not only to depictions which relate to reality, but also to his nonrepresentational or abstract works.

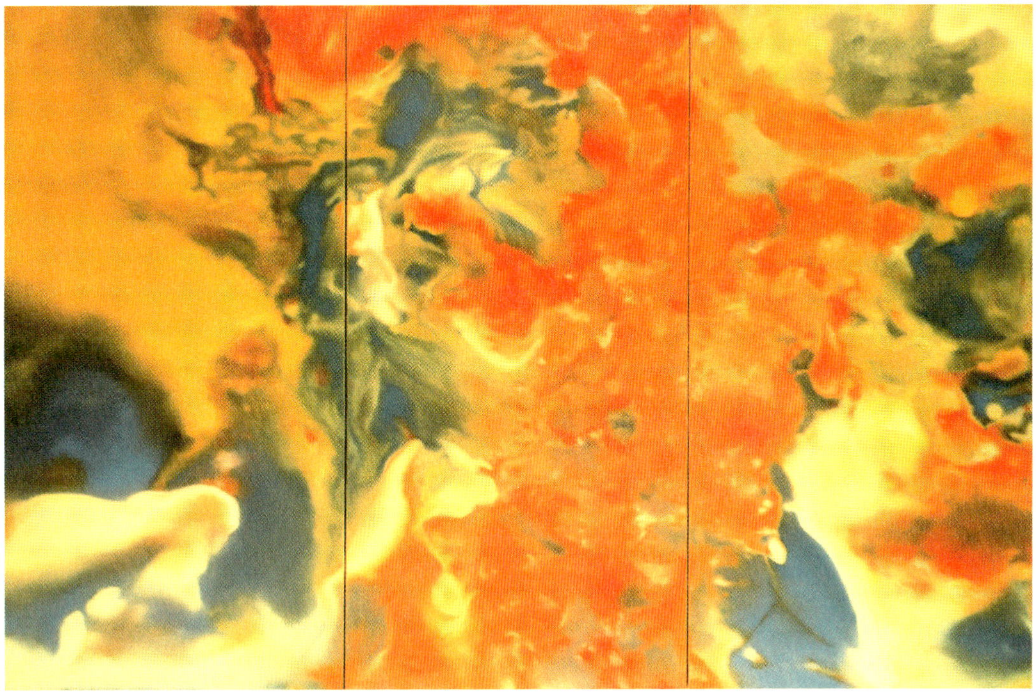

5 Gerhard Richter: *Detail* [291], 1971
Oil on canvas, 250 × 375 cm
Böckmann Collection, Berlin

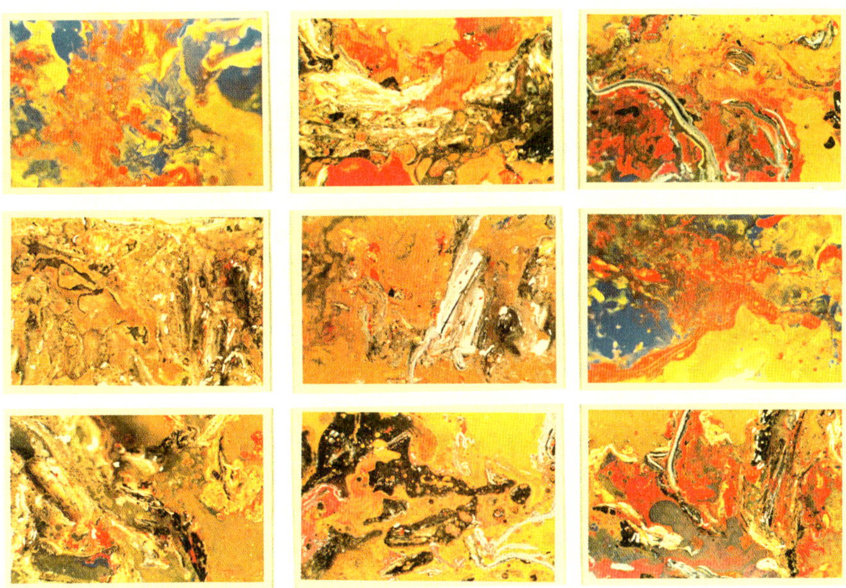

6 Gerhard Richter: *Atlas* (Photographic Details 1970) [Plate 89]
Städtische Galerie im Lenbachhaus und Kunstbau, Munich

Fiedler's writings bring us another step forward in our understanding of Richter's work, leading us into the twentieth century. In Fiedler's view, the artist manages "to move directly from vivid perception to vivid expression; his relationship with nature is not one of visual contemplation, but of expression."[27] Fiedler understood seeing—a psychophysical process—as "self-realizing reality." It is also self-referential: We see something and at the same time we can observe our seeing. Seeing, then, does not ascertain, does not duplicate reality, does not depict reality: Seeing interprets what it perceives. This tallies with the ideas of other artists, such as Paul Klee, who in 1920 summarized Fiedler's thoughts in a single sentence: "Art does not reflect what is visible, but renders visible."[28] Richter also seems to be moving in a similar direction with thoughts and observations similar to those expressed and theoretically underpinned by Fiedler several decades earlier.

In 1972, Richter said in an interview that he did not want to "rely on the picture of reality that we see, because we see it mediated through the lens apparatus of the eye, and corrected in accordance with past experience. And because that is not enough for us—because we want to know whether it can all be different—we paint."[29] One year later, Richter was describing painting "as an autonomous reality, with no relation to any given reality except itself."[30] His large painting *Red-Blue-Yellow* [333-2] (cat. 24), an Inpainting from 1972, makes that clear. He was possibly reflecting on works of this kind, but also bearing in mind later paintings, when he commented in 1990: "Each picture has to evolve out of a painterly or visual logic: it has to emerge as if inevitably."[31]

Even if there are differences which are equally fundamental, a reading of Fiedler's writings—first published in their entirety in Munich in 1913–14 in the form of a two-volume edition, and subsequently edited and annotated in 1971 and 1991 by Gottfried Boehm—can contribute to an understanding of several aspects of Richter's painting. Under the heading "Reality and Art," for example, Fiedler observed: "Just as what is conveyed to us by intuition can only ever be intuition and nothing more, so what is ours in the concept can hardly be anything to us but the concept." And a few lines further on he added: "This reality recognized as relative consists altogether of nothing but the forms in which it is given to our senses and our mind, to our faculty for vision and cognition, and if we delete these forms, then the whole reality vanishes without trace, absolutely nothing remains."[32] This means that what a work of art cannot show or what an expressive gesture cannot develop is artistically nonexistent. In the words of Boehm in his comments on Fiedler's text, this translates thus: "The meaning is neither before nor after the work, it is the work process itself—under conditions which no longer permit a distinction between form and content."[33] This might be compared to a proposition by Theodor W. Adorno, whose *Aesthetic Theory* first appeared in 1970: "The truth content of artworks cannot be immediately identified. Just as it is known only mediately, it is mediated in itself. What transcends the factual in the artwork, its spiritual content [...] does not hover above the work's facture; rather, artworks transcend their factuality through their facture, through the consistency of their elaboration."[34] Fiedler, who died in 1895, could not have predicted the future of art, and certainly not of nonrepresentational art. Yet it cannot be denied that abstract art—and with it large sections of Richter's oeuvre—bears the consistency of action on the work with self-reflective factors.

The role played by facture, and what happens when the facture itself is the theme and is thereby transfigured, are issues that Richter explored in the late 1970s. His artistic production during that period can be seen as a self-reflective process which, on the one hand, seems to indicate doubts about what he was doing, yet on the other gave rise to fascinating results, as happened in 1978 when Richter transformed relatively small abstractions, all of which signal something violent, surly, or desperate, into big, "soft abstracts" that mutate all the contradictions and dynamism into a visualization of great composure, sovereignty, and intriguing beauty. After an elaborate conversion, the *Abstract Painting* [398-2] of 1976 measuring 26 × 23 cm (fig. p. 31) became the "soft" *Abstract Painting* [421] with dimensions of 250 × 200 cm (cat. 31), significantly larger than the original.

Richter, too, is referring to physicality when he says "in painting thinking is painting," just as for Fiedler all mental—in this case, artistic—activity was always at one and the same time conjugated to physical action.[35] The possibility of "progress in the development of images [depends] on that mechanical activity"[36] and "everything [the artist] can achieve is bound to [this] external physical activity."[37] In Fiedler's view, it is only through such activity that the artist can "obtain the awareness that a side of the world has been granted him so that he can carry it to an independent, formed presence."[38]

Richter likewise assumes a close connection between physical activity and visuality. Certainly, "visual resources are of elementary importance," but when asked in an interview in 1990 whether the value of a painting had anything to do with brushwork and technique, he replied: "It has more to do with seeing, I think. The rest is manual; it's no problem. Anything can be painted. It's more difficult to see whether one is doing any good or not. But that's the only thing that counts. [...] Seeing is the decisive act, and ultimately it places the maker and the viewer on the same level."[39]

What did pose a problem to Richter was the raison d'être behind the aesthetic autonomy of his works. The "blowing up into big formats," i.e. transforming photographic enlargements of meagre paint residues on his palette or small pictures into large-format canvas paintings, unleashed skepticism and uncertainty in him. However strikingly beautiful and inspiring results like the *Abstract Painting* [421] of 1977 may look, it was tainted, as Richter observed, by the fact that it "allows you to cheat," which is to say it pretends to convey a "'message'" but does not actually do so.[40]

Reorganizing Details

Richter addressed the relationship between the hand and the eye, and the correspondence between form, structure, and visuality in an experiment. His book *128 Details from a Picture (Halifax 1978) II* was published in 1980. It contains black and white close-up photographs of the surface of the 1978 *Abstract Painting* [432-5], a study in oils on canvas measuring 52 × 78 cm (fig. 7). These are diverse views of the work's structure. Richter photographed the surface of the painting from different angles, at different distances, and in different light, and set out his methods in the book.

These photos (fig. 8) illustrate an unbridled, seemingly chaotic texture with sharp burrs, cracked bulges, broken surfaces, deep fissures, complemented or interrupted by undulating brushstrokes, scarred zones alternating with amorphous splashes, patches, wipings, and smearings. Although these black-and-white reproductions are of mediocre quality, they highlight the emphatic energy and differentiated structure of the painting and its informative abundance as a complex "message." At the same time, the photographs are presented as a conceptual or minimalist work, both consecutively in book form and simultaneously as a grid in the original work *128 Photographs of a Painting* [441]. Ten years later, Richter made a portfolio edition out of them under the title *128 Details from a Picture (Halifax 1978) II*, testifying to his recurrent interest in this project and its significance for his art (cat. 46).[41]

Richter's experiment is propaedeutic. It indicates that, while details and enlargements—usually referred to by the artist as "Abstract paintings"—expand the formal arsenal, the summation and reorganization of details from a sketch enhance the potential for inherent formation to such a degree that the repository of messages is quite inexhaustible. These messages are inevitably formal and lack transcendence.

Richter's experiment addresses the question of seeing. Rather than soft forms, these are fragmented, lacerated elements of paint which no longer blend into coherent structures but seem to float above gentle-hued backgrounds as if their surfaces had broken open. This achieves a further level of complexity and displays greater potential for abstract formations than the Inpaintings and "soft abstracts." Here too, an analogy can be made to ideas by Fiedler that Boehm called the "core of his entire thought."[42] Fiedler wrote that "in the most elementary attempts at visual art [...] the hand does not [do] what the eye has already done; rather, something new emerges, and the hand picks up the onward development of what the eye is doing at that very point and continues it as the eye itself reaches the end of its activity." Fiedler expounds further on this interrelationship between seeing and practical activity: "By merely drawing a line, or performing a gesture intended to represent something the eye has perceived, a person will [...] realize that he is doing something for his visual conception which the eye, the organ specialized in sight, does not have the power to achieve."[43]

For this the hand requires a tool, such as a brush. The movement can only be controlled if the distance between the hand and the canvas is small, and with a longer brush chance begins to play a part. When Richter uses a short brush, as in the photograph of him painting *Small Bather* [815-1] in 1994 (fig. 9), something different happens compared to when he is further away from the canvas working on a large abstraction (fig. 10). The opportunities for control are even smaller when brushes of different sizes and widths are replaced by a roller or squeegee, as can be observed in his oeuvre from the 1980s (see the essay by Matthias Krüger, pp. 58–69). With a squeegee that is long but not very wide, the paint across the entire height and breadth of the work is often altered in a single stroke. The opaque

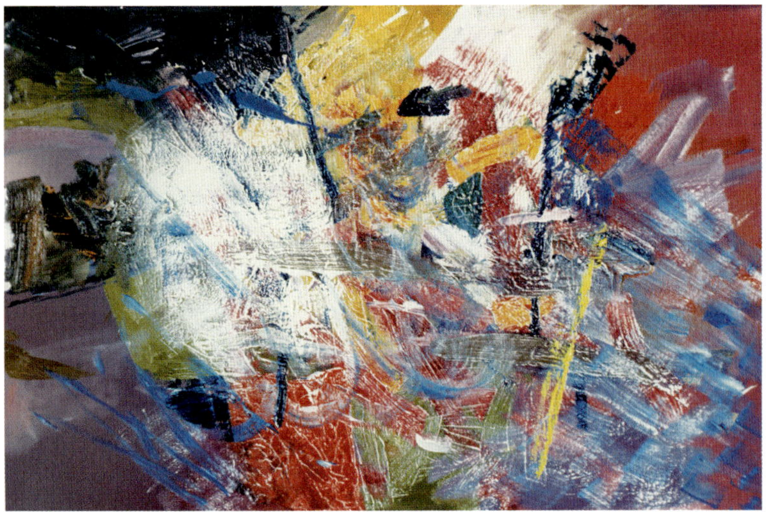

7 Gerhard Richter: *Abstract Painting (Halifax)* [432-5], 1978
Oil on canvas, 52 × 78 cm
Private collection

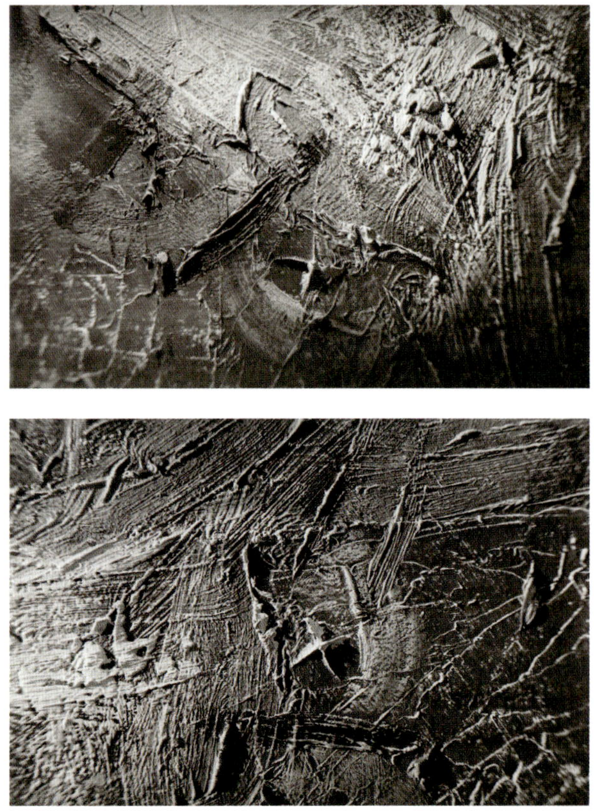

8 Photographs of *Abstract Painting (Halifax)* [432-5]

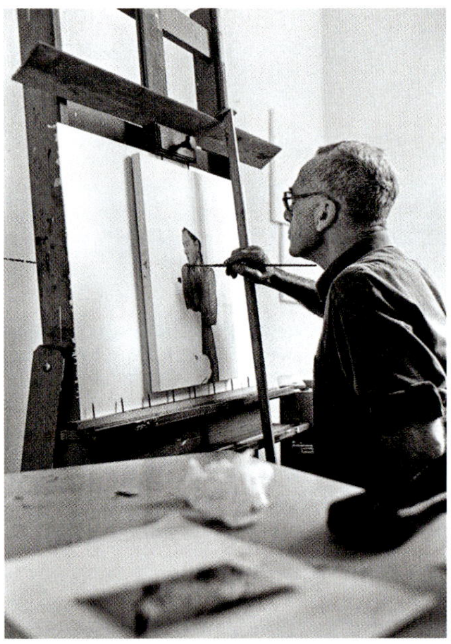

9 Gerhard Richter painting *Small Bather* [815-1], 1994

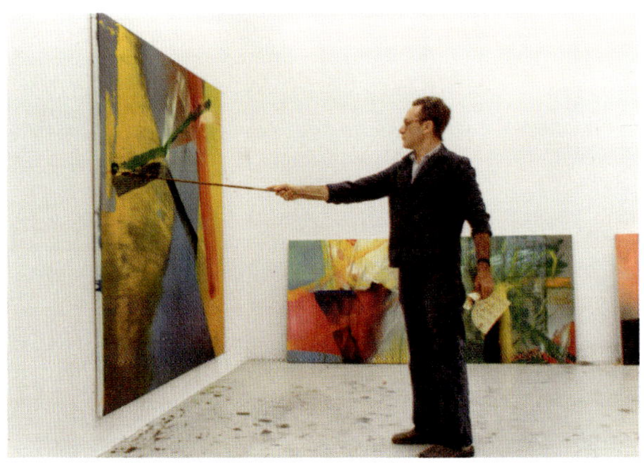

10 Gerhard Richter working on an Abstract painting in Cologne in the 1980s

material gains so much weight in this action that the operation becomes increasingly strenuous. The termination of the process, often after many stages, is its *ultima ratio*—the painting is either accepted as complete or else discarded and a new attempt begun.

The writings of Konrad Fiedler constitute one of the most interesting attempts in the latter half of the nineteenth century to plumb artistic production from a theoretical perspective. One might wonder whether Richter had similar ideas in mind when he coined his phrase "in painting thinking is painting." If so, what led him to this insight—his own practice, or an awareness of the sources available to him at the time? He had never heard of Fiedler, as he confirmed in conversation, and so quite possibly he had come across other literature. Willi Baumeister, for example, quoted Fiedler's quintessential statement—"The content of the work of art is nothing but the forming itself"[44]—in his widely read book, *Das Unbekannte in der Kunst*, which was reprinted in a second edition in 1960; and the philosopher Arnold Gehlen devoted a lengthy passage to Fiedler's ideas in his widely discussed book *Zeit-Bilder* (1960). Even if Fiedler could not have been aware of abstract art, his theory—as Otto Stelzer argues in his 1964 study on the prehistory of abstract art—might be read as an incitement to overcome boundaries and cast off the shackles of representation on the canvas itself, as Vasily Kandinsky (for one) did around 1913.[45] Nonrepresentational painting—including tachist and informalist works—thus finds in Fiedler "a previous theoretical justification. It is clearer and more compelling than most of what can be found on this matter in modern commentaries—and decades ahead."[46]

The Obscure Little Meaning of Colors

The practice described by Fiedler becomes even more significant in Richter's "pure" abstractions. The interaction of eye and hand found an important advocate not merely in Fiedler, whose influence did not gain traction until recent decades,[47] but can be observed in Richter's contemporaries—albeit with different motivations and accordingly expressed in different terms. Richter's thoughts, then, can be contextualized within the aesthetic discourse of the 1960s.

Richter's nonrepresentational paintings feature not only smears and gray tones, but also colors that have no specific significance per se and that have not been selected according to any kind of calculation (see the essay by Hubertus Butin, pp. 34–45). In this regard, Richter would have been able to draw on Sartre, whose book *What is Literature?* he had possibly read in the early 1960s. For Sartre, colors were not signs, for they did not refer to anything outside themselves. Painters, reasoned Sartre, were not interested in tracing signs on canvas; they "want to create a thing."[48] The yellow gash in the sky over Tintoretto's *Golgotha* (Scuola Grande di San Rocco, Venice) is not supposed to signify or provoke anguish; the gash *is* anguish and yellow sky at the same time.[49] No quality or sensation is so bare that it is not imbued with signification. "The obscure little meaning that inhabits colors [...], the light cheerful lightness, the shy melancholy, remains within them or envelopes them like a warm breath; it *is* color."[50] The painter, therefore, needs "a material that cannot be assimilated, because beauty does not dissolve into ideas." And the painter only achieves unconditional liberty "because he distinguishes radically between things and thoughts."[51] And when Sartre insists that "it is only in the course of writing that the writer forms his idea of the art of writing,"[52] he comes very close to Richter's formulation that "in painting thinking is painting."

The combination of both—the emergence of the aesthetic mindscape in the painting process and the obscure little meaning that makes no reference that can be found in the colors—imply the possibility of painting that does not directly generate meanings, and yet is meaningful. "In painting painting is thinking"—the idea that essentially reflects what Fiedler expressed, but in different terms—became a defining factor in Richter's practice. It led him to admire the European culture of painting and to oppose postmodernism, which adapts, varies, and modifies the revolutionary shifts in modernism and its strategies for constantly generating new codes—or in other words pursues practices that viewers presumably also think they can observe in Richter.

In February 1986, Richter noted: "The idea as a point of departure for the picture: that's illustration. Conversely, acting and reacting in the absence of an idea leads to forms that can be named and explained, and thus generates the idea ('In the beginning was the deed')."[53] The formulation "in painting thinking is painting" can hence also be taken to mean that Richter wishes to replace a traditionally metaphysical and essentialist model of form with a pragmatic one. The decisive factor is not what form represents, but what it does. The pragmatic takes priority over the semantic.[54] The painting process is thus primarily understood as "form reacting to form, something primary to something else primary," without anything else coming into play.[55] The artist confirmed as much in a statement in October 1986: "'What' is the hardest thing, because it is the essence. 'How' is easy by comparison. To start off with, the 'How' is frivolous, but legitimate. Apply the 'How,' and thus use the requirements of technique, the material and physical possibilities, in order to realize the intention. The intention: to invent nothing—no idea, no composition, no object, no form—and to receive everything: composition, object, form, idea, picture."[56] Richter could see this constant tension between intention and condition stretching all the way back to his early work: "Even in my youth [...] I very soon became aware of this problem of having no subject. Of course, I took motifs and represented them, but this was mostly with the feeling that these were not the real ones, but imposed, dog-eared, artificial ones."[57] The meaning of a work can no more be reduced to the conceptual than its aesthetic appearance can be reduced to the visual.[58]

Richter is no theoretician, but during his first years in Düsseldorf he gave some thought to the conditions that make painting possible, summing them up in the concise adage "in painting thinking is painting." This motto has also governed the practice of many other artists and informed a lengthy tradition in the art of the twentieth century. For Richter it was to prove extremely fruitful and amenable to development. This short essay illustrates that the formulation "in painting thinking is painting" holds true not only of Richter's early representational work, but also of the Streaks (cat. 3, 9), Inpaintings (cat. 21–24), Gray paintings (cat. 25–27), and Details (cat. 28, 29), as well as his later Abstract paintings (cat. 31–41, 63–74, and 80–86). The foundations for this conceptual continuity were laid early, then, and they were based on ideas that permeate modernism and have conditioned it to a greater or lesser extent. In Richter's case, the historical orientation gradually intensified as his art evolved, to the point where he was able, in 2002, to style himself with no hint of irony as the "keeper of tradition."[59]

Translated from the German by Kate Vanovitch

1 Richter pointed out the connection; see Cossje van Bruggen, "Gerhard Richter: Painting as Moral Act," in *Artforum* 24, no. 5 (May 1985), 82–91, here 85.

2 Ignazio Gardella's table, known in Italian as the *tavolo allungabile*, was designed in 1954 and won a gold medal at the 11th Triennale di Milano. See illustration in *domus* 293 (April 1954), 76, and 329 (August 1956), 46 ff. See *L'architettura di Ignazio Gardella*, ed. Marco Porta (Milan, 1985), 214, fig. 83.

3 It is questionable whether the picture, under cover of stylistic difference, was a dramatic attempt to articulate the aesthetic parallels between socialism and capitalism in order to express the iconographic and ideological instability of the Cold War. See John J. Curley, "Gerhard Richter's Cold War Vision," in Mehring et al. 2010, 18–35.

4 See Gelshorn 2012, 125.

5 New York 2002, 29.

6 See Benjamin H. D. Buchloh, "Richter's Abstractions: Silences, Voids, and Evacuations," in New York 2005, 7–27, here 11–12.

7 See *Gerhard Richter* (Aachen: Zentrum für aktuelle Kunst – Gegenverkehr e. V., 1969), fig. 1. Exhibition catalog.

8 Gerhard Richter, "Comments on Some Works" (1991), in Richter 2009, 259–70, here 259.

9 Immanuel Kant, *Critique of Judgment*, trans. Werner S. Pluhar (Indianapolis, IN: Hackett Publishing, 1987), § 44, 173.

10 Georg Wilhelm Friedrich Hegel, *Aesthetics*, vol. 1, trans. T.M. Knox (Oxford: Oxford University Press, 1975), 73.

11 Gottfried Boehm, "Zur Biographie," in Konrad Fiedler, *Schriften zur Kunst*, ed. Gottfried Boehm, vol. 1 (Munich: Verlag Wilhelm Fink, 1991), XLI–XLIV, here XLII.

12 Gerhard Richter, "Brief an Wieland Förster (February 4, 1962)," in Hamburg 2011, 50–51, here 50.

13 Gerhard Richter, "Notes" (1962), in Richter 2009, 14–15, here 15.

14 In 1989, Richter told Jan Thorn-Prikker in an interview: "If I work methodically, it just doesn't work. A picture has a logic that can't be verbalized until afterwards; it can't be designed." Gerhard Richter, "Conversation with Jan Thorn-Prikker concerning the *18 October 1977 cycle*" (1989), in ibid., 226–40, here 238. Eleven years later, talking to Astrid Kasper, he phrased it this way: "painting [is] like a substitute for thinking—a different way of thinking," Gerhard Richter, "Interview with Astrid Kasper" (2000), in ibid., 365–71, here 365. And in 2002, the artist remarked to Robert Storr: "Perhaps the seeing and deciding and doing is such a complicated, tricky procedure that I shouldn't upset it by trying to verbalize," Gerhard Richter, "MOMA interview with Robert Storr" (2002), in ibid., 397–439, here 417.

15 Richter 1962 (see note 13), 15.

16 Konrad Fiedler, "Über den Ursprung der künstlerischen Tätigkeit (1887)," in Fiedler 1991 (see note 11), 111–220, here 127.

17 Ibid., 175–76. Gottfried Boehm's introduction is key to understanding Fiedler's writing; see ibid., XLV–XCVII.

18 Richter 1962 (see note 13), 14. Richter is alluding indirectly to Klee's dictum in 1920: "Art does not reproduce the visible, but makes visible," which sums up the quintessence of Fiedler's thinking, see note 28.

19 Gerhard Richter, "Interview with Rolf Schön" (1972), in Richter 2009, 59–61, here 60.

20 Fiedler 1887 (see note 16), 191.

21 Ibid., 161–62. This creates something "that presents the visuality of the object to us, and as we do this we generate something new, something different from what previously constituted the appropriation of our visual conception."

22 Ibid., 192.

23 Ibid.

24 Konrad Fiedler, "Über die Beurteilung von Werken der bildenden Kunst (1876)," in Fiedler 1991 (see note 11), 1–48, here 37.

25 Konrad Fiedler, "Moderner Naturalismus und künstlerische Wahrheit (1881)," in ibid., 81–110, here 109.

26 Fiedler 1887 (see note 16), 140.

27 Ibid., 173.

28 Paul Klee, "Beitrag für den Sammelband *Schöpferische Konfession*" (1920), in Paul Klee, *Schriften. Rezensionen und Aufsätze*, ed. Christian Geelhaar (Cologne: DuMont, 1976), 118–22, here 118. See also Gottfried Boehm, "Die Logik des Auges. Konrad Fiedler nach einhundert Jahren," in *Auge und Hand. Konrad Fiedler Kunsttheorie im Kontext*, ed. Stefan Majetschak (Munich: Wilhelm Fink Verlag, 1997), 27–40, here 36–37.

29 Gerhard Richter, "Interview with Peter Sager" (1972), in Richter 2009, 64–67, here 65.

30 Gerhard Richter, "Interview with Irmeline Lebeer" (1973), in ibid., 72–83, here 79.

31 Gerhard Richter, "Interview with Sabine Schütz" (1990), in ibid., 251–58, here 256.

32 Fiedler 1991 (see note 11), vol. 2, 107–94, here 151.

33 Gottfried Boehm, "Anschauung als Sprache. Nachträge zur Neuausgabe," in Fiedler 1991 (see note 11), vol. 1, VII–XXII, here XVII.

34 Theodor W. Adorno, *Aesthetic Theory*, trans. Robert Hullot-Kentor (London & New York: Continuum, 2002), 129.

35 Fiedler 1887 (see note 16), 167.

36 Ibid., 168.

37 Ibid., 175.

38 Ibid., 191.

39 Richter 1990 (see note 31), 257. In 2002, Richter told Robert Storr: "I am no virtuoso at all. [...] But I do have the ability to judge whether something is good or bad," Richter 2002 (see note 14), 399.

40 Gerhard Richter, "From a letter to Benjamin H. D. Buchloh" (May 23, 1997), in Richter 2009, 93–94, here 93.

41 See Butin et al. 2014, nos. 99–101.

42 Boehm 1997 (see note 28), 37.

43 Fiedler 1887 (see note 16), 165.

44 Willi Baumeister, *Das Unbekannte in der Kunst* (1947), second ed. (Cologne: DuMont, 1960), 52.

45 See Otto Stelzer, *Die Vorgeschichte der abstrakten Kunst* (Munich: Piper, 1964), 212.

46 Ibid., 216.

47 On Fiedler's influence on the philosophy, aesthetics, and art history of the twentieth century and on artists such as Henri Matisse, Yves Klein, Francesco Lo Savio, and others, see Udo Kultermann, "Konrad Fiedler und die Kunsttheorie der Gegenwart," in Majetschak 1997 (see note 28), 55–70.

48 Jean-Paul Sartre, *Qu'est-ce que la littérature?* (Paris: Gallimard, 1948), 14. It is not certain whether Richter had read Sartre, but on April 25, 1961 he wrote to Wieland Förster: "Bought Sartre on literature," Hamburg 2011, 41.

49 Sartre 1948 (see note 48), 15.

50 Ibid., 14.

51 Ibid., 121. Fiedler puts it this way: "There is something truly discouraging about the recognition that all theoretical holds on reality are verbal holds. Even when thinking comes very close to sensuality, [...] even there one finds oneself [...] severed by the unbridgeable chasm from the sensual substance of experience," Fiedler 1887 (see note 16), 126.

52 Sartre 1948 (see note 48), 211.

53 Gerhard Richter, "Notes" (1986), in Richter 2009, 158–63, here 159.

54 See Klinger 2013, 21.

55 Ibid., 64.

56 Richter 1986 (see note 53), 162.

57 Ibid.

58 Adorno 2002 (see note 34), 150.

59 In 2002, for example, in his interview with Robert Storr, Richter 2002 (see note 14), 439.

Richter's Squeegee: The Artist and His Tools

Matthias Krüger

Gerhard Richter's squeegee technique, which is particularly important to the series of Abstract paintings he has been making since the 1980s, is one in a long list of experimental painting techniques to have influenced the course of modern art. As early as the nineteenth century, painters were increasingly turning away from inherited techniques. But it was only during the period of postwar modernism, when all traditional artistic values were being fundamentally challenged, that there was a radical break with the old methods. Conventional tools were also abandoned. Jackson Pollock's action painting was trailblazing in this regard (fig. 1), with the artist declaring in 1947: "I continue to get further away from the usual painter's tools such as easel, palette, brushes, etc. I prefer sticks, trowels, knives and dripping fluid paint or a heavy impasto with sand, broken glass and other foreign matter added."[1]

In subsequent years, artists discarded the traditional tools of their trade and tried out new utensils and methods instead: shaking, dripping, and spraying paint onto the picture surface from buckets or tin cans, slitting the canvas with razor blades, lashing their work with whips, shooting at it with rifles, painting with their hands, feet, and hair, and using naked models as live brushes.[2] Each of these tools called for its own handling, each left different traces on the surface, had its own texture, contributed differently to the meaning of the work it was used to create. The same goes for Richter's squeegee, as the following discussion of his work will demonstrate.

The Method

Richter's squeegee technique has been widely imitated. There are various instructions online and in print aimed at enabling others to "squeegee" their own abstract painting à la Richter.[3] Anyone who prefers not to get dirty can use Photoshop to make a squeegee image. The popularity of the technique can be attributed to Corinna Belz's film *Gerhard Richter Painting*, which was screened in cinemas in 2011 and offered an insight into Richter's painterly practice.[4] It is also the basis for the following description of his squeegee technique.

The film shows how Richter begins a work by painting the canvas in different colors with a broad brush. He then proceeds to repeatedly paint over this original arrangement in the first few sessions, often with a broad brush, later usually with one of his squeegees. The artist has a whole range of these at his disposal—"completely my own design," he insists (figs. 2, 3).[5] They are comprised of a rectangular plexiglass blade and a wooden handle, but they vary in length and breadth—the longest measuring several meters. To make them easier to use, an angled wooden strip is mounted onto the plexiglass. In the longer versions, which often require the whole body to operate them, this handle has grip holes.[6]

Richter's squeegee sessions can vary considerably. Nevertheless, there are a few hallmarks. First, paint is applied to the squeegee. Then Richter usually drags it across the canvas in a horizontal or vertical direction. If he is using one of his larger squeegees, he will often cover the entire surface with a new layer of paint in a single pass. Frequently, after only a few repetitions, the original layer of paint is no longer visible.

The surface structures that Richter creates with the squeegee can turn out very differently, depending on how dry the underlying layer of paint was, on the angle at which Richter applies the squeegee, and on how much pressure and speed accompany its trajectory across the canvas. As a squeegee never spreads the paint evenly, the lower layers are not fully concealed. Besides, the artist keeps exposing patches in the lower strata by dragging a clean squeegee across the canvas like a slicer, or by scratching away small patches with a knife.

The process not only involves working on the picture, but also stepping back from the canvas repeatedly to appraise the work in progress from a distance, and to contemplate the next step in the process or, indeed, to postpone the decision and let the work "mature" a little first. In this manner, the creation of a work can take weeks, with the painting in question undergoing numerous metamorphoses, its character sometimes being radically transformed several times over before the artist is satisfied with the result (see the essay by Armin Zweite, pp. 46–57).

The Squeegee

Even the name used for Richter's working utensil is problematic. The German term *Rakel* poses a grammatical riddle, because although a German dictionary identifies the noun as feminine, a masculine article is repeatedly used in the literature on Richter. *Rakel* has been borrowed from the French. The French word *racle* is the noun that goes with the verb *racler*, which translates as "scrape," "scratch away," "scour," "scrub out," or "wipe off." *Racle* or *Rakel* are therefore used to describe a tool that is employed to scrape, scratch, scrub, or wipe a substance away. In German, the term is primarily used these days in the realm of printing and coating technologies. Here, the *Rakel* is an instrument used by screen printers to press viscous pigment through a screen onto the surface of a work.

Screenprinting is a technique that was developed around 1900 for applying labels to glass bottles, wood, and metal surfaces—and very soon it was adopted for commercial graphics.[7] The best-known artistic use of screenprinting is by Andy Warhol. It makes sense to see this as a reference point for Richter, given that Warhol had previously also provided inspiration for Richter's works based on photographs. In 1960, two years before Richter, Warhol had begun manually transferring press photos onto large canvases in oils, before switching in 1964 to the photomechanical screenprinting technique (fig. 4). This step, as Andy Warhol explained in a programmatic statement in 1980, had been motivated by the desire to "completely remove all the hand gesture from art and become non-committal, anonymous."[8] The artist's personal style should no longer be visible in the finished work, and the creative process was to be replaced by a mechanical technique.

Although Richter used his squeegee for painting rather than printing, he had a similar motive for choosing to use it. He, too, sees it as a tool for eliminating his own subjectivity and restricting his control over the work process—faithful to the programmatic statement in his 1985 notes: "Letting a thing come, rather than creating it."[9]

Richter's squeegee technique is not only a reference to Warhol, however, but also to Karl Otto Götz, his teacher at the Düsseldorf Art Academy, who in the early 1950s had already repurposed the printer's squeegee to manipulate paint in his works (fig. 5, fig. p. 10). In contrast to what Richter would later go on to do, though, Götz used the tool almost entirely to remove, break open, or fling away paint, thereby inscribing negative forms in his paintings.[10] Götz was not the only informalist artist to use the squeegee. Around the same time, K. R. H. Sonderborg had discovered it too, but unlike Götz he also used the squeegee to apply paint. Moreover, both Götz and Sonderborg played around with window or windshield wipers, which are comparable in many respects to the squeegee, with the artists sometimes not making any distinction between the different tools. Götz, for example, when asked to describe squeegees in a television interview, once said vaguely: "They are those rubber window-cleaning things."[11]

English uses the same word for the screenprinting gadget as for the window-cleaning gadget: "squeegee." The result of this is that in the Anglo-American literature on Richter, his implement has repeatedly been associated with a device for removing water from windows, thereby invoking a very old topos: In 1435, Leon Battista Alberti published his treatise *Della Pittura*, describing a painting as a *finestra aperta*, an open window. This metaphor, however, was coined for pictorial compositions founded on central perspective. Central perspective was one of the most important achievements of early modern painting, because it enabled artists to lend their paintings illusory depth. Whereas a painting constructed around a central perspective suggests transparency, like a window opening onto a landscape beyond, Richter's Abstract paintings convey opacity. There is nothing diaphanous about them. The thick paint impedes the view of anything that might possibly lie behind it. Where the top layer has been torn open by a squeegee, all we can see is another layer of paint underneath. Our gaze seems to be hopelessly blocked out or walled in.

If calling Richter's working tool a squeegee encourages English-language writers to invoke the old metaphor of the painting as window in their discussion of the squeegee paintings, the thick paint at least obliges them to modify the image. In his monograph *The Artwork of Gerhard Richter* published in 2016, for instance, the Australian artist and art writer Darryn Ansted compared the paths traced by Richter's squeegee on the surface of his *Cage* paintings [897-1 to 897-6] with the trail of suds a window cleaner leaves on a windowpane (fig. 6).[12]

Sometimes Richter's squeegee is actually equated to a squeegee used for cleaning windows, as in Hilary Sample's 2016 book *Maintenance Architecture*. The subject of the book is the upkeep

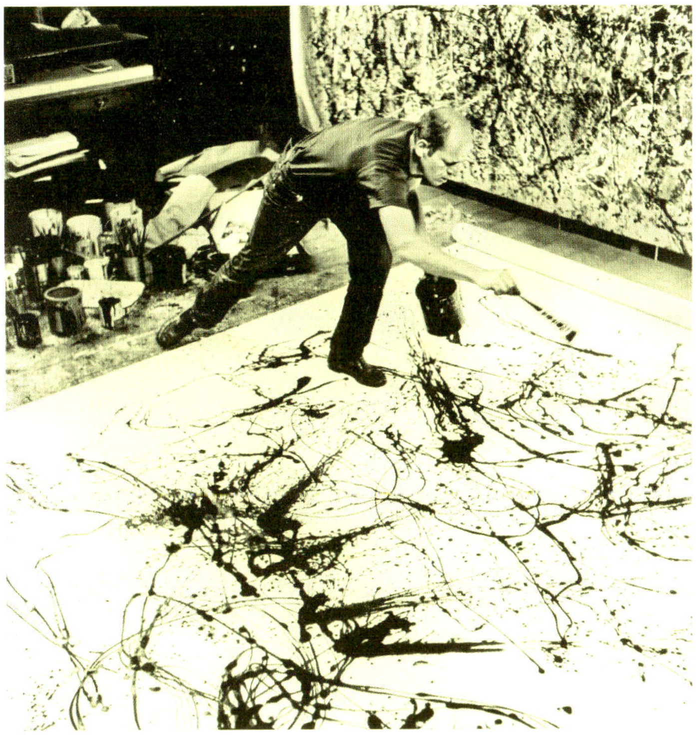

1 Hans Namuth:
Jackson Pollock working on *Autumn Rhythm*, 1950

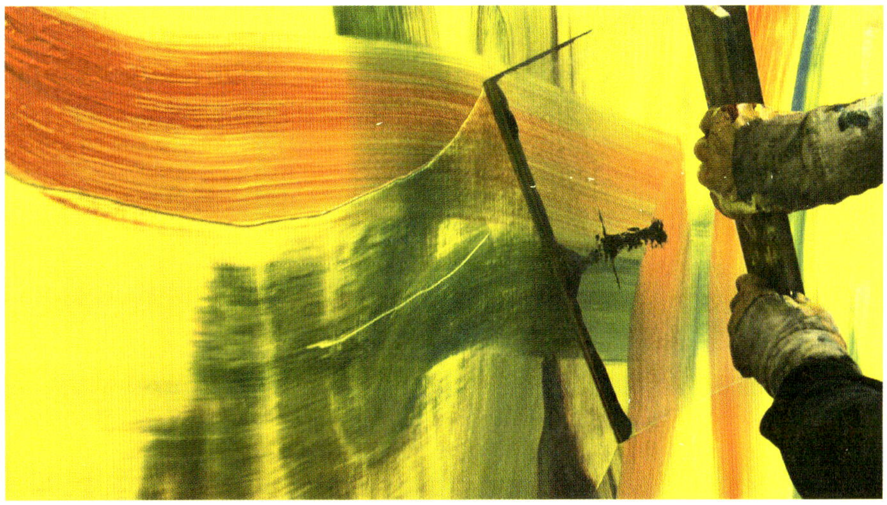

2 Richter working on *Abstract Painting* [910-2]
Still from *Gerhard Richter Painting*, 2011, directed by Corinna Belz

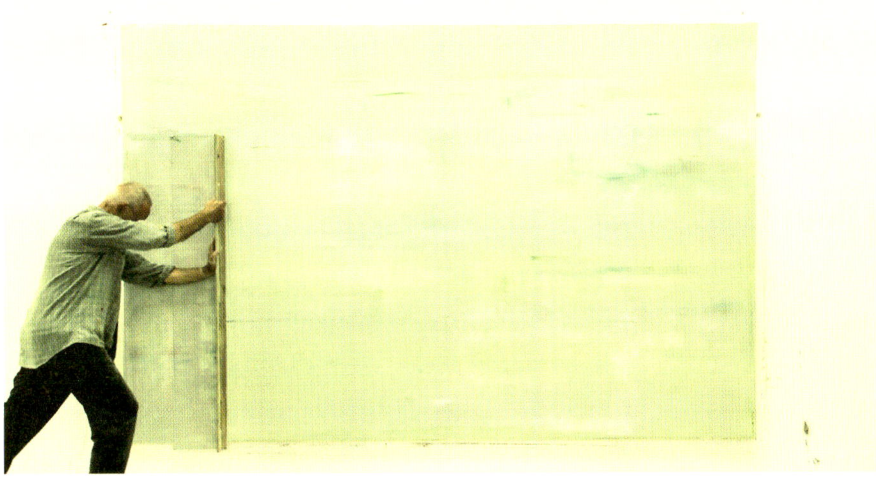

3 Richter working on *Abstract Painting* [911-4]
Still from *Gerhard Richter Painting*, 2011, directed by Corinna Belz

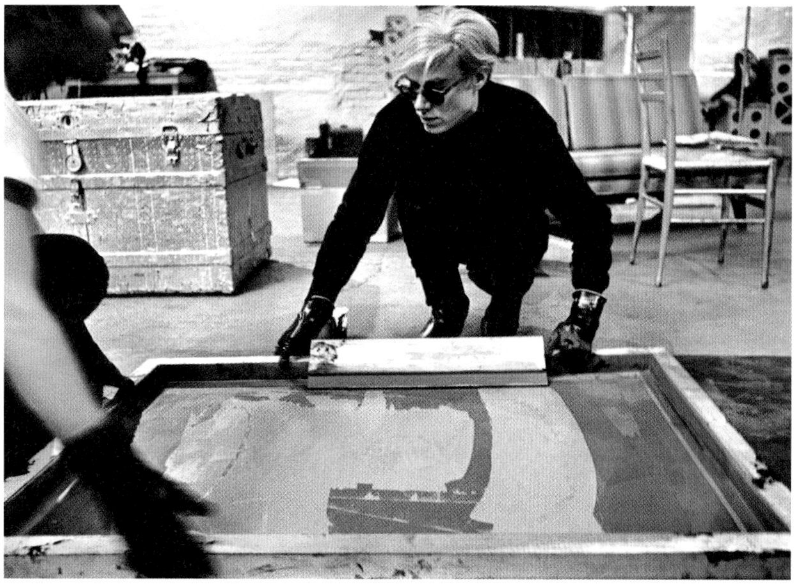

4 Andy Warhol making a silkcreen print at the Factory,
New York, 1964

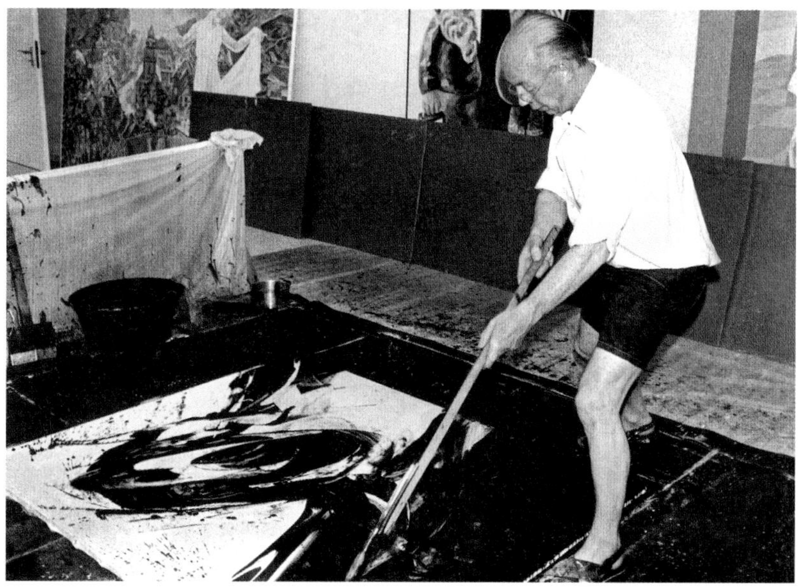

5 Karl Otto Götz painting with a squeegee,
June 26, 1976

of buildings, and the author devotes considerable detail to ways of cleaning them. It is in this context that she pays tribute to the modern-day T-shaped window squeegee designed by the Italian Ettore Steccone (fig. 7). Steccone emigrated to the United States in 1922 and worked his way up from a window cleaner to become a millionaire. Although rarely celebrated, the squeegee he patented in 1936 was one of the most important inventions in the history of building maintenance. Compared with its predecessor, the Chicago squeegee, which was quite awkward to use, Ettore Steccone's version was not only easier to handle, but was also more efficient, and this made it possible to wash the large glass surfaces so beloved of modern architecture. In Sample's eyes, the modern qualities of the squeegee—baptized "New Deal" by Steccone—are additionally demonstrated by its use as a tool in Richter's work, because "[w]hile the practical activity of applying paint is fundamentally different from removing dirt and dust, both should nevertheless be viewed as worldly transformations."[13]

Richter does not describe his work with such melodrama, but for him too the squeegee conveys "modernity" and "technical coolness, because painting with a brush is very old-fashioned," as he once said during an interview in his studio.[14] And it stands to reason that Richter would discern modernity in the efficiency of an implement that allowed him to process the large formats of his Abstract paintings more rapidly than would have been possible with a brush.

The connotations vary, then, depending on whether Richter's utensil is compared with a screenprinting squeegee or a window squeegee, and these connotations influence how people have perceived and understood his working methods. In fact, the device used by Richter resembles neither the version used by printers nor the one used by window cleaners, as it does not have that flexible rubber edge that is so crucial to printing and window cleaning. In screenprinting, this rubber is key to the even distribution of the paint, and in window cleaning to a smear-free pane. Had Richter decided to paint with a screenprinting squeegee or a window squeegee, the look and structure of his paintings would have been substantially different. The result would be a more homogeneous surface—and not those rugged textures that endow his squeegee paintings with their distinctive character.

The Spatula

The tool that Richter uses for his Abstract paintings is often not called a squeegee, but quite simply a spatula; the bigger version is accordingly known as the giant spatula, or as the *Riesenspachtel* or *spatule géante* in German and French.[15] Richter refers to the implement in an interview simply as a "*große Spachtel*"—a big spatula—and in the book *Text: Writings, Interviews and Letters 1961–2007* edited by Dietmar Elger and Hans Ulrich Obrist—a compilation of statements, letters, and interviews by and with the artist—the word "*Rakel*" is only used by people who interview Richter, and never by the artist himself.[16]

Originally intended for preparing paint on the palette, the spatula or palette knife was already being repurposed in the seventeenth century to apply the paint to the canvas—a practice popularized by Gustave Courbet in the nineteenth century (fig. 9). The *couteau à palette* (fig. 8) might be regarded as the precursor of Richter's squeegee, even if it is distinctly smaller and easier to handle. By including Courbet's name in the titles of two of his Abstract paintings, Richter has paid tribute to his palette-knife art. Like the squeegee, the knife not only spreads the paint over a larger area but can similarly function as a "random generator" among painterly techniques.[17]

Chance plays an important part in Richter's work. Firstly it is a thematic element—like in his Cloud paintings, which reference the centuries-old aleatory paradigm in art theory (see the essay by Ortrud Westheider, pp. 8–21).[18] In Richter's Color Charts, chance operates on a different level: In them, Richter says he arranges the colors according to a random principle (see the essay by Hubertus Butin, pp. 34–45). The factor of chance takes a different form again in his Abstract paintings, which owe their random structures to the painter's utensil. True, the squeegee technique is not an autopoietic process, as some have suggested, because the artist selects the color, sets the squeegee at a particular angle, and determines how much pressure to exert as he pulls or pushes it across the canvas; but even so, the end result of the application of paint is never fully predictable when a squeegee is used. The artist can guess at what structures are likely to emerge as he moves the squeegee over the surface in a certain way, but he cannot plan in advance for the individual scratches, scuffs, and streaks traced by the squeegee. According to Richter, this aspect was of crucial significance for him: In 1999, asked in an interview how far he was able to control the result with his knives and squeegees, he replied: "It's a

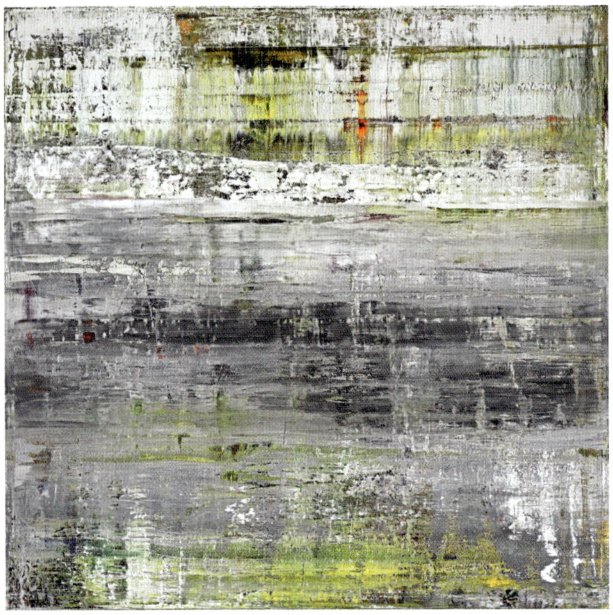

6 Gerhard Richter: *Cage* [897-2], 2006
Oil on canvas, 300 × 300 cm
Tate Modern, London,
on permanent loan from a private collection

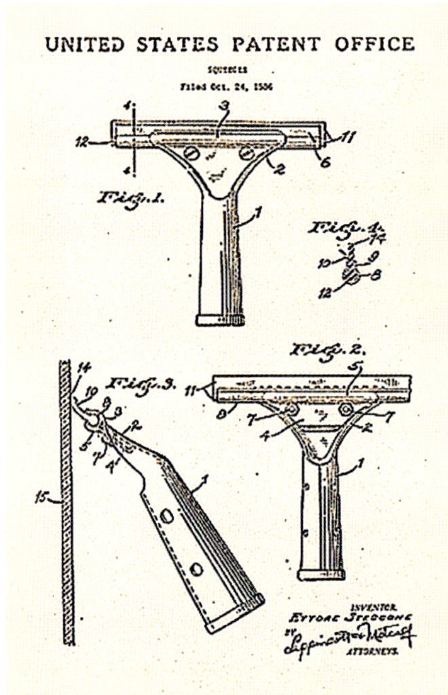

7 The squeegee designed by
Ettore Steccone, awarded US patent
2123638 A in 1936

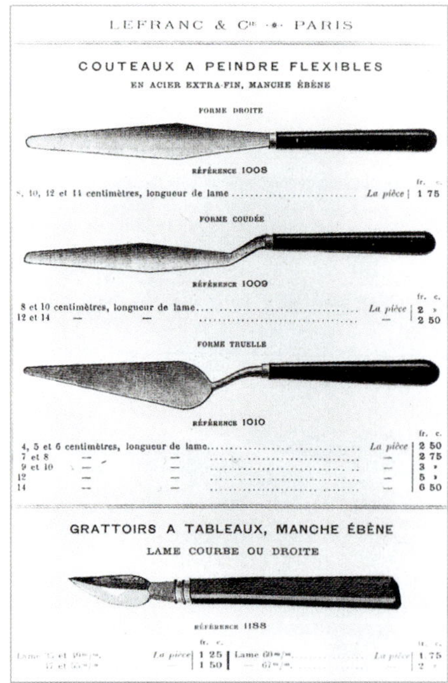

LEFRANC & Cie · PARIS

COUTEAUX A PEINDRE FLEXIBLES
EN ACIER EXTRA-FIN, MANCHE ÉBÈNE

FORME DROITE

RÉFÉRENCE 1008

		fr. c.
8, 10, 12 et 14 centimètres, longueur de lame	La pièce	1 75

FORME COUDÉE

RÉFÉRENCE 1009

		fr. c.
8 et 10 centimètres, longueur de lame	La pièce	2 »
12 et 14 — —	—	2 50

FORME TRUELLE

RÉFÉRENCE 1010

		fr. c.
4, 5 et 6 centimètres, longueur de lame	La pièce	2 50
7 et 8 — —	—	2 75
9 et 10 — —	—	3 »
12 — —	—	5 »
14 — —	—	6 50

GRATTOIRS A TABLEAUX, MANCHE ÉBÈNE
LAME COURBE OU DROITE

RÉFÉRENCE 1188

		fr. c.			fr. c.
Lame [illegible]	La pièce	1 25	Lame [illegible]	La pièce	1 75
[illegible]	—	1 50	— [illegible]	—	2 »

8 Range of palette knives
from the Lefranc catalog, 1900

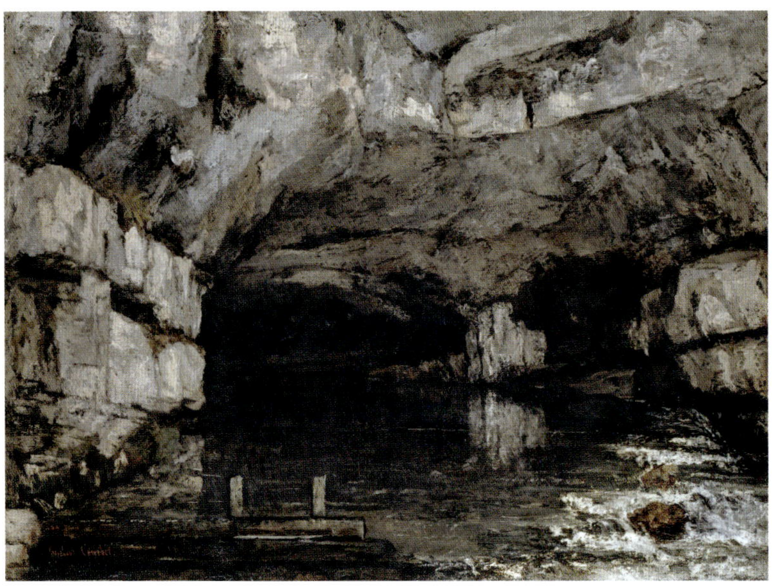

9 Gustave Courbet: *Cave on the Loue River*, 1864
Oil on canvas, 98 × 130.5 cm
Hamburger Kunsthalle

good technique for switching off thought. I can't consciously calculate what will emerge. Subconsciously though, I have an inkling of it. It's a pleasant state of limbo."[19] He expressed similar views in a conversation in 2007 when he defined the role played by chance in both the *Cage* paintings [897-1 to 897-6] and in his Abstract paintings in general as "substantial": "Despite all my technical experience, I cannot always exactly foresee what will happen when I apply or remove large amounts of paint with a scraper. Surprises always emerge, disappointing or pleasant ones, which in any case represent changes to the painting."[20]

The question of the aleatory factor dominated critical discourse about palette knives and spatulas early on. Both were seen as tools which were less easy to control than the brush, leaving painterly execution to some extent open to chance. As early as 1784, in a talk delivered to the Royal Academy, Joshua Reynolds extolled the palette knife as a means of using chance productively in the working process: "Rembrandt, in order to take the advantage of accident, appears often to have used the pallet-knife [sic] to lay his colors on the canvass [sic], instead of the pencil. Whether it is the knife or any other instrument, it suffices, if it is something that does not follow exactly the will. Accident, in the hands of an artist who knows how to take the advantage of its hints, will often produce bold and capricious beauties of handling and facility, such as he would not have thought of, or ventured, with his pencil, under the regular restraint of his hand."[21] However, for Reynolds and other authors, exploiting chance was only admissible for certain subjects, such as rocks—a motif for which Gustave Courbet, for one, used his palette knife.

In general however, the palette knife was not held in high esteem, precisely because it is not as easy to guide as the brush. That was why art critics repeatedly took issue with Courbet's apparently obsessive recourse to the palette knife as a risky gamble. Camille Lemonnier, one of the artist's earliest biographers, was especially harsh: The brush, he explained to his readers, fully obeyed the brain of the artist, whereas the knife was "the blunt tool of the laborer. It is insentient, irresponsible, and mechanical. It directs the hand and collaborates with chance."[22] Tellingly, the adjectives attributed by Lemonnier to palette-knife painting are almost the same ones that Richter chose a good century later to describe his squeegee technique—except that for Richter, the connotations are positive.

Palette Waste

The radical reevaluation of chance in art theory promoted in postwar modernism had its roots in the late nineteenth century, notably in the essay "Du hasard dans la production artistique" published in 1894 and authored by the Swedish playwright August Strindberg. It is certainly no accident that Strindberg's highly experimental painting and photography was rediscovered in the 1960s, for it appeared to make him a forerunner of abstract art.[23] One of those to express such views was the art critic Franz Roh, who wrote of Strindberg's painting in an article for the art journal *Das Kunstwerk* in 1963: "Really this is already action painting."[24] Roh quotes passages from the aforementioned essay, which Strindberg began by describing various examples of chance being harnessed in art, such as the Malay custom of drilling holes in bamboo stalks to hear the music of the wind whistling through them, or the weavers who used a kaleidoscope to "discover new designs, leaving it to blind chance to assemble the bits of colored glass,"[25] and the wooden panel in a tavern frequented by the artists' colony at Marlotte displaying what he calls "*grattures de palette.*" Roh translated this into German as *Palettenabfall* (palette waste), whereas the first full German translation of Strindberg's essay, which appeared a year later in *Der Merkur*, prefers the term *Palettenreste* (palette residues). The aptest English translation for this is "palette scrapings."[26] The wooden panel, Strindberg recounts, stemmed from a procedure popular among artists at the time: "that when an artist has finished working, he scrapes the remnants of the colors together, and if he feels so inclined, uses them to make a rough sketch. [...] Now freed from the trouble of finding the right colors, the soul of the painter enjoys the freedom to elicit shapes, and as his hand manipulates the spatula at random, still retaining nature's model in mind without seeking to copy it, the result reveals itself as a charming combination of the conscious and the unconscious. This is natural art, where the artist works in the same capricious way as nature, without a specific aim."[27]

The painting described here by Strindberg is a kind of capriccio, then, a pleasurable adventure on which the artist embarks after his work is done. The raw material is supplied by residues of paint scraped from the palette (Strindberg uses the French verb *racler*, from which the squeegee, as we saw above, acquired its German name). So the procedure is a kind of playful recycling of waste. For

Strindberg, it is also an inspiration for his attempts at painting, for which—he insisted—he only ever used palette knives, given that he did not own a single brush (fig. 10).

It is evident from the accounts by Hans Ulrich Obrist and Georg Imdahl that Richter adopted a similarly playful method to the *grattures de palette* when using up paint residues to overpaint photographs, which he often did at the end of the day "after finishing work on one of his large-format abstract paintings" (fig. 11, cat. 56–61).[28] Richter always kept a box—Imdahl even calls it a crate—of photographs to hand in his studio so he could "fish out" one or more whenever he felt the need. These were no art prints, as Obrist makes clear, "but quite ordinary snapshots," mostly taken on vacation. Both the time of day (after work) and the material being painted over (private vacation photos) suggest that this was a leisurely pursuit on the part of the artist. To overpaint the photos, Richter would use the paint "still clinging to the wide squeegee." It is hard to say for certain whether Richter was familiar with the paint scraping procedure described by Strindberg. One argument in favor could be the undisputed evidence that the artist drew on a variation of this unorthodox technique for another series in his oeuvre.

The Details produced in 1970–71 began—for the most part—with remnants of paint, but in this case not with the residue clinging to the squeegee after a day's work. This series predates the squeegee paintings, and the remnants concerned were sourced from the palette the artist had been using. Richter would photograph one or two square centimeters of these leftovers and then transfer this detail onto a large canvas in oils. The subtitle of one of these paintings is the decisive clue here, because in *Detail (Makart)* [288] (cat. 29) Richter pays homage to Hans Makart, a fashionable artist in imperial nineteenth-century Vienna, who was a forebearer in terms of detail painting. In 1899, the art historian Cornelius Gurlitt published a book on German nineteenth-century art—*Die deutsche Kunst des Neunzehnten Jahrhunderts: Ihre Ziele und Thaten*—and he included the following anecdote about Makart, who was a pupil of the Munich history painter Carl Theodor von Piloty: "Hans Makart's work was the epitome of Piloty's treatment of color. Another student of the Munich master told me how the youngsters at the academy composed paintings in those days. They would stir the remnants of paint on their used palette with a broad brush, and then they would take a piece of paper from which they had cut out a rectangle, the future picture, and move it around this blend until they found a place where it framed an effective, coherent harmony of color. And then they tried to sketch human figures in the pretty patch, thus finally devising a sense for them, the idea."[29]

It is thus clear that Makart and other pupils in Piloty's studio used their palettes as a springboard for new pictorial compositions (fig. 12). Compared with Richter's method, there is a vital difference. In the procedure described by Gurlitt, the remnants serve as inspiration for a figurative work, insofar as the artist projects figures onto the paint mixture on the palette. The artist's role consists not merely of selecting the demarcation, but also transforming the detail into a figurative composition. The amorphous brew of color gives rise to an idea. Richter, by contrast, confines himself to enlarging the selected detail, painting without the addition of a representational component.

A similar conclusion can be made about his Abstract paintings. While Strindberg draws on structures generated with the aid of chance, letting intention intervene to suggest something figurative, Richter dispenses with such retrospective reworking. Although he has persistently maintained that abstract configurations inevitably invite projections, his Abstract paintings leave these to the viewer. Only with titles like *Wall* [808] (cat. 70), *Forest* [731], and *Rain* [676-1, 676-2] does the artist occasionally participate in interpreting content. Unlike Strindberg with his palette scrapings, Richter does not use chance simply as the point of departure for a painting, but instead allows it to carry on operating on his behalf until he feels that the fruits of this aleatory process have resulted in a coherent, finished work.[30]

Performance

The adoption of new tools in modern art was not just a response to the desire to broaden the formal options available to painting. The tools acquired additional significance in the context of painting performances, a phenomenon prevalent since the 1950s, and not only confined to the Western art world. Theater historian Erika Fischer-Lichte concludes that these works heralded a "performative turn" that began in the early 1960s.[31] In fine art, this phenomenon was reflected in action painting, a term coined by Harold Rosenberg. As early as 1952, the American art critic had observed a trend

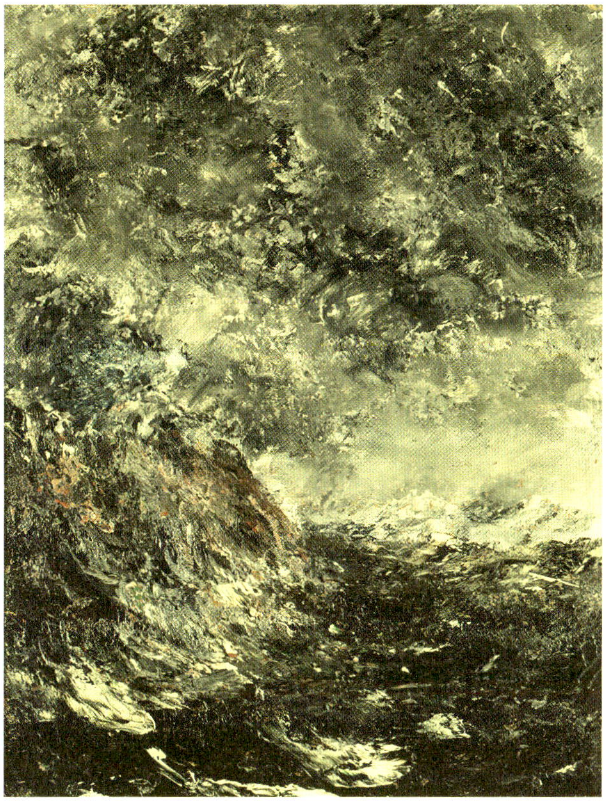

10 August Strindberg: *Sea with Cliff*, 1894
Oil on cardboard, 45 × 30 cm
Musée d'Orsay, Paris

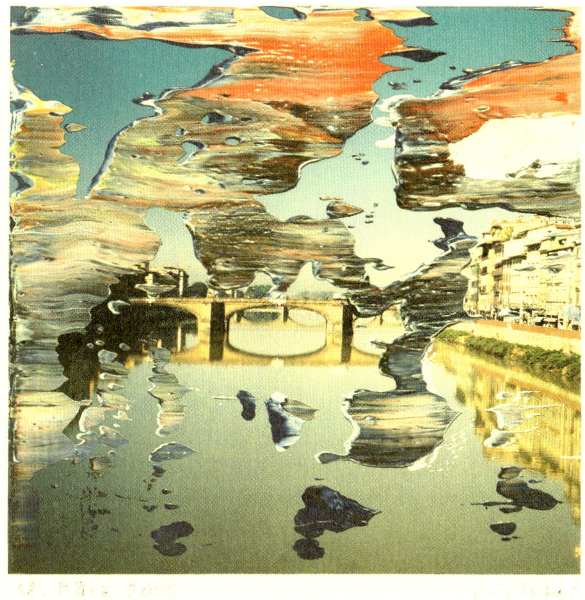

11 Gerhard Richter: *18 March 2000 (Florence)*, 2000
Oil on color photograph, 12 × 12 cm
Private collection

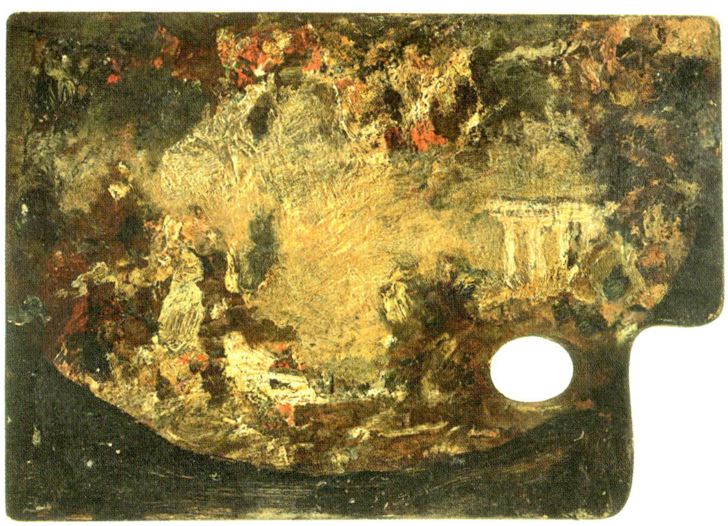

12 Hans Makart's palette
with a temple landscape, ca. 1865
Salzburg Museum

among contemporary artists toward treating the canvas as an "arena in which to act. [...] What was to go on the canvas was not a picture but an event."[32] The photographs that Hans Namuth took of Jackson Pollock at work helped to reinforce this understanding of painting (fig. 1). These photographs have arguably been even more influential in art history than Pollock's paintings themselves.[33]

Richter's contribution to this performative turn was relatively small. Richter remained largely true to the traditional notion of artwork; the layout of his catalogue raisonné is in itself an indication of that. According to the art historian Benjamin H. D. Buchloh, Richter's art delimits itself from the "looming fate of a total 'spectacularization' affecting all artistic techniques and practices" to which Jackson Pollock and Yves Klein had fallen prey.[34] Richter—unlike many artists of his generation—never gave painting performances. He allowed himself to be photographed and filmed while at work, but these painting scenarios are far removed from action painting. Indeed, they avoid the slightest hint of spontaneity. There is nothing impulsive about the way Richter applies paint, in contrast to action painting and its European counterpart, informalism. This becomes clear in the contrast between how Richter works with the squeegee and the approach taken by his teacher Karl Otto Götz (fig. 5). For Götz—as he reveals in his memoirs—"the speed of brush strokes and squeegee runs played an important role. The new medium [a paint and gouache hybrid] permitted a rapid style. The speed was a crucial way of keeping conscious control to a minimum. The speed also gave rise to the traces, passages, and textures (streaking and spraying) that I could not have achieved with slower, more controlled painting."[35]

Richter, too, was keen to minimize his control over the execution, likewise with the aim of creating textures he could not have produced intentionally, but that did not result in his working quickly. Quite the reverse. In the film *Gerhard Richter Painting*, we see him push the squeegee across the surface of the painting with deliberation and without haste, and in one scene he even draws the brush across the canvas at a provocatively slow pace. Whereas Götz used rapid execution to add dynamism to his signature style, Richter wanted to renounce such a style altogether. Instead of the uninhibited strokes typical of Götz, he shifts his squeegee over the picture surface in straight, strictly horizontal and vertical lines.

As mentioned previously, the sequences that show Richter at work on his painting are accompanied by scenes in which he steps back and subjects his work to a critical appraisal. His verdict is at times harsh: "They are good," he says in one scene of the film, adding sardonically: "They are good for two hours, maybe a day."[36] Richter claims that this scrutiny of his works is even more important than the act of painting itself. In an interview in 1990, responding to an observation that for many artists the action of painting, the process, is paramount, he commented: "What counts is always the seeing. The physical act can't be avoided, and certainly it is sometimes necessary to paint with the whole body—but all in the cause. And these 'Actionists'—you only have to look at what comes out of that."[37]

In another interview in 2004, Richter argued that skill and virtuosity were "no longer necessary for painting pictures,"[38] and when asked to define what made things "specifically artistic," he replied: "First the enjoyment, the wanting to do it. And then being able to see whether something looks good or not, looks serviceable." That, Richter explained, was why Marcel Duchamp was so important to him. After all, the readymade was nothing more than "a process that emphasizes the basic skill at the heart of the matter: the ability to visualize something."[39] Elsewhere, in the same vein, Richter compares his Abstract paintings to readymades (see the essay by Hubertus Butin, pp. 34–45). The decisive task, Richter maintains, is to recognize when chance has presented him with a picture of the desired quality, as if his role in the genesis of a work consisted merely in establishing the endpoint and required no personal involvement. However, in reasoning this way, the artist denies the very painting technique whose significance this essay has highlighted. But if it were as insignificant as he would have us believe, Richter could have left the execution of his squeegee paintings to an assistant.

Translated from the German by Kate Vanovitch

I am indebted to Anne Röhl for her critical reading.

[1] Jackson Pollock, "My Painting" (1947), in *Interviews, Articles, and Reviews*, ed. Pepe Karmel (New York: H.N. Abrams, 1999), 17–18, here 18.

[2] See Matthias Krüger, "Werkzeuge," in *Metzler-Lexikon Kunstwissenschaft. Ideen, Methoden, Begriffe*, ed. Ulrich Pfisterer (Stuttgart: J.B. Metzler Verlag, 2011), 489–93, here 492.

[3] See, for example, Deborah Foreman, *Paint Lab: 52 Exercises Inspired by Artists, Materials, Time, Place, and Method* (Beverly, MA: Quarry Books, 2013), 26–27; Gerda Lipski, "Acrylmalerei Techniken Strukturen mit der Rakel/ structures with the squeegee," February 25, 2014, accessed January 12, 2018, https://www.youtube.com/watch?v= yW8L7u3RPKQ.

[4] Belz 2011. On technique in Richter's Abstract paintings, see Kasper 2003, 46–52.

[5] Georg Imdahl, "Meister des Abstrakten. Atelierbesuch bei Gerhard Richter," in *Kölner Stadt-Anzeiger*, October 14, 2008, accessed January 12, 2018, https://www.ksta.de/meister-des-abstrakten-atelierbesuch-bei-gerhard-richter-13757300.

[6] See the description of Richter's squeegee technique in Storr 2009, 69.

[7] See Walter Koschatzky, *Die Kunst der Graphik* (Salzburg: Bertelsmann Verlag, 1972), 317–18.

[8] Andy Warhol and Pat Hackett, *POPism: The Warhol Sixties* (New York: Harcourt Brace Jovanovich, 1980), 8.

[9] Gerhard Richter, "Notes" (1985), in Richter 2009, 140–44, here 141.

[10] See Götz's own description of his painting technique in Karl Otto Götz, *Erinnerungen*, vol. 2: *1945–1959* (Aachen: Rimbaud, 1994), 113.

[11] Obituary for Karl Otto Götz, *Tagesschau*, August 21, 2017, accessed October 29, 2017, https://www.tagesschau.de/inland/k-o-goetz-101.html.

[12] See Ansted 2017, 202. See also Robert Storr, "Gerhard Richter: Forty Years of Painting," in New York 2002, 11–90, here 73.

[13] Hilary Sample, *Maintenance Architecture* (Cambridge, MA: MIT Press, 2016), 149.

[14] Imdahl 2008 (see note 5).

[15] Richter's squeegee paintings were initially known as "spatula paintings," see Heribert Heere, "Gerhard Richter. Die Abstrakten Bilder. Zur Frage des Inhalts," in Bielefeld 1982, 9–20, here 14.

[16] Gerhard Richter, "Interview with Hans Ulrich Obrist" (2007), in Richter 2009, 528–33, here 531.

[17] On this see Matthias Krüger, "Gespachtelter Zufall. Gustave Courbet und die Messermalerei," in *Werkzeuge und Instrumente*, ed. Philippe Cordez and Matthias Krüger (Berlin: De Gruyter, 2012), 109–27.

[18] See Johannes Stückelberger, *Wolkenbilder. Deutungen des Himmels in der Moderne* (Munich: Wilhelm Fink Verlag, 2010), 301–65.

[19] Gerhard Richter, "Interview with Stefan Koldehoff" (1999), in Richter 2009, 349–53, here 353.

[20] Gerhard Richter, "Interview with Hans Ulrich Obrist" (2007), in ibid., 528–33, here 531.

[21] Sir Joshua Reynolds, *Discourses Delivered at the Royal Academy*, vol. 2 (London, 1820), 92.

[22] Camille Lemonnier, *G. Courbet et son œuvre* (Paris: Alphonse Lemerre, 1878), 62.

[23] See Grischka Petri, "August Strindbergs moderne Malerei und der Zufall im kunsthistorischen Schaffen," in *August Strindberg. Der Dichter und die Medien*, ed. Walter Baumgartner and Thomas Fechner-Smarsly (Munich: Wilhelm Fink Verlag, 2003), 83–112, here 83–88.

[24] Franz Roh, "Strindberg als Avantgardist der Malerei," in *Das Kunstwerk* 17 (1963), 2–4, here 2.

[25] August Strindberg, "'The New Arts! or The Role of Chance in Artistic Creation" in *The Cambridge Companion to August Strindberg*, trans. Michael Robinson (Cambridge: Cambridge University Press, 2009), 103–07, here 103.

[26] Hans Ulrich Obrist, *Kuratieren!* (Munich: C.H. Beck, 2015), 111–12; Imdahl 2008 (see note 5).

[27] Strindberg 2009 (see note 25), 103.

[28] Hans Ulrich Obrist, *Kuratieren!* (Munich: C.H. Beck, 2015), 111–12; Imdahl 2008 (see note 5).

[29] Cornelius Gurlitt, *Die deutsche Kunst des Neunzehnten Jahrhunderts. Ihre Ziele und Thaten* (Berlin: Georg Bondi Verlag, 1899), 386–87.

[30] See Dario Gamboni, *Potential Images: Ambiguity and Indeterminacy in Modern Art* (London: Reaktion Books, 2002), 230.

[31] See Erika Fischer-Lichte, *Ästhetik des Performativen* (Frankfurt am Main: Suhrkamp Verlag, 2004), 22.

[32] Harold Rosenberg, "The American Action Painters (1952)," in *The Tradition of the New* (New York: Horizon Press, 1959), 35–47, here 36.

[33] See Caroline Jones, *Machine in the Studio: Constructing the Postwar American Artist* (Chicago, IL: University of Chicago Press, 1996), 72.

[34] Benjamin H. D. Buchloh, "Geste, Faktur, Index. Abstraktion in der Malerei von Gerhard Richter," in Cologne 2008, 8–17, here 10–11.

[35] Götz 1994 (see note 10), 127.

[36] Gerhard Richter in the film interview with Corinna Belz, Belz 2011 (see note 4).

[37] Gerhard Richter, "Interview with Sabine Schütz" (1990), in Richter 2009, 251–58, here 257.

[38] Gerhard Richter, "Interview with Jan Thorn-Prikker" (2004), in ibid., 464–79, here 476.

[39] Ibid.

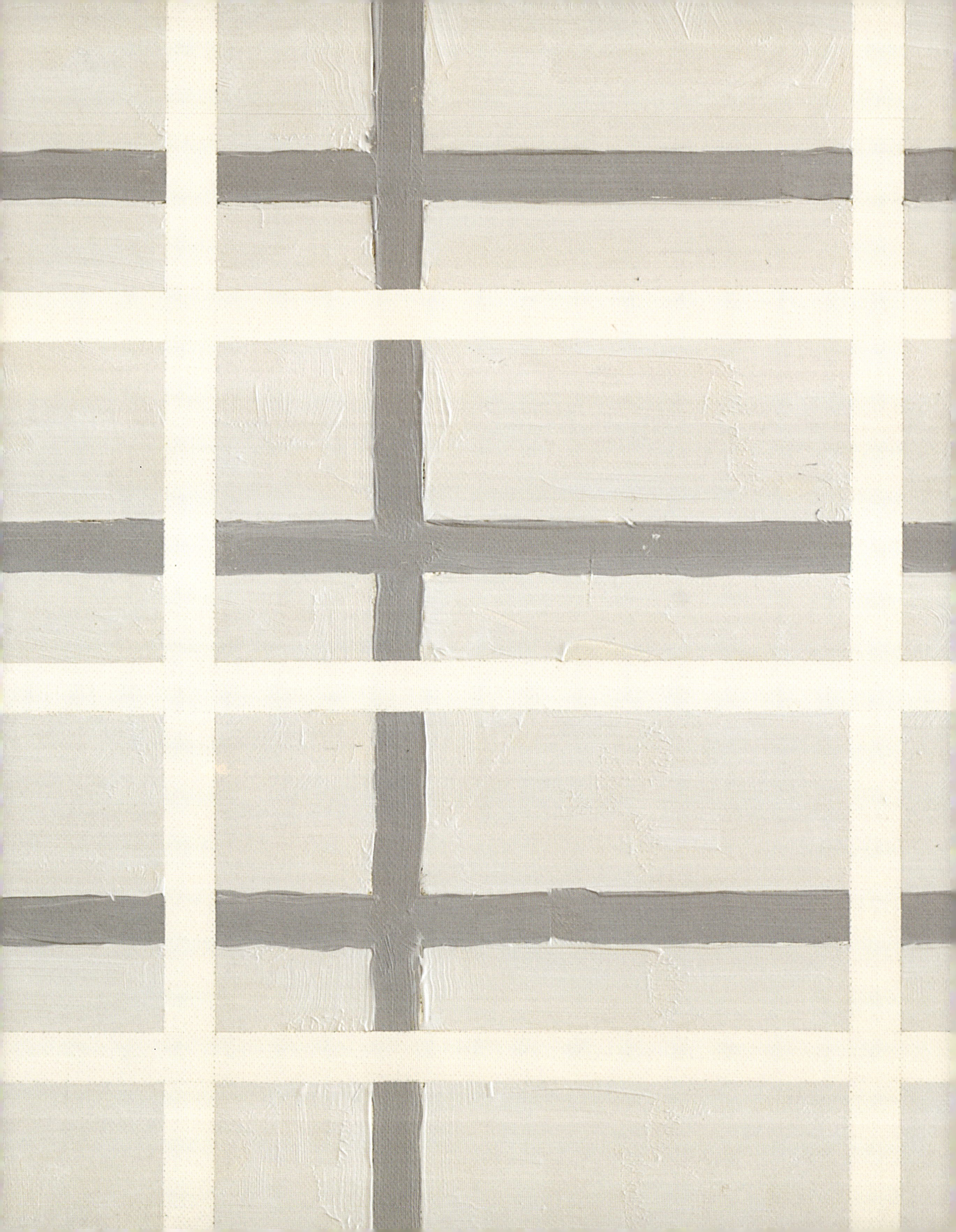

Structures and Illusions: Abstract Works in the 1960s

Valerie Hortolani

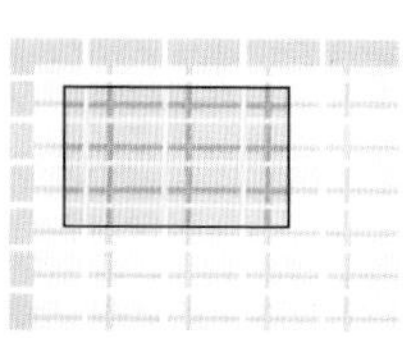

cat. 4

At a time when painting was losing significance, Gerhard Richter's work was a defense of the medium. To avoid the burden of imputed meaning, he turned to photographs in the 1960s. Austere compositions and grids offered neutral motifs, shifting the focus to structures and illusions. By copying and alienating details, he liberated painting from its role of representation. The form of abstraction thus generated was new. Instead of abstracting from the object as Vasily Kandinsky did, Richter centered on pictorial resources such as streaks, gestural brushwork, and shadows.

Gerhard Richter chose to begin his catalogue raisonné with *Table* [1] from 1962 (figs. pp. 10, 24), a decision that reflected his exploration of figurative and abstract art (see the essays by Ortrud Westheider, pp. 8–21, and Dietmar Elger, pp. 22–33). He spent much of the next ten years repeatedly examining this question. His many artworks from this period were dominated by the color gray.[1] Although this is said to have been a result of the artist's use of the black-and-white aesthetics of photography, gray in the form of grisaille has a long tradition in art history, and Richter's works can be seen as belonging to this tradition.[2] Despite his conspicuous utilization of this color—or perhaps precisely because of it—Richter has said very different things about the meaning of gray, describing it both as an absolute color[3] and as the color of indifference or nothingness.[4]

In concentrating upon planar motifs such as curtains, windows, and doors, and industrial structures such as corrugated metal, grids, and tubes, Richter approached abstraction via formal simplicity and close observation. While his early Photo paintings sought to reproduce an object based on photographic source material, the Curtain paintings (1964 onward) were no longer based on a specific image. Rather, they visualize imaginary images (cat. 1, 2). They are the first pieces in which Richter approached his (still) figural motifs via an idea.

Between 1964 and 1967, he produced twelve paintings with curtain motifs. In the series of works showing a drawn curtain hanging in folds, Richter developed this motif into a nonhierarchical, rhythmic division of the picture surface in vertical stripes.[5] All of the works in the series present the curtain as a closed, opaque structure obstructing the observer's view of whatever lies behind. It is not the depiction of the material qualities of the fabric, but the exploration of the formal aspects of the pictorial surface that is crucial. While an eighth of the picture surface in *Curtain* [58-1] (cat. 1) is devoted to the floor in the foreground, thus indicating a sense of depth, the floor in *Curtain III (Light)* [56] (cat. 2) is reduced to a narrow black strip, leaving just enough space for the hem of the curtain. Here, the motif has become almost entirely abstract.

The series is rooted in the art historical tradition, with references to the anecdotes of classical antiquity (see the essay by Ortrud Westheider, pp. 8–21), but it is also anchored within contemporary international movements such as pop, op, and minimal art. The series Corrugated Iron, Grids (cat. 5), and Shadow paintings (cat. 4) allude to the stripped-down aesthetics of American minimalism by artists such as Carl Andre, Sol LeWitt, and Donald Judd, whose work Richter saw early on in the Düsseldorf gallery of his friend, Konrad Fischer.[6] *Grid* [166] (cat. 5) and *Shadow Picture* [209-8] (cat. 4) in particular can be interpreted as explorations of the grid—a pattern that is central to minimal art.[7] However, Richter would not have adapted these ideas uncritically, due to his insistence upon specific, painterly qualities, such as a playing with illusion and soft focus. Paradoxically, by deemphasizing the painterly and revealing doubt in his own medium, Richter asserted himself even more forcefully as a painter.

As late as 1964–65, in a note about his paintings based on photographs, Richter wrote, "All that interests me is the gray areas, the passages and tonal sequences, the pictorial spaces, overlaps and interlockings. If I had any way of abandoning the object as the bearer of this structure, I would immediately start painting abstracts."[8] He finally stepped into nonobjective territory in 1966 with the painting *Untitled* [194-9] (cat. 7). In this painting, Richter monumentalized the brushstroke as a strategic gesture, freeing it from the object. Like the sky, the diffuse gray background seems to blur into brightness from the bottom to the top of the painting, and it alone awakens the final traces of representationalism, showing the constant fluctuation between abstraction and semblance in Richter's oeuvre (see the essay by Dietmar Elger, pp. 22–33).

In the series of three *Star Pictures* [224-13 to 224-15], completed in 1969 (cat. 10–12), the chain of ideas is reversed: These results of experiments in abstract painting with monochromatic smears of paint gain their evocative character solely from the ex post facto titles of *Star Picture*. Richter's search for new paths in abstract art manifests itself here. Simultaneously, the Star paintings mark a transition to the series of Inpaintings and Gray monochromes he began making in the 1970s (see the chapter "Gestures and Blendings: Inpaintings and Gray Paintings," pp. 104–19). On the one hand, the Star paintings offered Richter room to play, to experiment with methods of painting and ways of applying paint; on the other hand, he was aware of the aesthetic weakness of these apparently rough and noncomposed paintings. As he stated in 1991, "the painting itself is not interesting."[9] He might very well have destroyed the paintings, had the discrepancy between title and painting not appealed to him.

Translated from the German by Allison Moseley

[1] See Gregor Wedekind, "Grau als Modus des Uneigentlichen bei Gerhard Richter," in *Die Farbe Grau*, eds. Magdalena Bushart and Gregor Wedekind (Berlin: De Gruyter, 2016), 267–85.

[2] See *Monochrome: Painting in Black and White* (London: The National Gallery, 2017). Exhibition catalog.

[3] "Gray is, after all, also a color, and sometimes it is the most important one to me," Gerhard Richter in an interview in *Deutsche Zeitung*, 1972, quoted in Burgdorf 2005, 50.

[4] "Gray. It makes no statement whatsoever; it evokes neither feelings nor associations; it is really neither visible nor invisible. Its inconspicuousness gives it the capacity to mediate, to make visible, in a positively illusionistic way, like a photograph. It has the capacity that no other color has, to make 'nothing' visible. To me, gray is the welcome and only possible equivalent for indifference, noncommitment, absence of opinion, absence of shape." Gerhard Richter, "From a letter to Edy de Wilde" (February 23, 1975), in Richter 2009, 91–92, here 92; "... in the Gray pictures it's lack of differentiation, nothing, nil, the Beginning and the End," Gerhard Richter, "From a letter to Benjamin H. D. Buchloh" (May 23, 1977), in ibid., 93–94, here 93.

[5] See Elger 2011–2017, vol. 1, 32; Christoph Schreier, "Befragung der Sphinx," in Bonn 2017, 17–24.

[6] See *Wolke & Kristall. Die Sammlung Dorothee und Konrad Fischer* (Düsseldorf: Kunstsammlung Nordrhein-Westfalen, 2016). Exhibition catalog.

[7] See Rosalind E. Krauss, "Grids," in Krauss, *The Originality of the Avant-Garde and Other Modernist Myths* (Cambridge, MA: MIT Press, 1985), 8–22; see also *Rasterfahndung. Das Raster in der Kunst nach 1945* (Stuttgart: Kunstmuseum, 2012). Exhibition catalog.

[8] Richter, "Notes" (1964–65), in Richter 2009, 29–35, here 33.

[9] Richter, "Comments on Some Works" (1991), in ibid., 259–70, here 263.

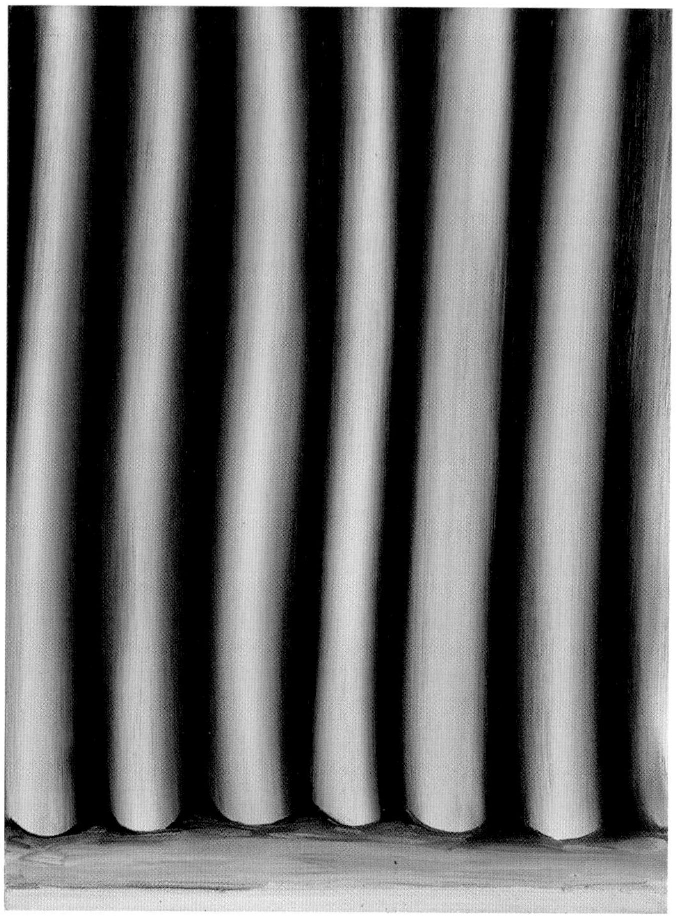

1 *Curtain (Vorhang)* [58-1], 1964
Oil on canvas, 65 × 47 cm
Block Collection, Berlin

2 *Curtain III (Light) (Vorhang III [hell])* [56], 1965
Oil on canvas, 199.5 × 189.5 cm
Staatliche Museen zu Berlin, Nationalgalerie

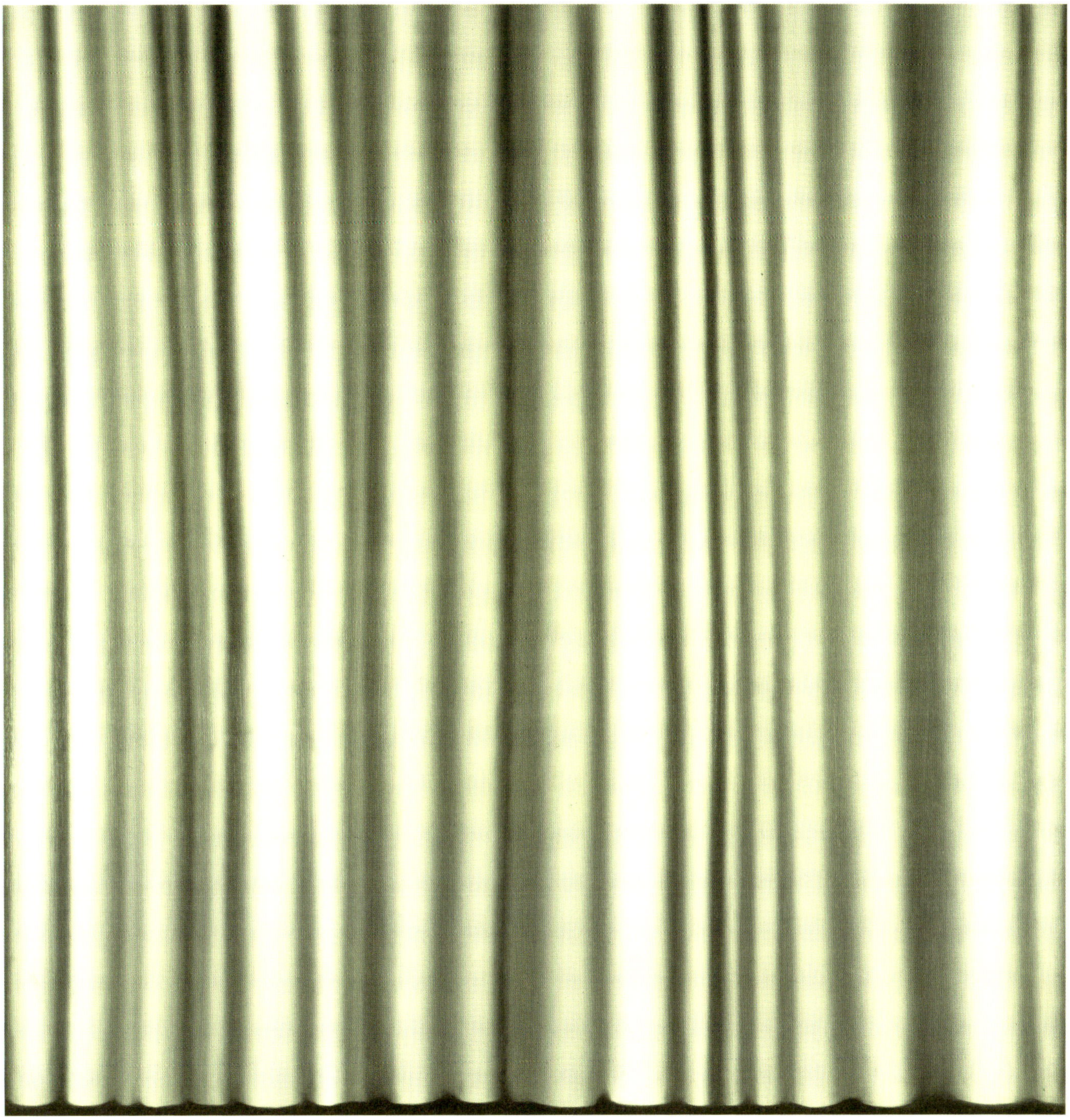

3 *Gray Streaks (Grauschlieren)* [192-1], 1968
Oil on canvas, 200 × 200 cm
Gerhard Richter Archive,
Staatliche Kunstsammlungen Dresden,
loan from a private collection

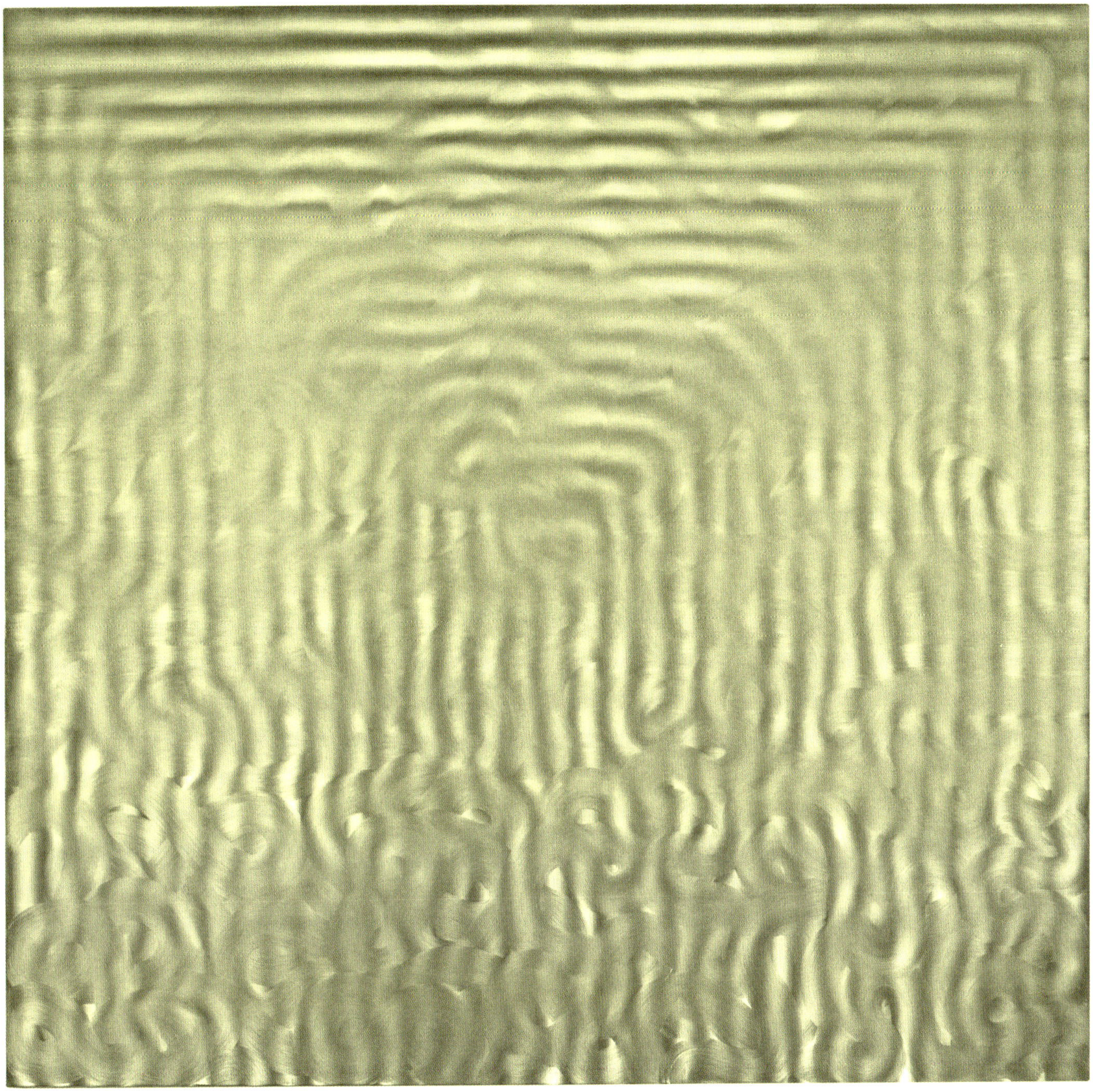

4 *Shadow Picture (Schattenbild)* [209-8], 1968
Oil on canvas, 67 × 87 cm
Collection Fundação de Serralves,
Museu de Arte Contemporânea, Porto,
acquired 1998

5 *Grid (Gitter)* [166], 1967
Oil on canvas, 155 × 130 cm
Vanmoerkerke Collection, Ostend

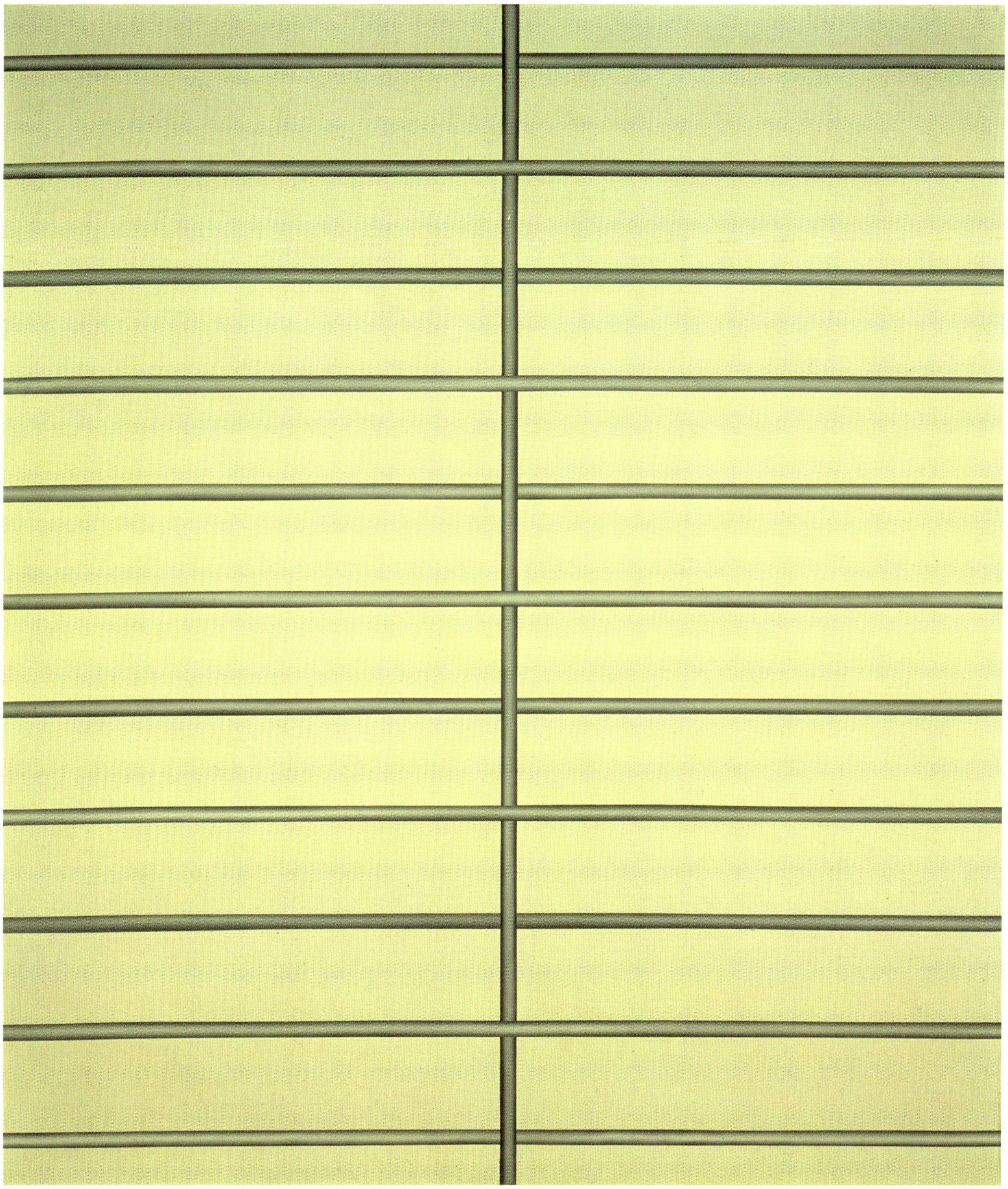

6 *Christmas Market (Weihnachtsmarkt)* [198], 1968
Oil on canvas, 67 × 87 cm
Private collection

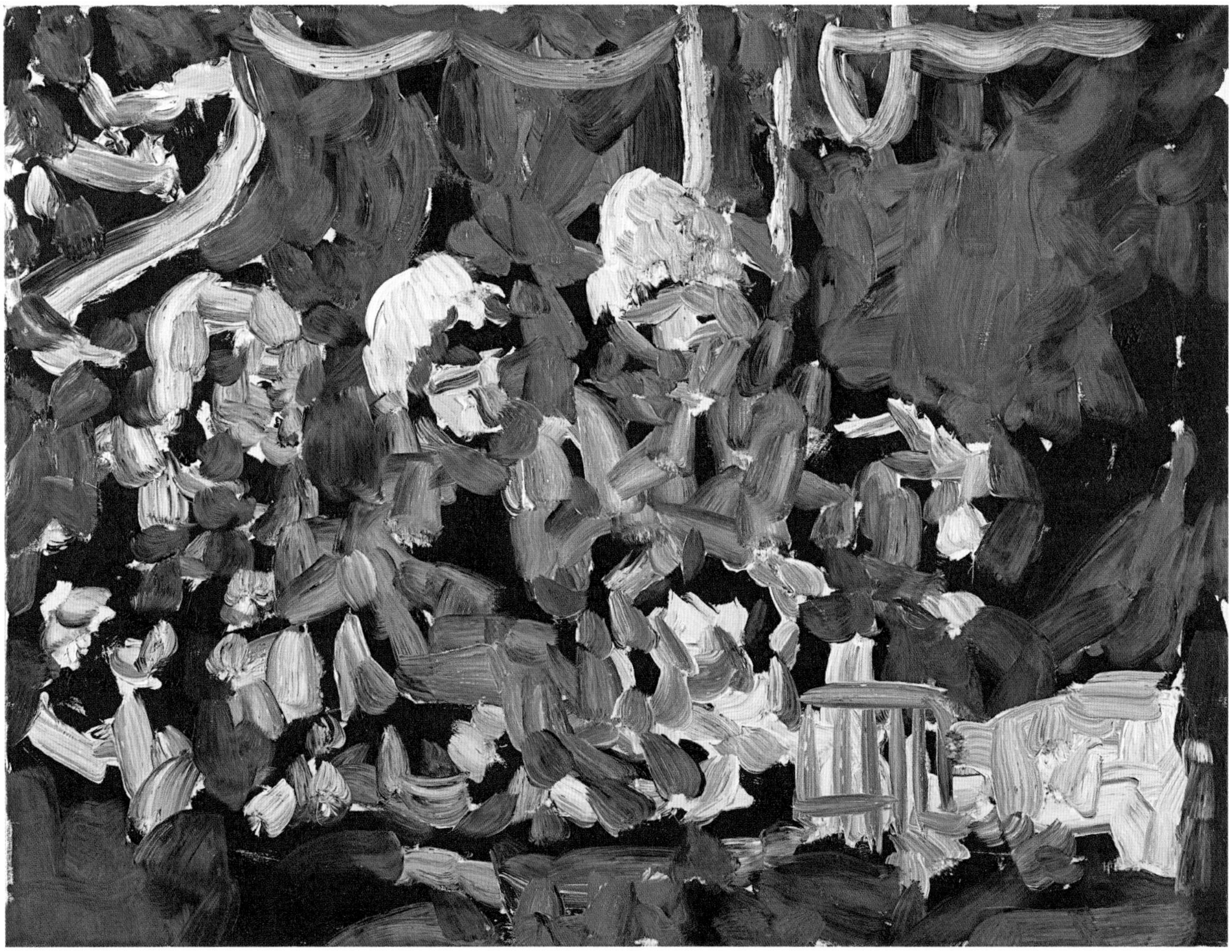

7 *Untitled* [194-9], 1966
Oil on canvas, 80 × 40 cm
Hamburger Kunsthalle, permanent loan from
the Elisabeth and Gerhard Sohst Collection

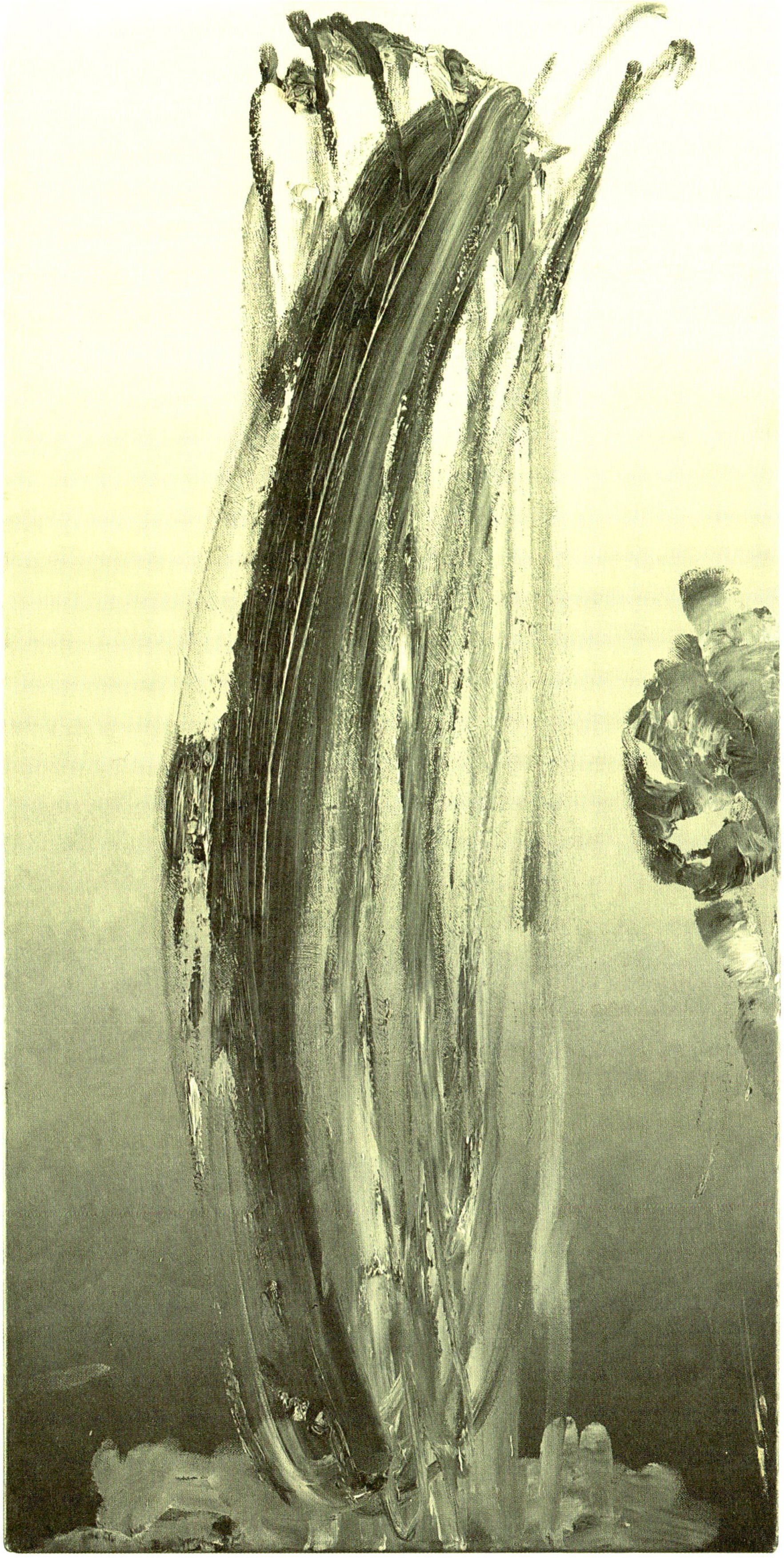

8 *Cloudy (Wolkig)* [194-11], 1968
Oil on canvas, 50 × 50 cm
Museum Wiesbaden

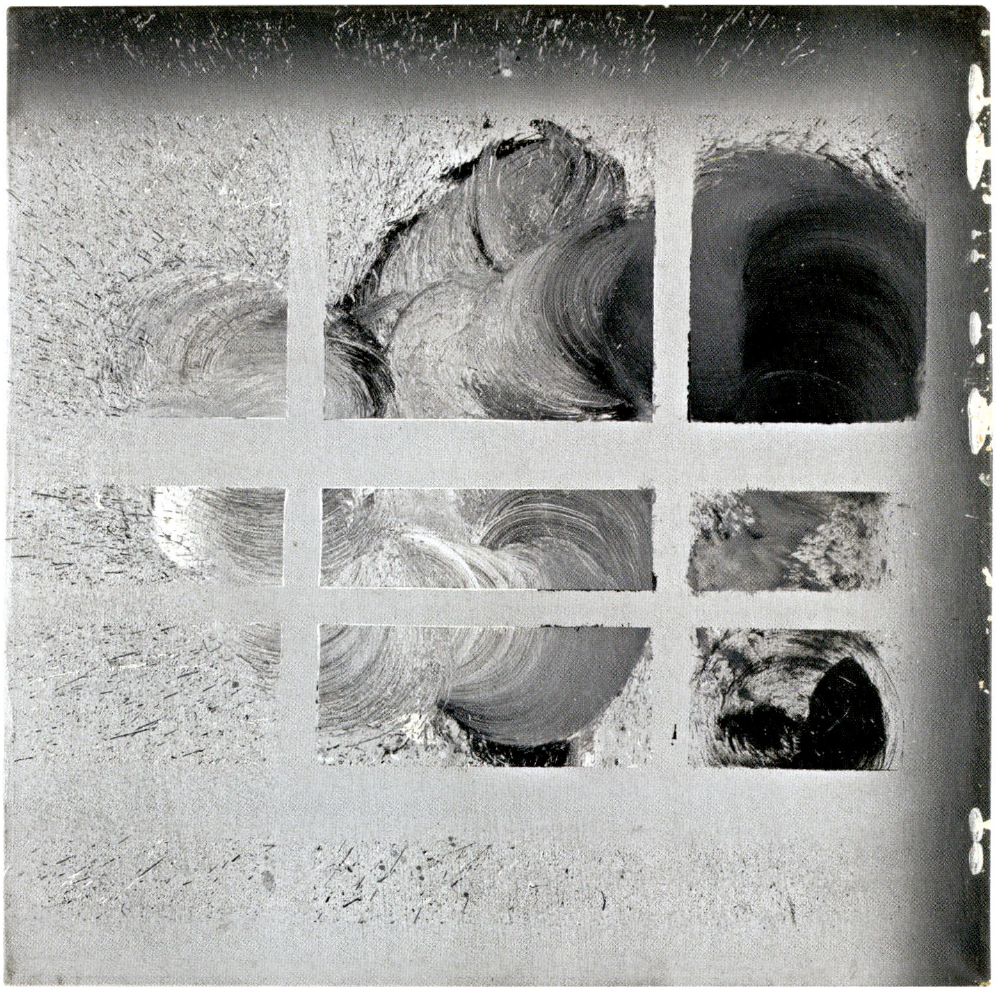

9 *Grid Streaks (Gitterschlieren)* [194-5], 1968
Oil on canvas, 65 × 50 cm
Museum Wiesbaden

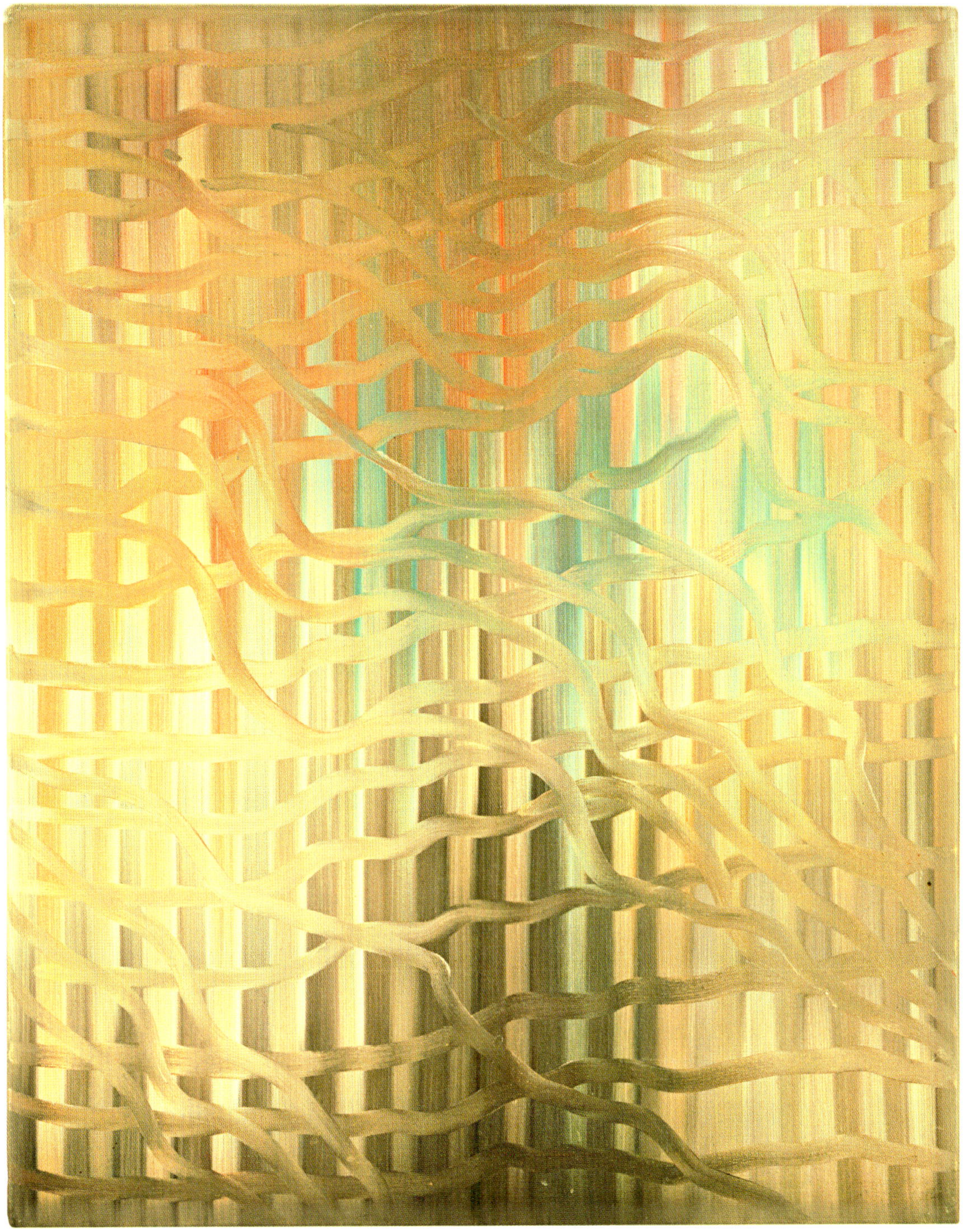

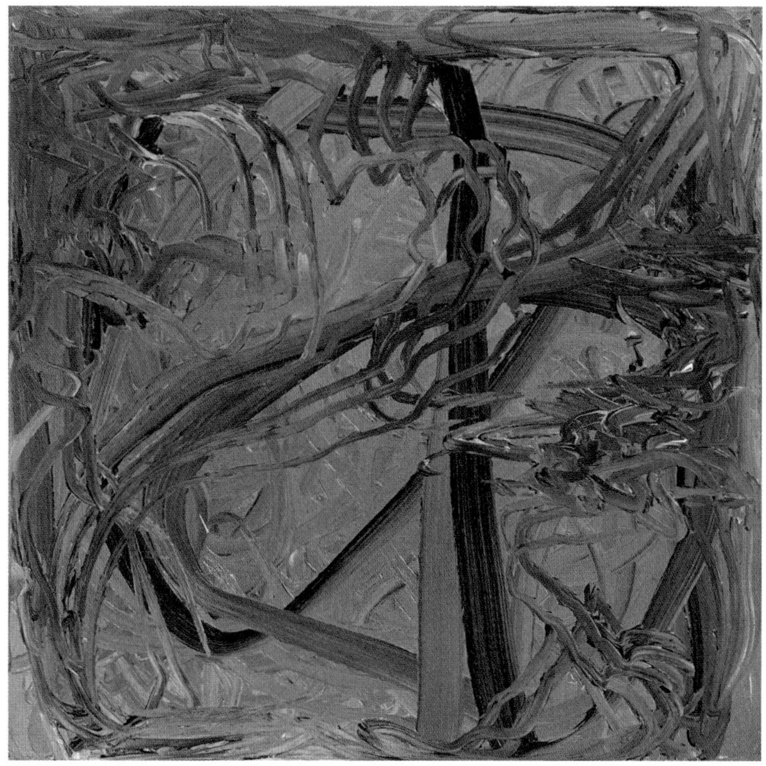

10 *Star Picture (Sternbild)* [224-13], 1969
Oil on canvas, 70 × 70 cm
Private collection of Stefan Asbrand-Eickhoff, Hesse

11 *Star Picture (Sternbild)* [224-14], 1969
Oil on canvas, 70 × 70 cm
Private collection of Stefan Asbrand-Eickhoff, Hesse

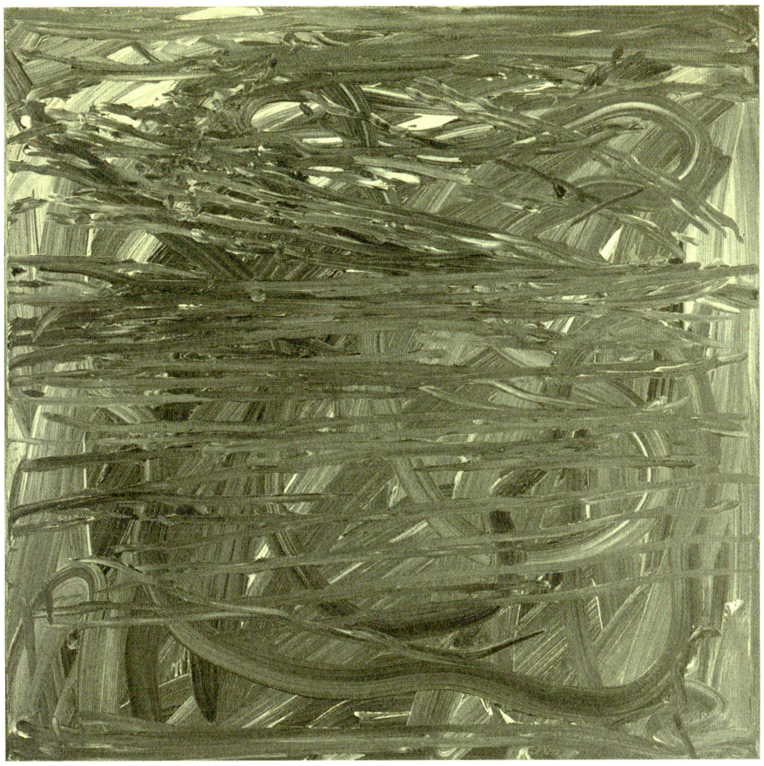

12 *Star Picture (Sternbild)* [224-15], 1969
Oil on canvas, 70 × 70 cm
Private collection of Stefan Asbrand-Eickhoff, Hesse

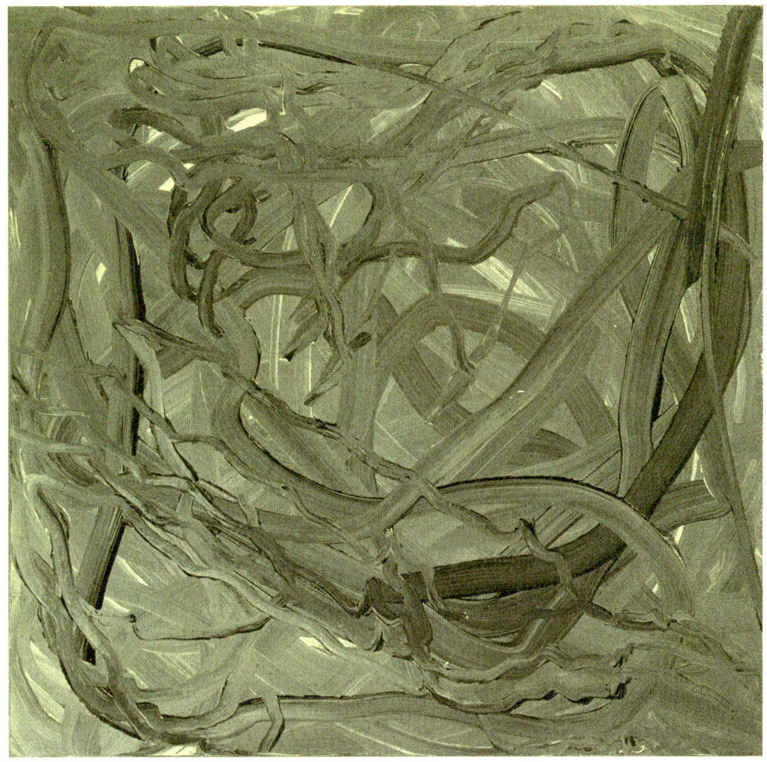

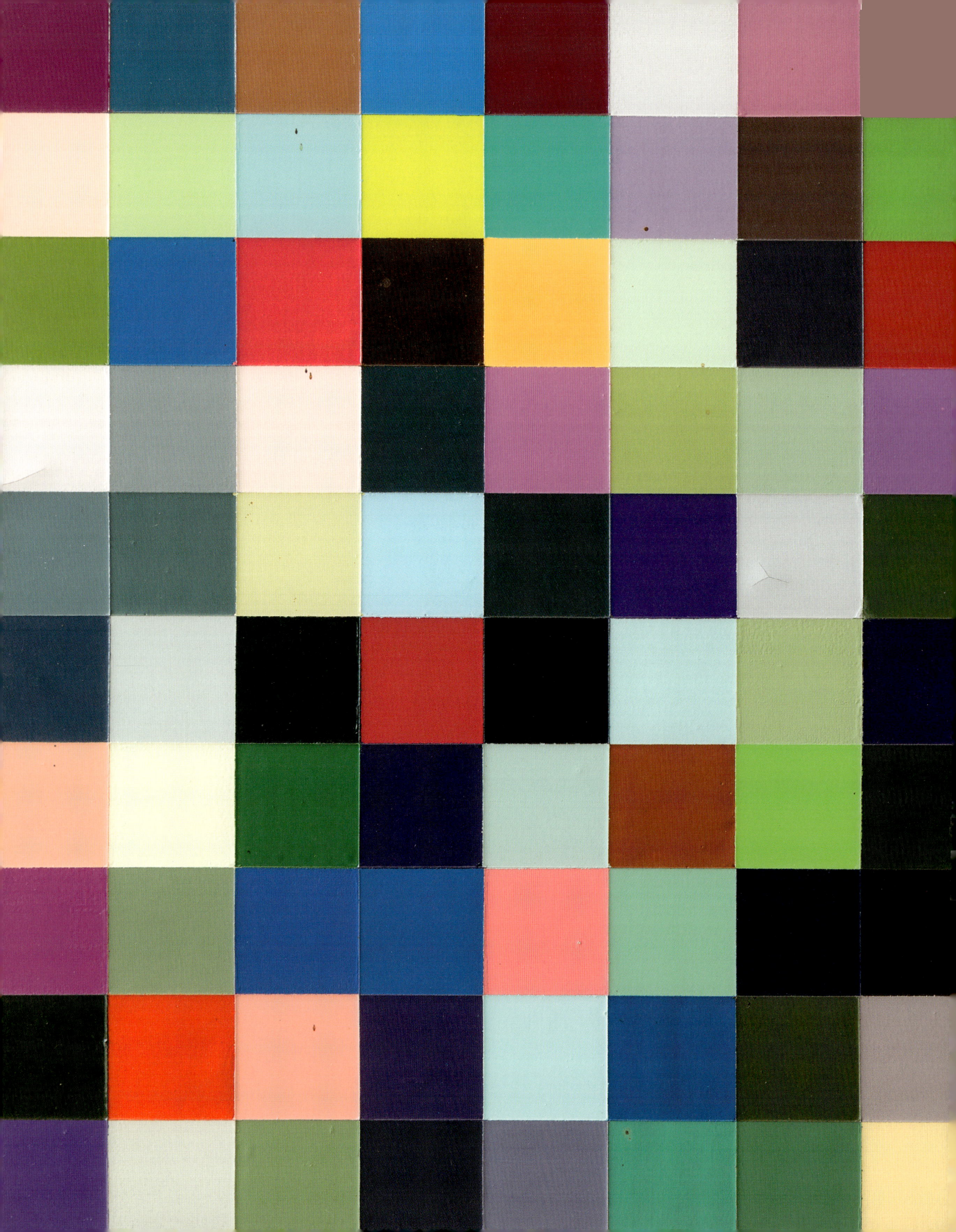

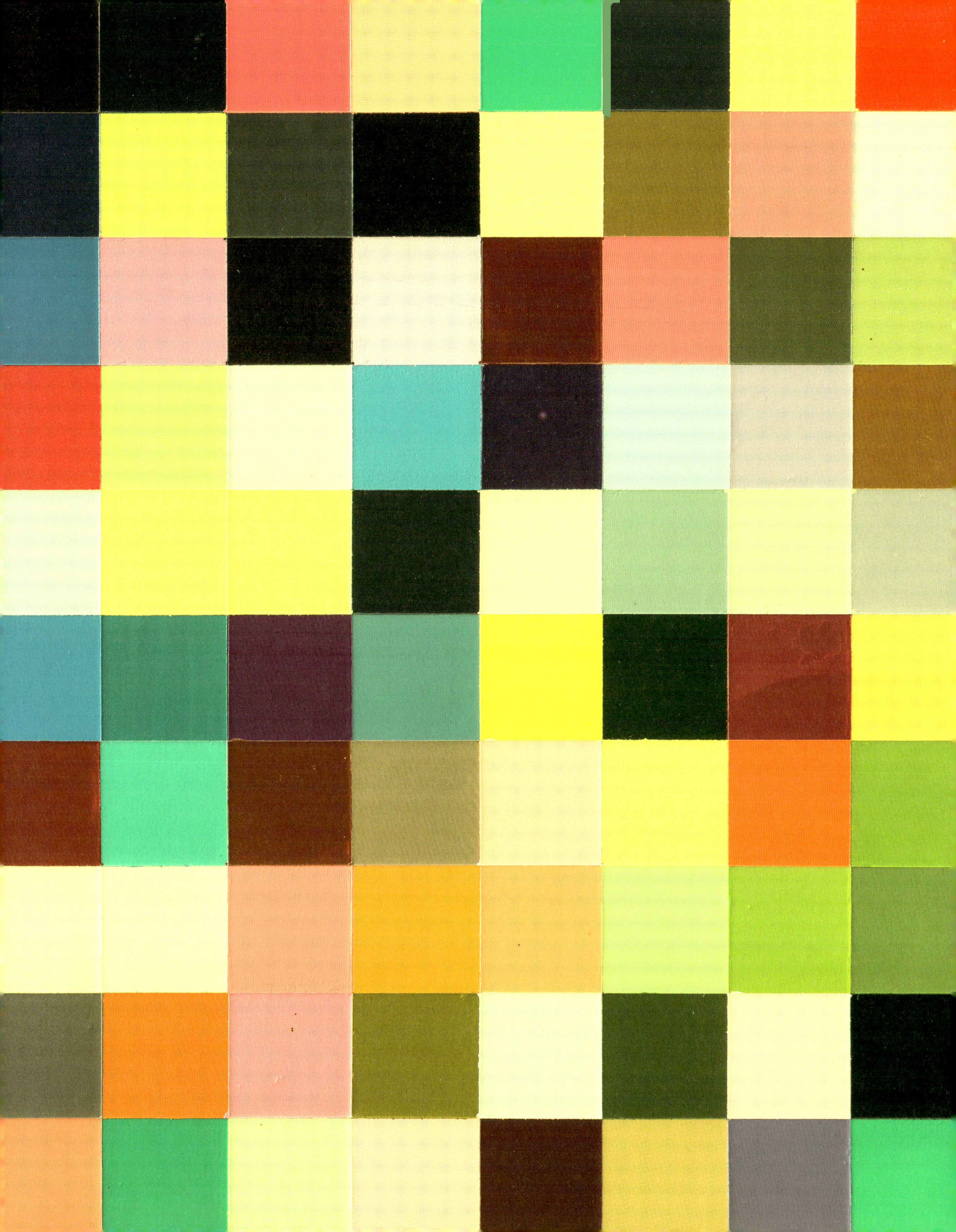

Chance and Concept: Color Charts

Dietmar Elger

cat. 18

In the color theories propounded by Isaac Newton and Johann Wolfgang von Goethe, colors slot into a hierarchy defined by relationships. Richter discarded these principles and devised his own concept. He used chance to determine the distribution of monochrome squares. As in his previous abstract paintings and Photo paintings, the Color Charts peeled away the subjective element in painting. Abstract expressionism had already emancipated color from the object, treating every point on the canvas equally. Richter's Color Charts reflected this development, but whereas Jackson Pollock and others emphasized artistic self-expression, Richter presented the materiality of paint.

In 1966, Gerhard Richter produced nineteen Color Charts, including the paintings *192 Colors* [136] (cat. 13) and *Six Colors* [142] (cat. 15), and the work *Two Grays, One upon the Other* [143-2] (cat. 14), confined to two tones of gray. These paintings formed the foundation for one of Richter's first series not based on photographs from magazines or photo albums. The Color Charts did have a source of their own, however, as the artist related in 1966: "In early January I went into a paint shop [...] and there I saw the usual sample cards with the full array of shades in a collection, the sort of thing we're all familiar with. Suddenly I couldn't help telling myself: 'You can't do a better job than that! Those are perfect pictures.'"[1] What initially appealed to Richter about those sample cards was a commercial aesthetic typical of American pop art (see the essay by Hubertus Butin, pp. 34–45).

The first Color Chart Richter painted was *192 Colors* [136] (cat. 13). The work measures 200 × 150 cm and depicts 192 squares of different colors arranged in strict grid formation and separated by white bars. Richter selected the colors at random and arbitrarily allocated them to the squares, outlined beforehand in fine-tipped pencil. For this first Color Chart he used traditional oil paints, but he soon switched to industrial paints more in keeping with his artistic intentions.

This decision to change paints was not simply a technical choice, but a programmatic alignment. The smooth, high-gloss surfaces offered by industrial lacquers reinforced the nonartistic, deindividualized, neutral character these works had for Richter, just as he sought to avoid any hint of artistic composition or personal taste by haphazardly distributing the randomly selected shades. Another of the artist's decisions is worth noting in this context: Since it was the first of the Color Charts, *192 Colors* [136] should really have been given the lowest number in this series in his catalogue raisonné, but to conceal the correction he had made by changing materials, Richter defied chronology and cataloged this painting between the other Color Charts executed in industrial paints.

After the gray, representational Photo paintings which preceded them, the Color Charts of 1966 were a radical new departure. At first, Richter was by no means sure about the quality of these works, a concern that would recur with later series. His doubts were quashed by his fellow artist and friend Konrad Lueg, who, after a visit to his studio, waxed lyrical about the new paintings. After an exhibition in October 1966 at the Friedrich & Dahlem gallery in Munich, Richter stopped working on the series for a while.

He did not return to his Color Charts until 1971. Compared with the earlier examples, these paintings were more neutral, more complex, and more systematic (cat. 16–18). For the Color Charts in 1966, Richter had merely made a show of allocating the shades spontaneously, whereas now he introduced a strict procedure and drew lots to determine their distribution on the canvas (fig. p. 231). Looking back, he described these phases of development as follows: "The first color charts were unsystematic. They were based directly on commercial color samples. They were still related to Pop Art. In the canvases that followed, the colors were chosen arbitrarily and drawn by chance. Then, 180 tones were mixed according to a given system and drawn by chance to make four variations of 180 tones."[2]

In the 1970s, the practical production of the Color Charts was so elaborate that Gerhard Richter began to employ students from the Düsseldorf Art Academy as assistants. To create the up to 1,024 different shades of color for these new works, he methodically mixed the three primary colors red, yellow, blue, and also green[3] in the correct proportions and gave each shade a number. The numbers were noted on little pieces of paper and then assigned, and this dictated the sequence for applying the shades to the canvas (fig. p. 43). Compared with the earlier Color Charts, Richter had increased the systematic complexity, neutrality, and size of the canvases.

It was not until 1974, however, that this development entered another decisive phase with Color Charts such as *1024 Colors* [356-2] (cat. 18). Richter had already recognized that "each color adapts marvelously to whatever other color is used"[4] as a result of drawing lots, but despite this, he had continued to separate the shades with white bars, deliberately preventing any interaction between the individual colors. Only now did Richter allow the fields of color to collide directly. He discovered that the colors retained their autonomy and did not blend optically.

After 1974, Richter returned only occasionally to his Color Charts—the most spectacular example of which was his 2007 *Cologne Cathedral Window* [900] (fig. p. 44)—and in 1997, there was an unusual rendering in the form of two small-scale Abstract paintings (cat. 19, 20). In both works, Richter expands the creative potential of his Color Charts, in one case by testing their illusionary qualities (cat. 19), and in the other by devising a composition that makes it seem as if the colors and shapes were distributed randomly (cat. 20).

Translated from the German by Kate Vanovitch

1 Gerhard Richter in "Wolfgang Christlieb: Galerie Friedrich und Dahlem," in *Abendzeitung,* October 22–23, 1966, 6.

2 Gerhard Richter, "Interview with Irmeline Lebeer" (1973), in Richter 2009, 72–83, here 82.

3 See Gerhard Richter, "*1024 Farben* in 4 Permutationen," in *Andre, Broodthaers, Buren, Burgin, Gilbert & George, Richter* (Brussels: Palais des Beaux-Arts, 1974), unpaginated. Exhibition catalog. Even in this first edition, gray is erroneously given as a fourth color in addition to red, yellow, and blue. Richter corrected the error in 2006 in "Notes for a press conference" (July 28, 2006), in Richter 2009, 517–18, here 517.

4 Richter 1973 (see note 2), 83.

13 *192 Colors (192 Farben)* [136], 1966
Oil on canvas, 200 × 150 cm
Hamburger Kunsthalle, permanent loan from the Elisabeth and Gerhard Sohst Collection

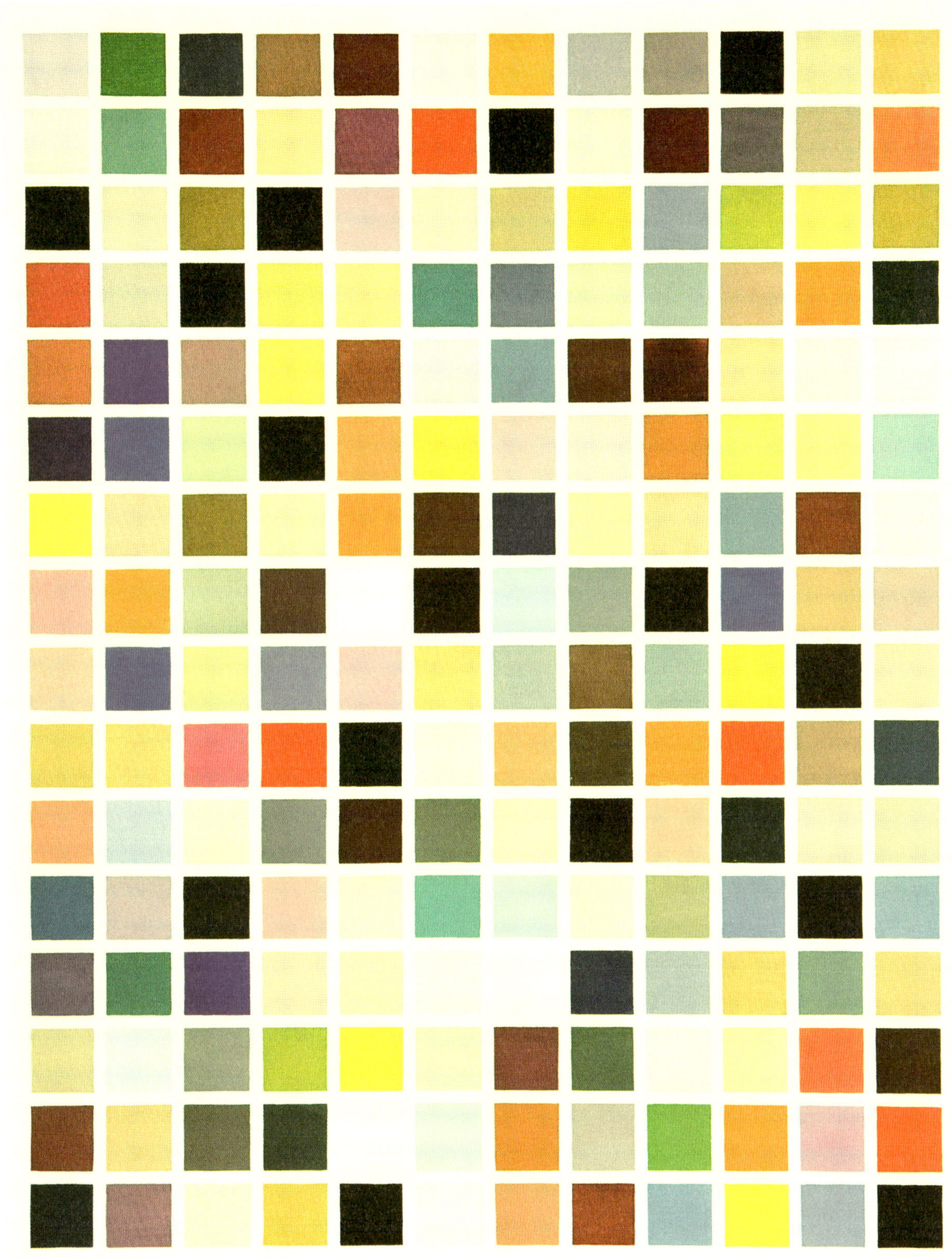

14 *Two Grays, One upon the Other (Zwei Grau übereinander)* [143-2], 1966
Lacquer on canvas, 200 × 130 cm
Olbricht Collection, Essen

15 *Six Colors (Sechs Farben)* [142], 1966
Lacquer on canvas, 200 × 170 cm
Neues Museum. Staatliches Museum für Kunst und Design, Nuremberg, permanent loan from a private collection

16 *1024 Colors (1024 Farben)* [351], 1973
Lacquer on canvas, 299 × 299 cm
Kunstmuseen Krefeld

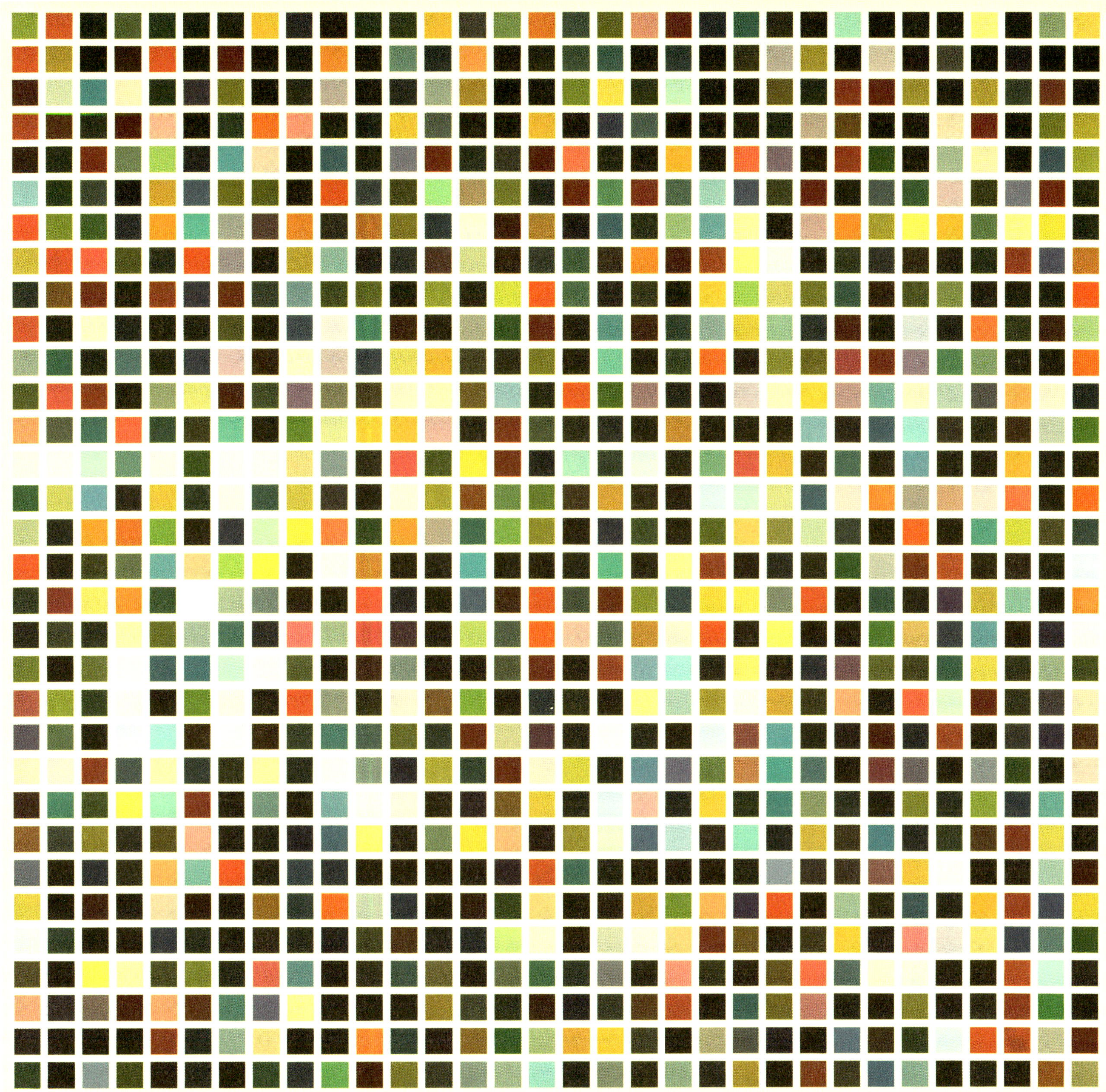

17 *1025 Colors (1025 Farben)* [357-3], 1974
Lacquer on canvas, 120 × 123.5 cm
Private collection, Cologne

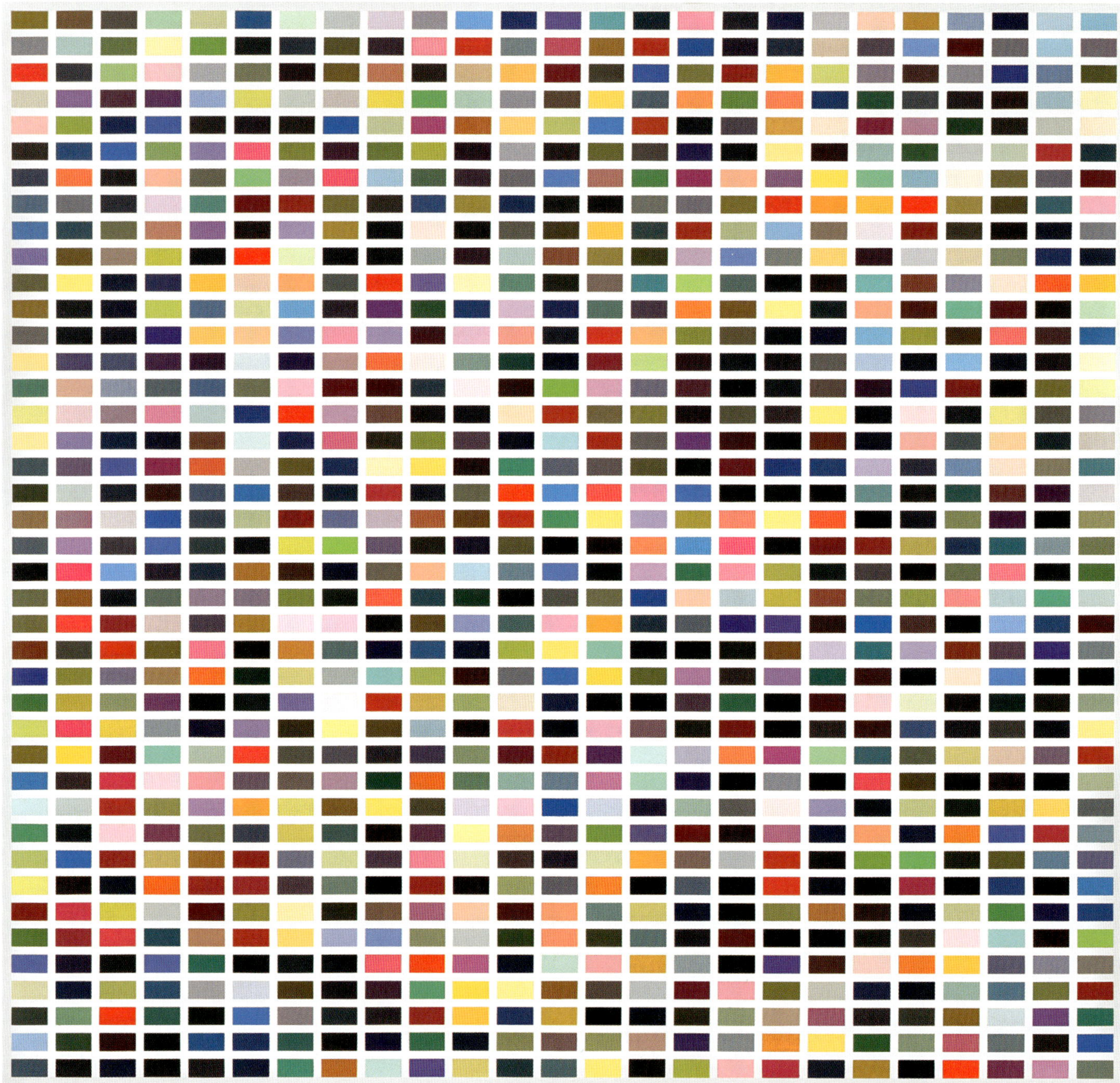

18 *1024 Colors (1024 Farben)* [356-2], 1974
Lacquer on canvas, 96 × 96 cm
Collezione Prada, Milan

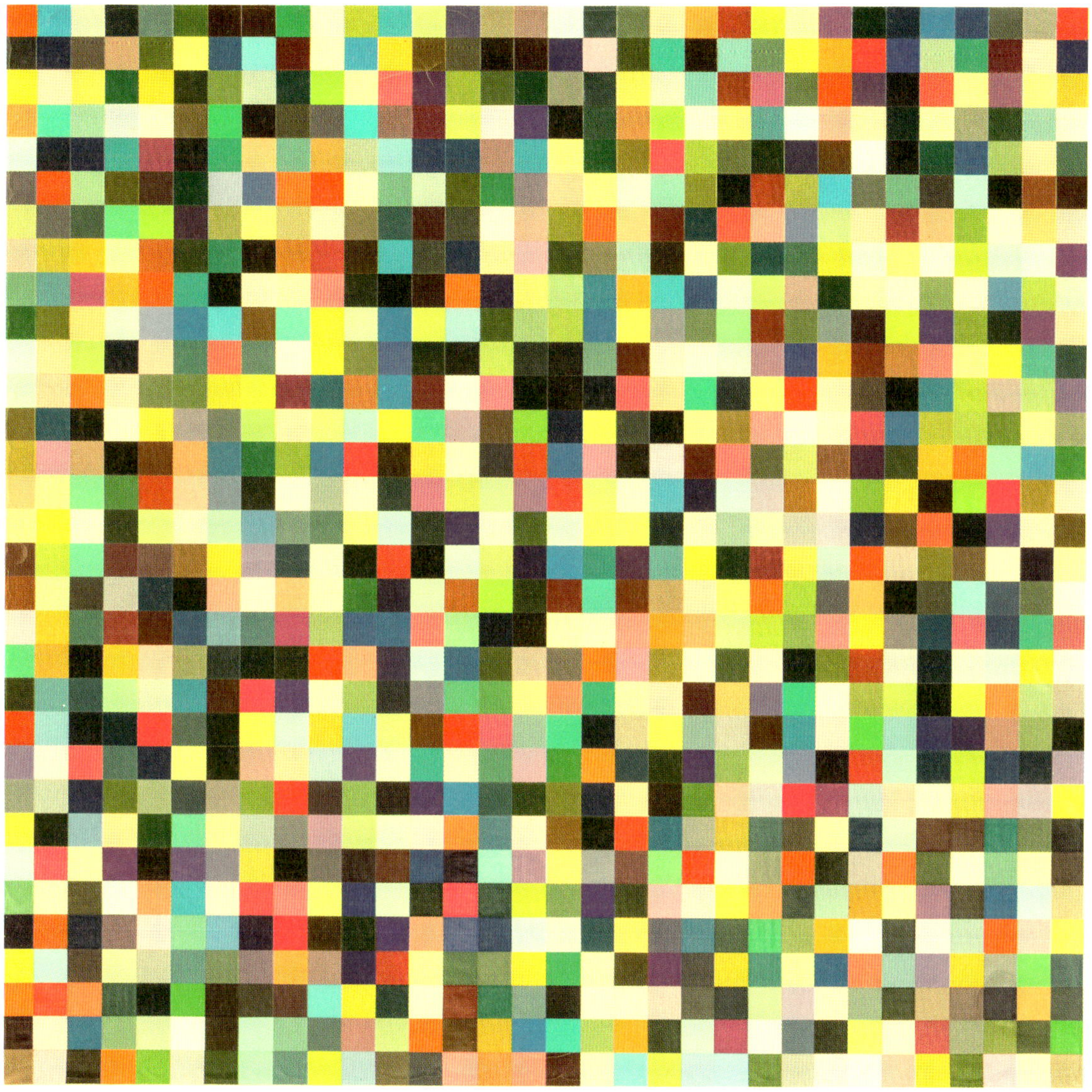

19 *Abstract Painting (Abstraktes Bild)* [848-10], 1997
Oil on canvas, 36 × 51 cm
Private collection

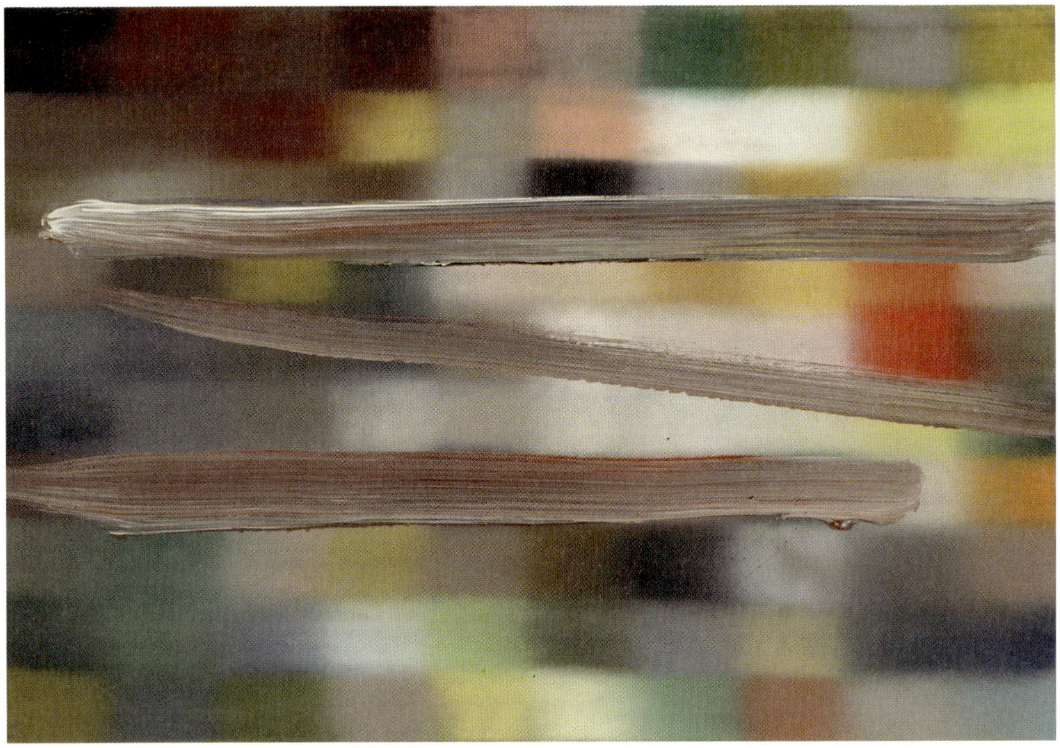

20 *Abstract Painting (Abstraktes Bild)* [848-11], 1997
Oil on aluminum Dibond, 46 × 41 cm
Private collection

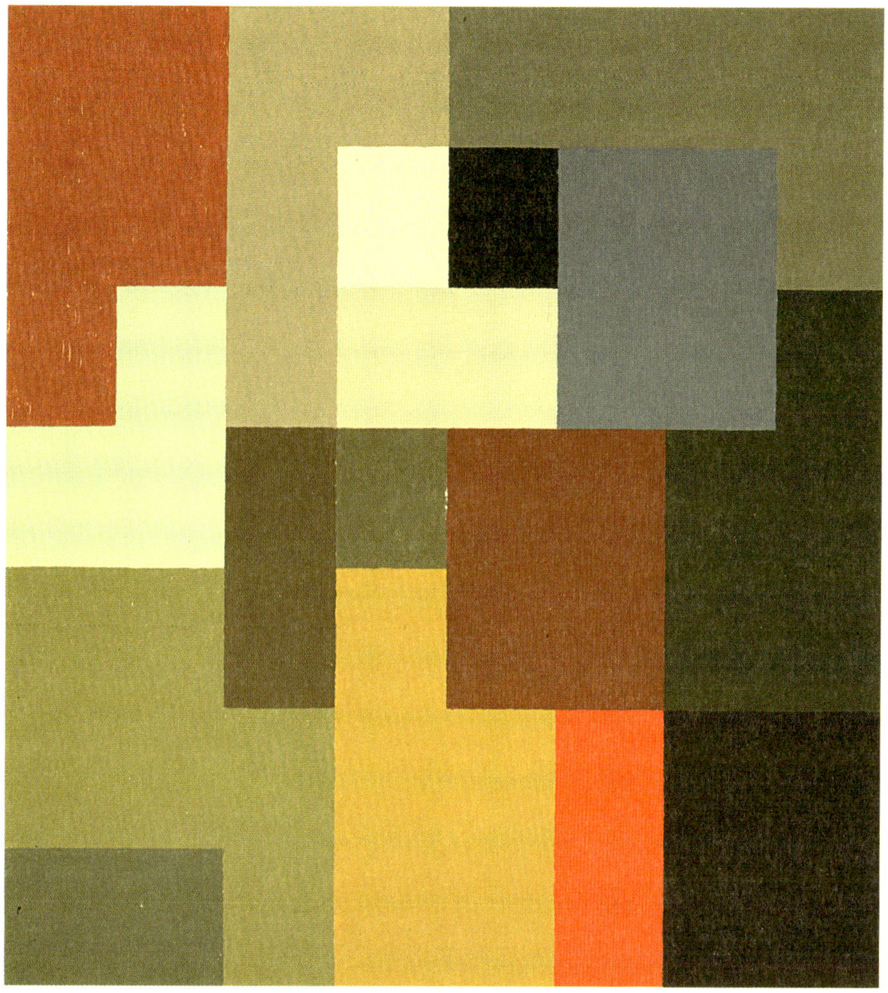

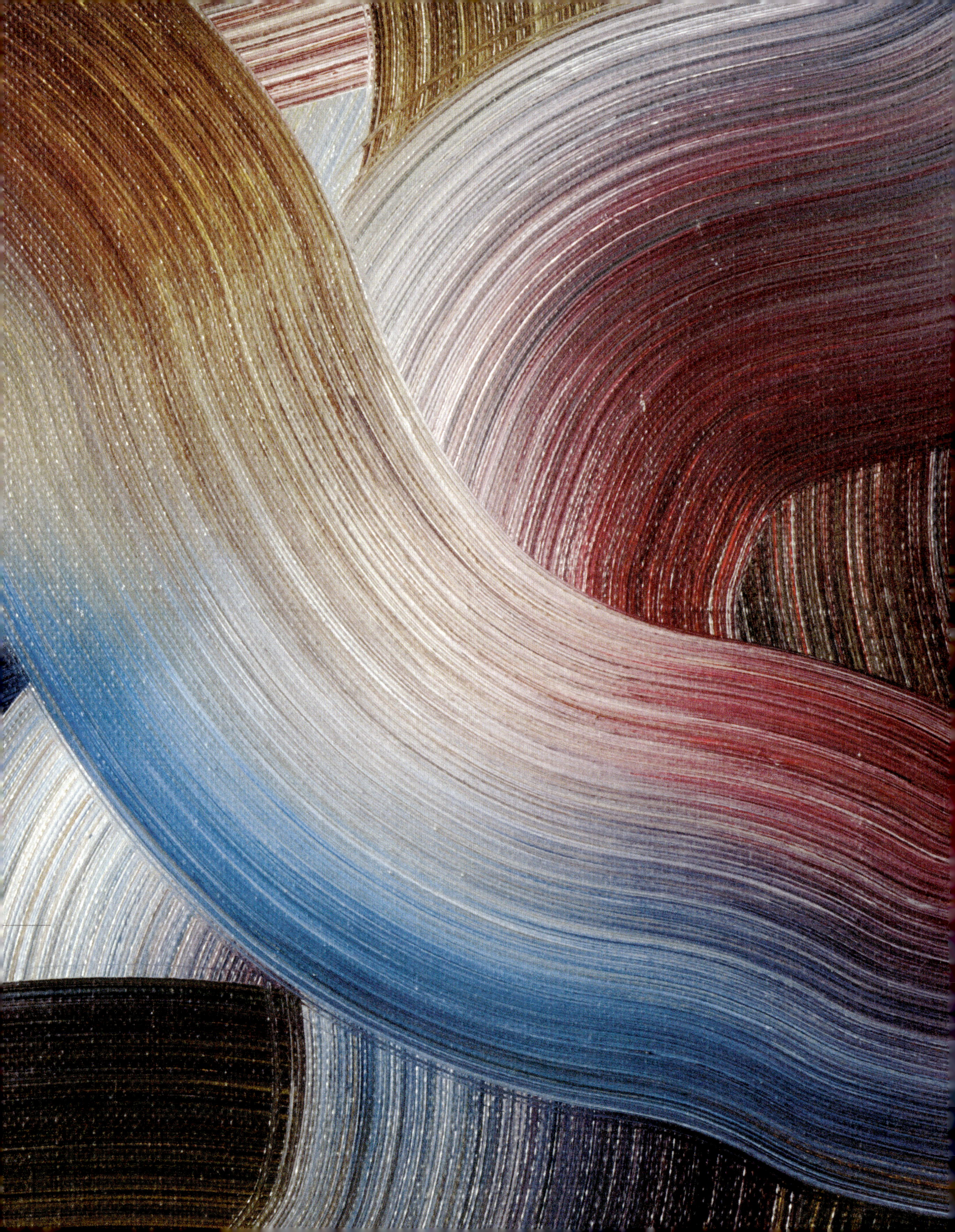

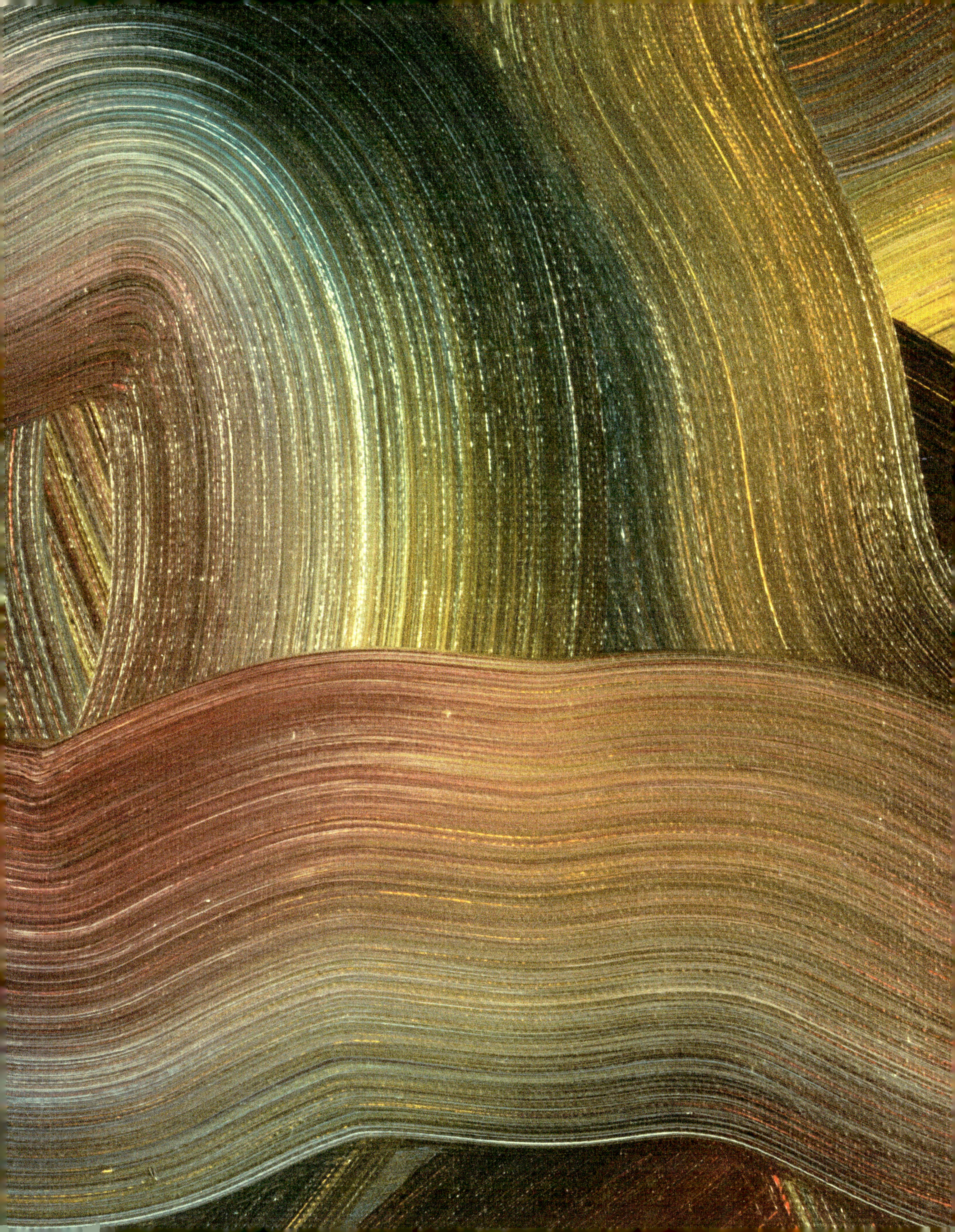

Gestures and Blendings: Inpaintings and Gray Paintings

Valerie Hortolani

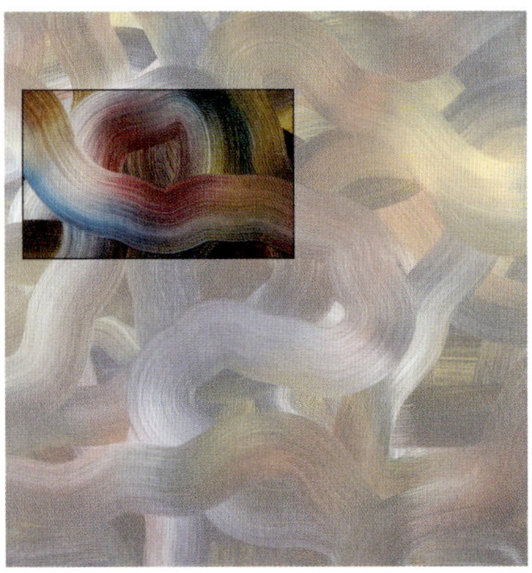

cat. 23

Early avant-garde artists linked the primary colors red, blue, and yellow with idealist concepts, associating these colors with notions of purity. Richter liberated the primary colors from idealist transfiguration. In his Inpaintings, the primary colors mingle and are provocatively impure. Richter thus releases them from their explicitness and highlights their materiality. The same applies to the monochromatic Gray paintings, which focus the gaze on the textures produced by the application of paint. In an age where ideology was under critique, Richter continued to value polysemy and an insistence on artistry.

In his series of Inpaintings begun in 1971, Gerhard Richter continued his exploration of painterly principles by examining how colors mix and how the brush travels over the canvas.[1] The sequence in his catalogue raisonné suggests that the abstract Inpaintings evolved out of a previous period of representational landscapes. Beginning with trees painted with strong brushstrokes in two *Park Pieces* [310 and 311] (1971, private collection and mumok Museum moderner Kunst Stiftung Ludwig Vienna), Richter gradually filtered out the representational elements until all that remained in the triptych *Untitled (Green)* [315-1 to 315-3] (cat. 21) were thick strokes of green paint to fill the space with what he described as "artistic jungles."[2] Richter has never talked about abstraction and representation as if they were polarities. If anything, the two principles pervade his art in a permanent interplay, and one may always harbor characteristics of the other. Opposites are resolved in Richter's work by tackling problems on a higher plane and constantly interrogating his own technique.

The Inpaintings are the result of moving the brush across the canvas in broad, apparently unbroken loops, often combining the primary colors red, blue, and yellow (cat. 23, 24). Richter described the procedure in a letter in 1973: "Three primary colors, as the source of endless sequences of tones [...]. The shades and forms emerge through the constant blending of brushstrokes; they create an illusionistic space, without any need for me to invent forms of signs. The brush goes on its allotted way, from patch to patch of paint, first mediating and then to a greater or lesser degree destroying, mixing, until there is no place left intact. It is almost a soup, a non-hierarchical interweaving of form with space and color."[3]

Because the gestural movement remains visible to the viewer, the brushwork becomes a theme of the series. This is underscored by the deliberately unpoetic, rather technical title of the series: Inpaintings. The canvas turns into a palette, allowing the artist to improvise with the brush. Richter's adage "in painting thinking is painting"[4] finds ample expression in these works (see the essay by Armin Zweite, pp. 46–57). Richter described this simultaneous process of reflection and genesis in his Inpaintings when he called them "[p]ictures which emerge, which result from the making. Not creations; definitely not creative [...] but creaturely."[5] With this phrasing, he plays down his artistic authorship, attributing a backseat role to his creative idea and implying that the works developed autonomously.

Although there are similarities between the visibility of the painting process in the Inpaintings and the gestural painting observed in informalism and abstract expressionism, Richter's works—unlike, say, Jackson Pollock's drip paintings (fig. p. 61) or the works of his Düsseldorf Art Academy teacher Karl Otto Götz (figs. pp. 10, 62)—are by no means expressive or random. Richter countered the spontaneity of his artistic colleagues by adopting a painterly motion of the brush with a slowly meandering, unemotional rhythm.

The primary colors red, yellow, and blue, which have featured for centuries in color theory discourse (see the essays by Ortrud Westheider, pp. 8–21, and Hubertus Butin, pp. 34–45), merge with varying intensity in many of the Inpaintings. At times they even blend into a homogenous noncolor which, although three separate colors are acknowledged in the title, can ultimately only be perceived as "indifferently colorful."[6] The Inpaintings combine aspects of nonhierarchy, noncomposition, and noncolor. In some Inpaintings, Richter reinforced this indifference to color by working with a spectrum of grays, moving closer toward the monochrome (cat. 22).

The color gray, already significant in Richter's early work (see the chapter "Structures and Illusions: Abstract Works in the 1960s," pp. 70–87), was to be the subject of one of his most prolific series, the Gray paintings produced between 1969 and 1976.[7] In these Gray paintings, streaks of color reminiscent of the Inpaintings blend into an opaque gray surface structure. Gray paint, supposedly monotonous, offered the artist tremendous potential for experimenting with a variety of painting surfaces, brushes, and application techniques (cat. 25–27). A gestural approach makes some of these Gray paintings look like achromatic Inpaintings, but with more emphasis placed on surface qualities (cat. 26). Gray comes across here as dull, sober, and demure compared with the transcendental pathos of monochrome compositions by Kazimir Malevich and Yves Klein. Richter later continued his work on the color gray in a series of gray Mirrors (cat. 75). By taking the reduction of content, shape, and color to the extreme, Richter was able to fully embody diversity in unity.

Translated from the German by Kate Vanovitch

[1] See Elger 2008, 232–35.

[2] Gerhard Richter, "From a letter to Jean-Christophe Ammann" (February 1973), in Richter 2009, 70–73, here 71.

[3] Ibid.

[4] Gerhard Richter, "Brief an Wieland Förster" (February 4, 1962), in Hamburg 2011, 50–51, here 50.

[5] Richter 1973 (see note 2), in Richter 2009, 71.

[6] Elger 2008, 235.

[7] See Burgdorf 2005; Friedrich 2009.

21 *Untitled (Green) (Ohne Titel [grün])* [315-1 to 315-3], 1971
Oil on canvas, three parts, 200 × 150 cm each
Museum Küppersmühle für Moderne Kunst, Ströher Collection, Duisburg

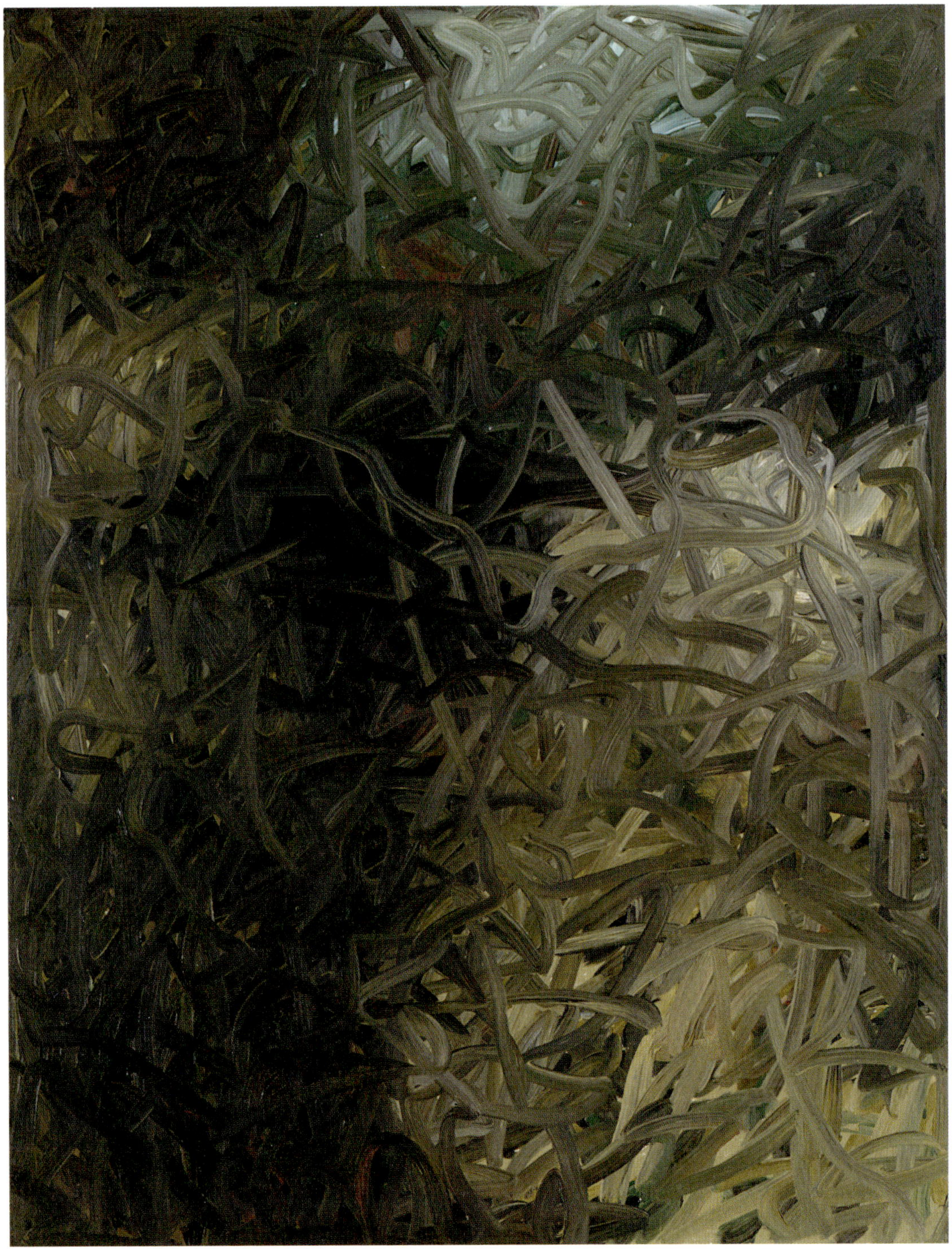

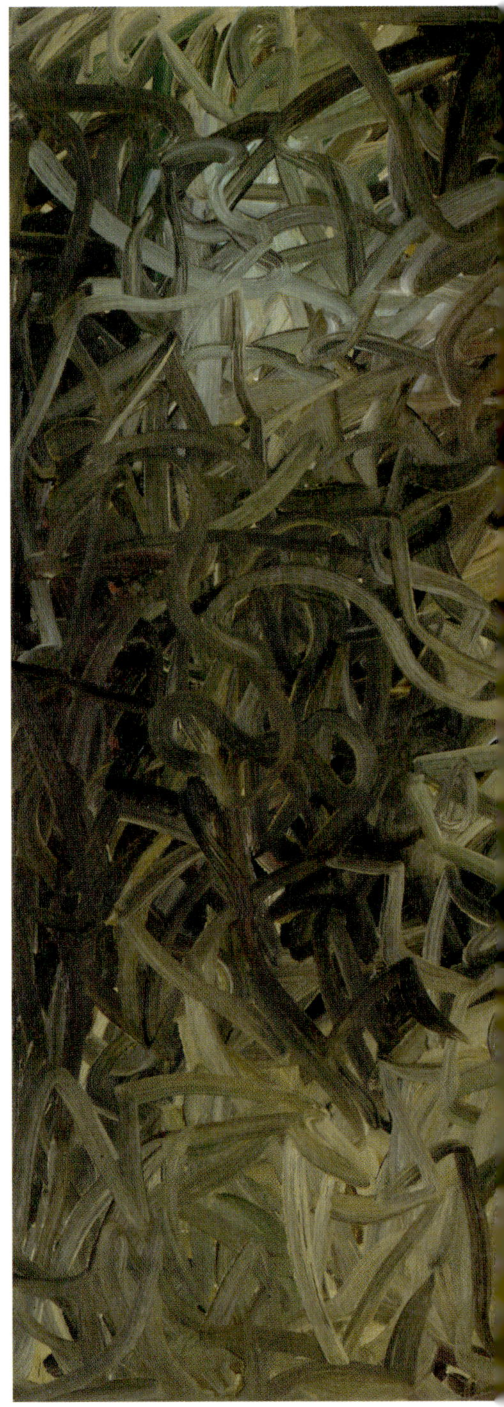

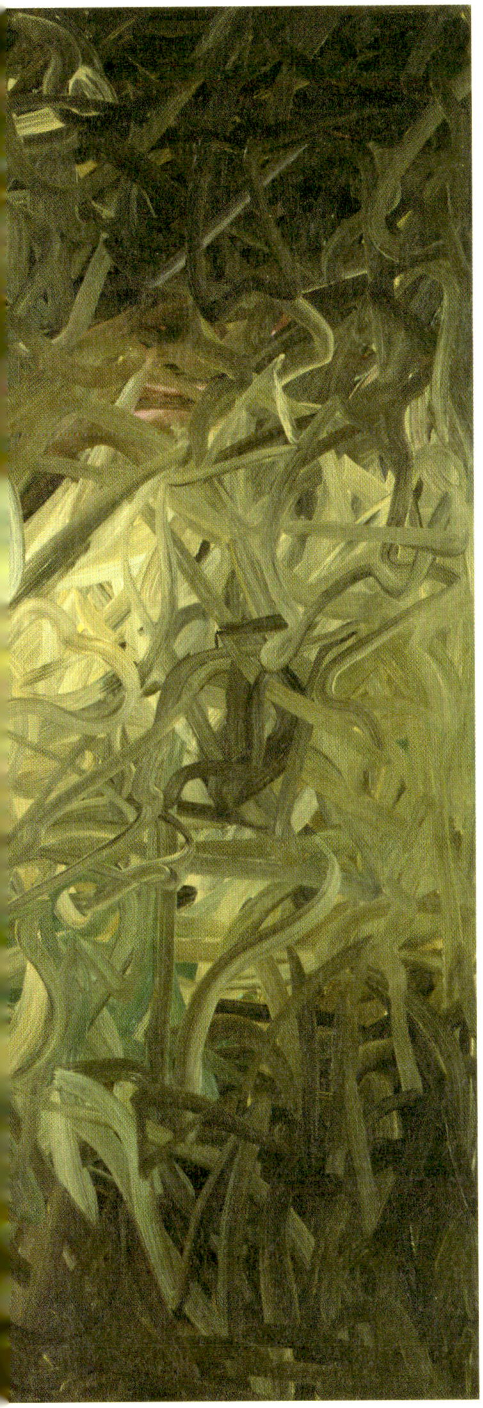
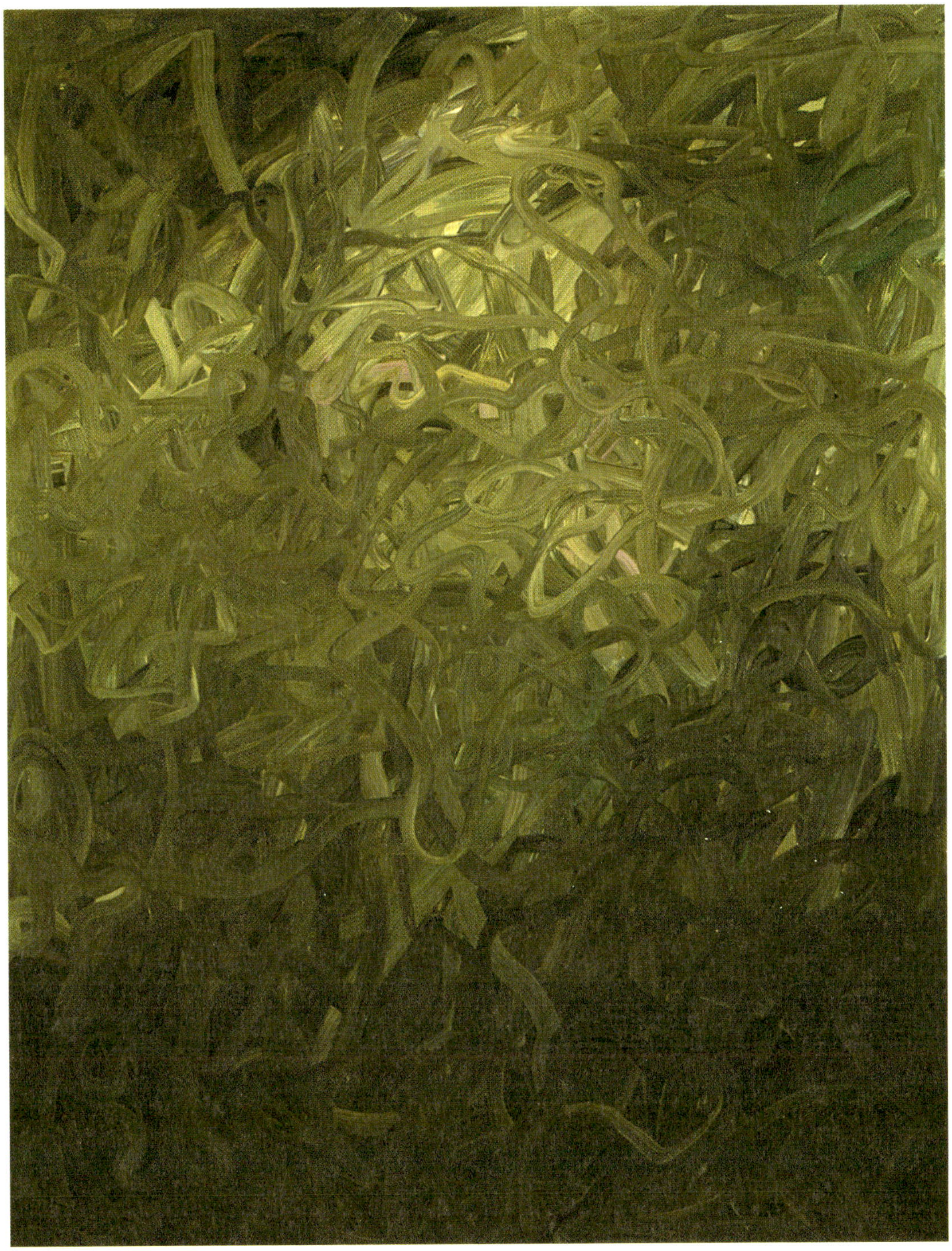

22 *Inpainting (Vermalung)* [326-7], 1972
Oil on canvas, 70 × 55 cm
The "M" Art Foundation, Belgium

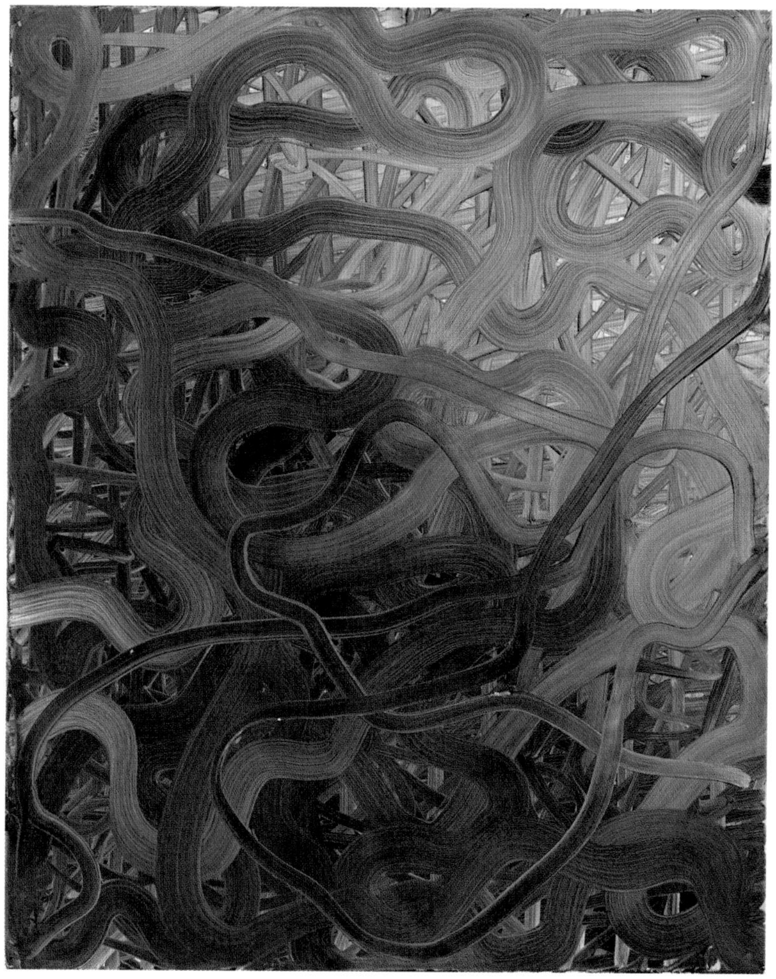

23 *Red-Blue-Yellow (Rot-Blau-Gelb)* [339-4], 1972
Oil on canvas, 98 × 92 cm
Private collection, Switzerland

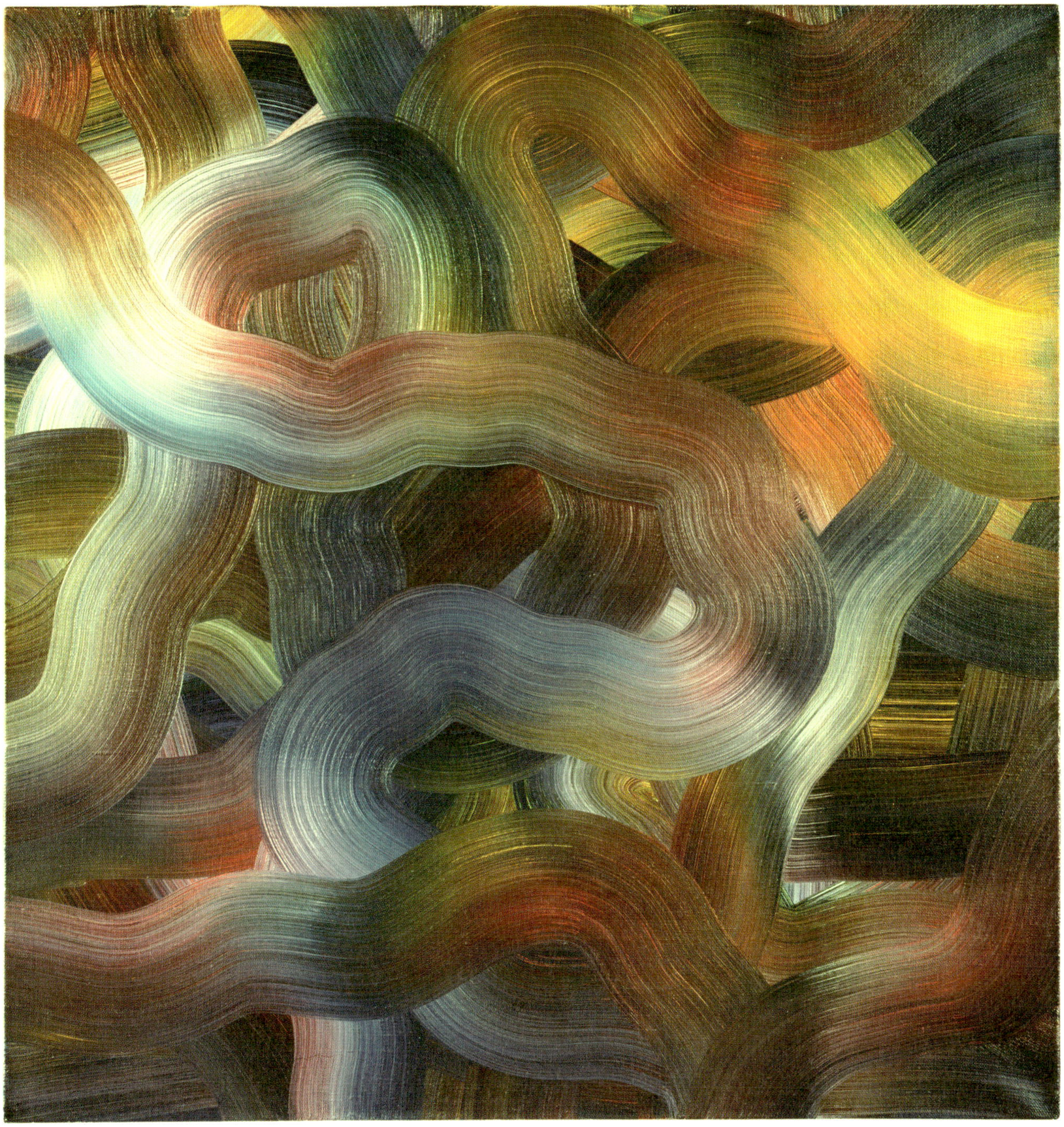

24 *Red-Blue-Yellow (Rot-Blau-Gelb)* [333-2], 1972
Oil on canvas, 251 × 200 cm
Kunsthalle Bremen – Der Kunstverein in Bremen

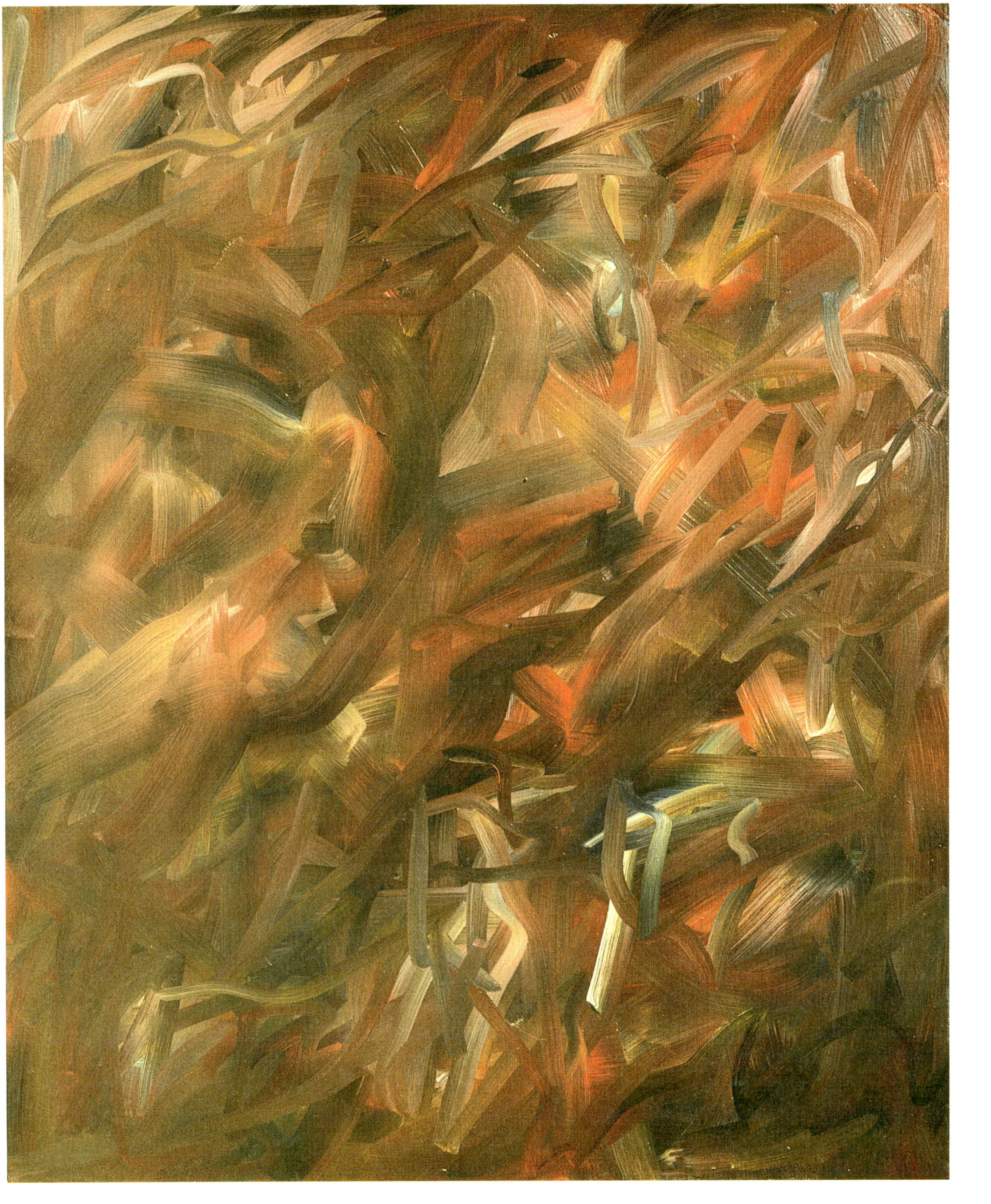

25 *Gray (Grau)* [334], 1972
Oil on canvas, 250 × 200 cm
Museum Küppersmühle für Moderne Kunst, Ströher Collection, Duisburg

26 *Gray (Grau)* [361-1], 1974
Oil on canvas, 250 × 200 cm
Museum Küppersmühle für Moderne Kunst, Ströher Collection, Duisburg

27 *Gray (Bark) (Grau [Borke])* [348-7], 1973
Oil on canvas, 90 × 65 cm
Private collection

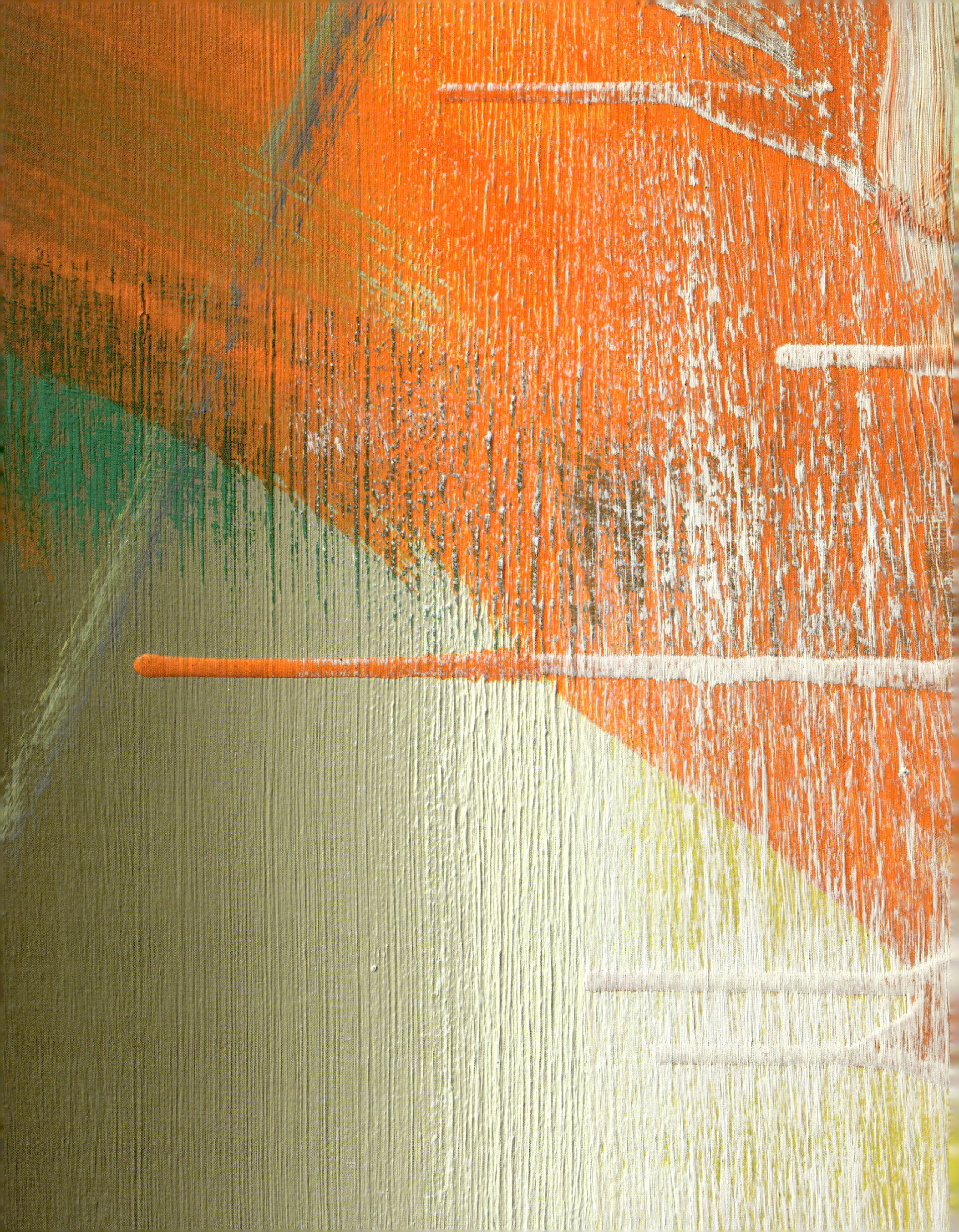

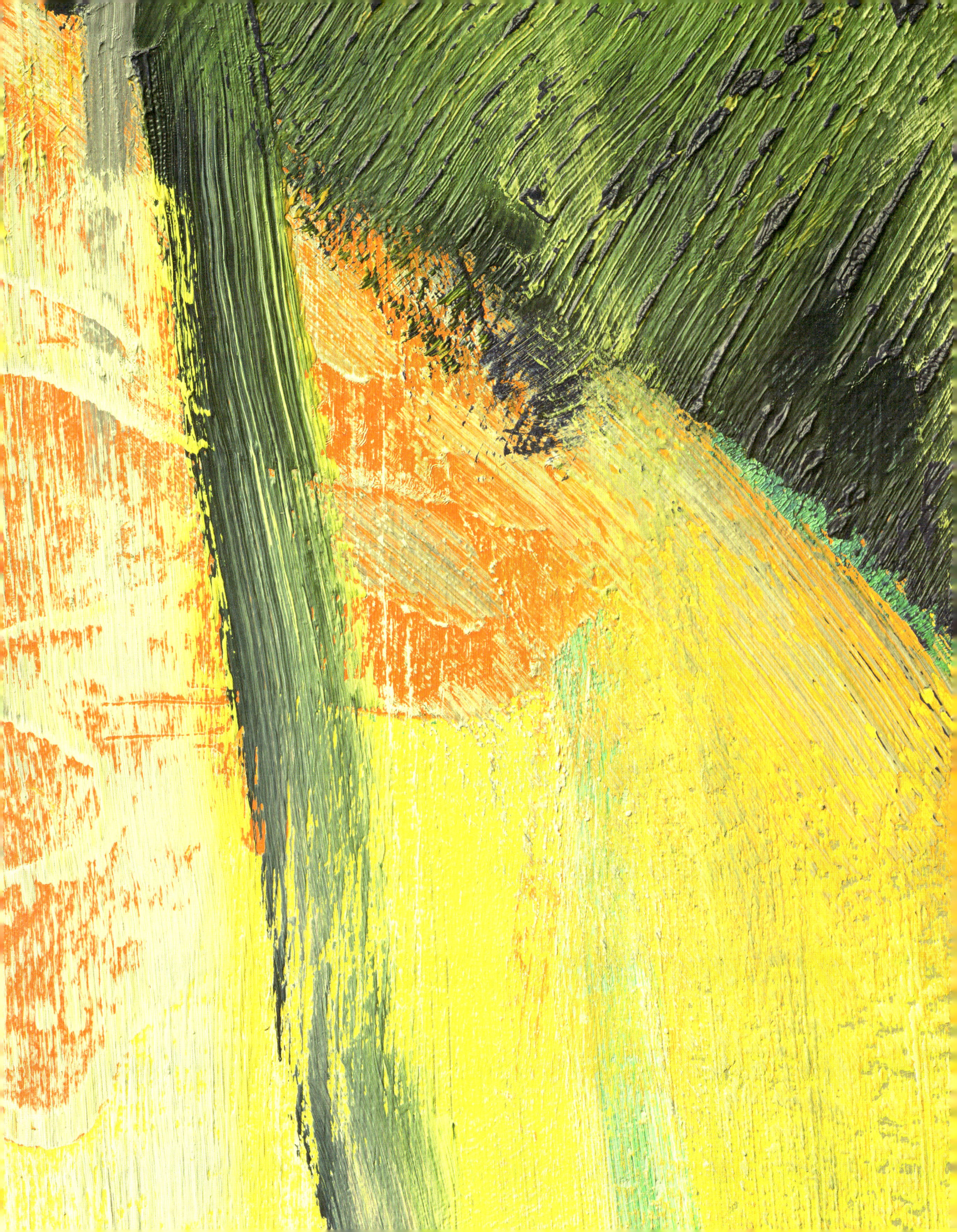

Blurrings and Close-Ups: Details and Early Abstract Paintings

Dietmar Elger

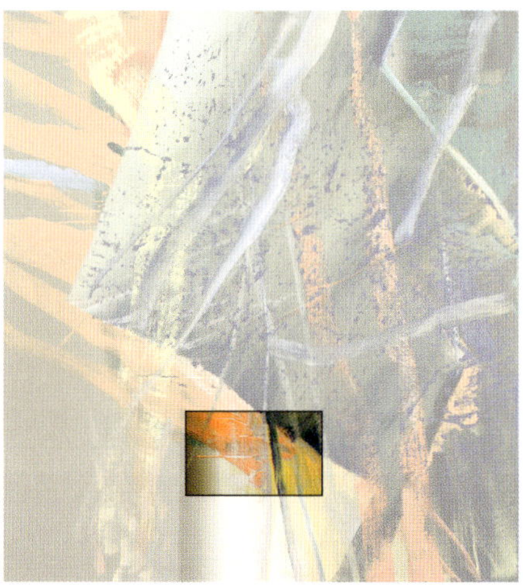

cat. 37

Richter took photographs of the patterns of paint he found on his palette. He then radically enlarged these close-up photographs and faithfully transposed them onto canvas. Richter's realistic replication went so far as to copy the blurring effect of the enlargement process. At the same time, the oversized scale has an alienating effect. The method creates an apparent abstraction—the object has been reproduced, but beyond recognition. In his series of Abstract paintings begun in 1976, Richter continued to develop his soft color gradients in a nonfigurative context, but even here the use of blurring can evoke figurative associations.

In the early 1970s, Gerhard Richter produced a small group of abstract paintings that he titled Details. These works in oil, which include the large-format *Detail (Red-Blue)* [273] from 1970 (cat. 28) and *Detail (Makart)* [288] from the following year (cat. 29), were the fruits of a busy phase of experimentation with changes of perspective and manipulations of reality. His seascapes of the same period, for example, were collaged, with the water and cloudy skies drawn from different source material. In these pictures, Richter is asking viewers whether what they recognize in the depictions is the same as what the motifs really show (see the essay by Dietmar Elger, pp. 22–33).

The Details of 1970–71 show painted photographic details of oil paints mixed on a palette. The originals were only a few square centimeters in size, but Richter projected and enlarged the motifs by painterly means, transferring them onto canvases of several square meters. From the results, however, it is impossible to reconstruct the process behind this switch of media and perspective, and so the paintings become, in Richter's words, "an abstract appearance of indeterminate 'beauty.'"[1] The painted images of details represent an illusionism built from empty shapes and motions that neither permits recognition nor generates meaning. Richter was aware of how easily these works could degenerate into kitsch.[2] Not without irony, he refers in the subtitle of the painting *Detail (Makart)* [288] to the decorative Viennese artist Hans Makart (1840–1884) and hence to bourgeois fashion in the art salons of the late nineteenth century (see the essay by Matthias Krüger, pp. 58–69). He first showed his painting *Detail (Red-Blue)* [273] in 1970 at a joint exhibition with Blinky Palermo that the artists had titled *For Salvador Dali*. Their homage, Richter later recalled, was meant to be polemical, an act of protest. "Dali [sic] was really out of favor, and in terms of social politics he was completely reactionary."[3]

In 1976, Richter began to feel that his explorations with Gray paintings over the last few years had reached a dead end (see the chapter "Gestures and Blendings: Inpaintings and Gray Paintings," pp. 104–19), and that he could only escape by painting the exact opposite.[4] The terms used to describe his new Abstract paintings were colorful, associative, random, polysemic, and devoid of meaning or logic.[5] The first work to fit this bill, an Abstract painting measuring 250 × 300 cm entitled *Construction* [389] (cat. 30), remained unique in his oeuvre. The paintings that followed were smaller in format, and initially he only accorded them the status of abstract sketches or sketches in oil. Whereas he had chosen an even, nonhierarchical application of paint for the Gray paintings and Inpaintings, the small Abstract paintings with their disparate shapes and colors are provocative. They parade their factual materiality, yet simultaneously create an abstract, illusionist, pictorial space. Flying in the face of the traditions of composition, these abstractions emphasize the role of chance and of detail in generating constellations of shape and color.

The traditional concept of a section of landscape framed by a window informed Richter's pictorial conception for the Abstract paintings from 1976 onward: Just as a view from a window crops the natural surroundings into a random, arbitrary detail, so too the Abstract paintings appear as contradictory, unintentional compositions. At the same time, just as he had done with his Color Charts, Inpaintings, and Gray paintings, Richter sought to banish his individuality and personal stance from the Abstract paintings. This challenge turned out to be a rather complex one, however, as every choice of paint and every brushstroke entails a personal decision. Richter tried to solve this problem by building in long gaps between stages in the work and by rotating the canvas during production. In addition, in the earlier years up to 1980, he would take a photo of an abstract motif, project it onto a large canvas, and copy it in an illusionist manner, seeking to establish the distance he wanted between the work and its author. For these paintings, which Richter called "'soft' abstracts,"[6] he adopted a similar technique to the one he had used for his Details in the early 1970s. *Abstract Painting* [421] (cat. 31) was made in 1977, based on the small-format *Abstract Painting* [398-2] of 1976 (fig. p. 31). By contrast, *Abstract Painting* [436] (cat. 32), painted in 1978, was based on a watercolor (fig. p. 31).

Not until 1981 did Richter succeed in transferring this freehanded application of paint to larger surfaces. The 1981 *Abstract Painting* [479-1] (cat. 34) is one of the earliest examples. The red and yellow Richter added contrasted strongly with the delicately colored background. Over this he added layers of paint with thick brushwork, creating an undefined, abstract, illusionist space.

Around this time, Richter began working with a new tool for applying paint, the squeegee (see the essay by Matthias Krüger, pp. 58–69). While he only made tentative use of the squeegee in the *Abstract Painting* [479-1] (cat. 34), by 1986 it had become a pivotal element in the structure of his paintings. Above all, the squeegee introduced the principle of chance and surprise into the production process. There was something liberating for Richter about working with the squeegee. From this point on, his Abstract paintings were the result of alternating between controlled brushwork and the random structure created by the squeegee. In *Hedge* [504] of 1982 (cat. 36), the orange trace of the squeegee covers almost the entire surface of the picture like a veil.

In an interview in 1999, Richter commented on the genesis of his Abstract paintings, and he came up with a surprising insight: "I am unable, for example, to produce a painting similar to painting X that I did a year ago."[7] This implies that specific Abstract paintings could only have been made at specific times. Their structures of shape and color are by no means as arbitrary, random, and detached as Richter himself has often claimed. Rather, the appearances of the Abstract paintings depend on when they were created and in what situation, and on how the artist was feeling at the time.

Translated from the German by Kate Vanovitch

1 Gerhard Richter, "Letter to Birgit Pelzer" (March 25, 1980), in Richter 2009, 115–16, here 115.
2 Ibid.
3 Gerhard Richter in an interview, in Elger 2009a, 182.
4 See Gerhard Richter, "Interview with Dorothea Dietrich" (1985) in Richter 2009, 145–58.
5 See Gerhard Richter, "Answers to questions from Marlies Grüterich" (September 2, 1977) in ibid., 94–95, here 95.
6 Gerhard Richter, "Notes" (1986), in ibid., 158–63, here 162.
7 Quoted in Dieter Schwarz, "Über Aquarelle und verwandte Dinge," in Winterthur 1999, 5–16, here 13.

28 *Detail (Red-Blue) (Ausschnitt [rot-blau])* [273], 1970
Oil on canvas, 200 × 300 cm
Private collection

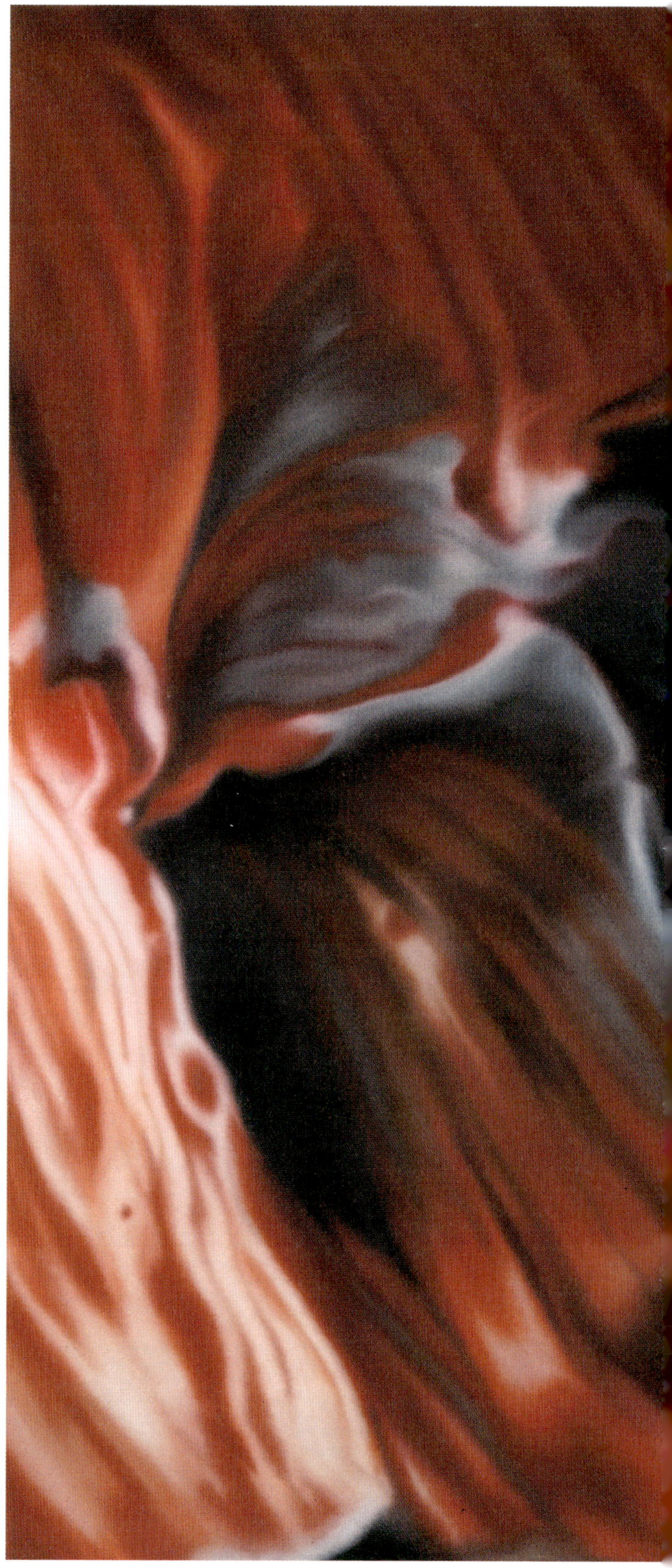

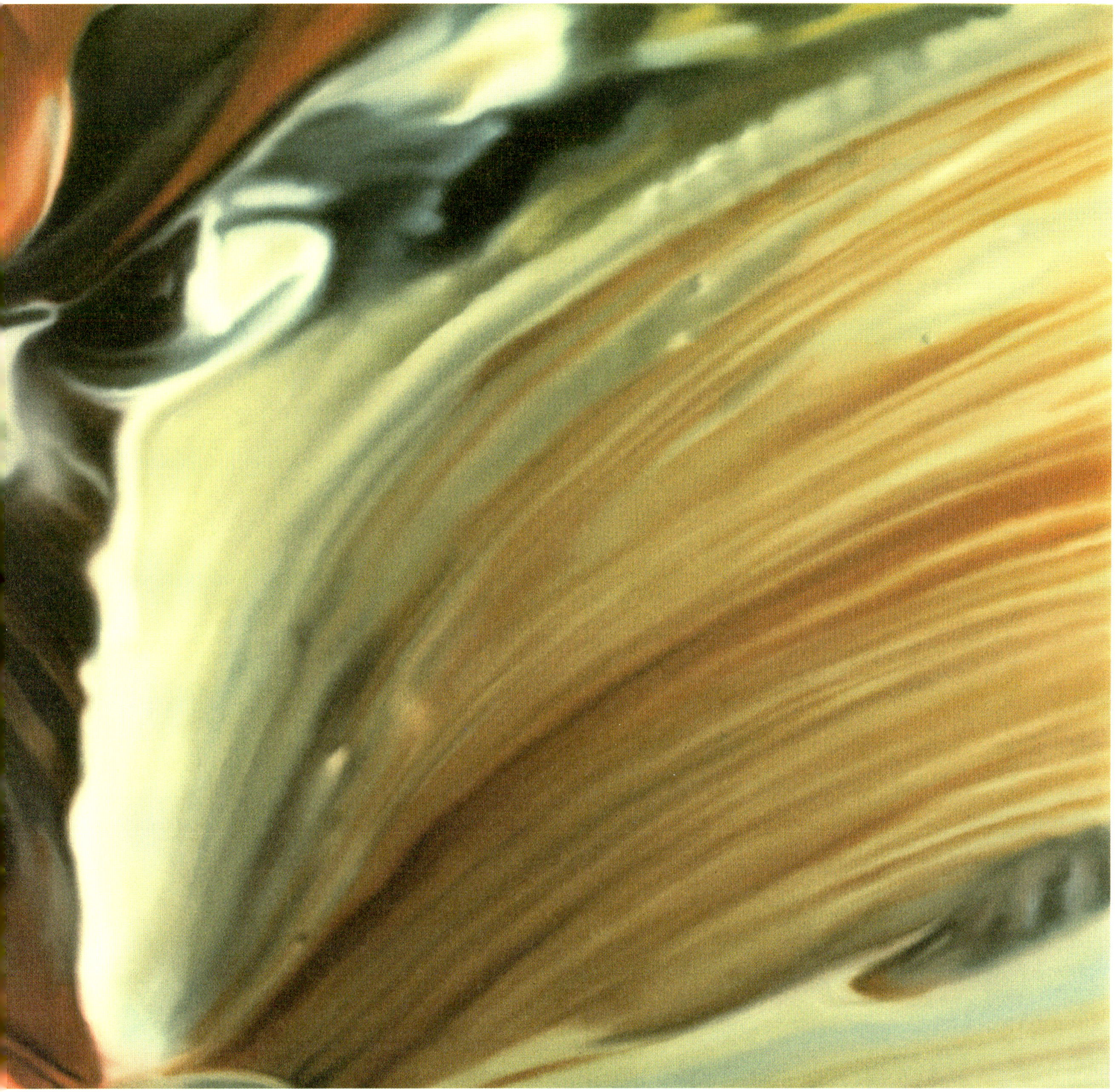

29 *Detail (Makart) (Ausschnitt [Makart])* [288], 1971
Oil on canvas, 200 × 200 cm
Museum Küppersmühle für Moderne Kunst,
Ströher Collection, Duisburg

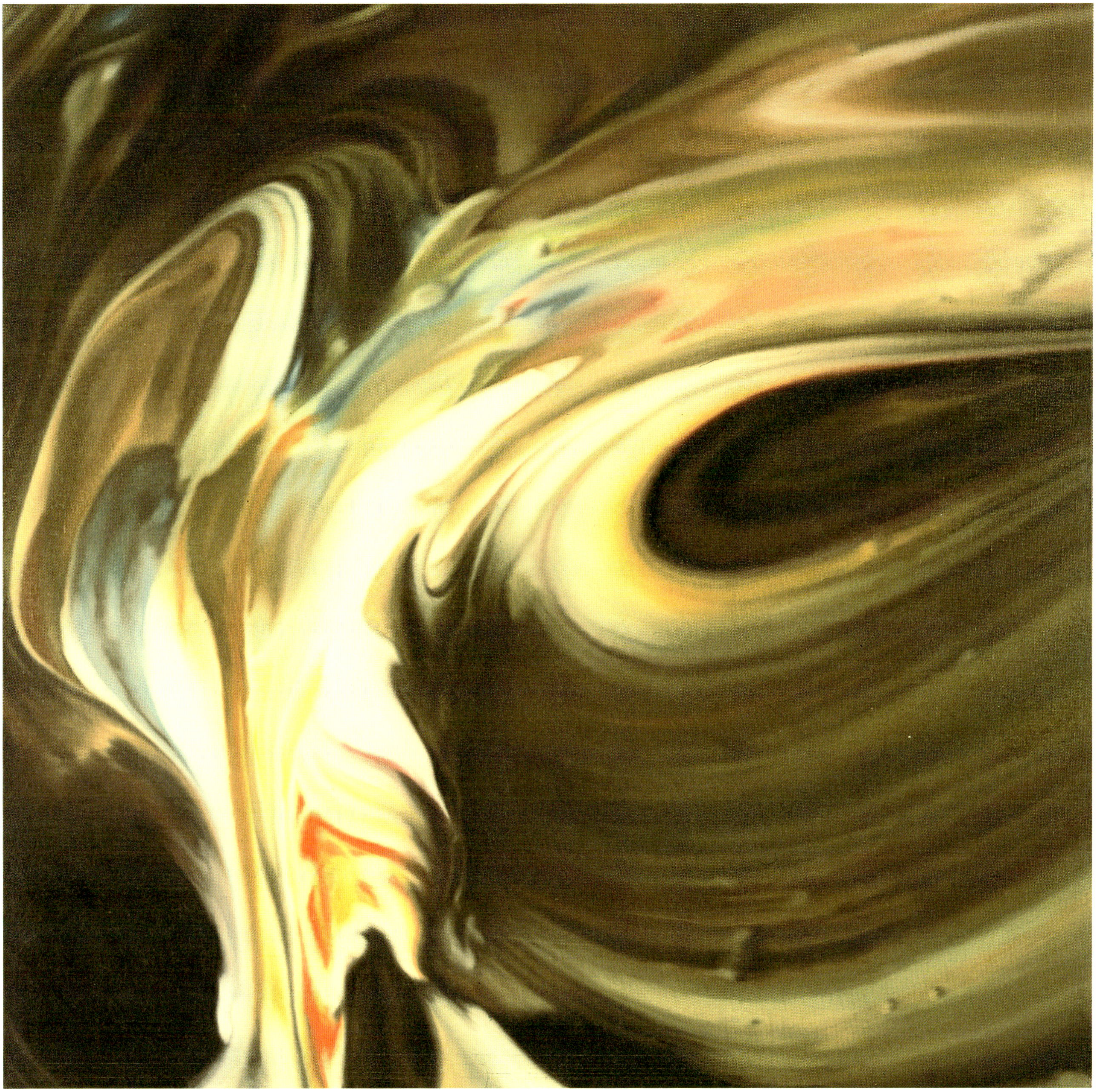

30 *Construction (Konstruktion)* [389], 1976
Oil on canvas, 250 × 300 cm
Neues Museum. Staatliches Museum
für Kunst und Design, Nuremberg,
permanent loan from a private collection

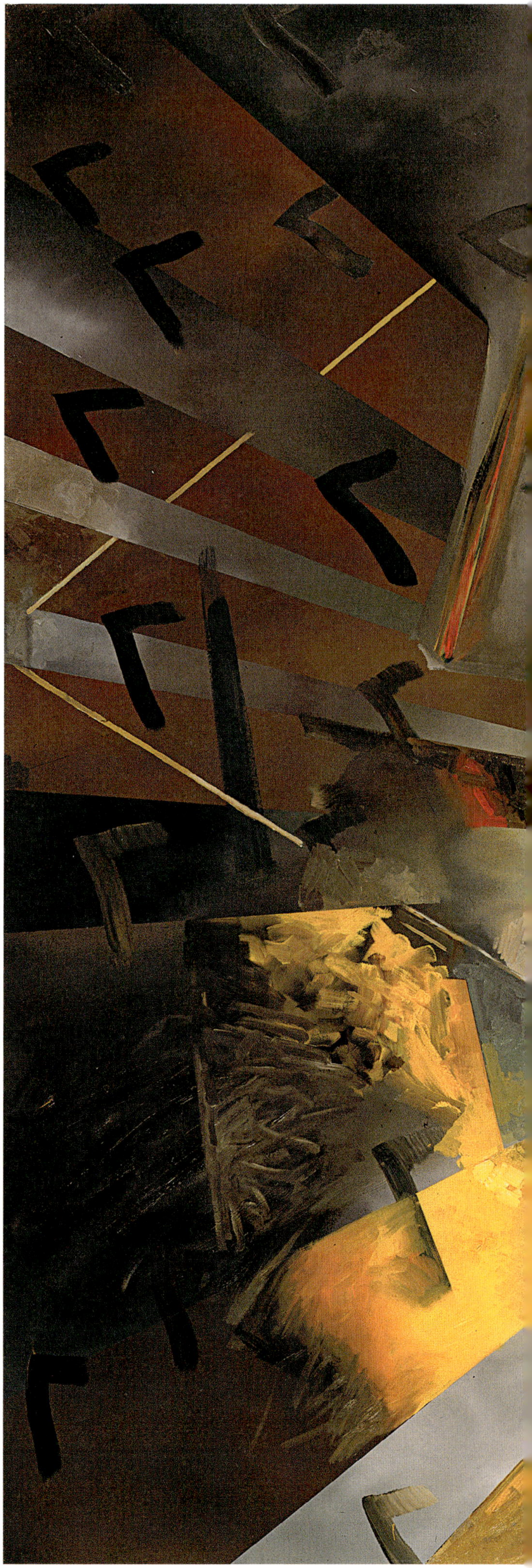

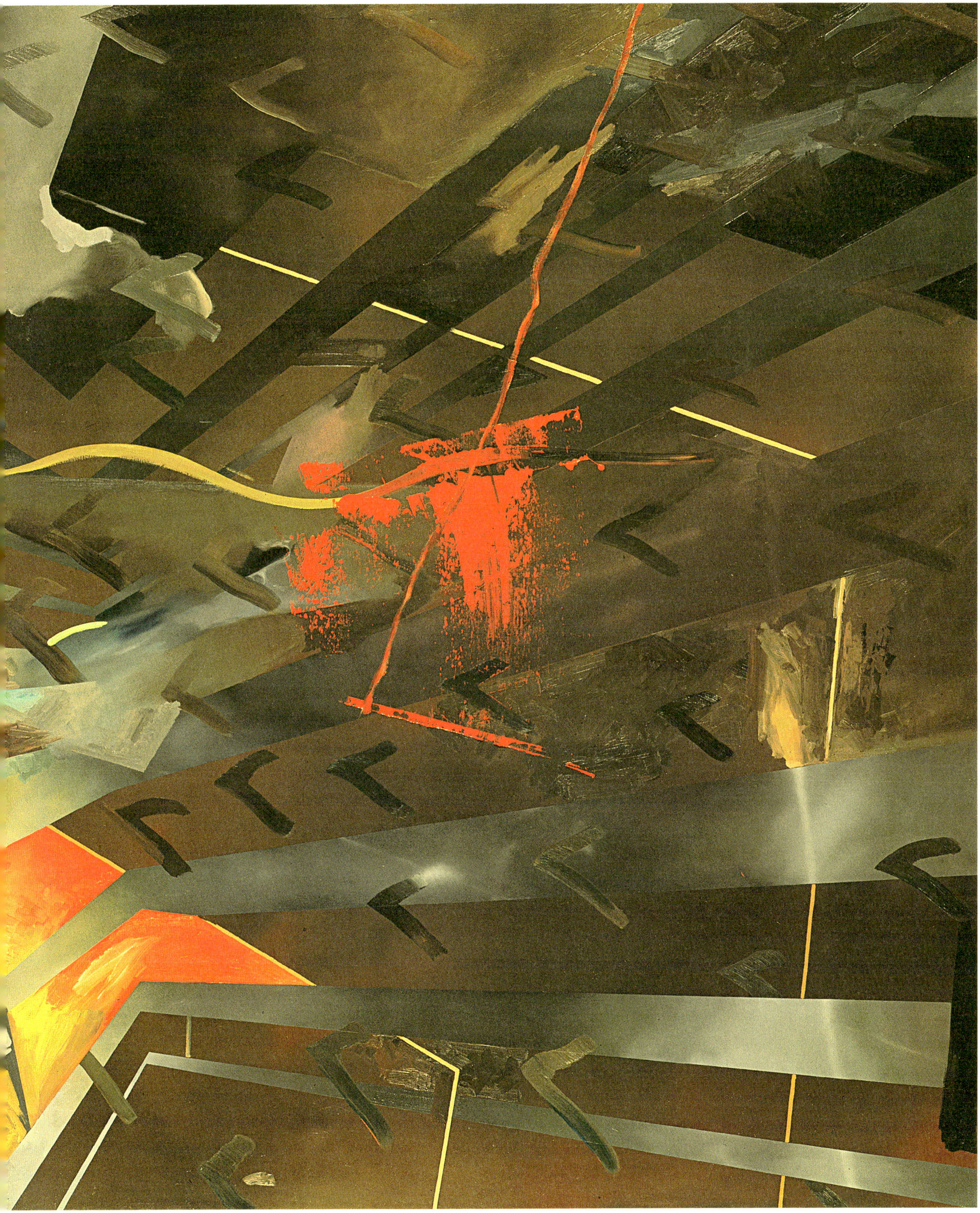

31 *Abstract Painting (Abstraktes Bild)* [421], 1977
Oil on canvas, 250 × 200 cm
Stedelijk van Abbemuseum, Eindhoven

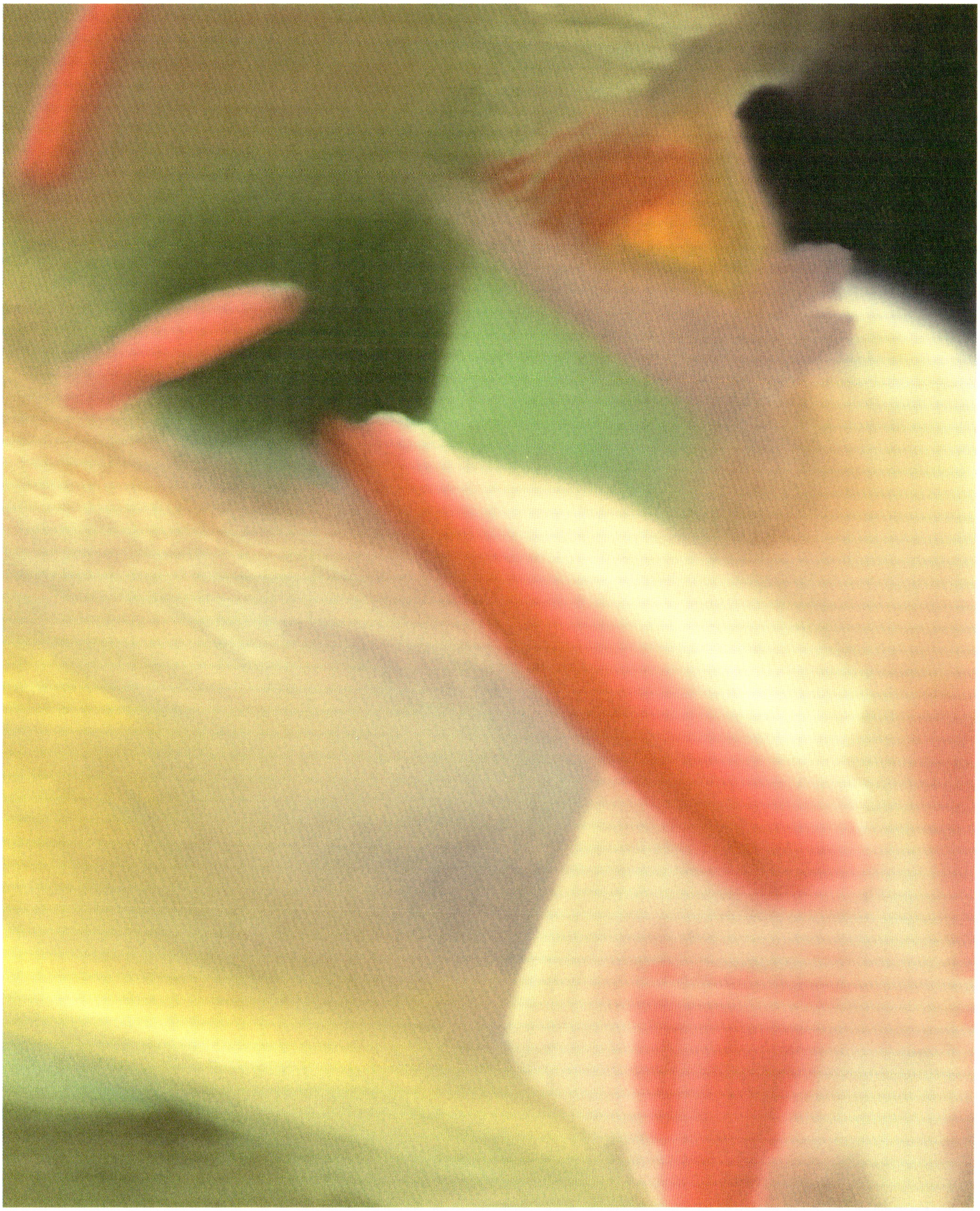

32 *Abstract Painting (Abstraktes Bild)* [436], 1978
Oil on canvas, 200 × 250 cm
Private collection, North Rhine-Westphalia

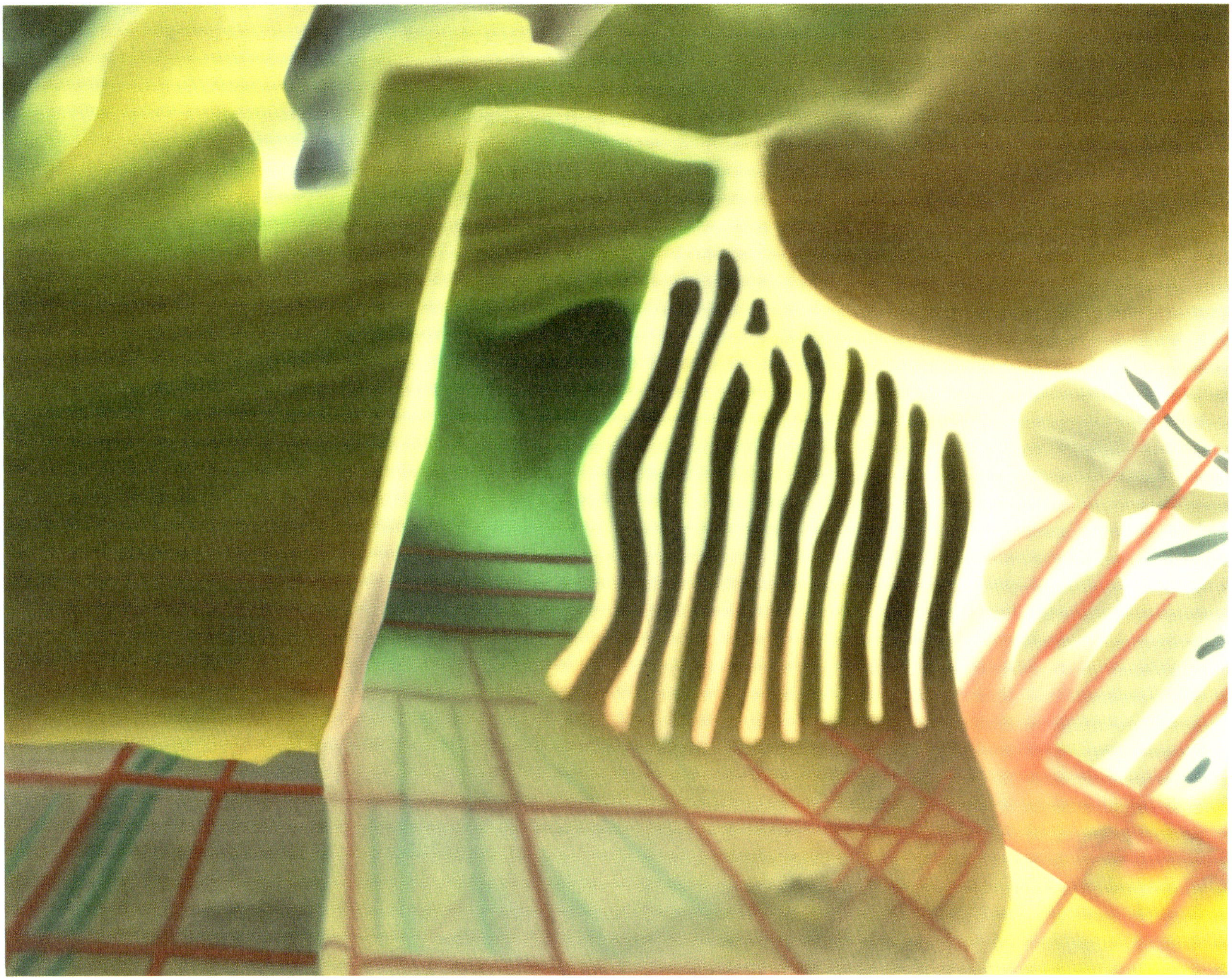

33 *Abstract Painting (Abstraktes Bild)* [449-3], 1979
Oil on canvas, 70 × 100 cm
Private collection, Switzerland

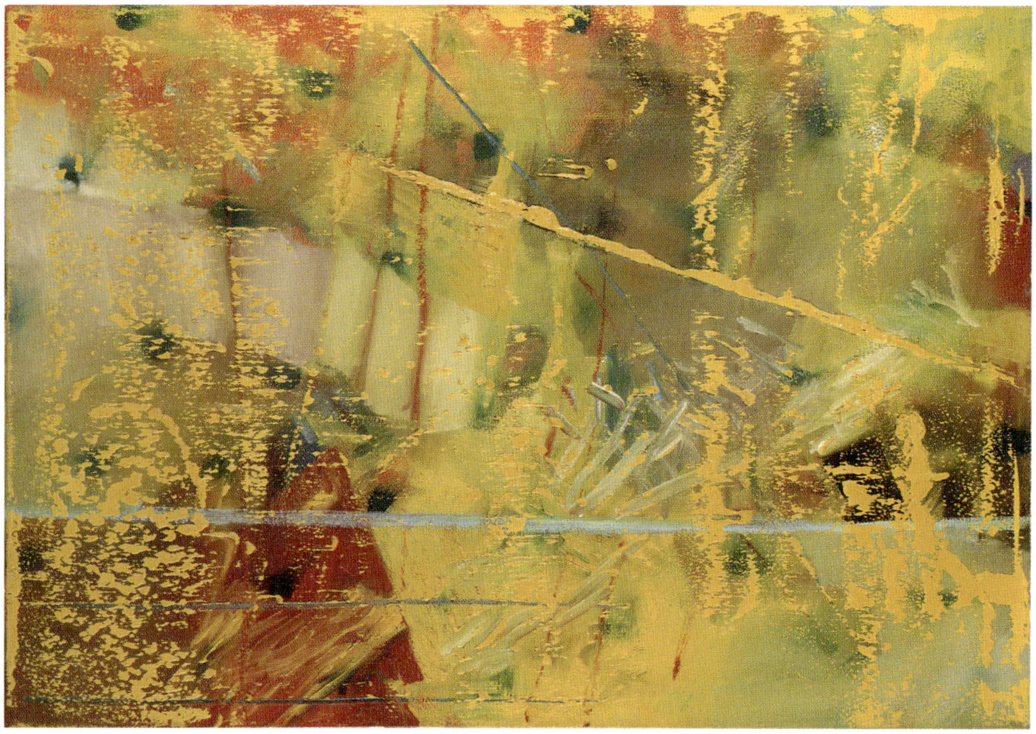

34 *Abstract Painting (Abstraktes Bild)* [479-1], 1981
Oil on canvas, 120 × 175 cm
Migros Museum für Gegenwartskunst, Zurich

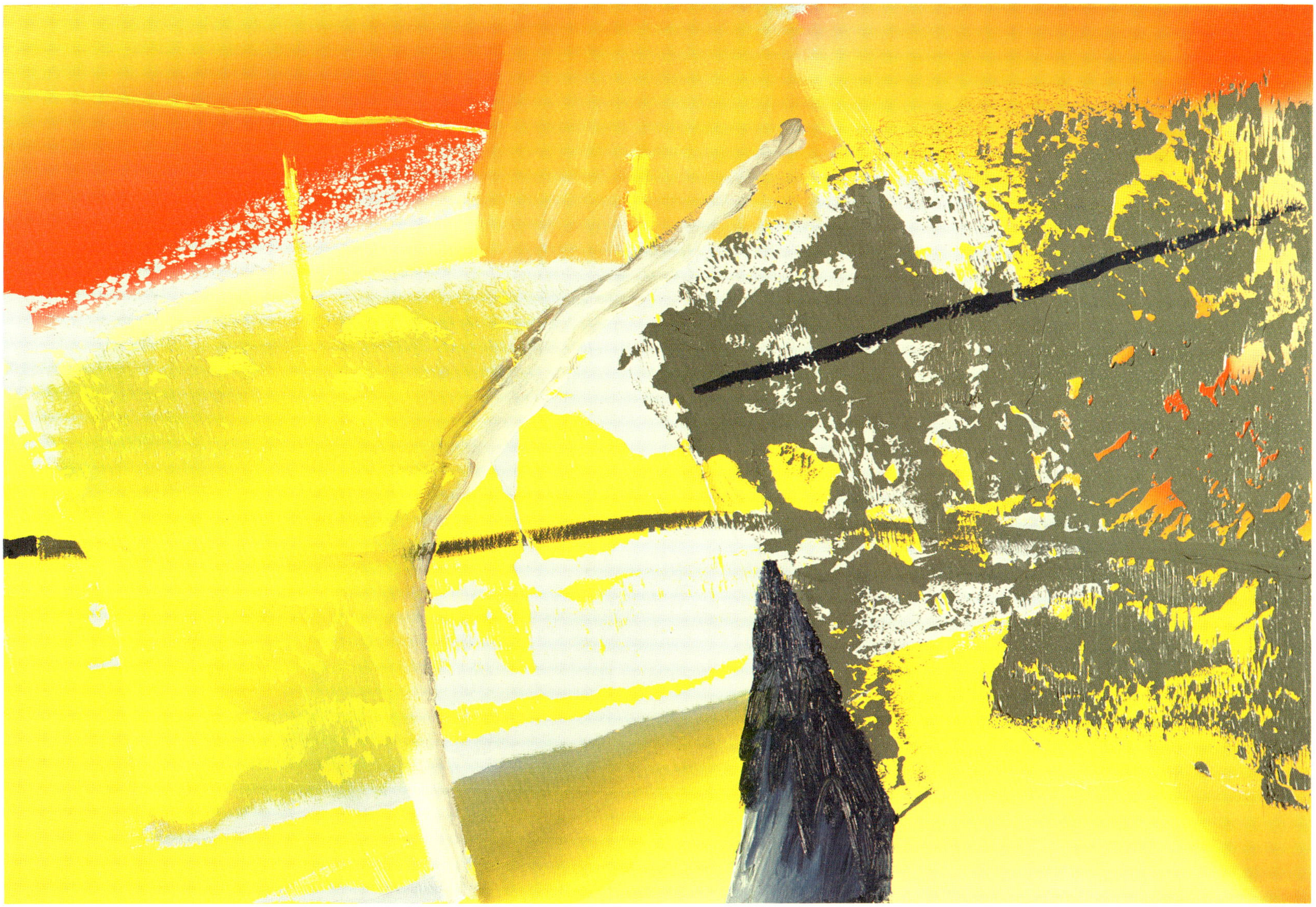

35 *Abstract Painting (Abstraktes Bild)* [520-6], 1983
Oil on canvas, 70 × 50 cm
Sprengel Museum Hannover,
permanent loan from a private collection

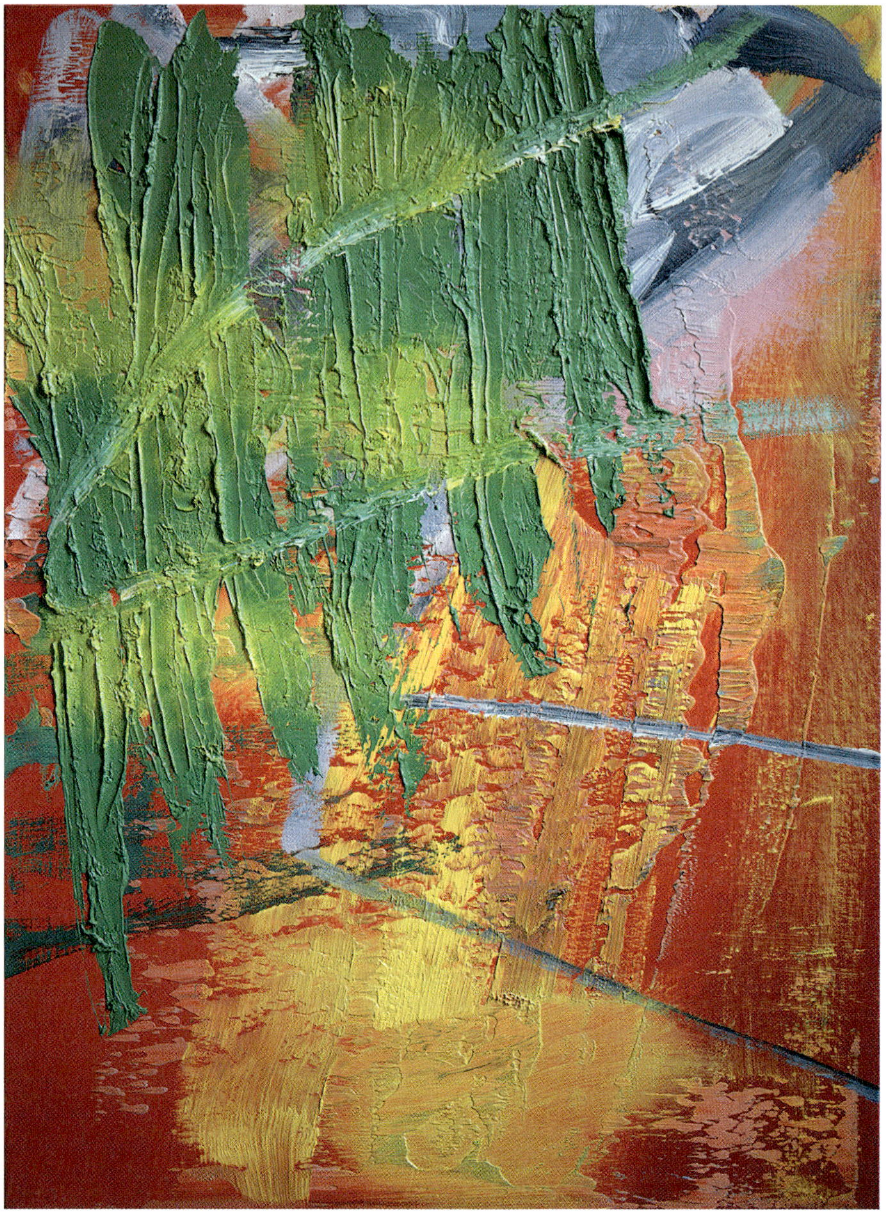

36 *Hedge (Hecke)* [504], 1982
Oil on canvas, 200 × 170 cm
Private collection, Hong Kong

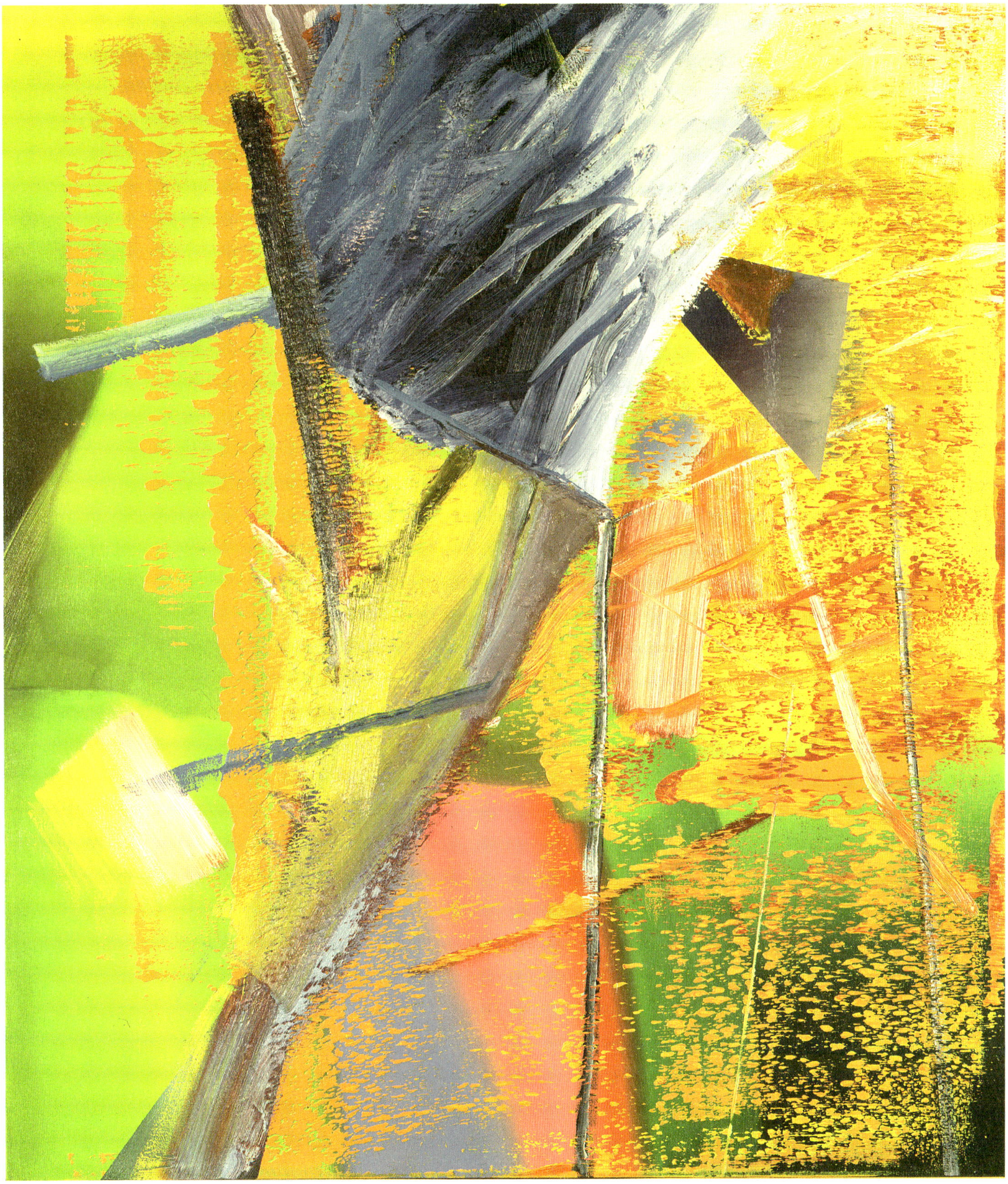

37 *Abstract Painting (Abstraktes Bild)* [568-1], 1984
Oil on canvas, 200 × 180 cm
Private collection

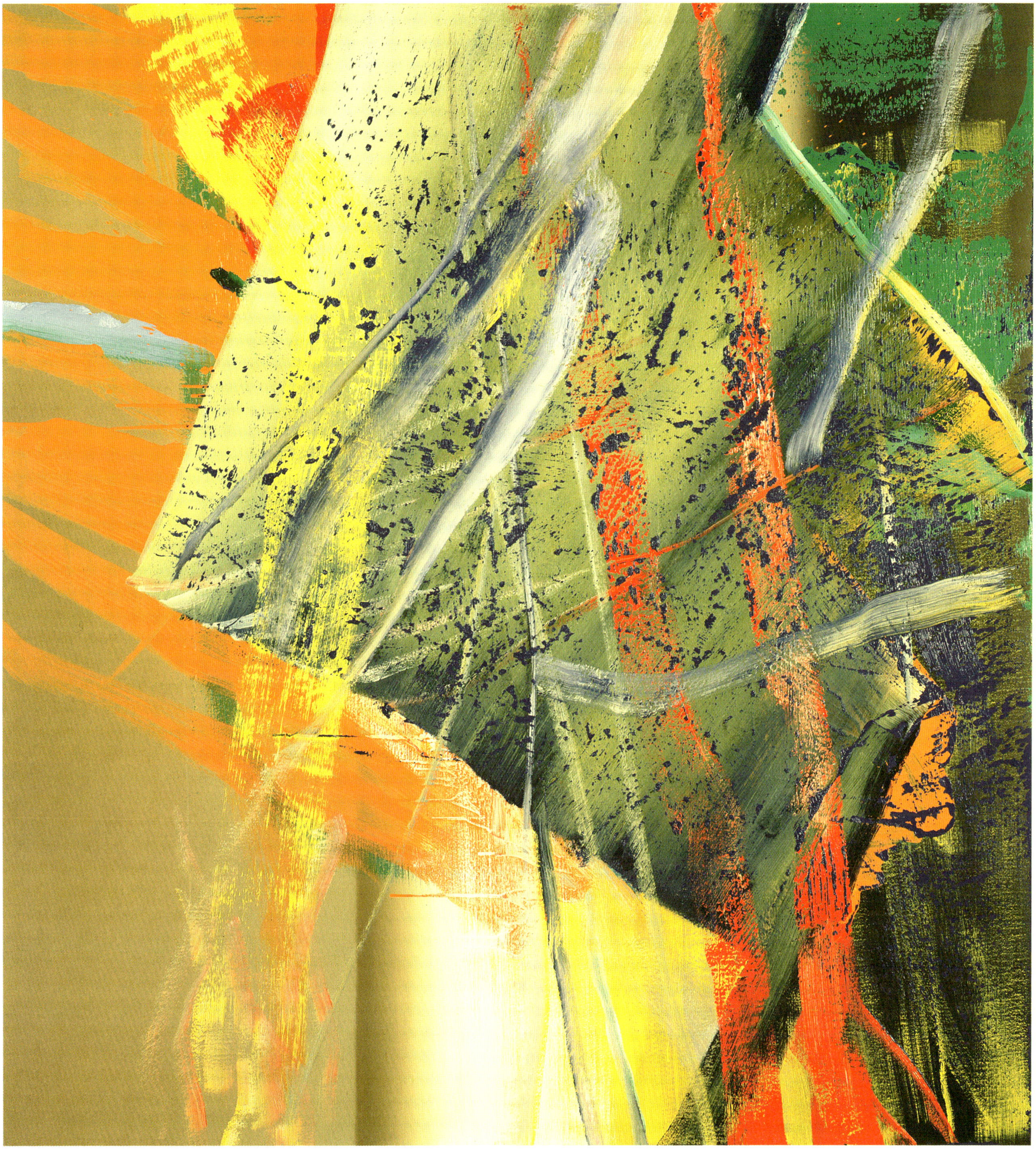

38 *Pyramid (Pyramide)* [522-2], 1983
Oil on canvas, 100 × 70 cm
Würth Collection, Künzelsau

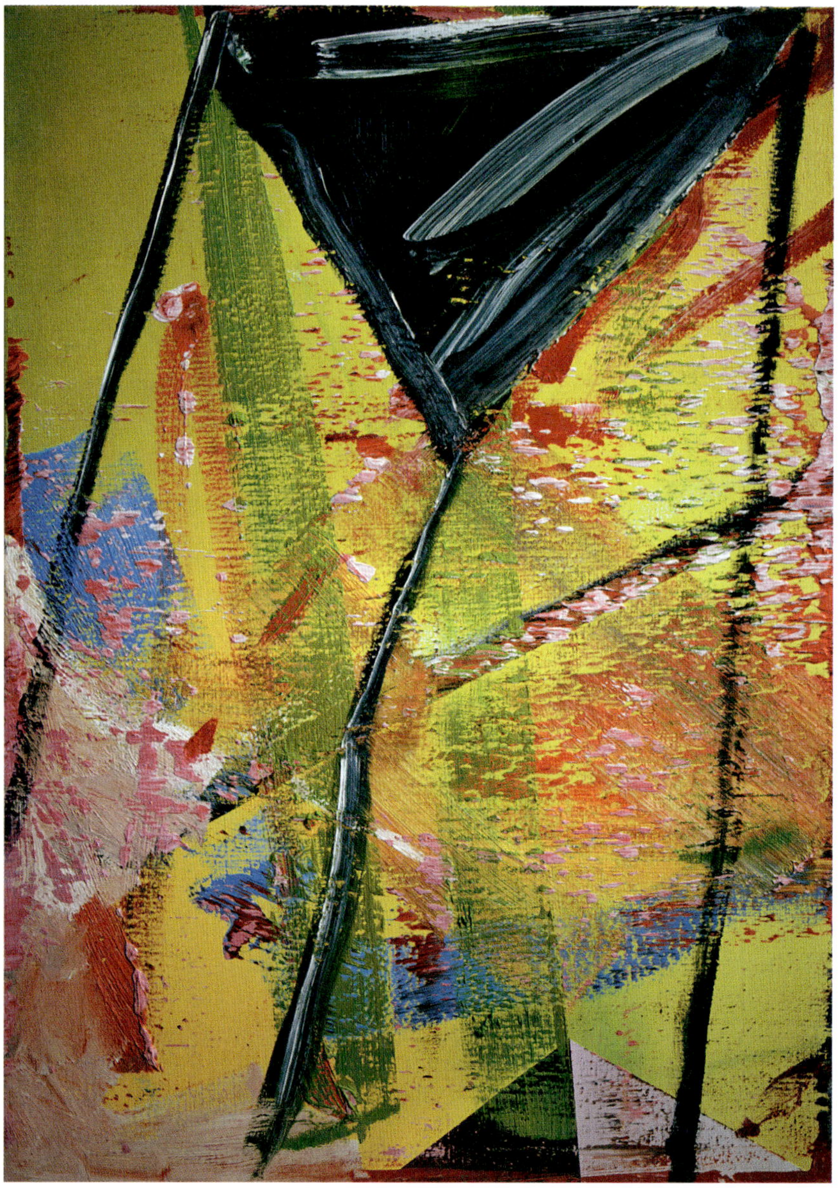

39 *Abstract Painting (Abstraktes Bild)* [563-1], 1984
Oil on canvas, 100 × 120 cm
Private collection, Hong Kong

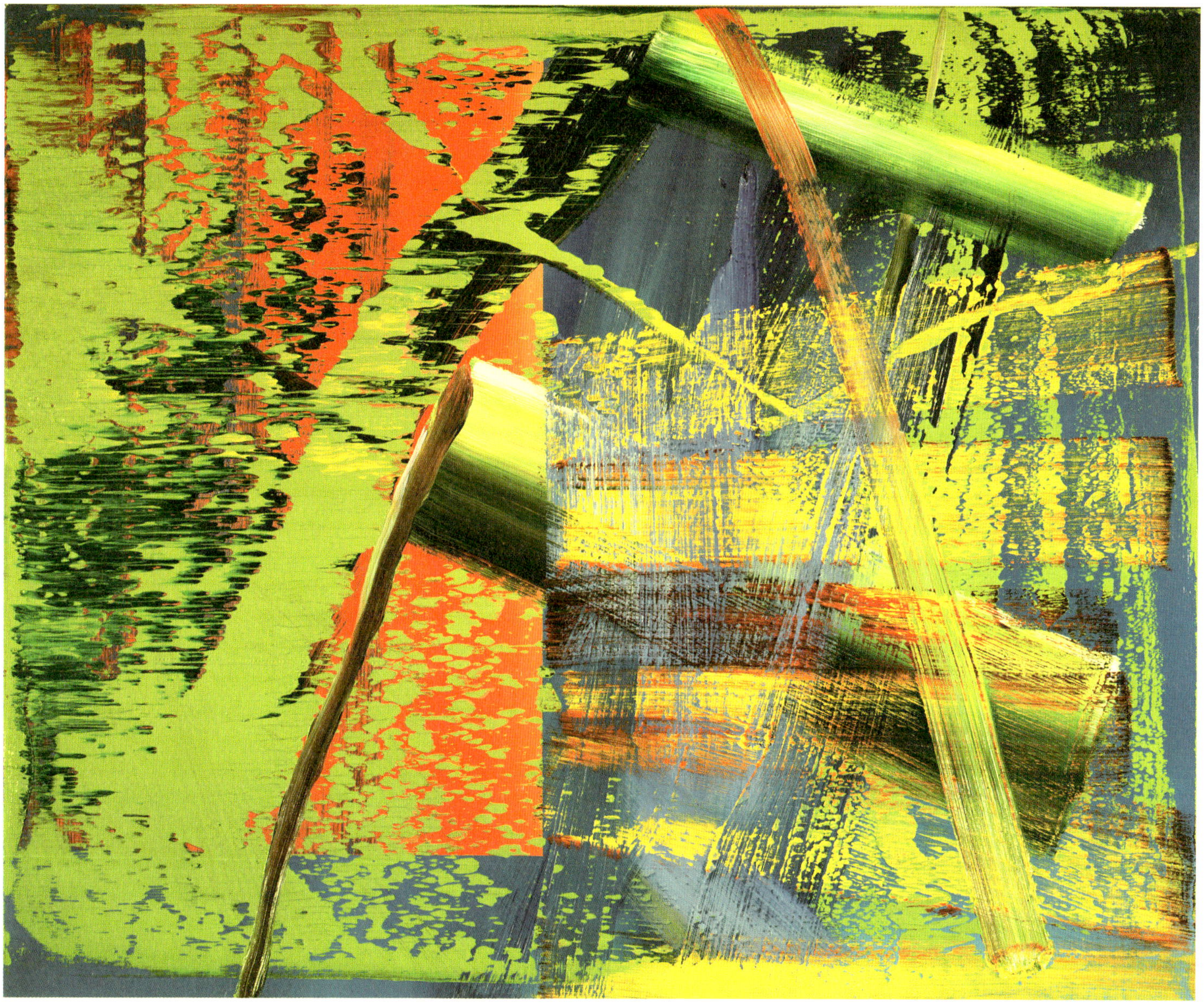

40 *Abstract Painting (Abstraktes Bild)* [605-2], 1986
Oil on canvas, 62 × 72 cm
Private collection

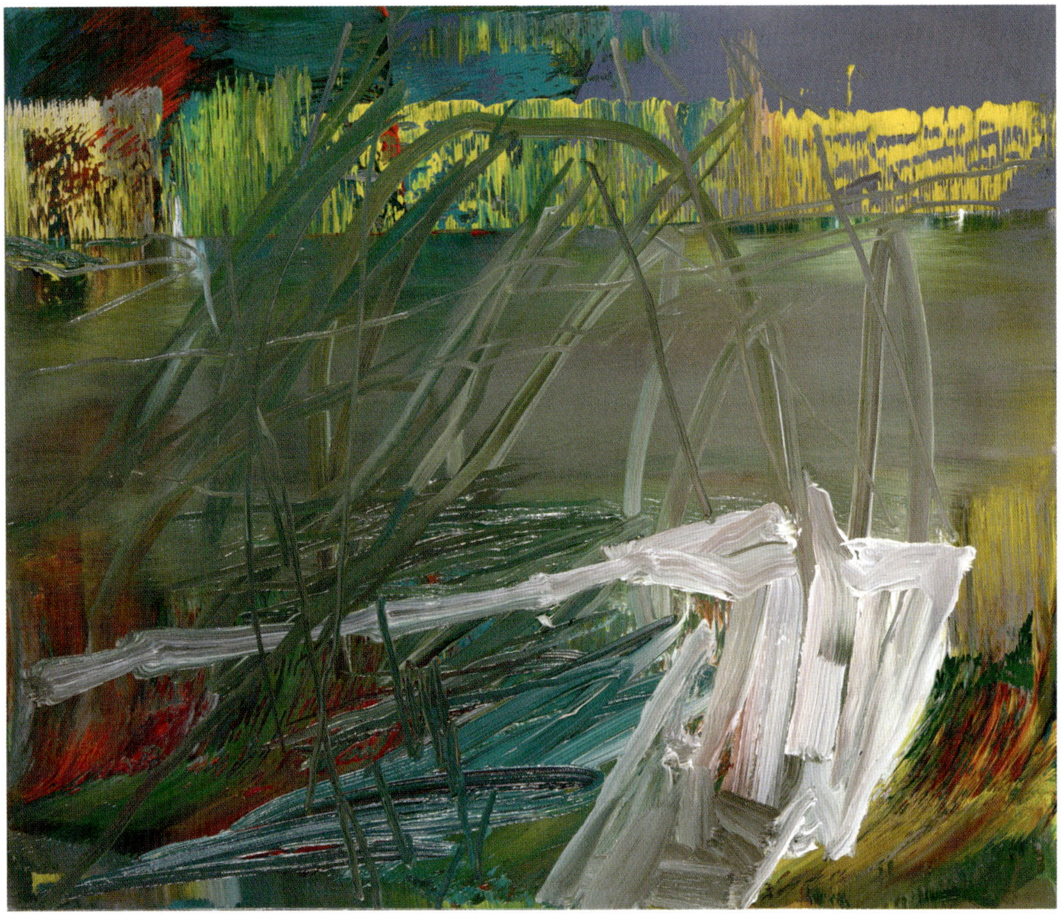

41 *Abstract Painting (Abstraktes Bild)* [578-3], 1985
Oil on canvas, 120 × 85.5 cm
Private collection

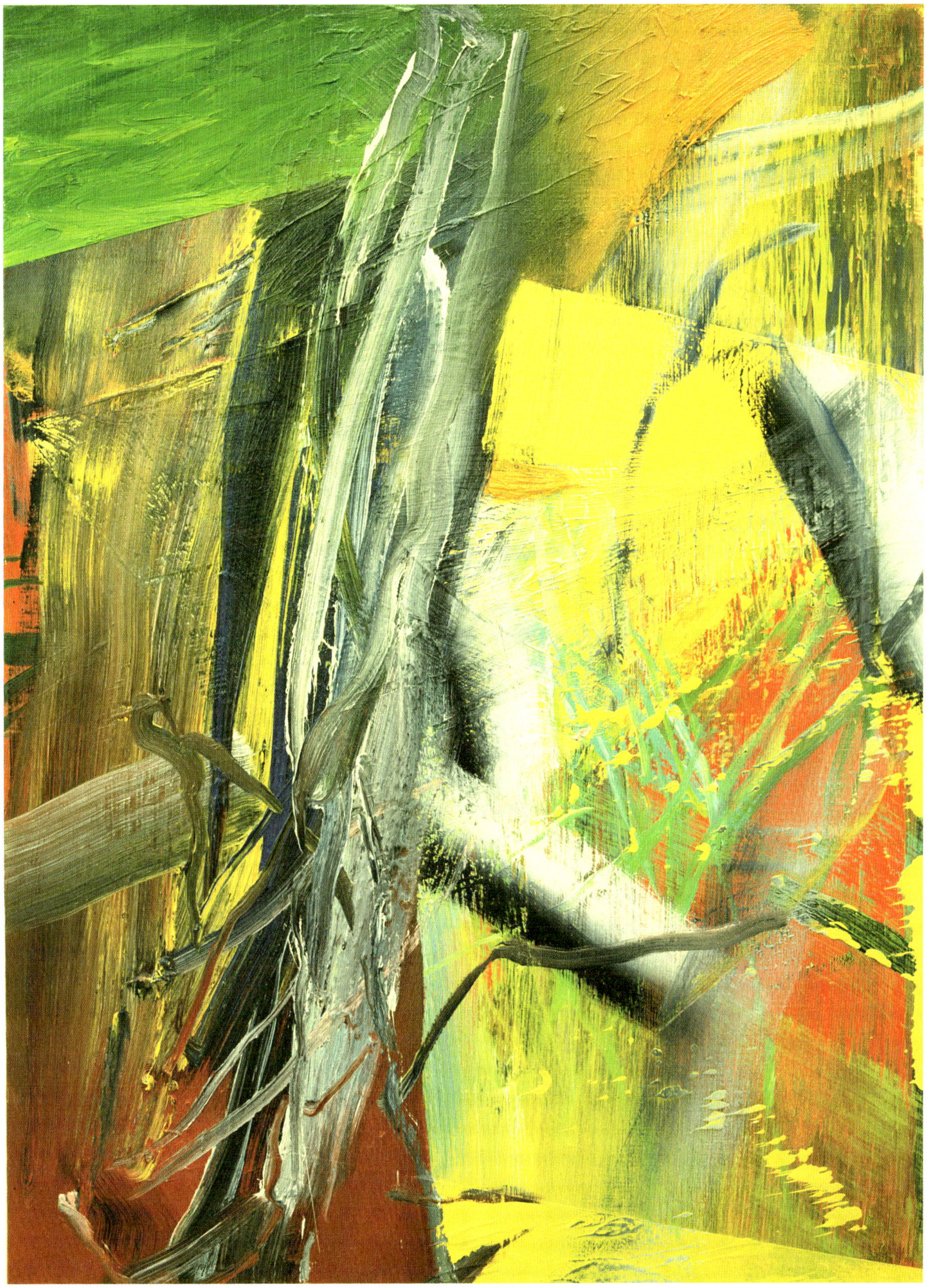

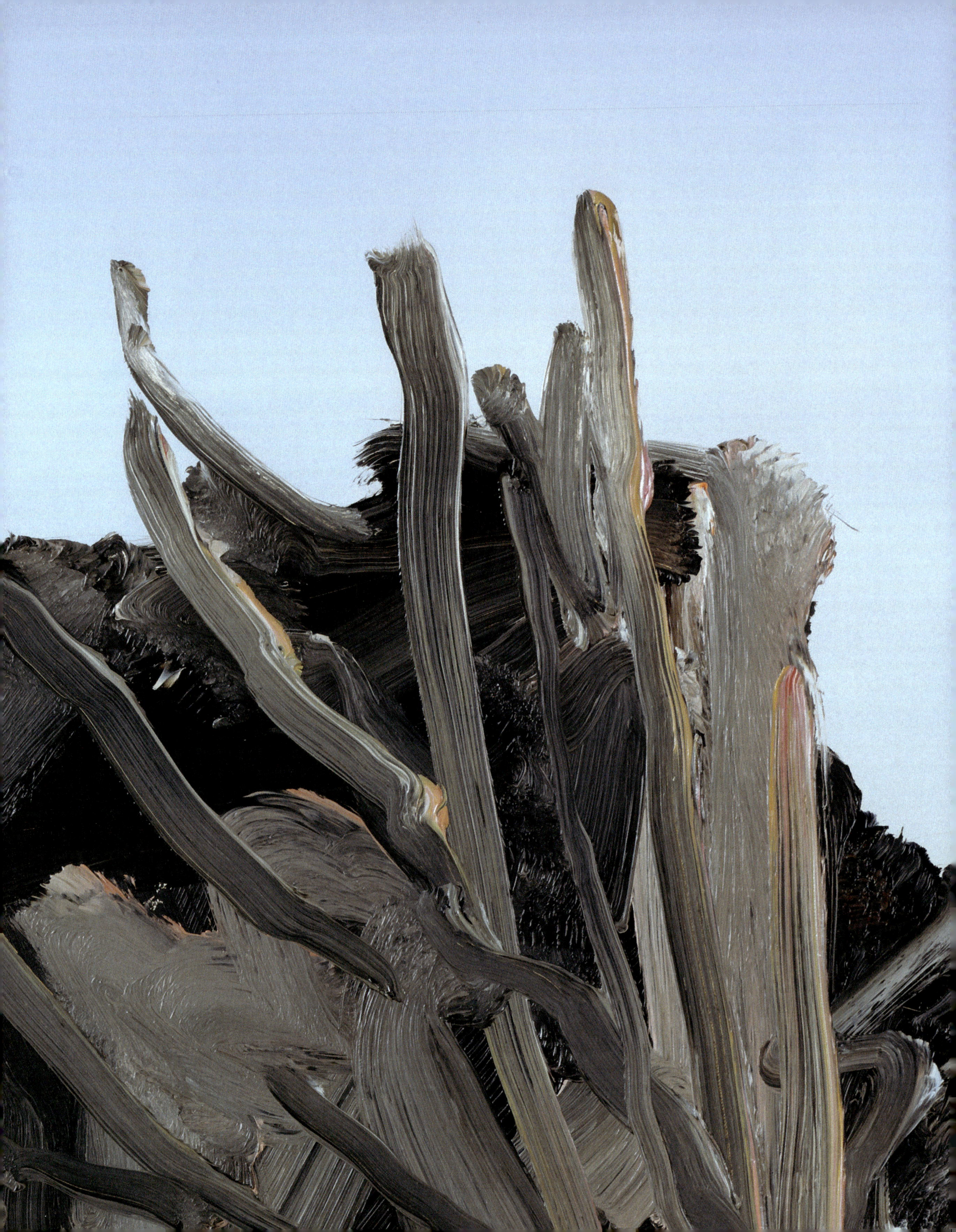

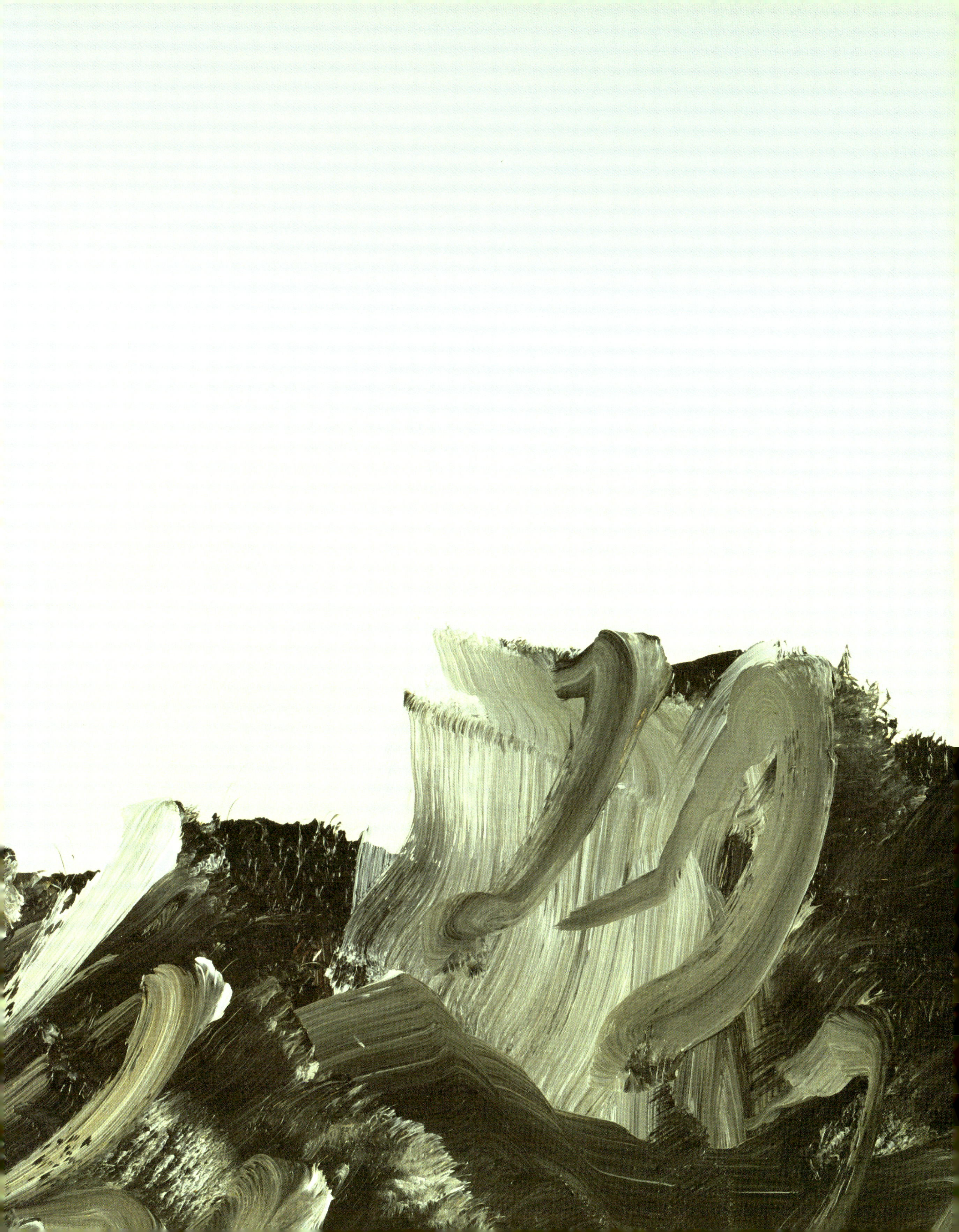

Nature and Materials: Abstract Landscapes

Dietmar Elger

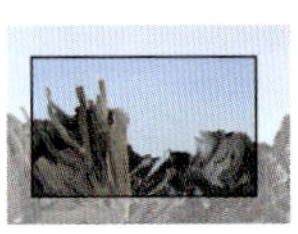

cat. 42

The pale blue and green colors suggest a landscape. There is a hint of a horizon. The painting seems legible because our habits of seeing draw associations. An Abstract painting appears to depict a landscape. Art that stimulates the imagination is not new: Leonardo da Vinci and eighteenth-century English landscape painters such as Alexander Cozens explored methods to achieve this aim. They sought to free the making of pictures from natural sources, using abstraction to apprehend the object. In Gerhard Richter's Photo Overpaintings, abstract streaks form layers over the figurative motif. Here too, Richter applied a principle of inversion, but in the opposite direction.

After Gerhard Richter moved from Dresden to Düsseldorf in March 1961, he initially turned to the international avant-garde of abstract art. During his first months in West Germany, Alberto Burri, Lucio Fontana, Jean Dubuffet, and Alberto Giacometti exercised a lasting influence on his painting. The following year, however, Richter radically shifted his artistic orientation, producing his first paintings based on photographs. Just two years later, he again explored strategies for abstract paintings, although their conception was at least as distant from his early abstract works as his simultaneously created gray Photo paintings (see the chapter "Structures and Illusions: Abstract Works in the 1960s," pp. 70–87).

Richter never developed his strategies for figural and abstract paintings as if they were direct opposites. Rather, he always maintained his relationship to natural source material, especially in his Abstract paintings (see the essay by Dietmar Elger, pp. 22–33). In an interview, he described his artistic ideal as a detail of a natural landscape that is presented as if one were looking through a window: "When I look out of the window, then truth for me is the way nature shows itself in various tones, colors and proportions. That's a truth and has its own correctness. This little slice of nature, and in fact any given piece of nature, represents to me an ongoing challenge, and is a model for my paintings."[1]

In his Abstract paintings, Richter does justice to this ambition in various ways, most directly when he gives his paintings titles that are associated with objects. As the title suggests, the striking dark form at the upper edge of the 1983 Abstract painting *Pyramid* [522-2] (cat. 38) recalls the silhouette of a pyramid. In his 1994 monumental composition *Wall* [808] (cat. 70), on the other hand, Richter seems to adhere to one of Leonardo da Vinci's famous precepts, in which he advises his pupils to school their imaginations on the abstract textures of walls and to discover faces, figures, and landscapes in them (see the essay by Ortrud Westheider, pp. 8–21).

In 1978, during his time as a visiting professor at the Nova Scotia College of Art and Design in Halifax, Richter took *128 Photographs of a Painting* [441] (Kunstmuseen Krefeld). Two years later, he produced an edition of these photographs in book form. In 1998, he produced another edition of the photos under the title *128 Details from a Picture (Halifax 1978) II*, turning them into a portfolio of eight pictures in an edition of sixty (cat. 46).[2] For this piece, he photographed 128 details of an Abstract painting removed from its frame, shooting the picture from different angles and distances, and under various lighting conditions (figs. pp. 31, 54). These became eight panels, each one with sixteen black-and-white prints. At first, he called the painting *Halifax*, after the place where it was made, but later gave the piece the more ambiguous title of *Abstract Painting* [432-5] (figs. pp. 54, 232). Richter's work recollects a Man Ray photograph titled *Dust Breeding*. Man Ray created it in 1920 by photographing the surface of Marcel Duchamp's *Large Glass*.[3] The photograph gives the viewer the impression of looking down from a height onto a complicated layout of airplane runways in a surreal desert landscape. And indeed, Man Ray initially published the photograph under the title *View from an Airplane*. The multiple details of Richter's Abstract painting's surface similarly redirect perception, and his description of the image as a view of another planet from an aerial perspective evokes the term employed by Man Ray.[4]

In 1984, Richter painted a number of small oils grouped together under the single work number 551 (cat. 42–45). Only the last painting was given a title referring to a place, *Arizona* [551-9] (private collection), even though the other works also recollect landscapes. A rough structure made up of sketchlike brushstrokes in mostly green and brown stretches out beneath a gently modulated blue plane in the upper half of the picture, which could be understood as a cloudless section of sky. The *Abstract Paintings* [551-1 to 551-3 and 551-6] (cat. 42–44; Galerie Bernd Lutze, Friedrichshafen) are animate, landscape-like sketches that walk a fine line, approaching natural motifs without losing their unique, abstract character. In the artist's catalogue raisonné, these paintings immediately follow a group of realistically painted, romanticized landscapes [549-1 and 549-2, 550-1 to 550-3]. At the same time, the small Abstract paintings anticipate the landscapes made in the following year [572-1 to 572-5] (figs. p. 24).

Translated from the German by Allison Moseley

[1] Gerhard Richter, "Interview with Christiane Vielhaber" (1986) in Richter 2009, 189–92, here 192.

[2] He also produced another version of the book, as well as a special edition, each with a unique overpainted photograph. See Butin et al. 2014, nos. 99–101.

[3] Richter spent several years in a productive competition with Duchamp. Two of Richter's most famous works, the 1996 *Ema (Nude on a Staircase)* [134] (Museum Ludwig, Cologne) and *4 Panes of Glass* [160] (fig. p. 15) of the following year, were created as a kind of objection to Duchamp and would not be understandable without reference to Duchamp.

[4] See Hans Ulrich Obrist, "Interview mit Gerhard Richter," in Obrist/Schwarz 2013, 55.

42 *Abstract Painting (Abstraktes Bild)* [551-1], 1984
Oil on canvas, 43 × 60 cm
Private collection, Switzerland

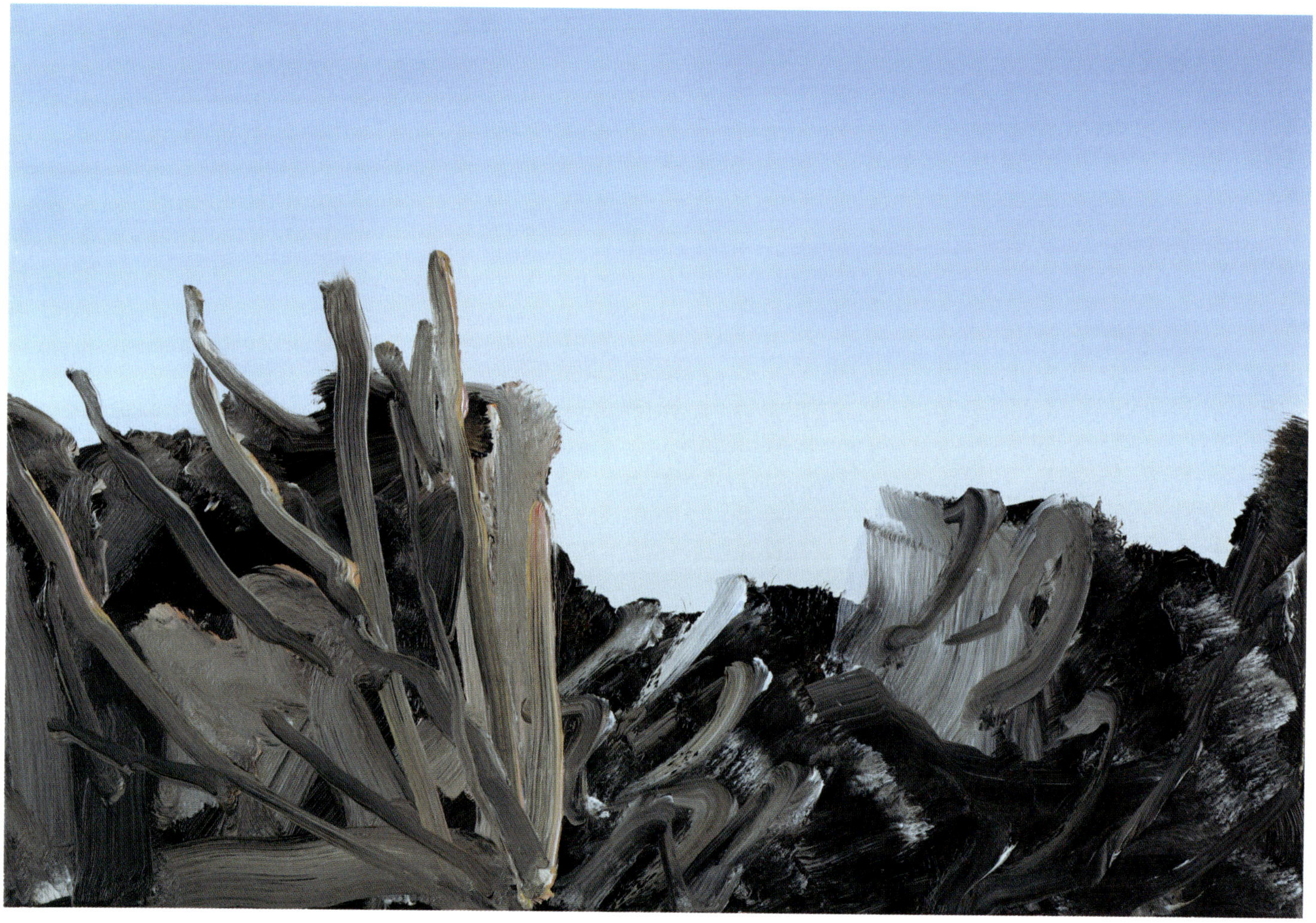

43 *Abstract Painting (Abstraktes Bild)* [551-2], 1984
Oil on canvas, 43 × 60 cm
Private collection, Switzerland

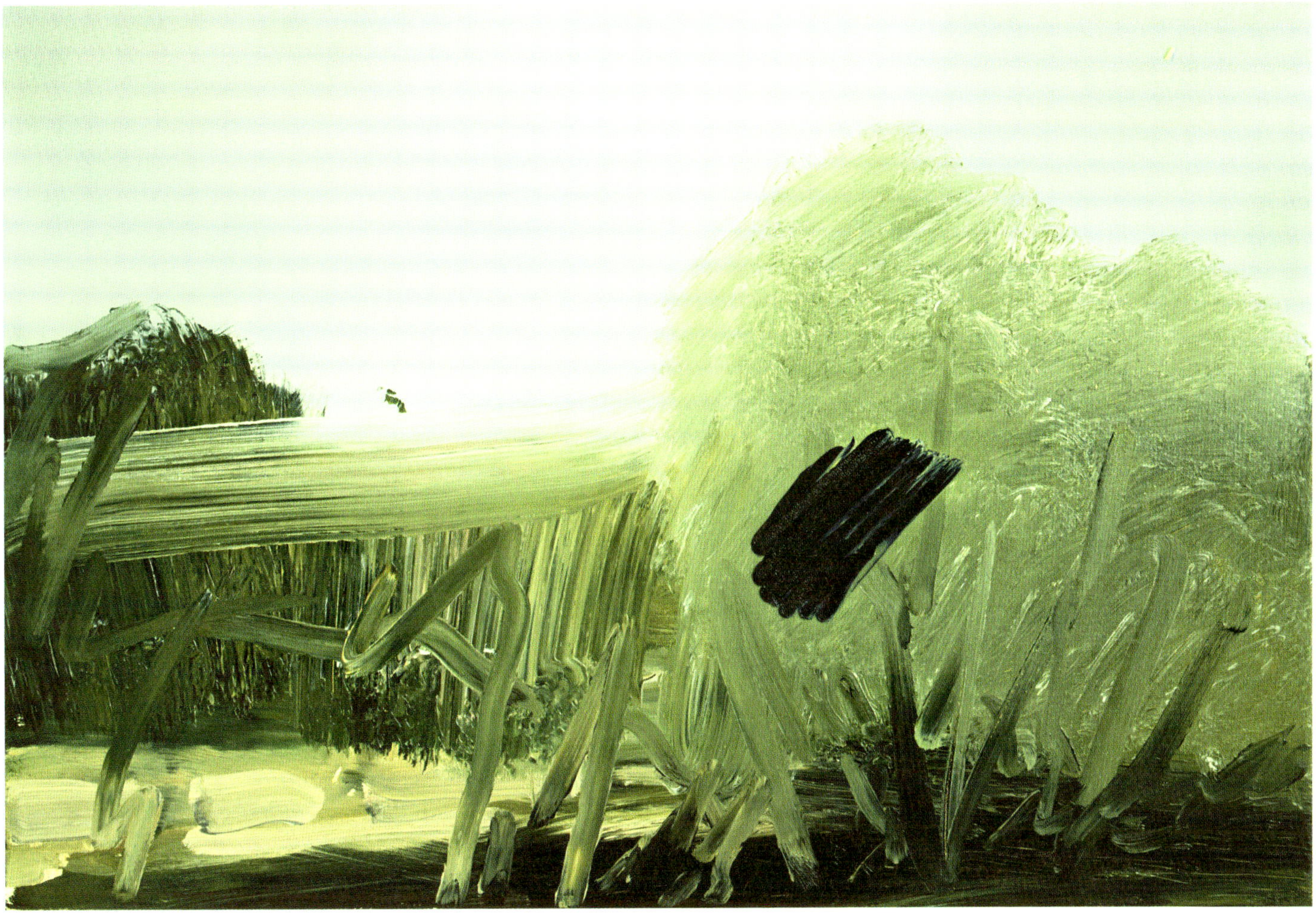

44 *Abstract Painting (Abstraktes Bild)* [551-3], 1984
Oil on canvas, 43 × 60 cm
Private collection

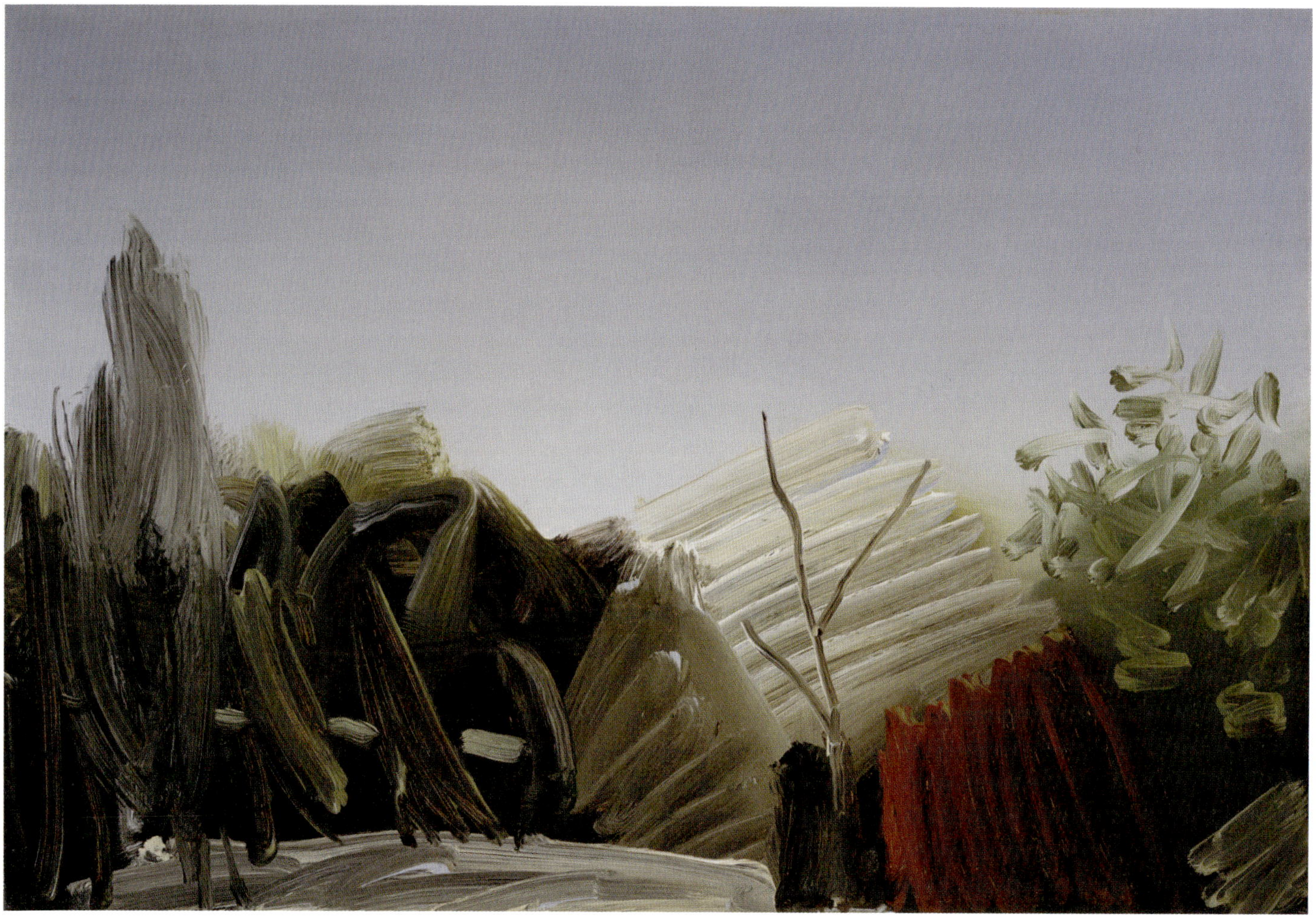

45 *Abstract Painting (Abstraktes Bild)* [551-8], 1984
Oil on canvas, 65 × 80 cm
Private collection, Switzerland

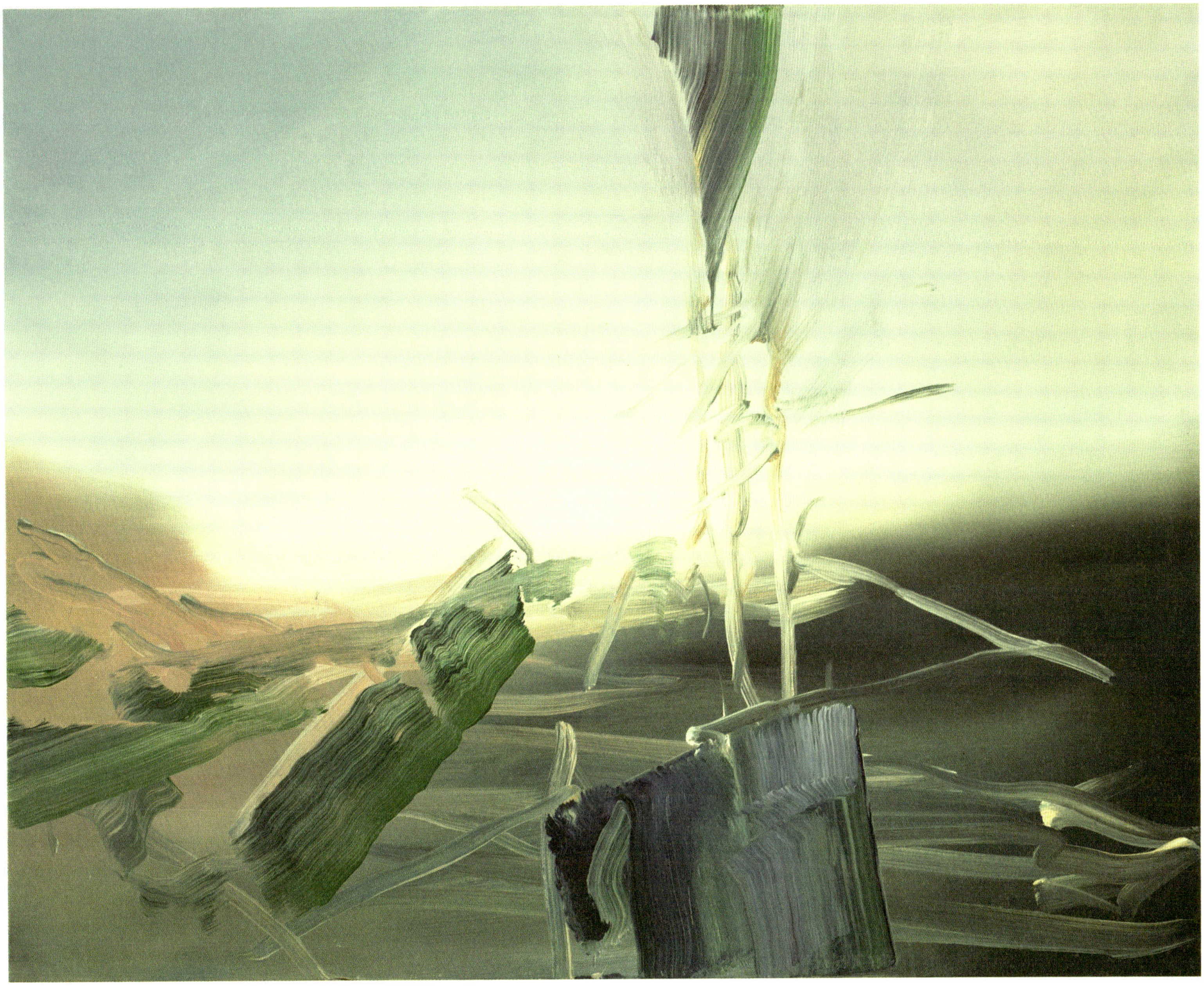

46 *128 Details from a Picture (Halifax 1978) II*
(128 Photos von einem Bild [Halifax 1978] II) [Editions 99], 1998
Eight offset prints in black and gray on cardboard, 64.2 × 100.6 cm each
Private collection

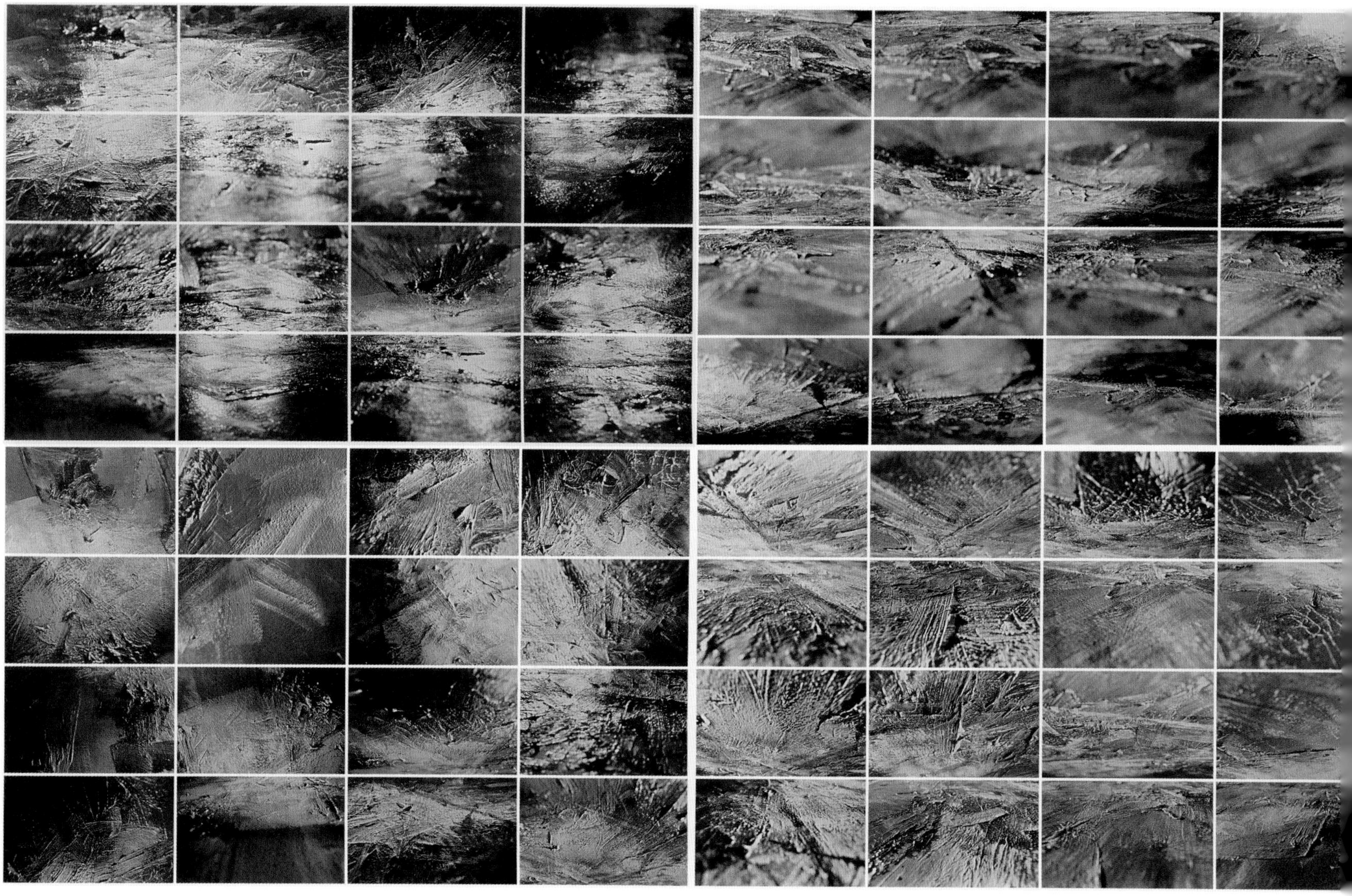

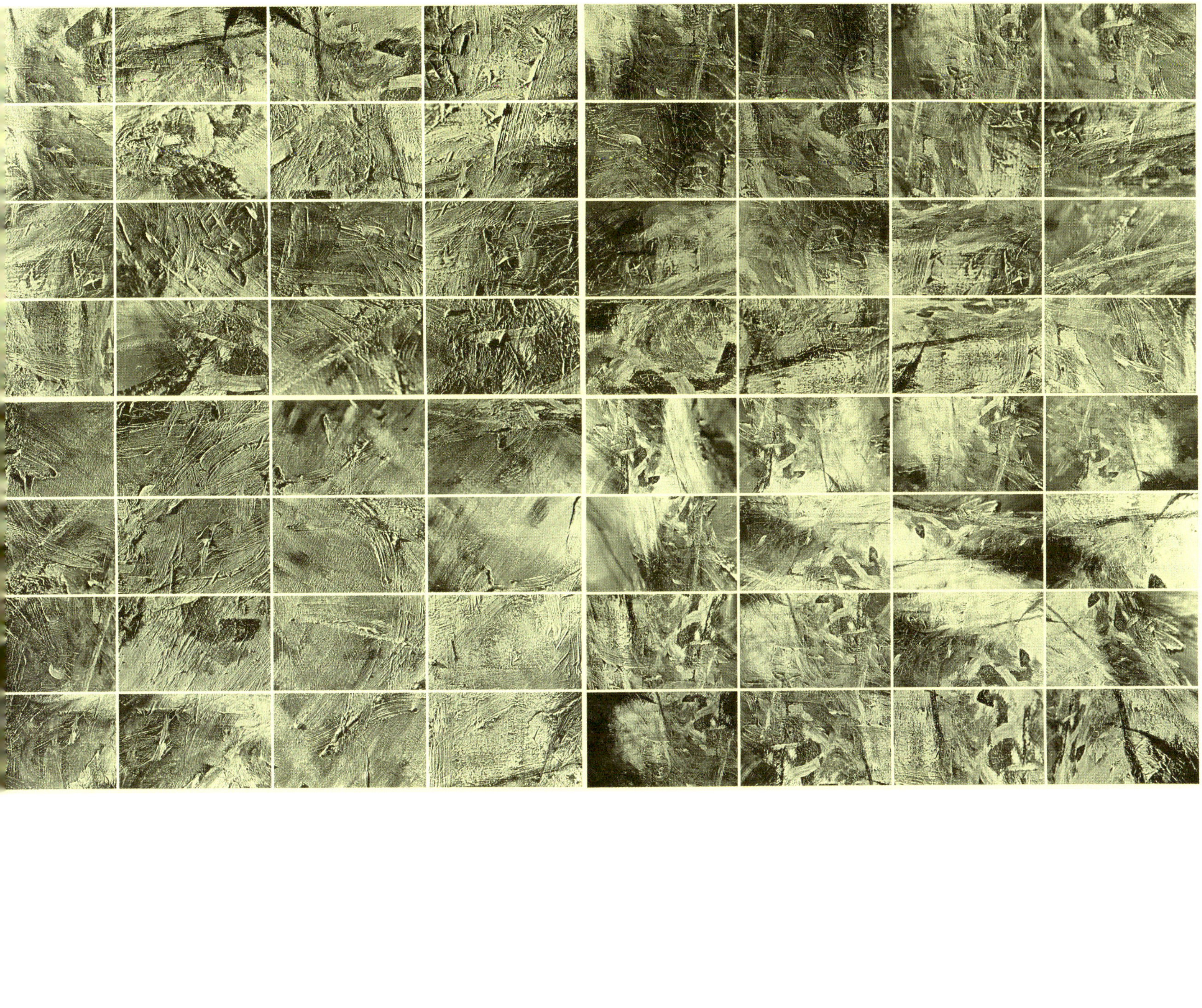

47 *Elbe* [Editions 155], 1957/2012
Thirty-one digital inkjet prints on cardboard, 29.5 × 21 cm each
Gerhard Richter Archive, Staatliche Kunstsammlungen Dresden

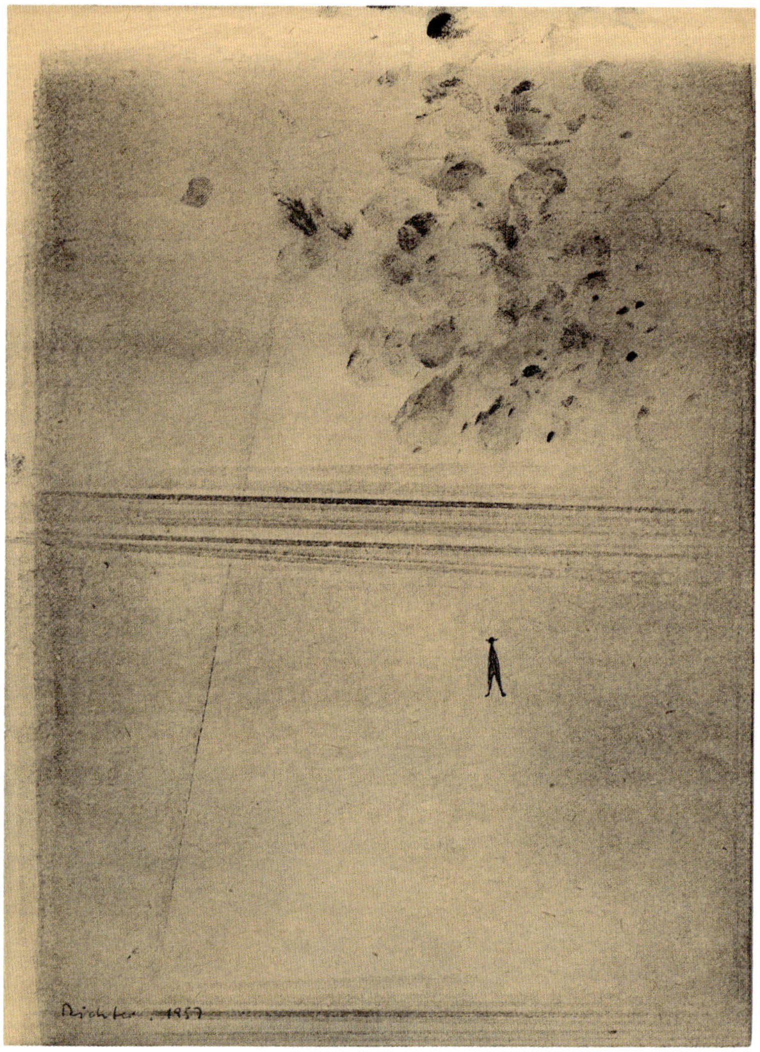

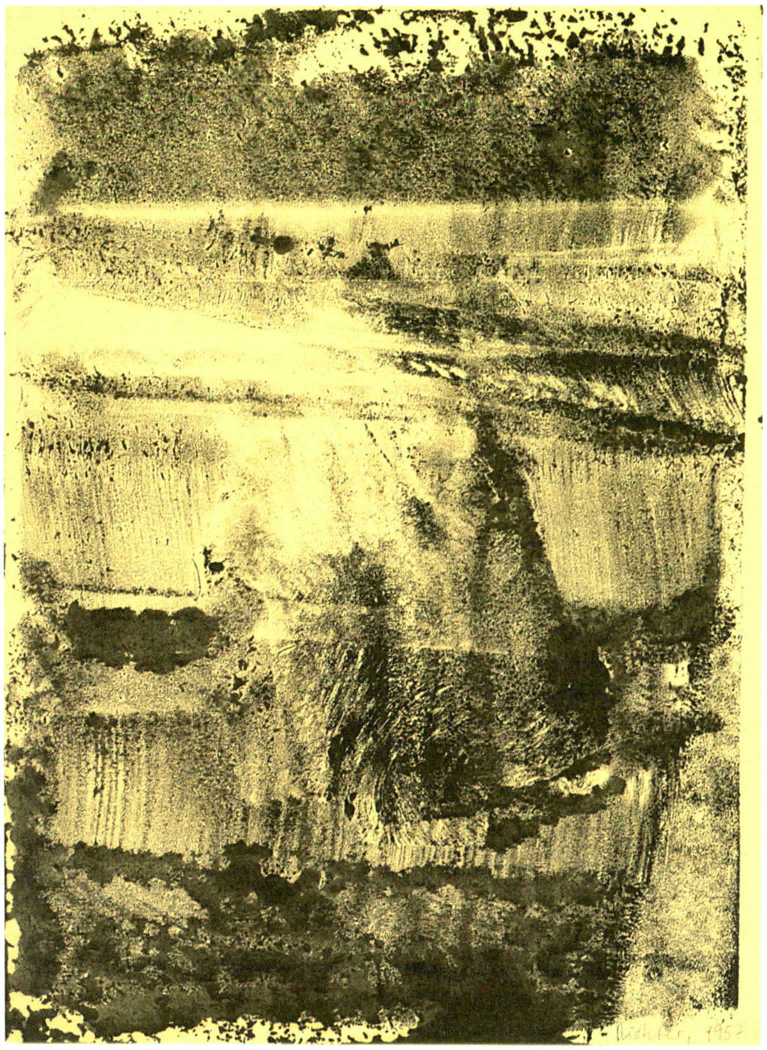

48 *Gray Forest (Grauwald) (10.1.08)*, 2008
Lacquer on photograph, 18.6 × 12.6 cm
Private collection

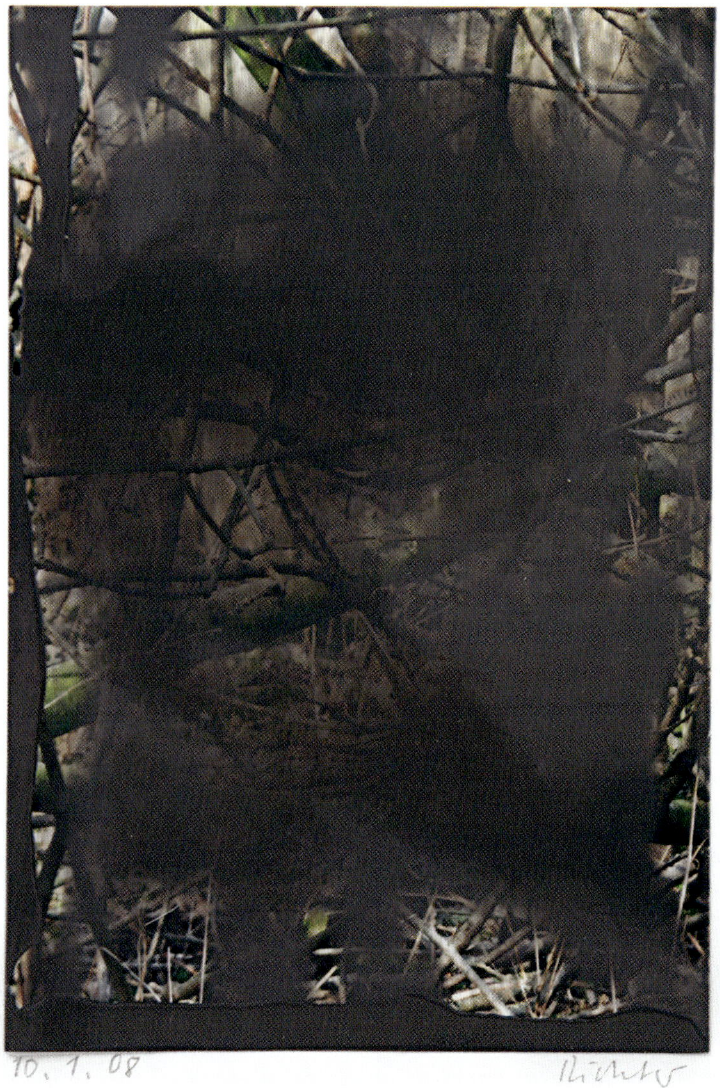

49 *Gray Forest (Grauwald) (11.1.08)*, 2008
Lacquer on photograph, 18.6 × 12.6 cm
Private collection

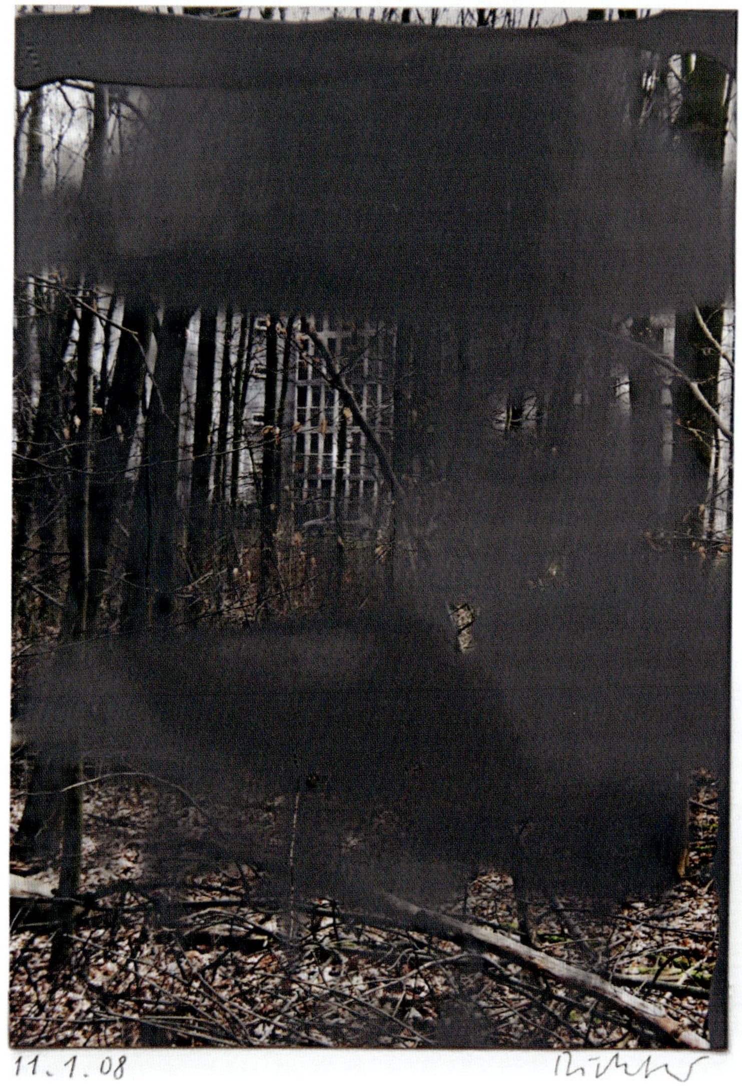

50 *Gray Forest (Grauwald) (12.1.08)*, 2008
Lacquer on photograph, 18.6 × 12.6 cm
Private collection

51 *Gray Forest (Grauwald) (22.1.08)*, 2008
Lacquer on photograph, 18.6 × 12.6 cm
Private collection

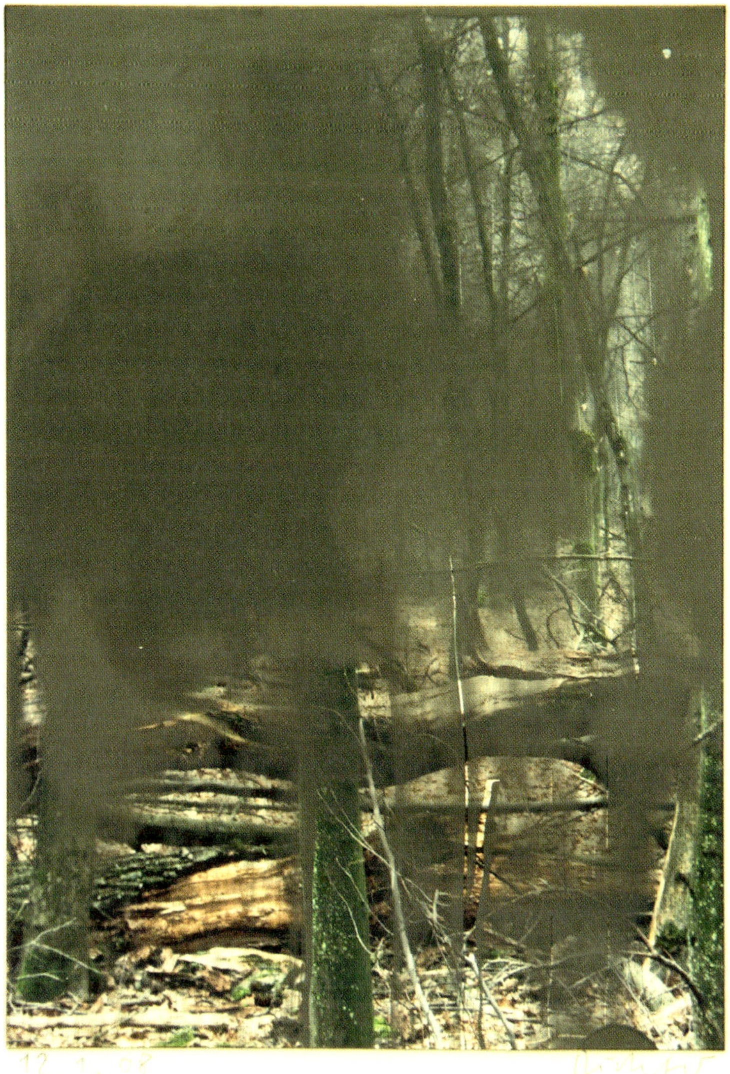

52 *Snow White (29.11.05)* [Editions 132], 2005
White acrylic and graphite on colored offset print, 22.5 × 32 cm
Private collection

53 *Snow White (13.12.05)* [Editions 132], 2005
White acrylic and graphite on colored offset print, 22.5 × 32 cm
Private collection

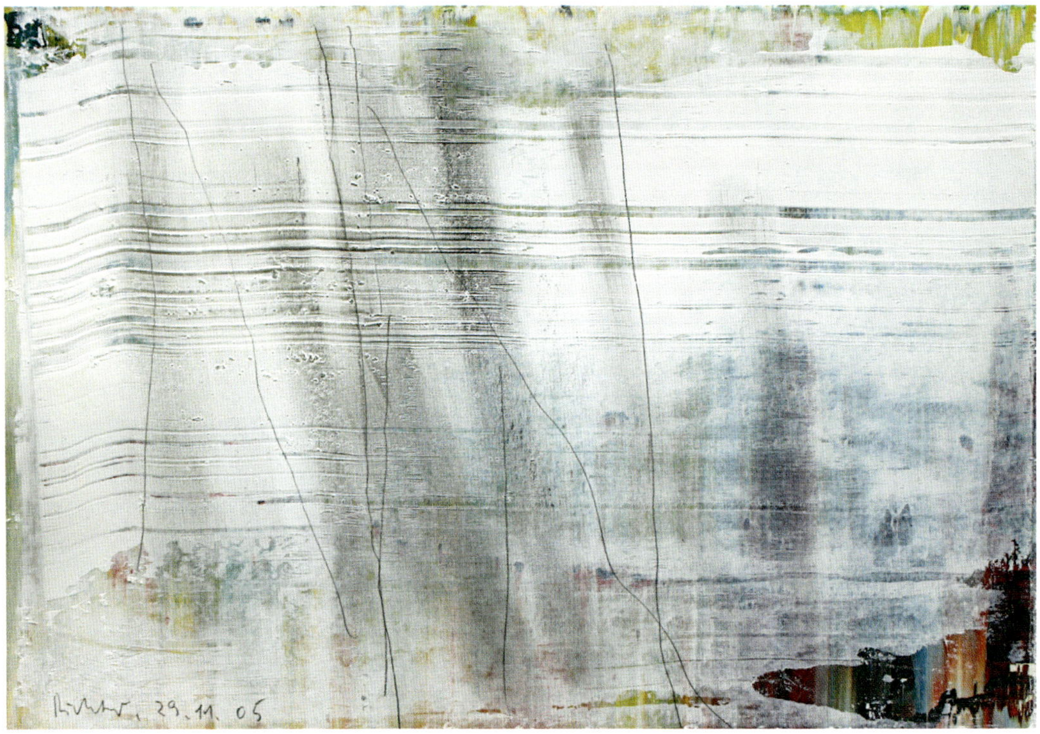

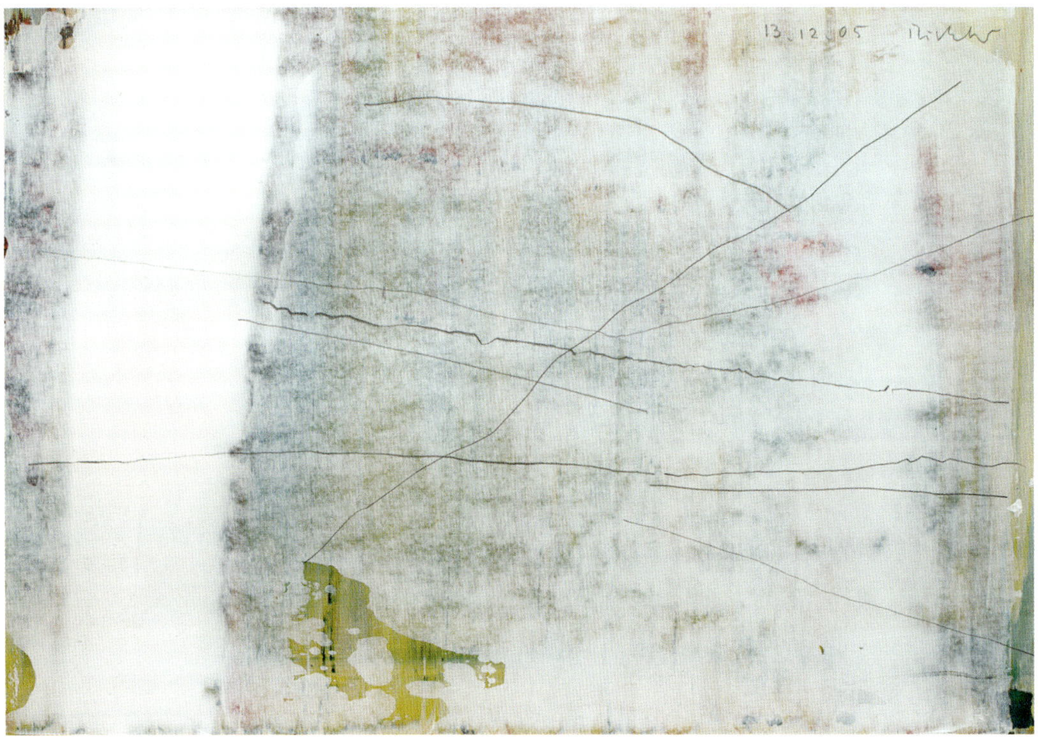

54 *Snow White (14.12.05)* [Editions 132], 2005
White acrylic and graphite on colored offset print, 22.5 × 32 cm
Private collection

55 *Snow White (1.1.06)* [Editions 132], 2006
White acrylic and graphite on colored offset print, 22.5 × 32 cm
Private collection

56 *MV. 72*, 2011
Lacquer on photograph, 10 × 15 cm
Private collection

57 *MV. 80*, 2011
Lacquer on photograph, 10 × 15 cm
Private collection

58 *MV. 12.9.11*, 2011
Lacquer on photograph, 10 × 15 cm
Private collection

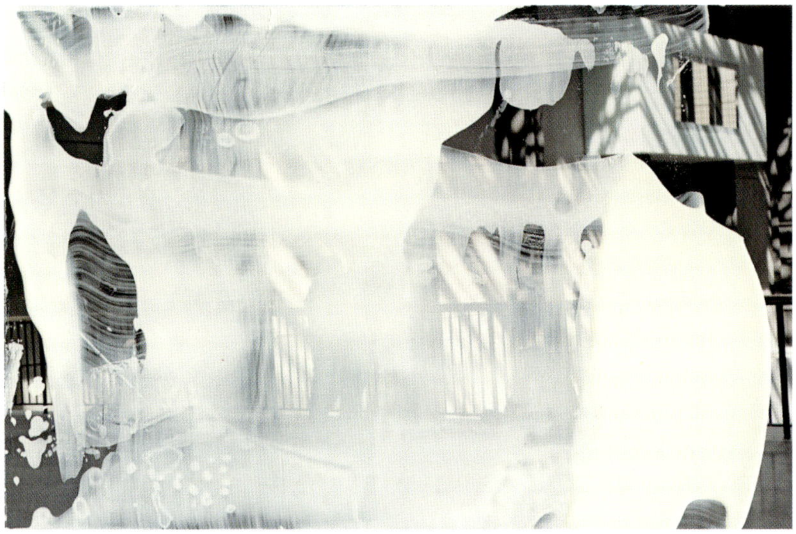

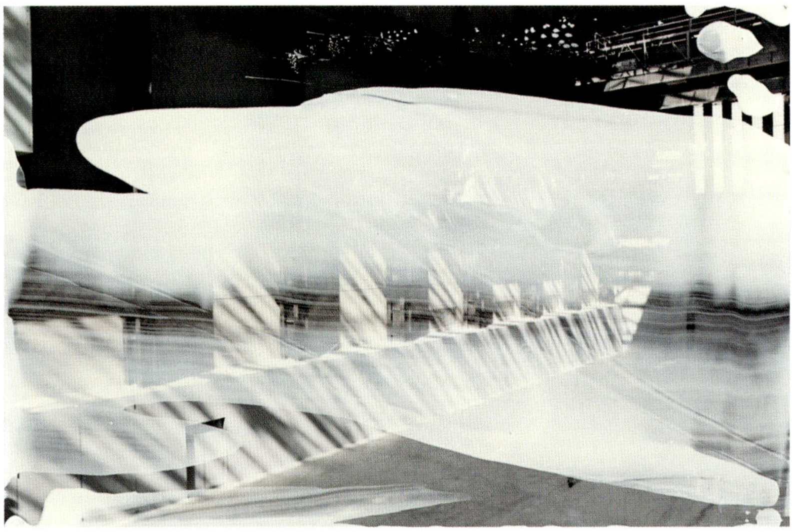

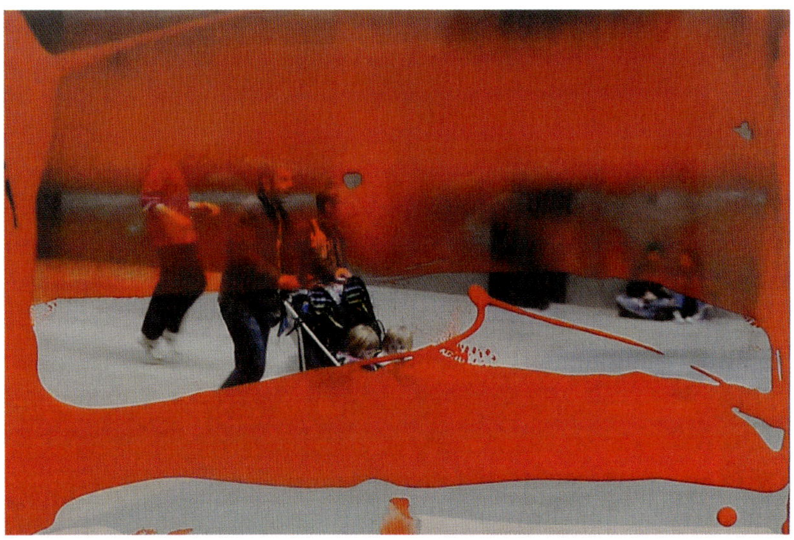

59 *MV. 209*, 2011
Lacquer on photograph, 10 × 15 cm
Private collection

60 *MV. 229*, 2011
Lacquer on photograph, 10 × 15 cm
Private collection

61 *MV. 233*, 2011
Lacquer on photograph, 10 × 15 cm
Private collection

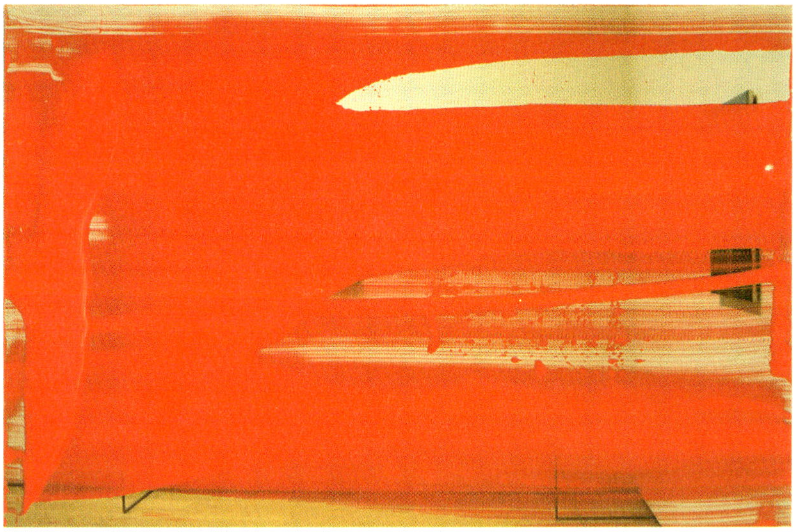

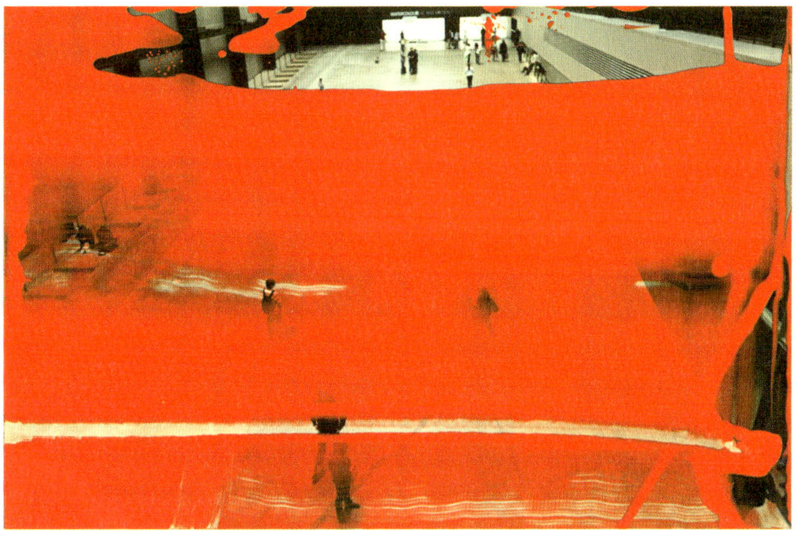

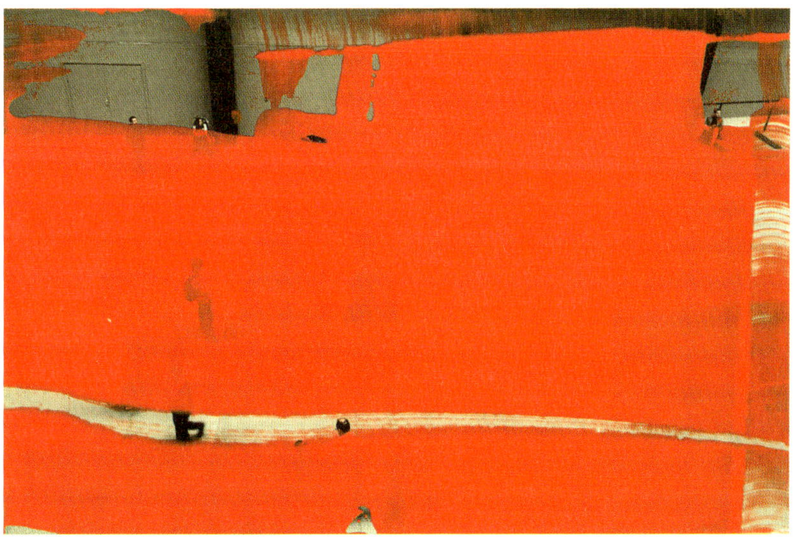

62 *40 Days (40 Tage)*, 2015
Colored offset print on paper, forty parts,
thirty-five sheets 21 × 29.7 cm each, five sheets 30 × 40 cm each
Private collection

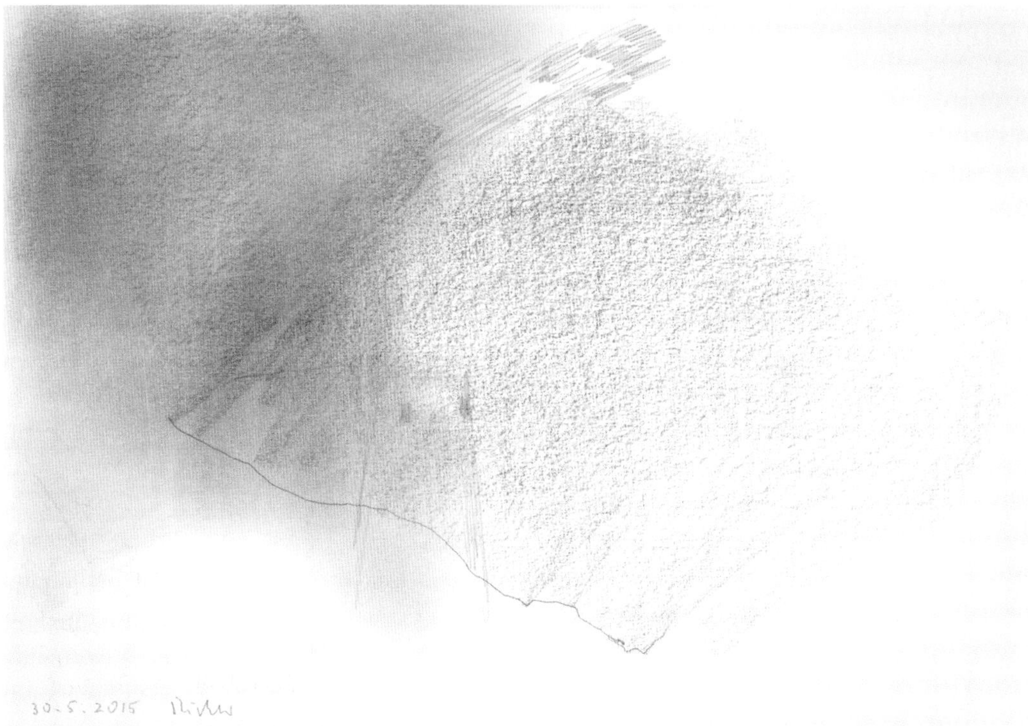

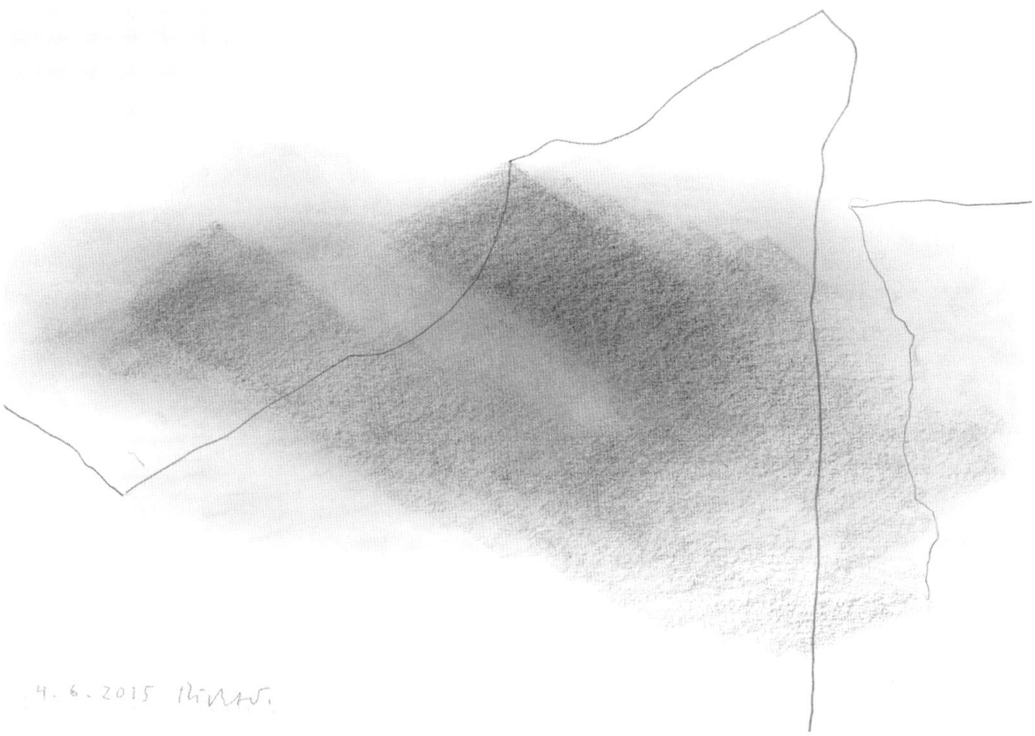

6. Juni 2015

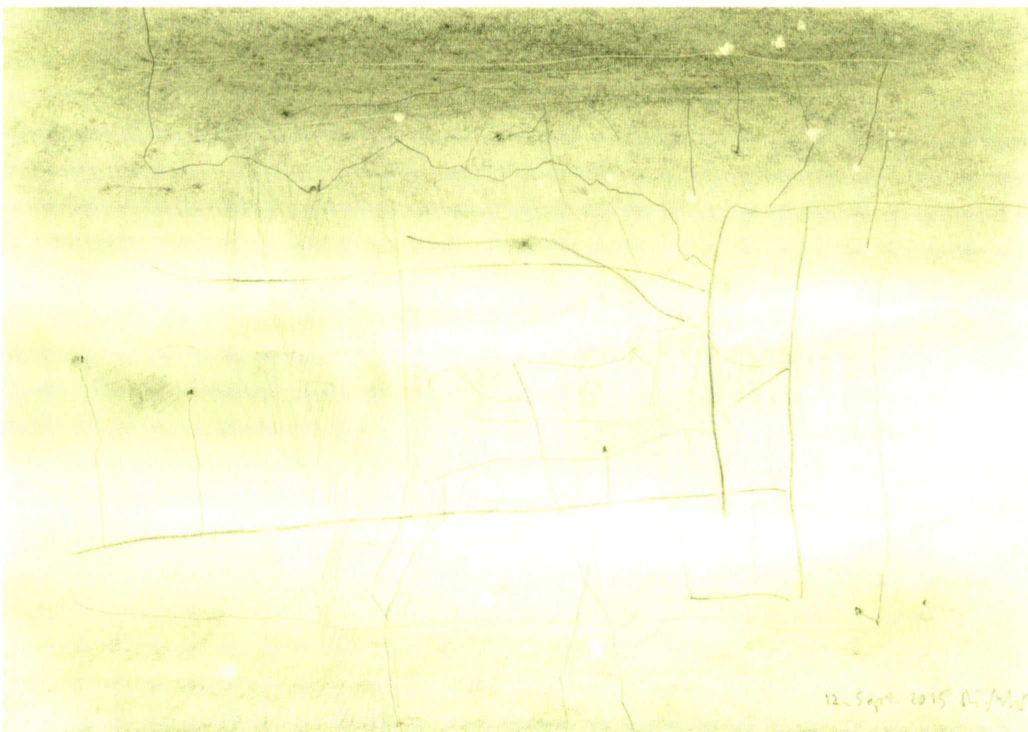
12. Sept. 2015

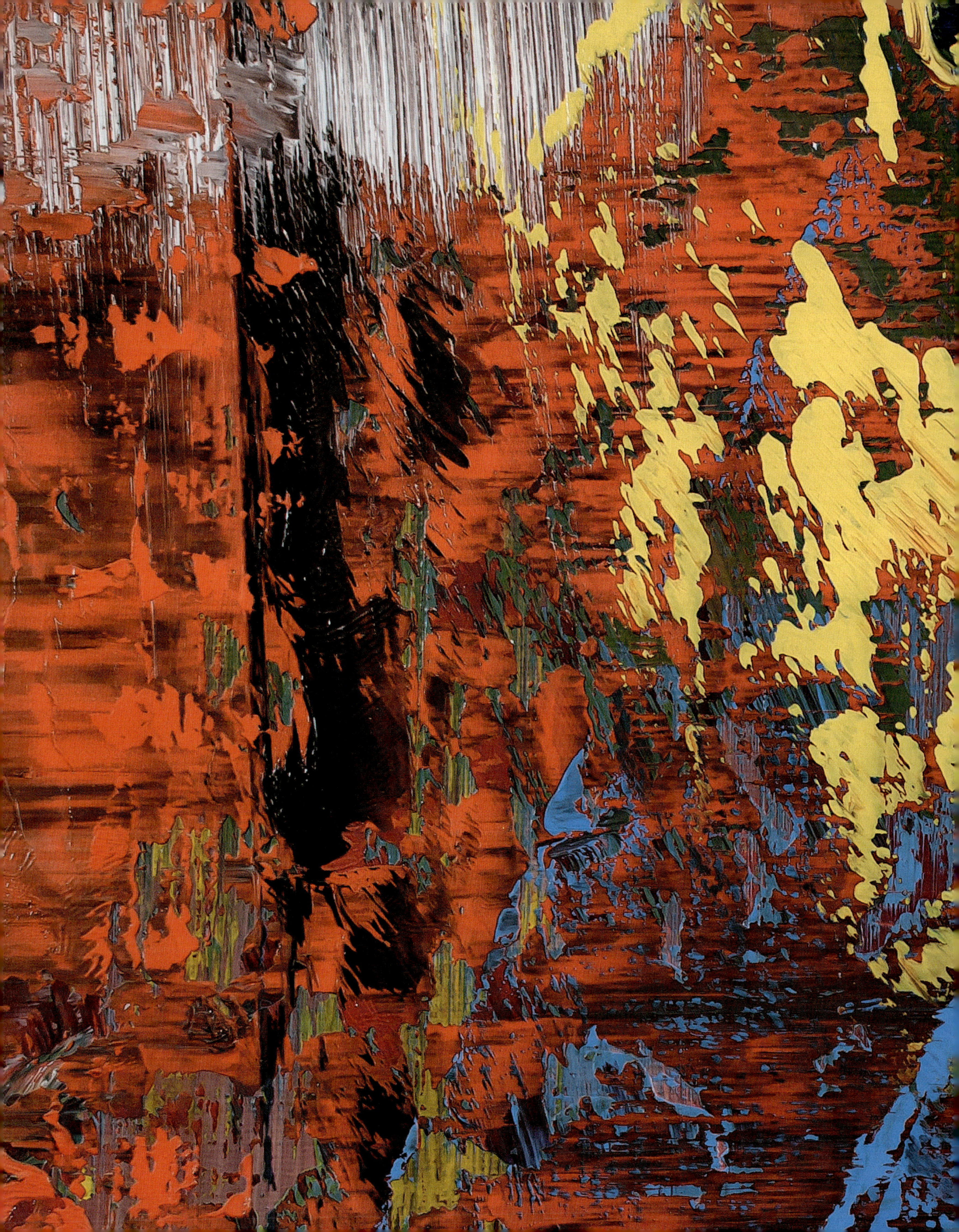

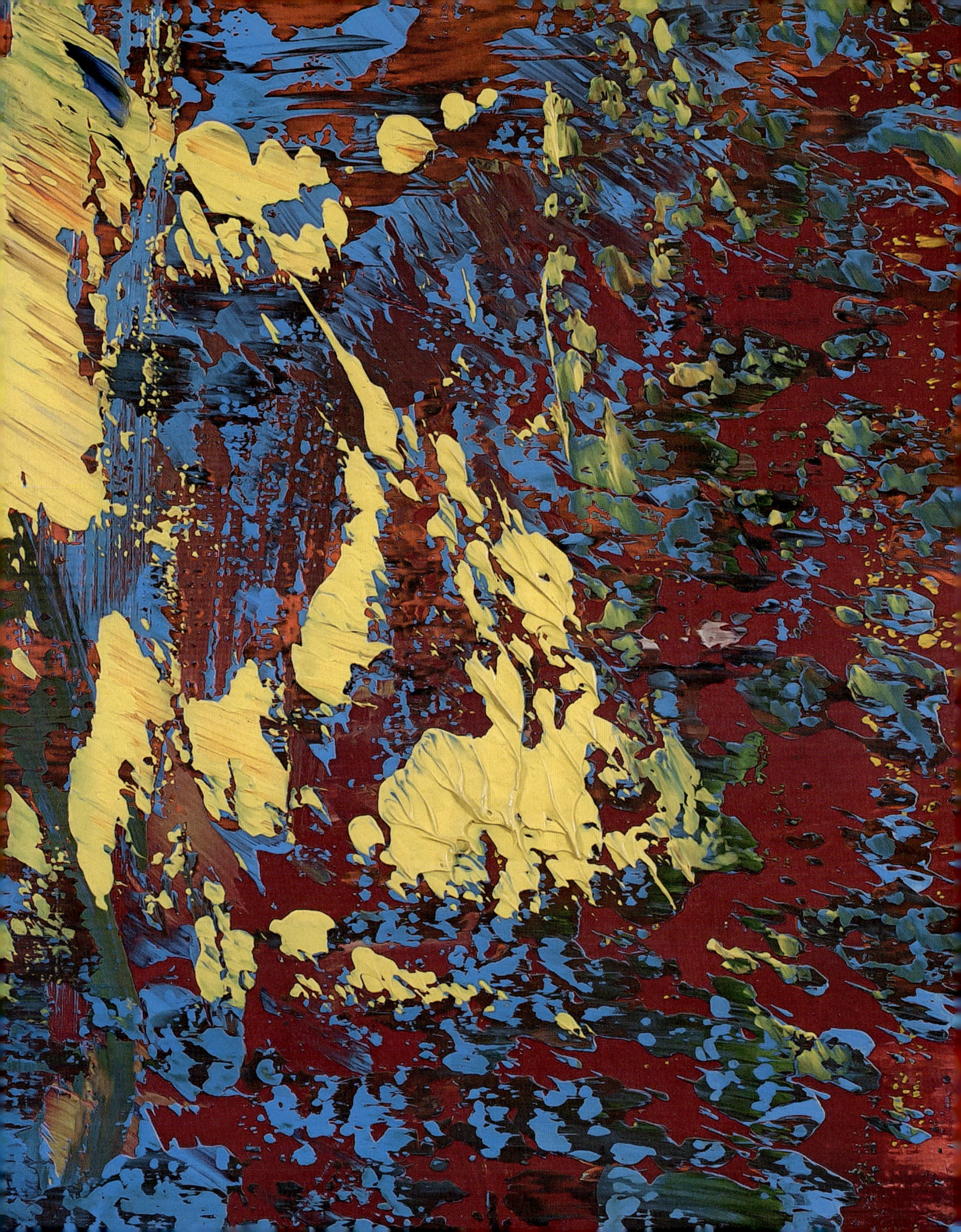

Paints and Layers: Abstract Paintings from 1986 to 2005

Kerstin Küster

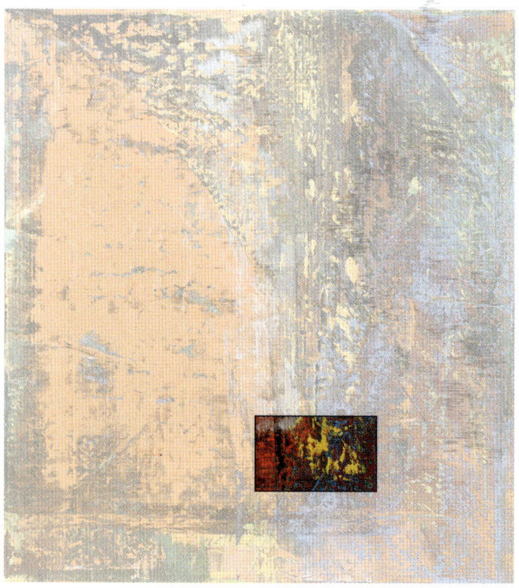

cat. 63

Richter's Abstract paintings are made in layers. Sometimes a photograph is the starting point. Overpainting can leave parts of the realistic picture uncovered and hence generate dimensionality. When overpainting, Richter again drew on chance to counteract conscious control of the painting process. From the 1980s, he used squeegees as tall as the canvas to spread paint across its surface in a single action. Richter had already applied a nonhierarchical principle in his Color Charts, treating every point in the painting as equally important. Layering remains important in these works too. Paint applied *alla prima* blends with the support, while unworked areas expose the underlying surface.

Gerhard Richter's first museum retrospective took place in 1986. The exhibition *Gerhard Richter: Paintings 1962–1985* (Gerhard Richter. Bilder von 1962–1985) was the most extensive presentation of his works until then and traveled to Düsseldorf, Berlin, Bern, and Vienna. The first published index of his works, featuring his paintings and sculptures numbered up to 794-3, also appeared as part of the exhibition catalog.[1]

The Abstract paintings, for which Richter made use of chance and arbitrariness, took up a great deal of space in this index. From the mid-1980s onward, the number of Abstract paintings increased with Richter's use of the squeegee as a painting tool (see the essay by Matthias Krüger, pp. 58–69). Brushes were mainly employed at the beginning of the painting process, or at the end, for producing controlled lineature. In a first step, the artist applied the oils across the whole canvas with brushes, often using two or three primary colors. On top of the diffuse colored ground he then added muted hues, using a variety of squeegees. For the monumental-sized pictures he used equally large squeegees, standing on a ladder to guide the tool across the entire surface of the canvas. Unlike a brush, the squeegee could be used not only to apply oil paint, but also to heavily impress the existing layers of paint, blending the damp layers of paint. When dried, they were partially scraped off and then covered again when completely dry (see fig. p. 61). In works such as *A B, Quiet* [612-4] (cat. 63), *Position* [660] (cat. 65), and *Abstract Painting* [666-2] (cat. 64), Richter applied somewhat less pressure on the squeegee for the last layer of paint, so that it only adhered to elevated spots. This careful application of paint closed off the Abstract paintings from the viewer as if with a delicate veil, partially concealing the layers of paint beneath.

In contrast to the large "soft abstracts," as Richter occasionally called them, which were executed between 1977 and 1980 (cat. 31, 32), these squeegeed visual carpets of color are the result of what was originally a vague idea of the artist's, coupled with the purposeful element of chance produced by the squeegee and the painter's constant corrections. The 1990 *Abstract Painting* [724-4] (cat. 67) is an exception to these frequently dark paintings. It is unusually colorful, a quality that Richter once again came to value twenty years later, when he used this piece as the foundation for his digital striped artworks, the Strips (see the chapter "Transparent and Reflected: Mirrors, Glass, and Strips," pp. 194–207, see cat. 78).

In the 1990s, Richter's Abstract paintings became more geometrical. Beside the squeegee, he made use of the spatula to scrape, apply, and again remove paint. This process of application, destruction, and layering produced uniform vertical and horizontal pictorial structures that recall Richter's structured paintings in the late 1960s (see the chapter "Structures and Illusions: Abstract Works in the 1960s," pp. 70–87). In these works, Richter eschewed dimensionality in favor of a quiet, self-contained surface texture defined by dark hues. The raised strips of color between the strokes of the spatula added rhythm to these works. *Abstract Painting* [776-3] (cat. 66) and *Abstract Painting* [780-3] (cat. 68), as well as the works *March* [807] (cat. 69) and *Wall* [808] (cat. 70), reflect the diversity of this period. Richter described the painting *March* in a 2004 interview thus: "The paint that was applied has been vertically scratched off. Pretty evenly, like a wooden fence. Underneath there are mainly horizontal brushstrokes, or marks made with a palette knife. It has reddish and light blue tones, and darker, soft brushstrokes underneath that have partly been scratched away. And with the traces of white the painting gets a light feeling, like a Chinese watercolor, a lightness. And to my mind, the remnants of snow convey a certain optimism, like just before spring."[2] *March* [807] and *Wall* [808] are among the few Abstract paintings to which Richter attributed concrete titles after finishing them. These titles are often associative and derive either from a shape in the painting that seems familiar to the artist, or from an experience that he associates with the creation of the painting (see the essay by Dietmar Elger, pp. 22–33).

In the late 1990s, Richter developed a new, more harmonious formal vocabulary for his Abstract paintings. Again, he replaced the spatula with the squeegee, but this time he applied multiple layers of paint after his destructive scraping. As in the early Abstract paintings, he created a diffuse, colored background, and then added several layers of paint by guiding the squeegee across it in powerful strokes. He no longer applied the squeegee in random motions across the canvas, but instead moved it from top to bottom, and from one side to the other. The uppermost layer of paint determines the overall impression the picture gives. The layers of paint beneath it only appear in fragmented spots, revealing a great wealth of details. Richter avoided strong color contrasts and instead returned to neutralizing white and gray hues, as he did in *Abstract Painting* [860-7] (cat. 71). In this way, he imbued these paintings with a greater sense of calm. Additionally, Richter did not execute the *Abstract Painting* [860-7] on canvas, as was his usual practice, but instead on aluminum Dibond. He first used this material in 1996 as the support for *Fuji* [839-1 to 839-110], his small-format, 110-part painting series. The smooth surface of this aluminum composite material reinforces the illusionistic quality of the paint, as well as its transparency, while also increasing the role of chance. For Richter, chance is not just a happy coincidence; it is also always a tool and a method, as he emphasized in an interview in 2004: "By accepting coincidence as an event that goes far beyond my faculties of imagination, even beyond all comprehension, I take on the role of someone who can only react to it—and yet, despite the helplessness of this position, can still make something out of it, to the point where it is no longer a coincidence any more. And then you have a new coincidence."[3]

Translated from the German by Allison Moseley

1 See Düsseldorf 1986.

2 Gerhard Richter, "Interview with Jan Thorn-Prikker" (2004), in Richter 2009, 464–79, here 477.

3 Gerhard Richter, "Interview mit Jan Thorn-Prikker über die Arbeit War Cut" (2004), in Richter 2008, 469–73, here 472.

63 *A B, Quiet (A B, Still)* [612-4], 1986
Oil on canvas, 225 × 200 cm
Museum Barberini, Potsdam

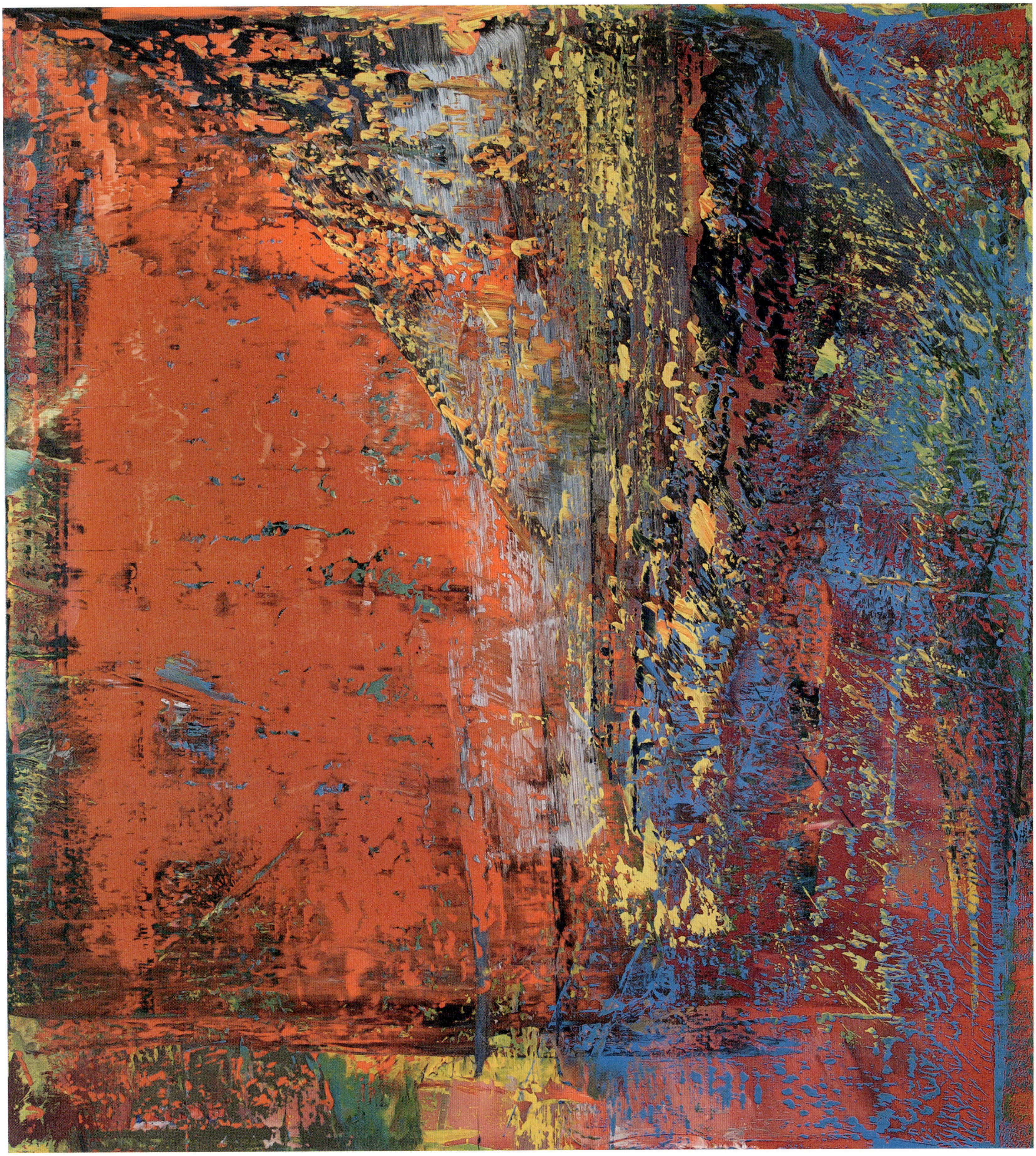

64 *Abstract Painting (Abstraktes Bild)* [666-2], 1988
Oil on canvas, 200 × 160 cm
Kunsthalle Emden –
Stiftung Henri und Eske Nannen und Schenkung Otto van de Loo

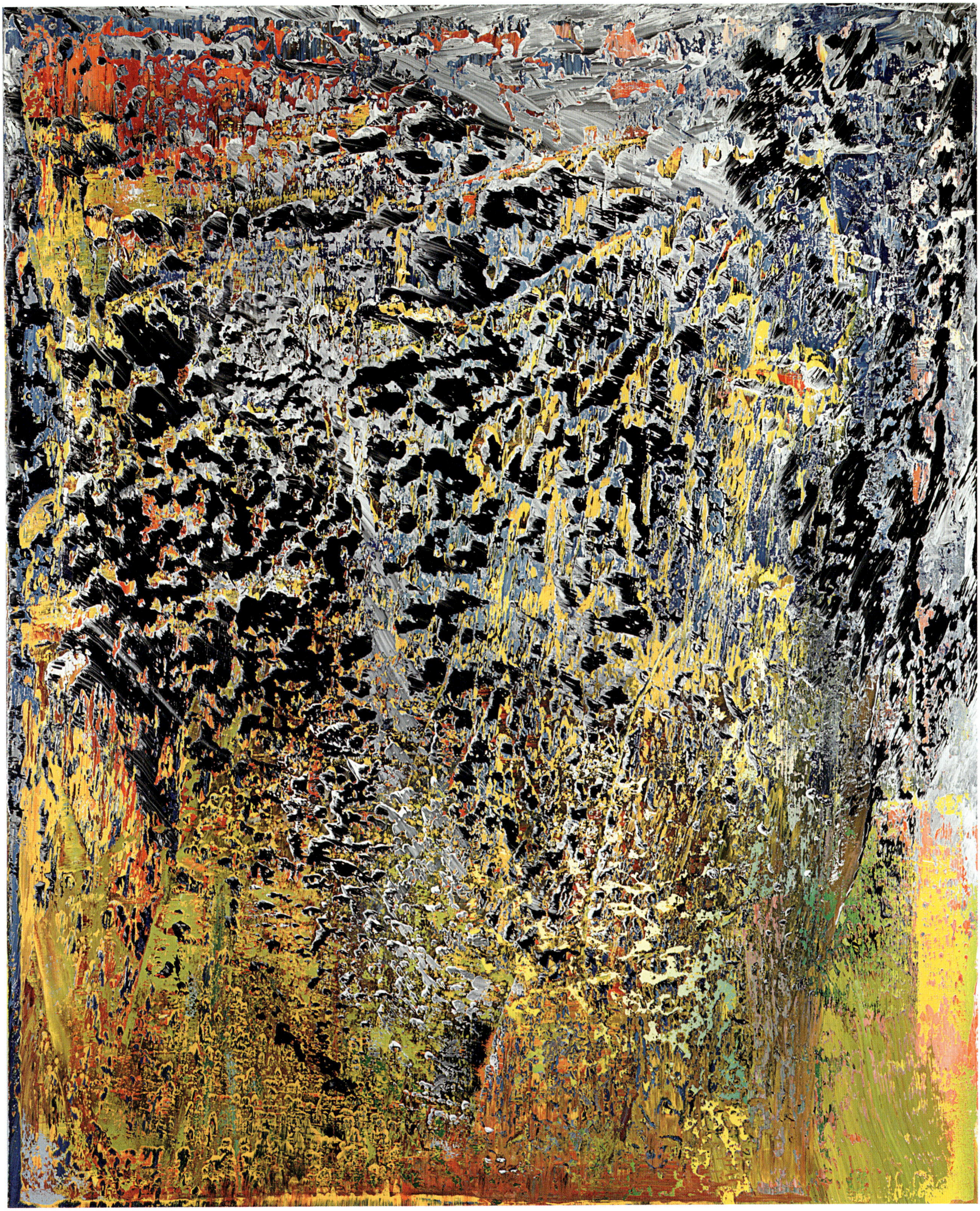

65 *Position (Stand)* [660], 1988
Oil on canvas, 300 × 250 cm
Museum Frieder Burda, Baden-Baden

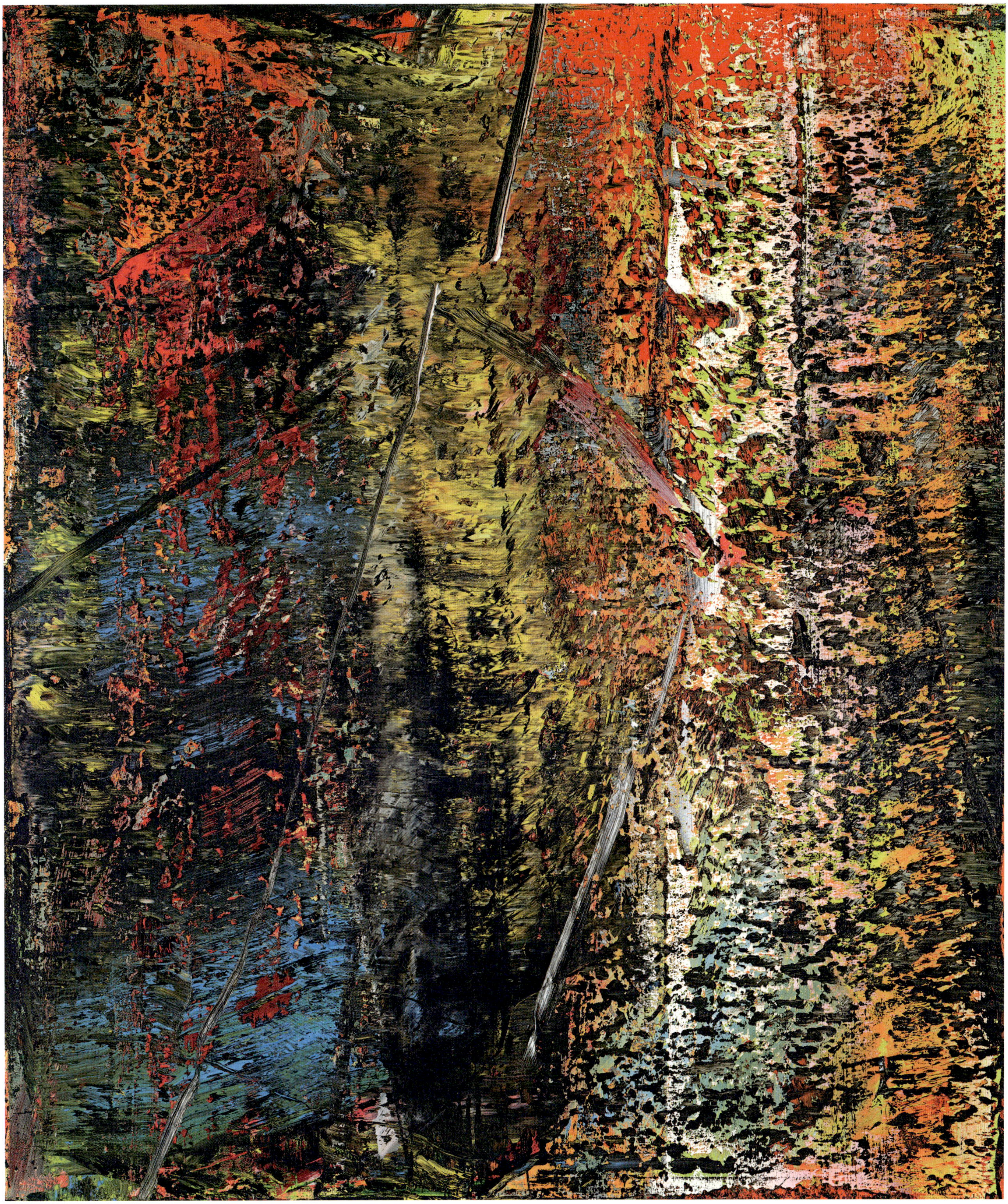

66 *Abstract Painting (Abstraktes Bild)* [776-3], 1992
Oil on canvas, 92 × 82 cm
Private collection, Switzerland

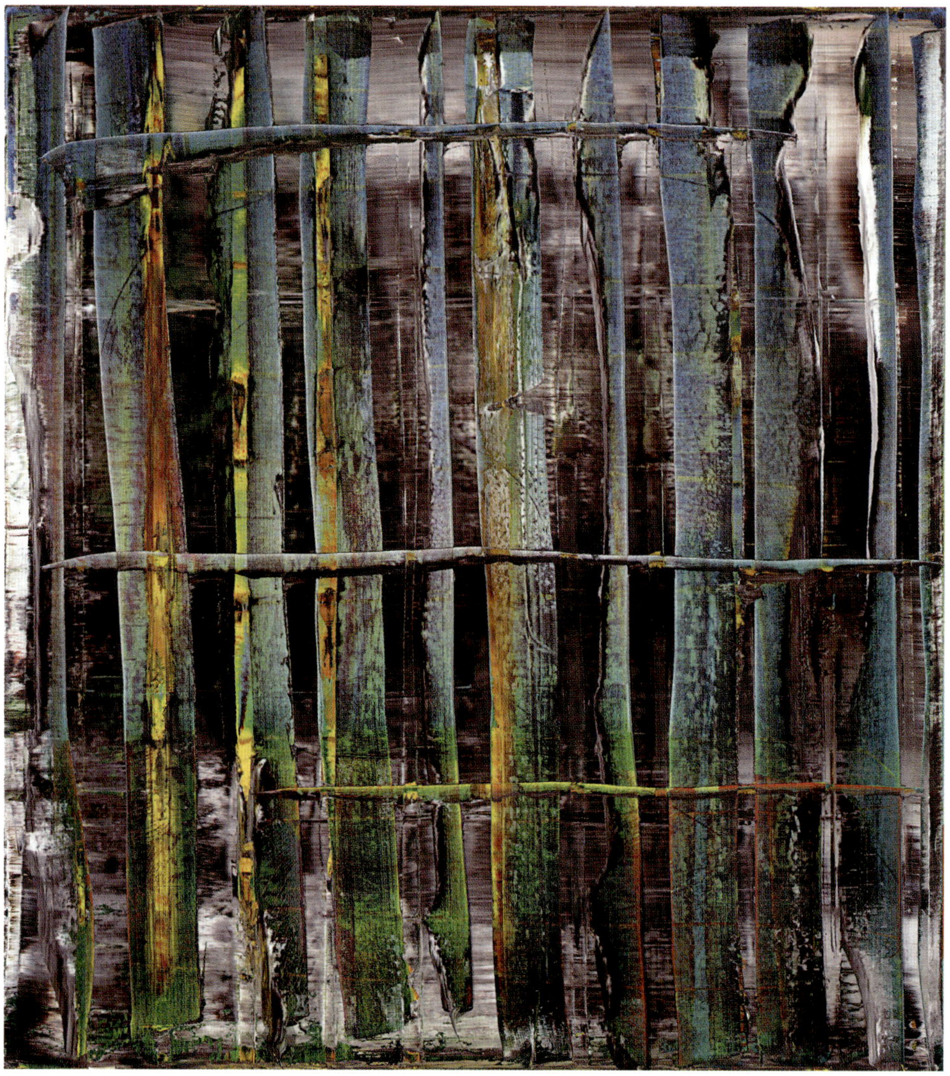

67 *Abstract Painting (Abstraktes Bild)* [724-4], 1990
Oil on canvas, 92 × 126 cm
Private collection

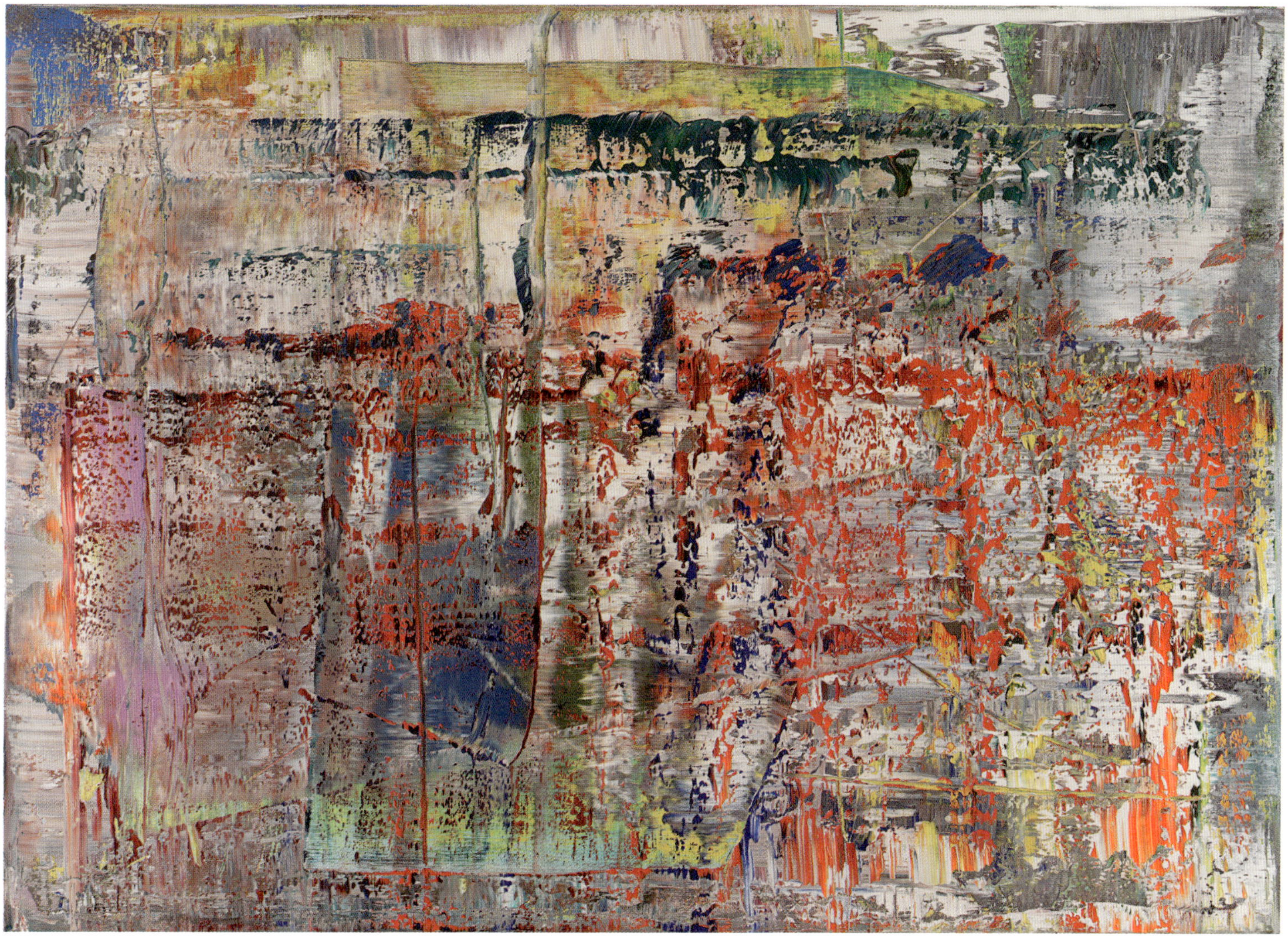

68 *Abstract Painting (Abstraktes Bild)* [780-3], 1992
Oil on canvas, 260 × 200 cm
Private collection

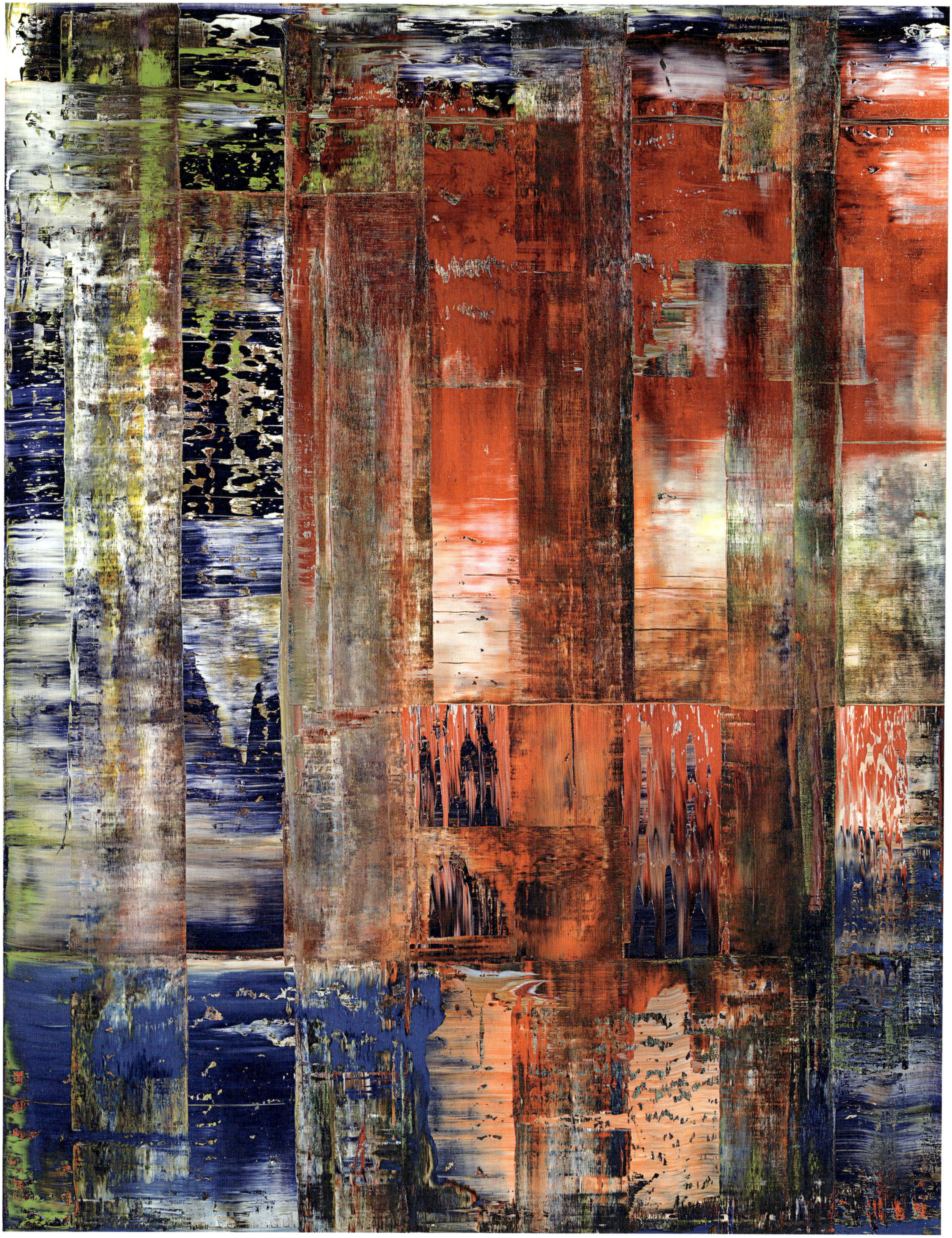

69 *March (März)* [807], 1994
Oil on canvas, 250 × 200 cm
Gerhard Richter Archive,
Staatliche Kunstsammlungen Dresden,
loan from a private collection

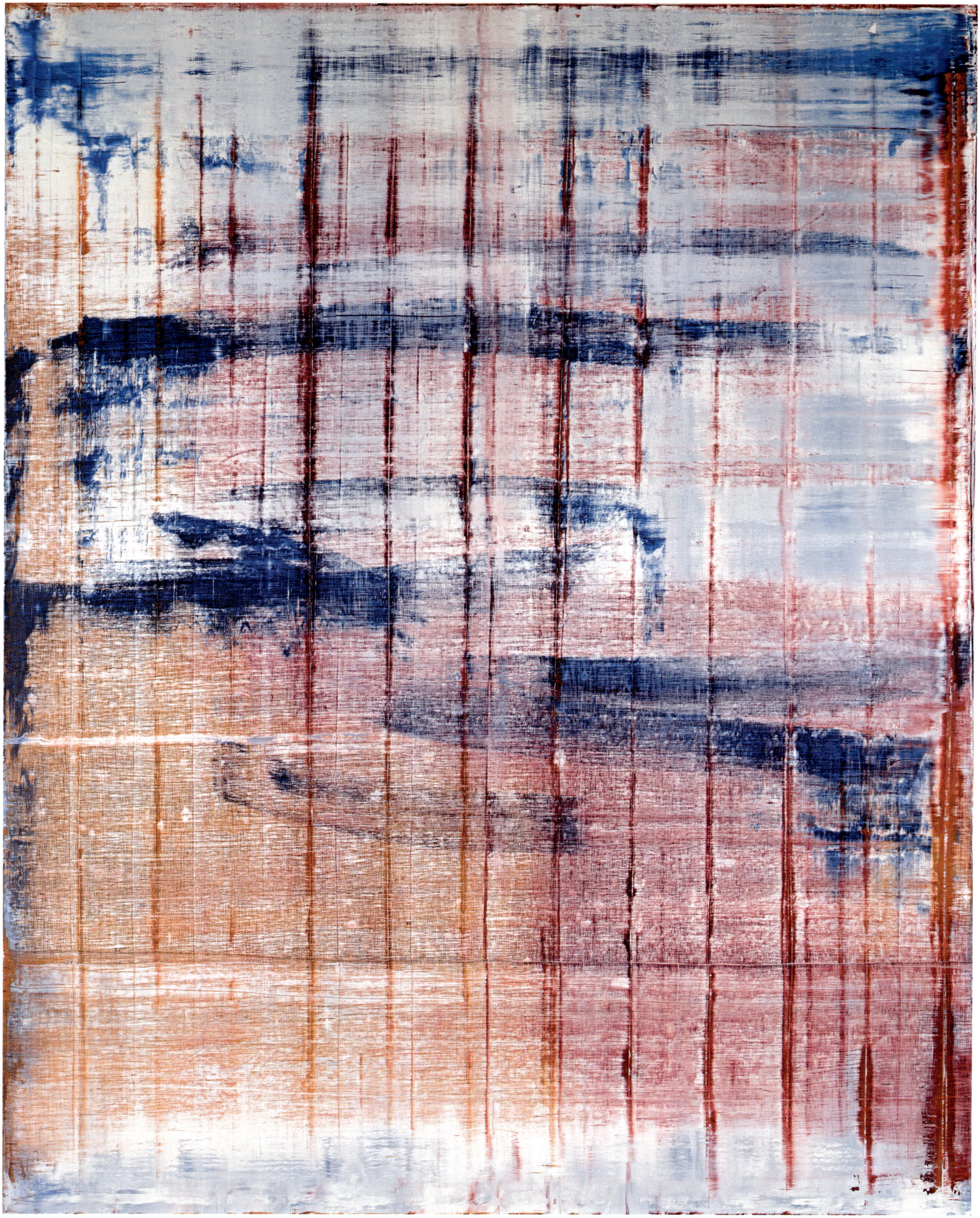

70 *Wall (Mauer)* [808], 1994
Oil on canvas, 250 × 200 cm
Private collection

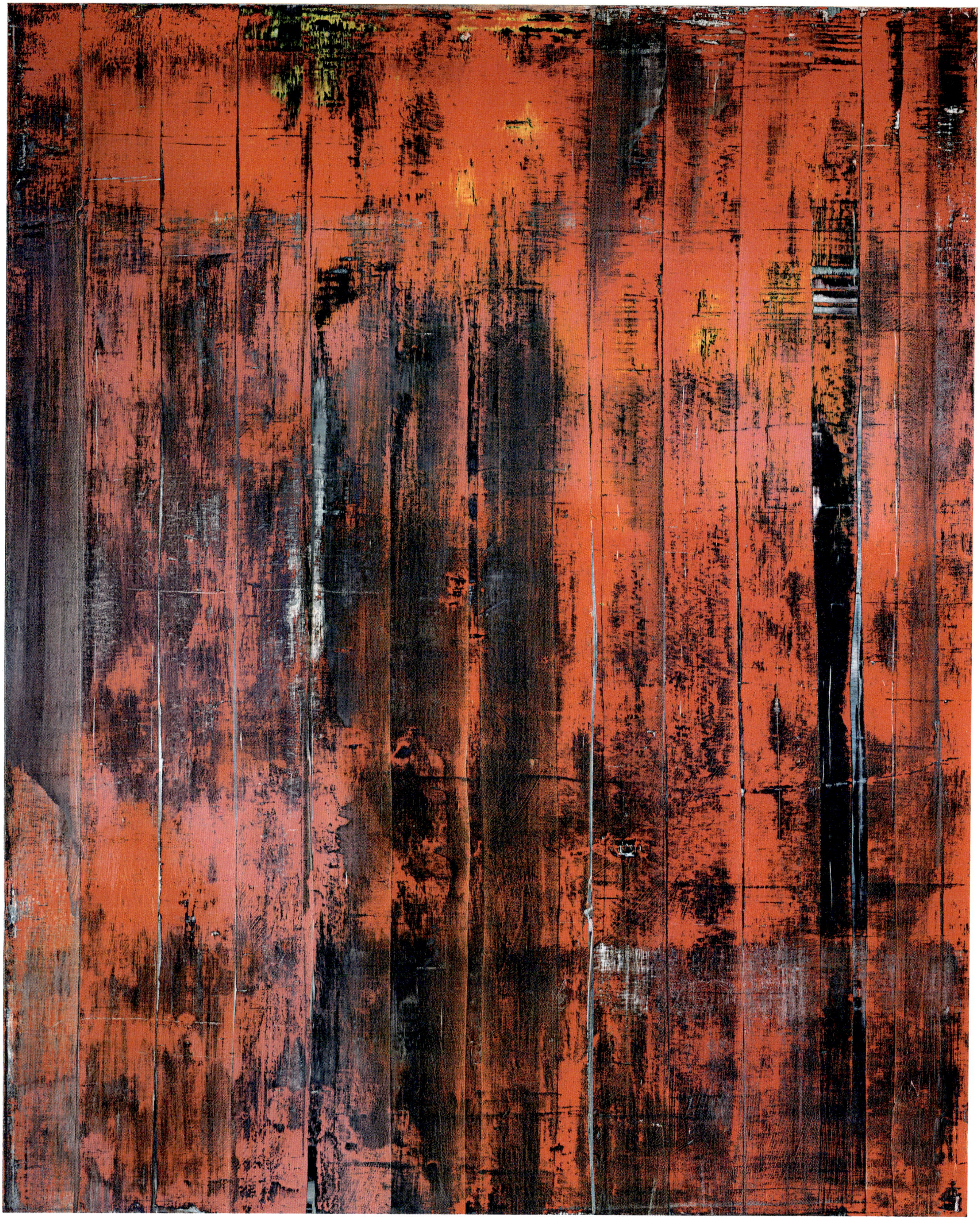

71 *Abstract Painting (Abstraktes Bild)* [860-7], 1997/1999
Oil on aluminum Dibond, 100 × 90 cm
Private collection

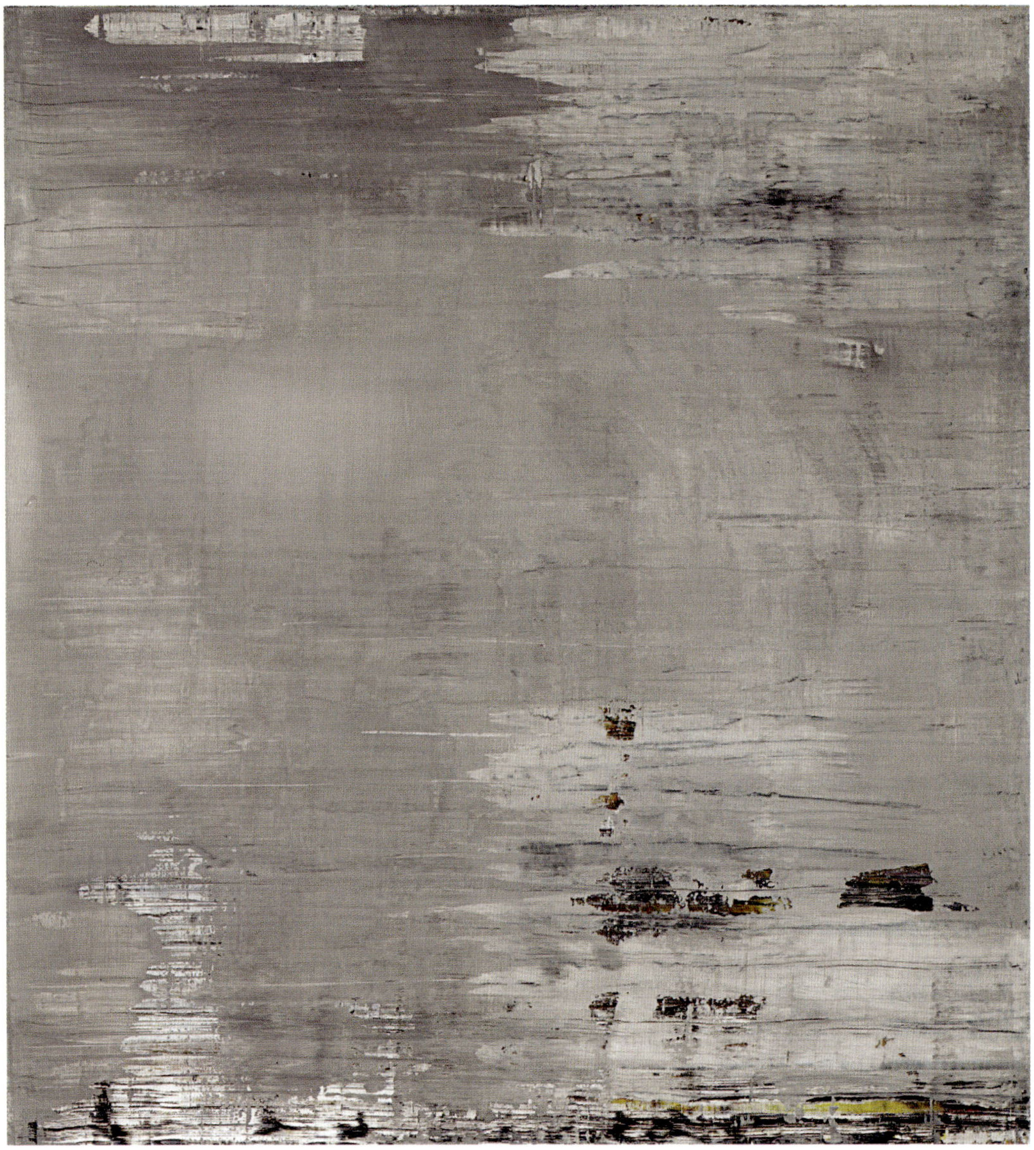

72 *Abstract Painting (Abstraktes Bild)* [891-4], 2005
Oil on canvas, 113.5 × 75 cm
Private collection

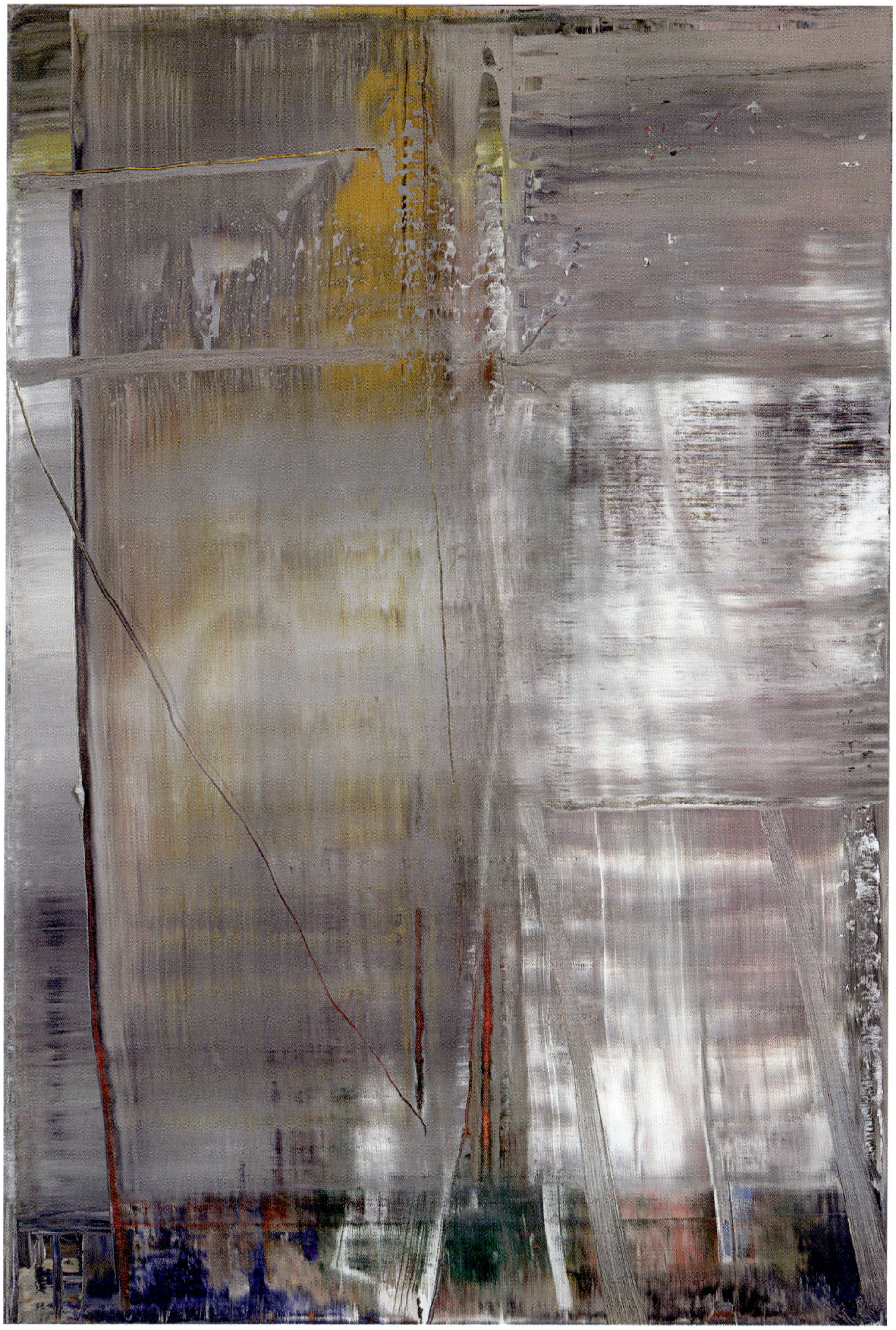

73 *Abstract Painting (Abstraktes Bild)* [865-2], 2000
Oil on canvas, 200 × 180 cm
Gerhard Richter Archive,
Staatliche Kunstsammlungen Dresden,
loan from a private collection

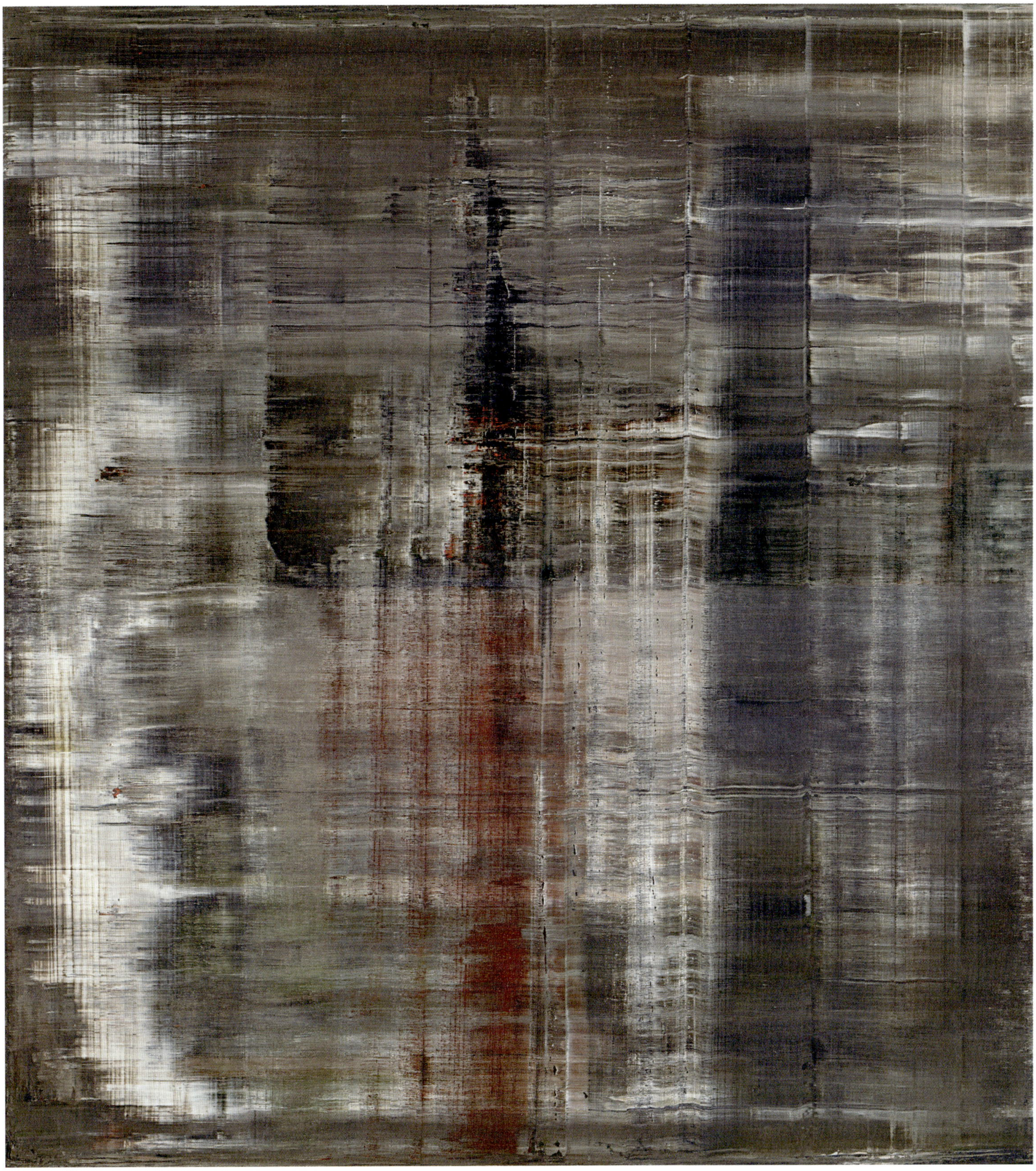

74 *Abstract Painting (Abstraktes Bild)* [889-10], 2004
Oil on canvas, 200 × 200 cm
Städtische Galerie im Lenbachhaus und Kunstbau, KiCo Collection, Munich

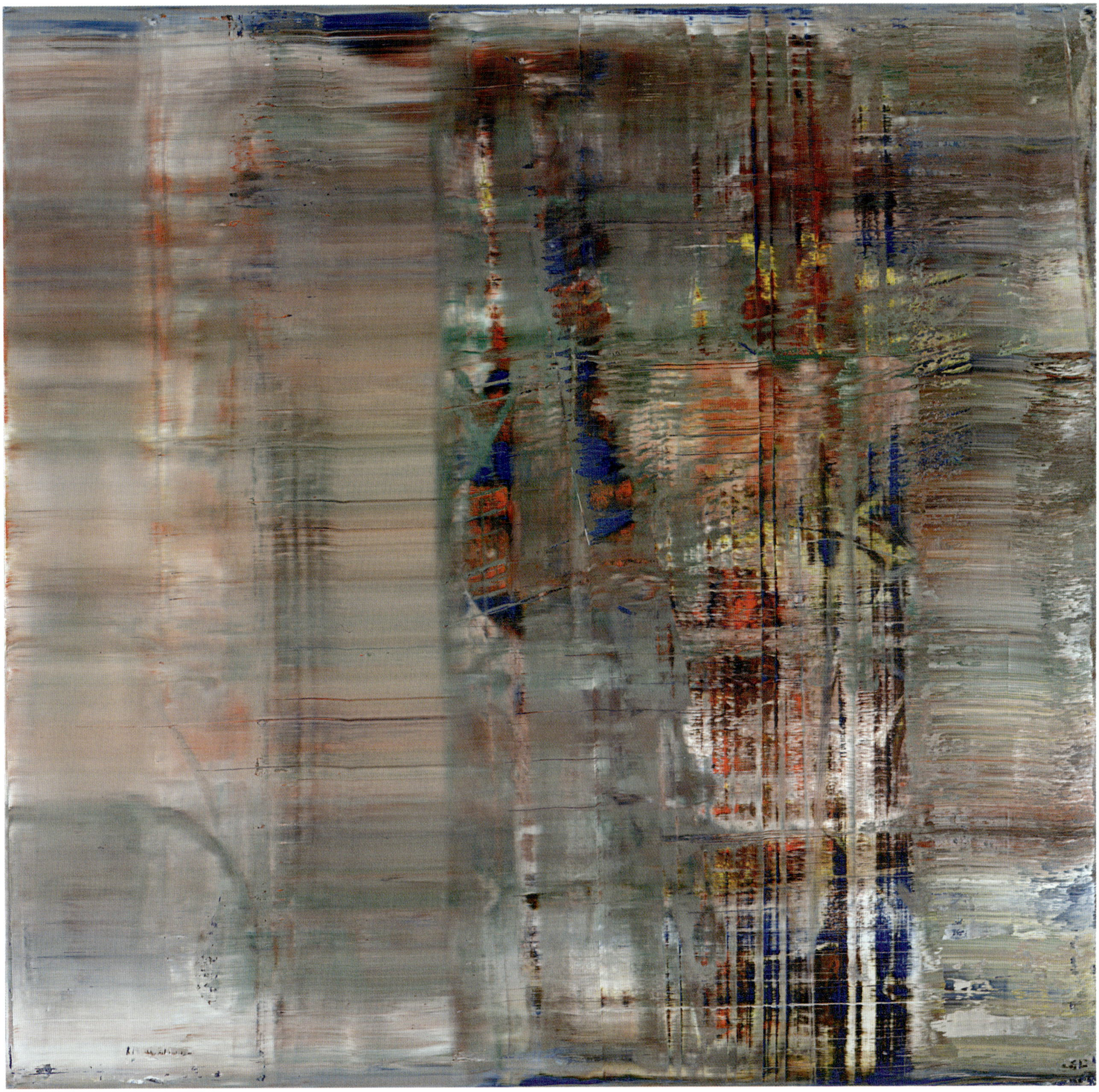

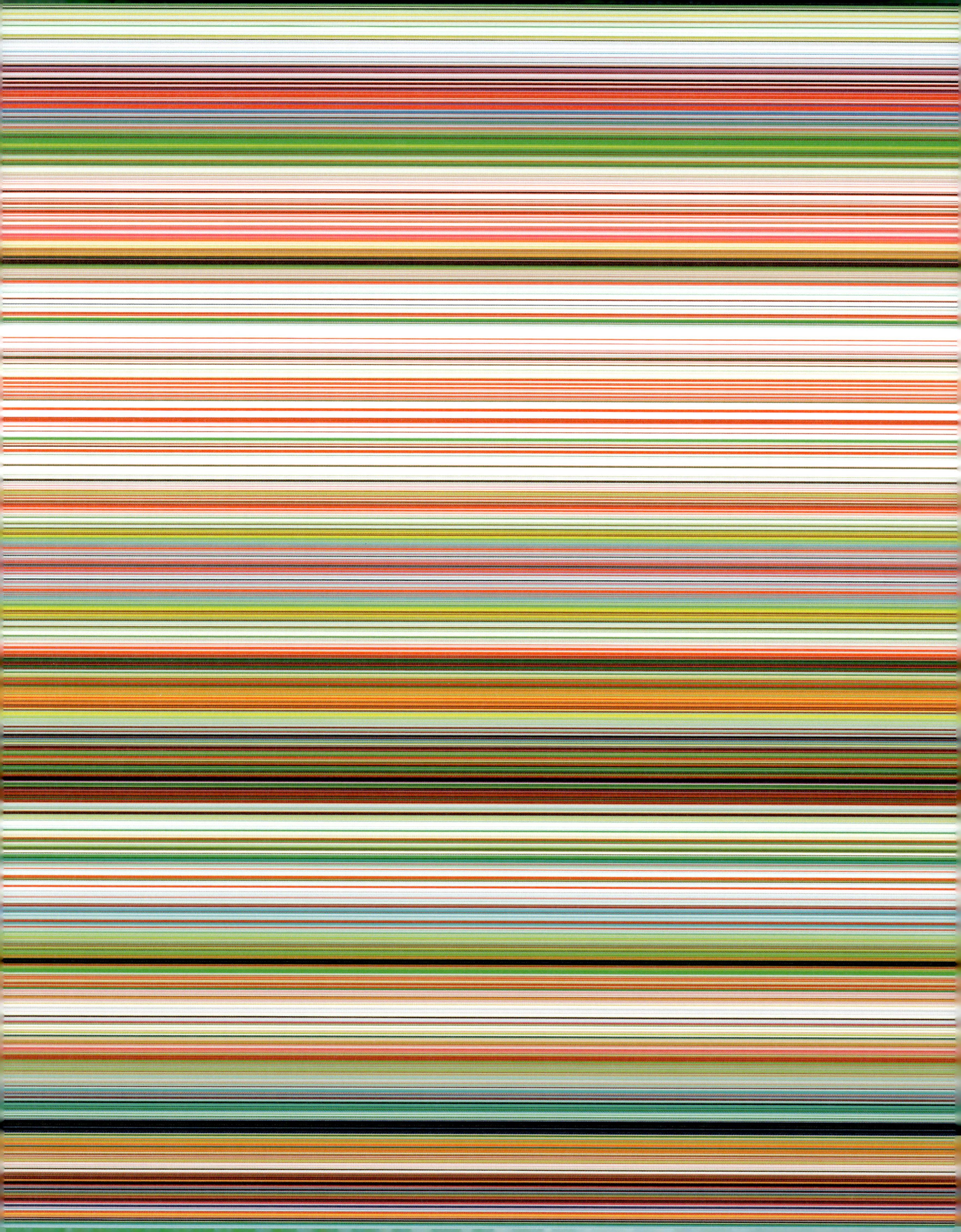

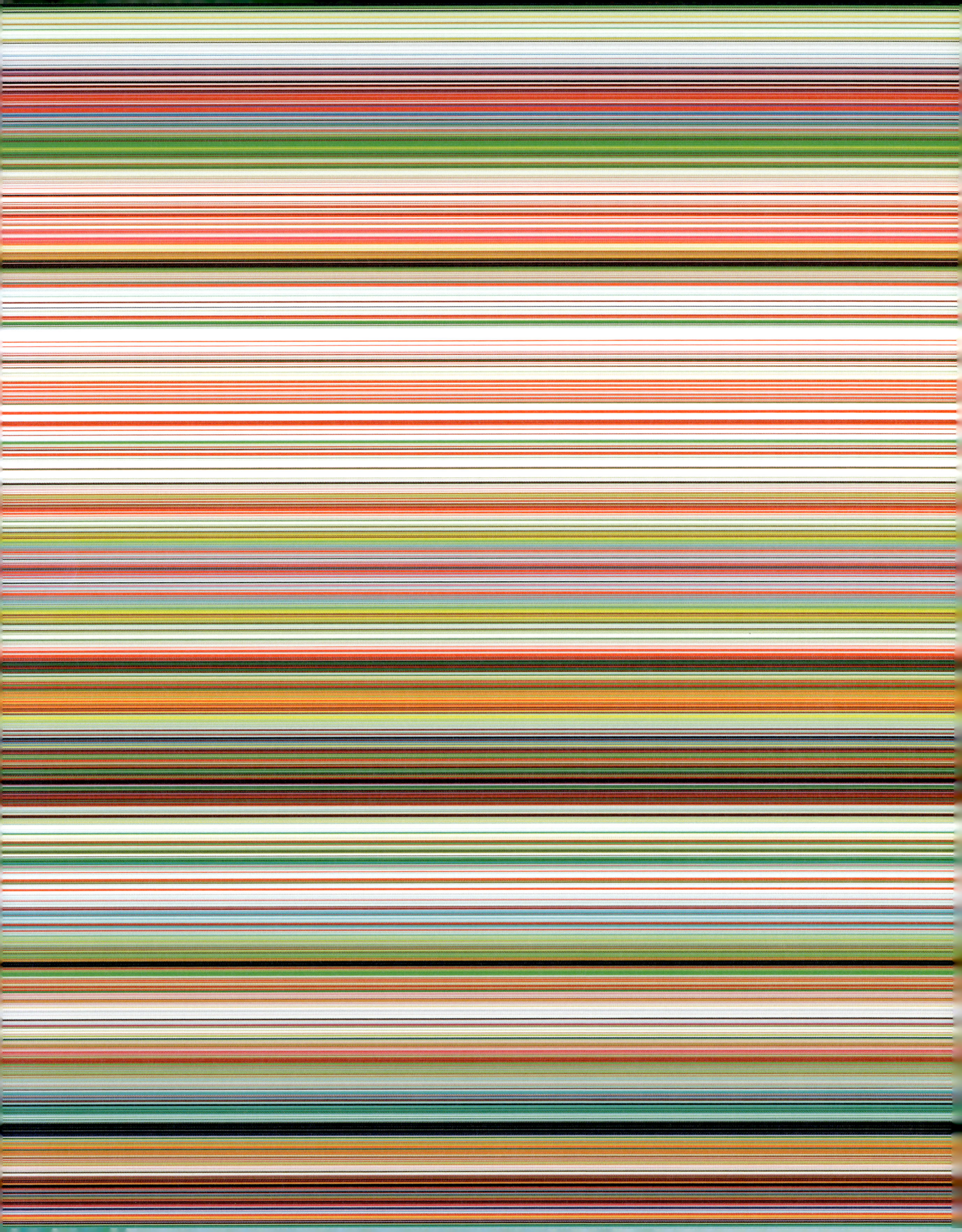

Transparent and Reflected: Mirrors, Glass, and Strips

Janice Bretz and Kerstin Küster

cat. 78

The shiny surface of a photograph was a factor in the nineteenth-century debate about photography and painting as rival media. This prompted artists such as Vincent van Gogh to adopt rough, dynamic brushwork. In Richter's versatile oeuvre, the spectrum arcs from his Gray paintings, with their focus on monochromatic textures, to Reverse-Glass paintings and sculptures made with glass panels. The latter reflect the space around them in changing ways, depending on the viewer's position and the sources of light. Glass provided Richter with another way of liberating the artwork from artistic pathos. In his Reverse-Glass works, his use of glass also achieved a greater chromatic intensity. As in his editions, his computer-generated Strips founded on tone values from an earlier Abstract painting play with the effect of a shiny surface.

"See all, grasp nothing" is the note Gerhard Richter made on a study for his first glass work in 1967. The *4 Panes of Glass* [160] (fig. p. 15) date from the same period as his realistic structural paintings (see the chapter "Structures and Illusions: Abstract Works in the 1960s," pp. 70–87). Richter showed both groups at the Heiner Friedrich gallery in Munich that same year, asking powerful questions about the representation of reality. The four panes in *4 Panes of Glass* [160] rotate individually and can come to a standstill at different angles. The image of the viewer is not simply mirrored here, but chopped into pieces and recomposed, depending on the position of the panes. Richter returned to this idea in 2013 with *7 Panes of Glass (House of Cards)* [932] (cat. 79). Like a house of cards, but with its fragility further underscored by the use of glass, the panes arranged on the floor slant toward each other, with small metal clasps fastening them to the ground and together at their few points of intersection. Although the installation—over 2.5 meters high, 6.5 meters wide, and 3.5 meters deep—occupies a large space, it nevertheless retains the lightness so vital to the artist. With its panes leaning against and partially concealing one another, the work resembles a prism. As viewers move around the work, their own images and the art on display in the room are reflected, refracted, and overlaid, creating new variations. Here, museum visitors are not spectators but creators, and they are confronted with the difference between the real exhibition space and the random reflection of reality in the glass. This difference lends the glass "house of cards" its particular quality: It is an invitation from the artist to think about seeing and what is seen as one potential reality among many. Seeing is situational, and reality always depends on the viewer.

Immediately before he produced *7 Panes of Glass (House of Cards)* [932], Richter had made numerous Strips and Reverse-Glass lacquer paintings in which he had thematized experimentation with transparency, optical illusions, and his trust in chance. The artist had already experimented with lacquer in 1985, but had destroyed the results due to his "disappointment at a kind of naturalism that was completely unusable, arty-crafty, kitschy."[1] Between 2008 and 2013, however, he picked up the idea again in his multipart series *Baghdad* [914-1 to 914-25], *Aladdin* [913-1 to 913-42], *Ifrit* [915-1 to 915-26], *Perizade* [916-1 to 916-21], *Abdallah* [917-1 to 917-100], and *Flow* [933-1 to 933-3, 934-1 to 934-18]. To make the works in this series, Richter poured various colored lacquers onto a smooth surface, spreading them now and then with a spatula. Then he abandoned the paints to their intrinsic material dynamics. Sometimes repelling, sometimes flowing into each other, they combined into unpredictable structures that were fixed at the moment the artist laid a glass plate over the paint, which he then carefully pulled back, allowed to dry, and sealed at the back with an aluminum Dibond panel. Fascinated by the independent behavior of the lacquers and the endless diversity of these pictures, Richter experimented with different formats. In reference to the image and its genesis, he called his hitherto most recent and largest Reverse-Glass paintings *Flow* [933-2 and 933-3] (cat. 76, 77). However, as each work measured 100 × 200 cm, he had to cut the glass in half to remove the paintings from the support without damaging them. There is something inherently mysterious about Richter's abstract Reverse-Glass paintings. They resemble agates or aerial views of the Earth (see the chapter "Nature and Materials: Abstract Landscapes," pp. 146–67). In 2008, the artist described this tendency to seek something identifiable in the nonfigurative: "As we do with every other image, every view, we examine it for resemblances to things and circumstances that we're familiar with and remember"[2] (see the essay by Dietmar Elger, pp. 22–33).

Richter's Strips defy every effort to detect a motif. They were made between 2011 and 2013, and, like the Reverse-Glass paintings, they were produced in various formats. The meticulous paper prints placed between plexiglass and aluminum Dibond reveal hardly anything of their creation process. All the Strips originated from the colorful small *Abstract Painting* [724-4] of 1990 (cat. 67). Richter had the 92 × 126 cm canvas scanned and then digitally modified, applying the principle "divide—mirror—repeat." The abstract template was divided along a longitudinal axis, then each half was separately mirrored and repeated. One picture was thus translated into two new abstract variations. After the vertical quartering of *Abstract Painting* [724-4] and the mirroring and repeating of the four picture segments, the works became reminiscent of the patterns in a kaleidoscope with their tiny, ornamental structures. As in his early Color Charts, Richter proceeded in powers of two: 2, 4, 8, 16, 32, and so on up to 4,096 (see the essay by Hubertus Butin, pp. 34–45, and the chapter "Chance and Concept: Color Charts," pp. 88–103). The computer-generated division of *Abstract Painting* [724-4] into 4,096 parts resulted in thin vertical 0.08 mm strips composed of single columns of colored pixels. Each vertical strip was mirrored and repeated multiple times, resulting in a Strip painting. The artistic impetus for the work lies in the original motif and the painter's involvement in cutting the sample printouts in his studio, rearranging the stripes, and choosing the size of the reproduction. As they take shape, Richter's Strips oscillate between rational mathematics and artistic curiosity. The outcome is needle-sharp, with precise colors and forms. As we step closer to these works, such as the ten-meter-long *Strip* [930-4] of 2013/2016 (cat. 78), they completely fill our field of vision, and the strips seem to move. With the technical perfection of his printed Strips, Gerhard Richter pushes the human faculty of sight to its physical limit and, just as he did in the late 1960s, interrogates seeing as perception and the medium of the image as a representation of reality.

Translated from the German by Kate Vanovitch

1 Gerhard Richter, "Notes" (1985), in Richter 2009, 140–44, here 141.

2 Gerhard Richter, "Abstrakte Bilder müssen eine Richtigkeit haben. Gerhard Richter im Gespräch mit Ulrich Wilmes," in Wilmes 2009, 45–55, here 49.

75 *Mirror, Gray (Spiegel, grau)* [735-3], 1991
Pigment on glass, framed, 280 × 165 cm
Private collection

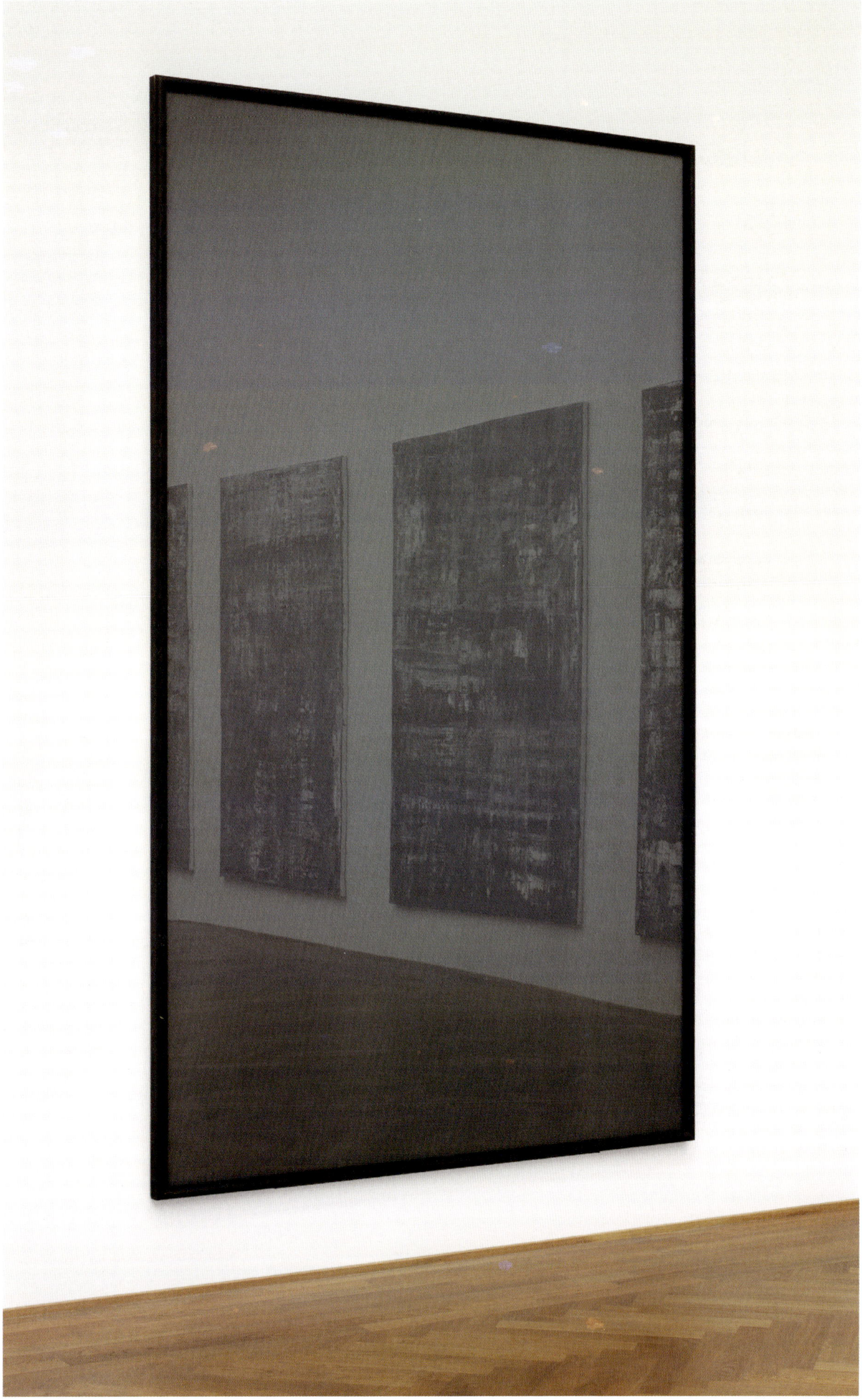

76 *Flow*, 2013/2016
Digital print on paper between glass and aluminum Dibond,
100 × 200 cm
Private collection

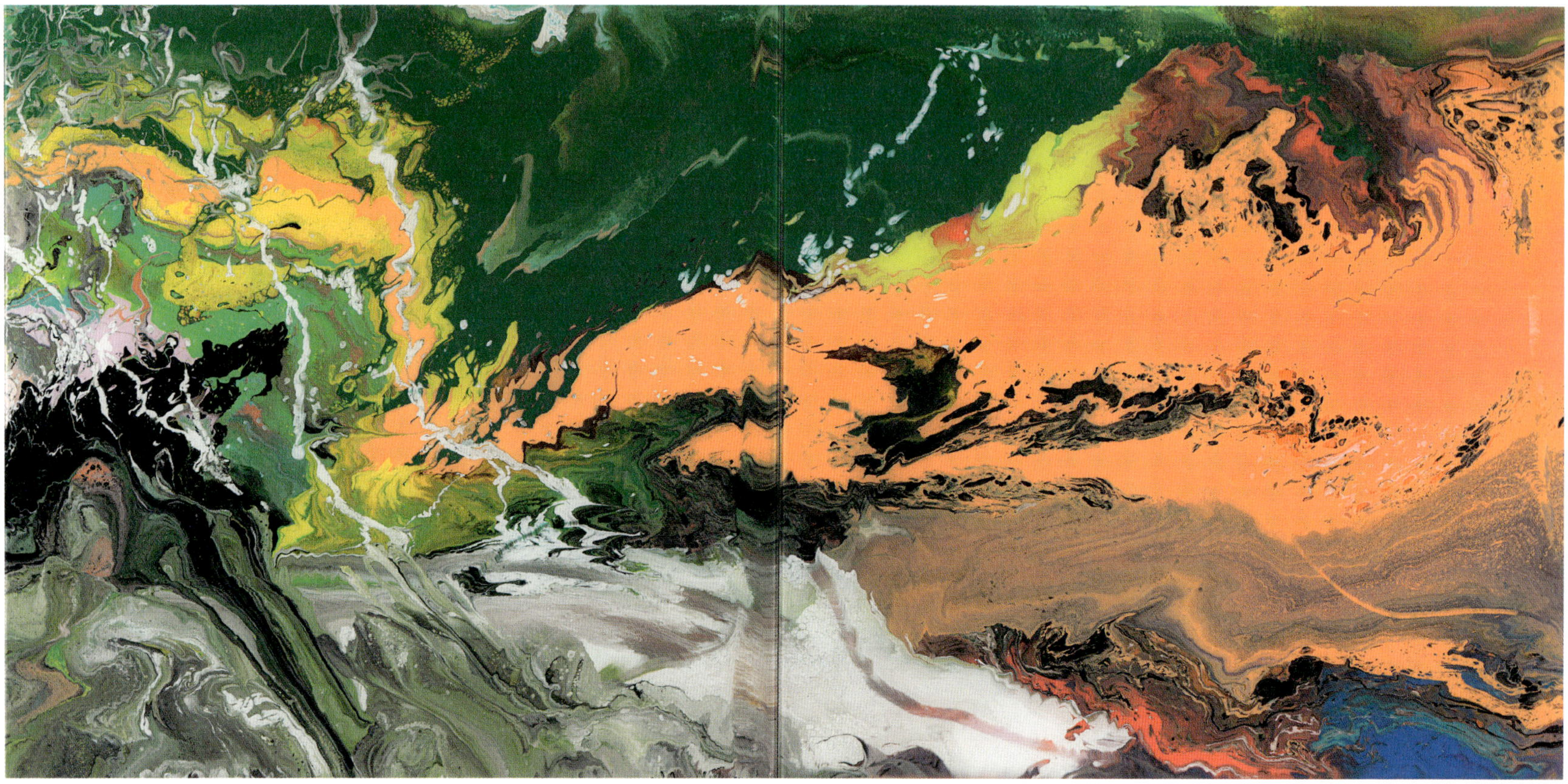

77 *Flow* [933-3], 2013
Lacquer on glass mounted on aluminum Dibond,
100 × 200 cm
Private collection

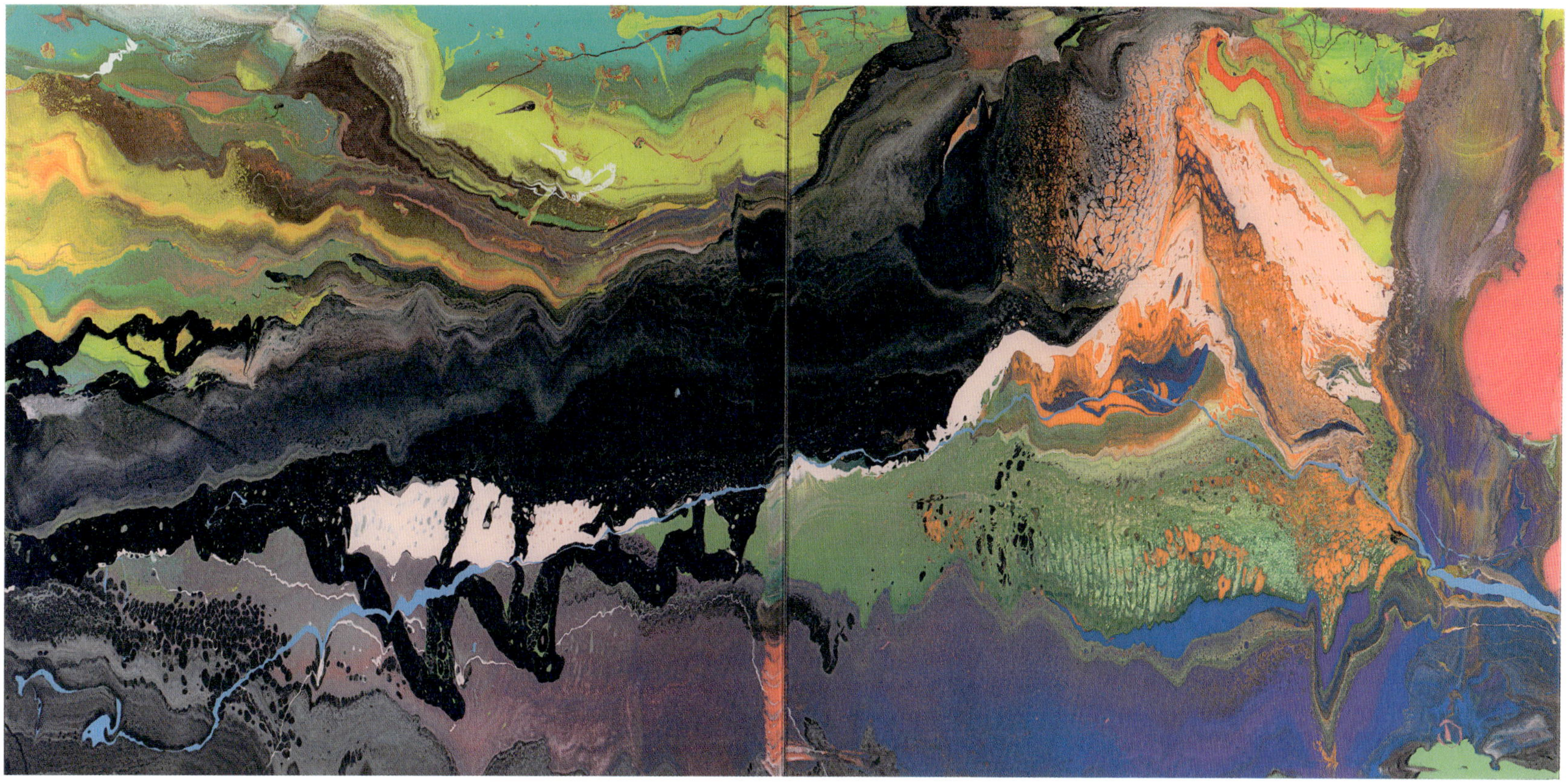

78 *Strip* [930-4], 2013/2016
Digital print on paper between aluminum Dibond and plexiglass,
200 × 1,000 cm (four panels at 200 × 250 cm each)
Private collection

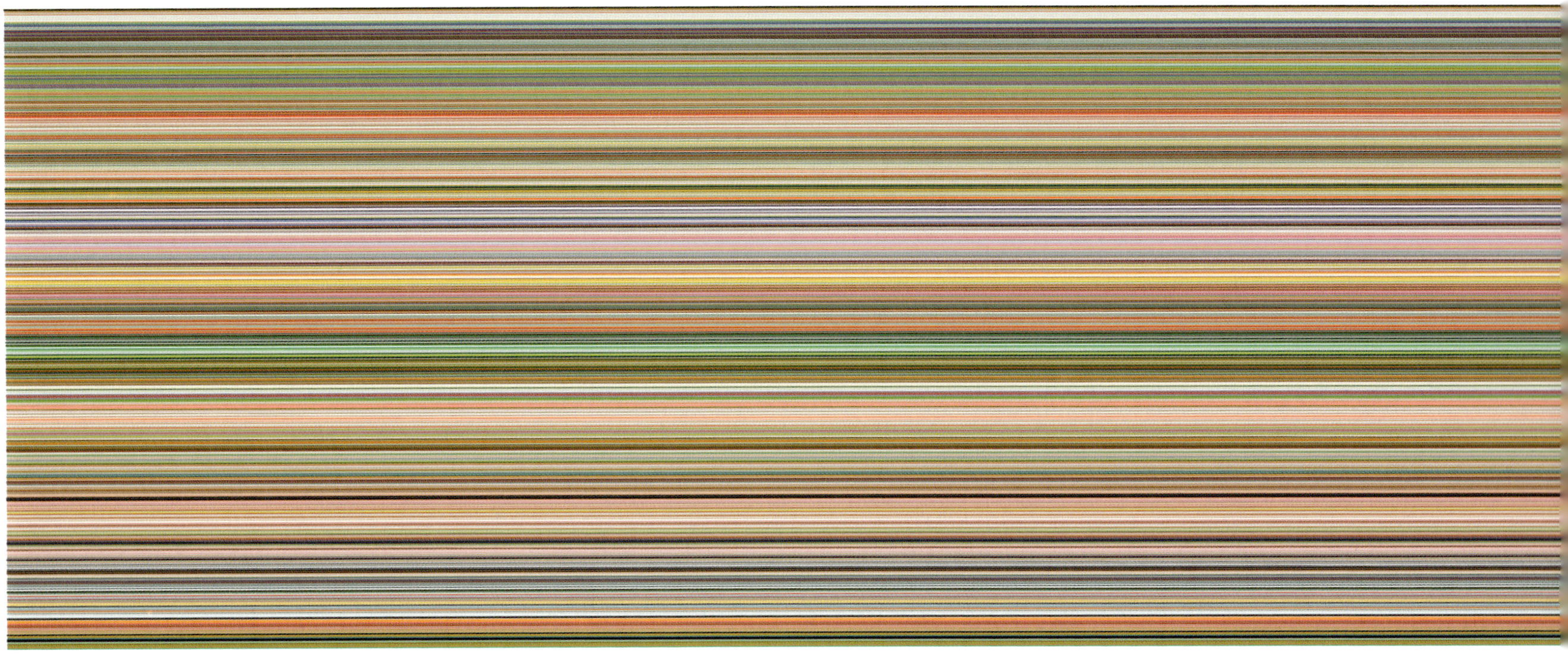

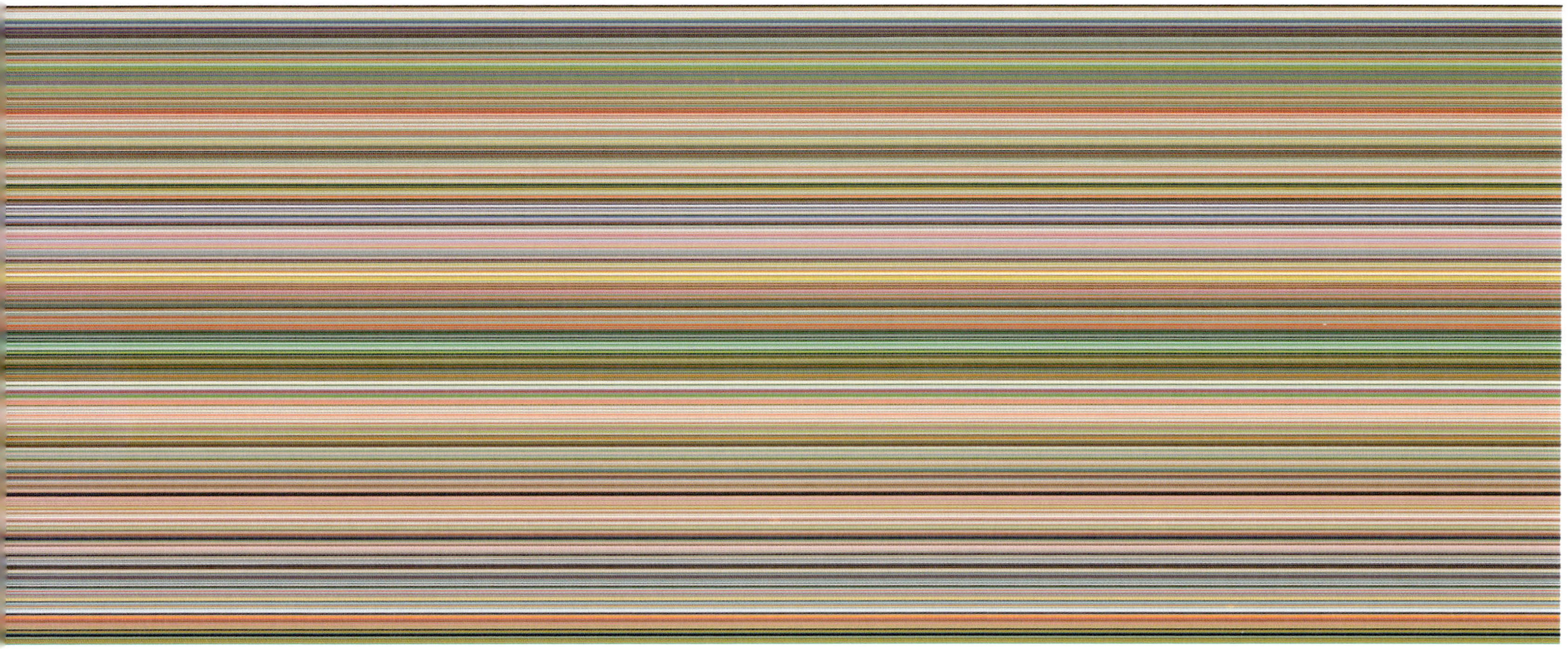

79 *7 Panes of Glass (House of Cards) (7 Scheiben [Kartenhaus])* [932], 2013
Glass and steel construction,
seven glass panes, 270 × 180 cm each,
257 × 650 × 360 cm in total
Private collection

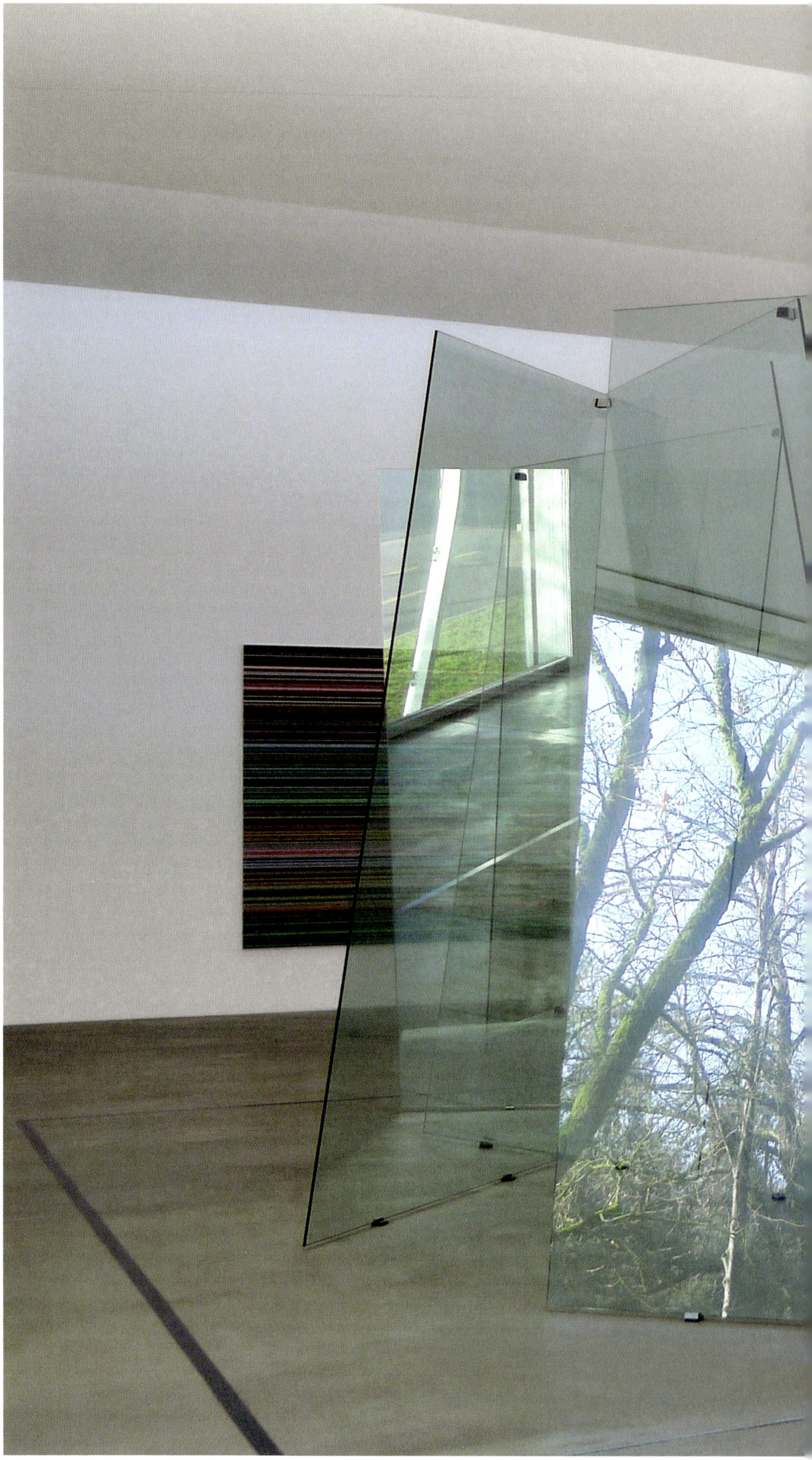

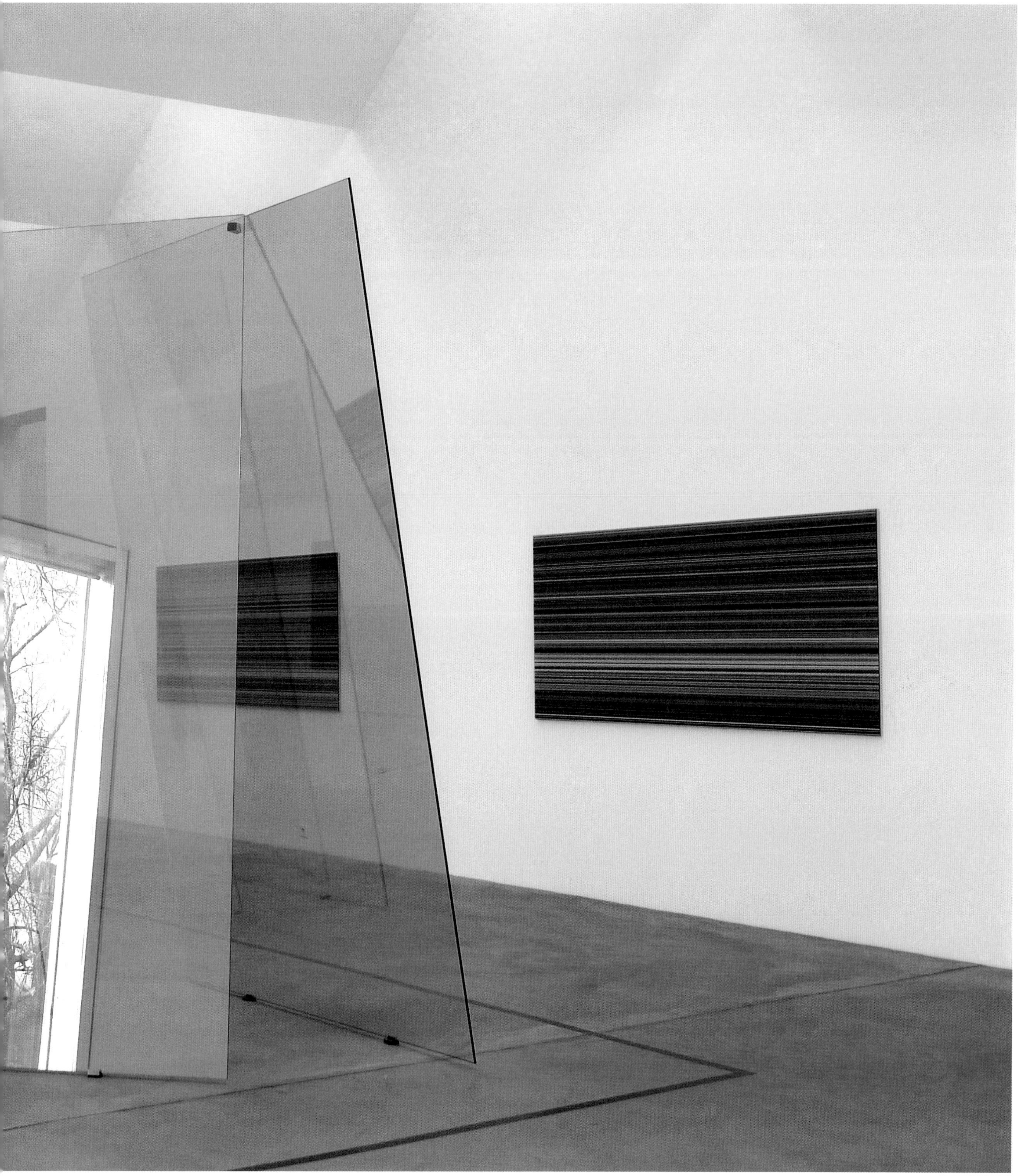

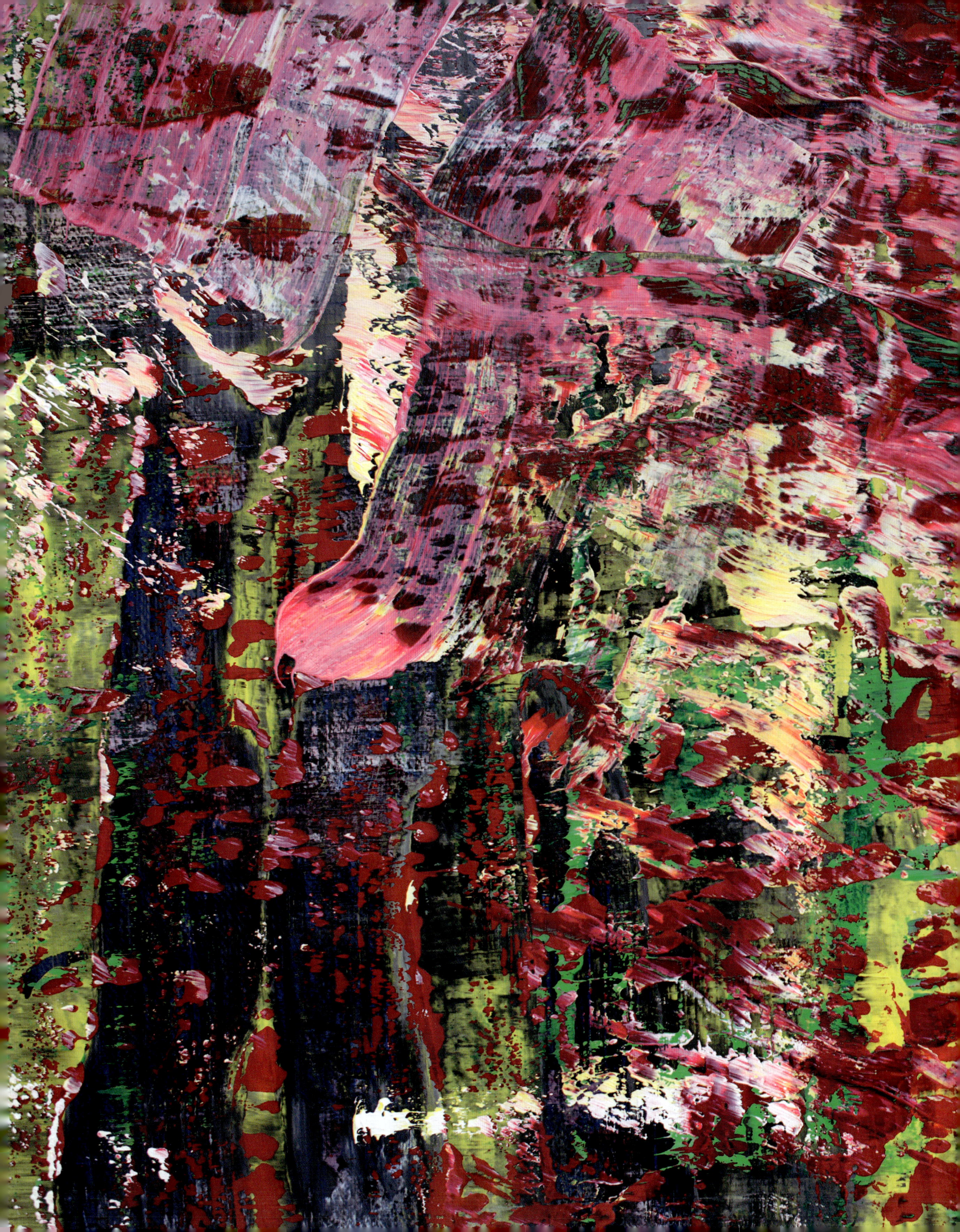

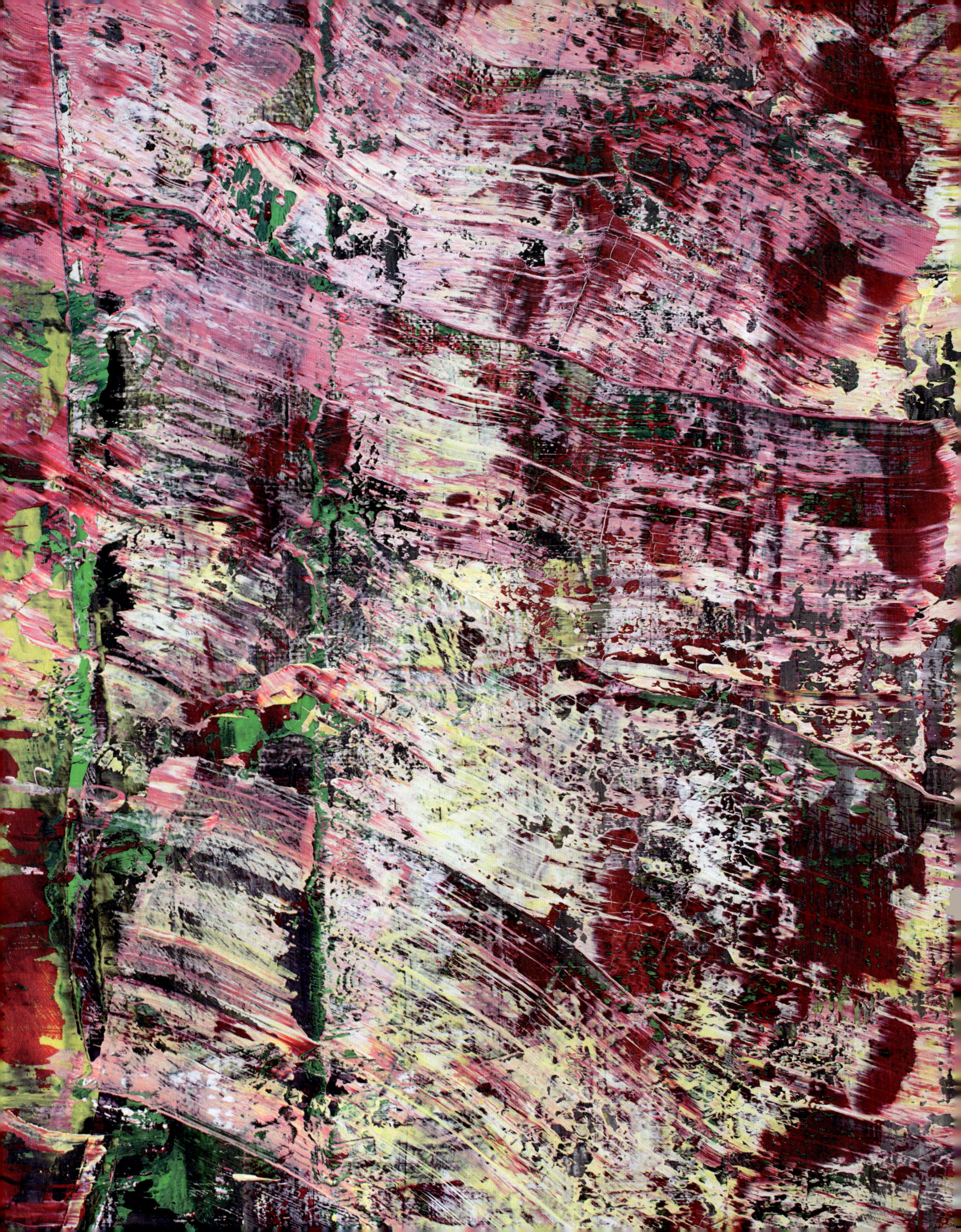

New Abstract Paintings from 2005 to 2017

Kerstin Küster

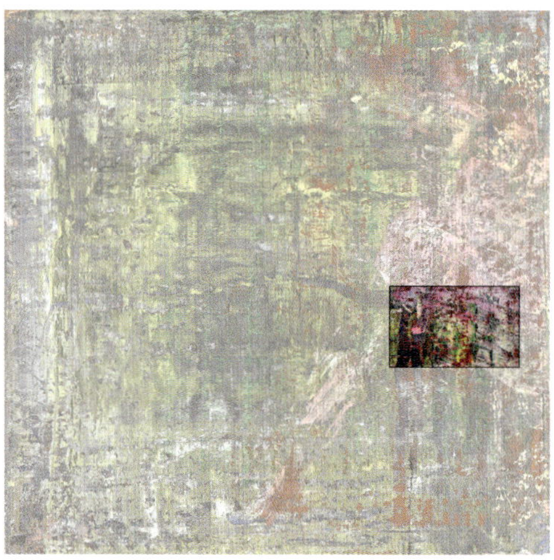

cat. 85

Richter's latest works advance the principles underlying his Abstract paintings. By layering and overpainting motifs, some taken from photographs, he extends the duration of the painting process. The formats are more varied here, as the artist experiments with different supports and tools. The vivid colors incorporate his experience making his Strips and Reverse-Glass paintings. He uses new painting tools to create a vibrant surface, making the colors shimmer and endowing his pictures with a quality of lightness. These recent paintings confirm that Richter never ceases to revisit and develop his artistic ideas and methods.

Between 2005 and 2009, Gerhard Richter painted the series *Forest* [892-1 to 892-12] (The Museum of Modern Art, New York) and *Cage* [879-1 to 879-6] (Tate Modern, London), as well as many nearly monochromatic white Abstract paintings distinguished by a sense of hermetically sealed self-containment. In 2011, the director Corinna Belz captured the protracted process of creating these Abstract paintings in her documentary film *Gerhard Richter Painting* (figs. p. 61).[1] It was during this period that Richter also produced the monumental *Cologne Cathedral Window* [900] (2007, fig. p. 44), turning to digital image processing for the first time. From 2008 onward, he turned away from painting on canvas almost entirely, instead experimenting with lacquer in the Reverse-Glass paintings (cat. 76, 77) and with digital techniques in the Strips (cat. 78) (see the chapter "Transparent and Reflected: Mirror, Glass, and Strips," pp. 194–207).

It was not until 2014 that Richter returned to his brush and squeegee and resumed working on canvas in his studio. In the cycle of paintings titled *Birkenau* [937-1 to 937-4] (private collection), Richter grappled with the Holocaust. He transferred four photographs taken by a Jewish prisoner at the Auschwitz-Birkenau concentration camp in August 1944 onto four canvases, each one measuring 260 × 200 cm. These documentary photographs became better known in Germany in 2007, when Georges Didi-Huberman published them in the German edition of his book *Images in Spite of All*.[2] After Richter had finished three realistic paintings, he squeegeed over the canvases. With each additional layer, the motifs shifted into the background until they disappeared entirely beneath a gloomy, abstract carpet of color given rhythm by flashes of contrasting red and green. These paintings are a continuation of Richter's explorations of the crimes of National Socialism begun in the early 1960s—an exploration that is an enduring personal need of his.[3]

Immediately after completing the *Birkenau* cycle, Richter turned to a less highly charged, simply more "beautiful" theme, which he discovered in landscapes. For Richter, landscape painting has always been connected with a sense of longing.[4] He produced two seascapes based on personal vacation photographs, painting the coastal motif, with its dark surf, low-lying horizon, and overcast gray sky, on 144 × 220 cm canvases in a realistically somber, diffuse painterly manner. As with the *Birkenau* paintings, he covered the realistic motif by squeegeeing over it almost completely. Only a vague horizon line and the ghost of a landscape in the *Abstract Paintings* [943-1] (cat. 80) and [943-2] (cat. 81) recall the original compositions. In contrast to *Birkenau*, Richter's choice of color and his method of applying paint are livelier in these paintings. In the *Abstract Painting* [943-1], the complementary colors of yellow and purple directly collide with each other (cat. 80). In the *Abstract Painting* [943-2], vertical and horizontal layers of red, yellow, and green combine to produce a luminous, open structure (cat. 81).

The abstract groups of works produced since then are distinguished by a dynamic surface that suggests a sense of ease. Intense colors, along with a complex fabric made up of layers of paint and traces of the painting process, define their impact. Richter experimented with sizes, techniques, grounds, and paint, which he varied in terms of coloration and texture. He went back to tried and true painting tools, but used them more freely in the painting process. He painted on wood, aluminum, and canvas, working on supports whose dimensions ranged from 50 × 50 to 200 × 200 cm. He guided the squeegee only to a limited extent, and applied it in random directions across the picture surface. He used the brush to apply trenchant lineature onto the surfaces of his paintings. A new technique was his use of a kitchen knife, employing its sharp blade to scrape off the paint down to the canvas as in the *Abstract Paintings* [950-3] and [950-4] from 2017 (cat. 83, 84). The painting style itself is impasto, which is unusual for Richter. He employed the squeegee in different directions in the four corners of the canvases and applied variable pressure. Thus the paintings feature blurred, layered, and scraped sections, bringing together techniques from earlier abstract series of works (see the chapter "Paints and Layers: Abstract Paintings from 1986 to 2005," pp. 168–95). The dynamic colors of the Reverse-Glass paintings (cat. 76, 77) are also echoed here. Like the earlier Abstract paintings, the most recent examples allow for an intense sensory experience.

Translated from the German by Allison Moseley

1 See Belz 2011.
2 Georges Didi-Hubermann, *Images in Spite of All: Four Photographs from Auschwitz* (Chicago: University of Chicago Press, 2012). Originally published in French as *Images malgré tout* (Paris: Les Éditions de Minuit, 2003). Published in German as *Bilder trotz allem* (Munich: Wilhelm Fink Verlag, 2007).
3 Buchloh 2016.
4 Gerhard Richter, "Interview with Dorothea Dietrich" (1985), in Richter 2009, 145–58.

80 *Abstract Painting (Abstraktes Bild)* [943-1], 2016
Oil on canvas, 144 × 220 cm
Private collection

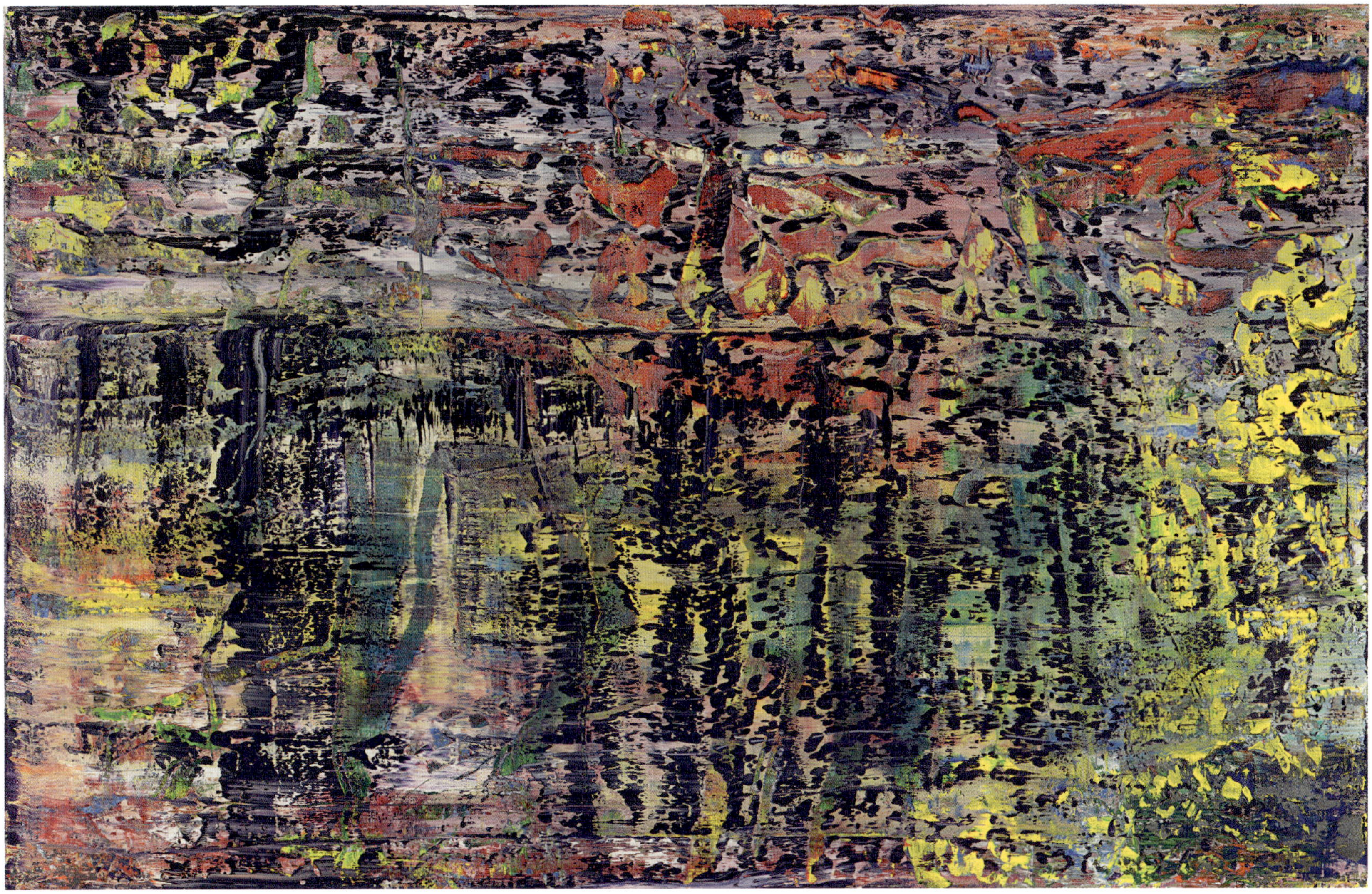

81 *Abstract Painting (Abstraktes Bild)* [943-2], 2016
Oil on canvas, 144 × 220 cm
Gion Collection, Japan,
Courtesy of Wako Works of Art

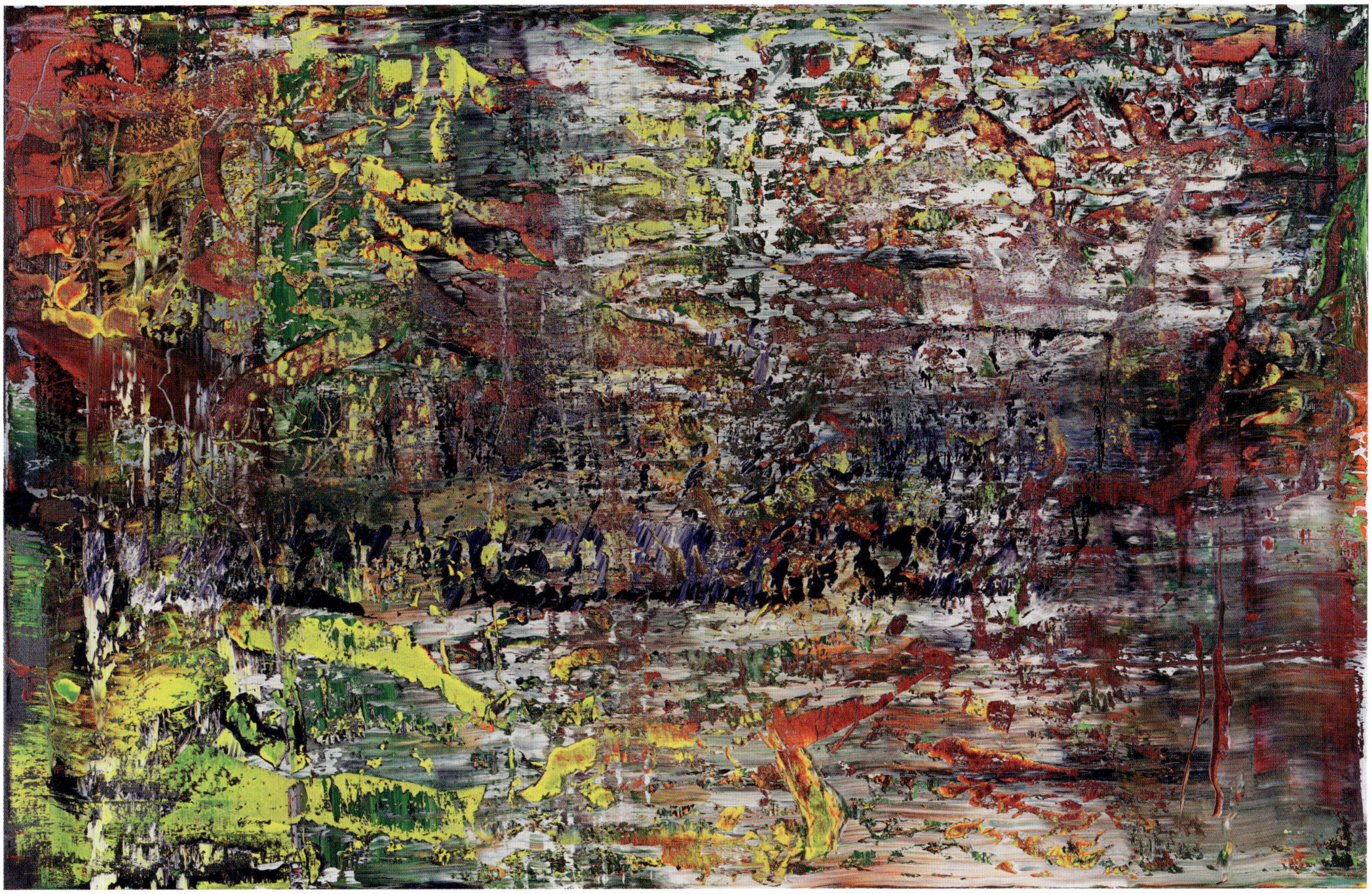

82 *Abstract Painting (Abstraktes Bild)* [946-3], 2016
Oil on canvas, 175 × 250 cm
Private collection

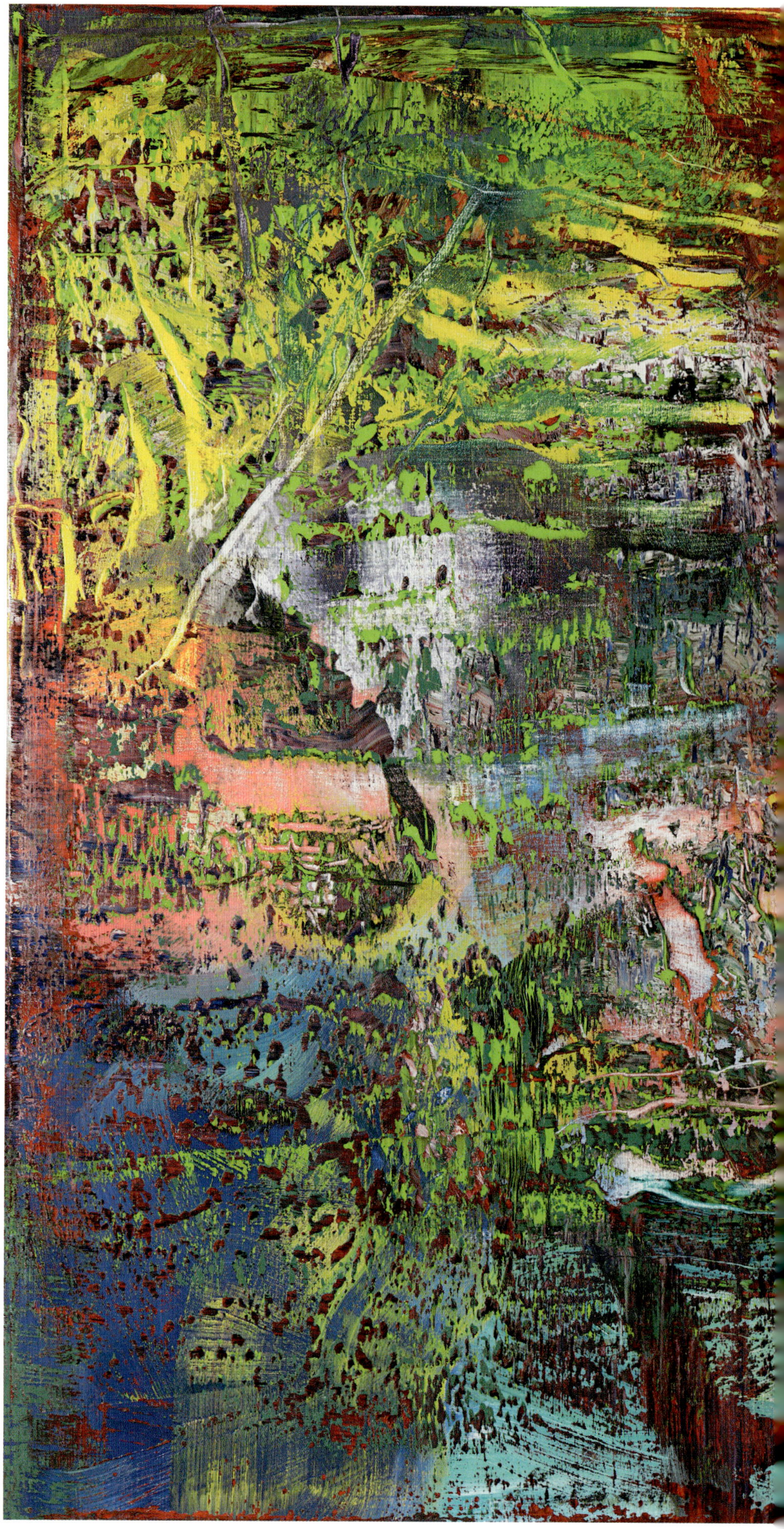

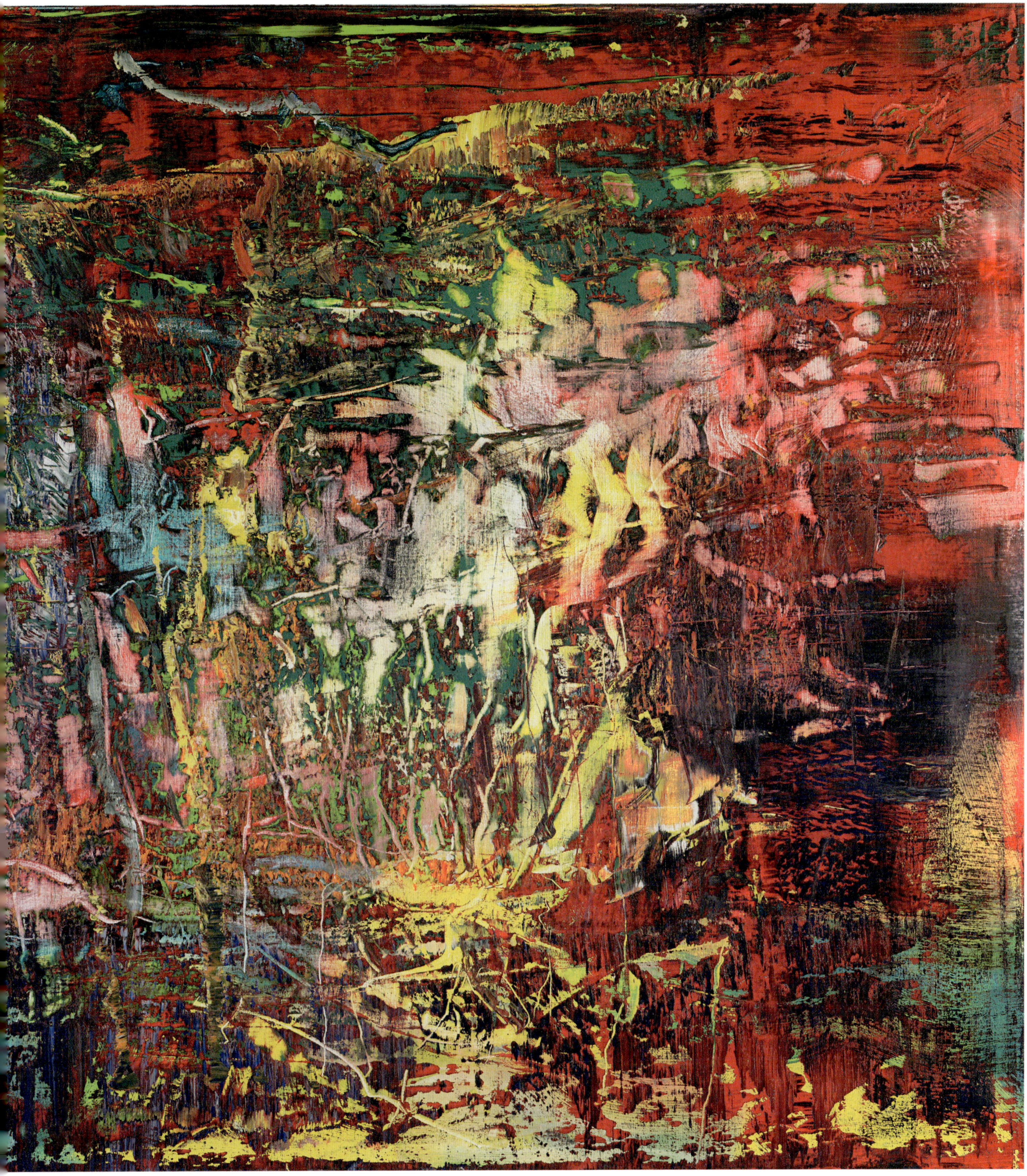

83 *Abstract Painting (Abstraktes Bild)* [950-3], 2017
Oil on canvas, 120 × 120 cm
Private collection

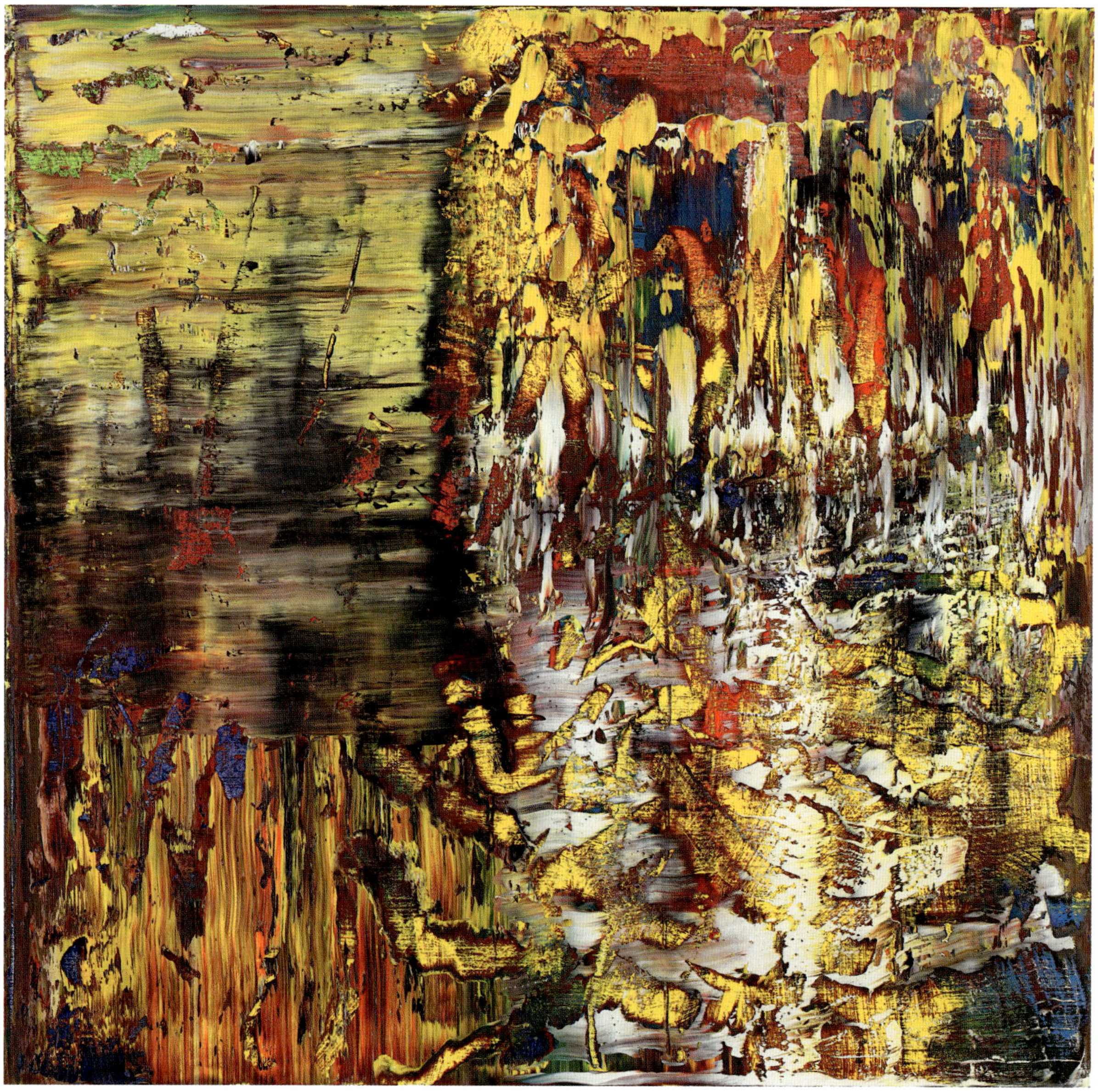

84 *Abstract Painting (Abstraktes Bild)* [950-4], 2017
Oil on canvas, 120 × 120 cm
Private collection

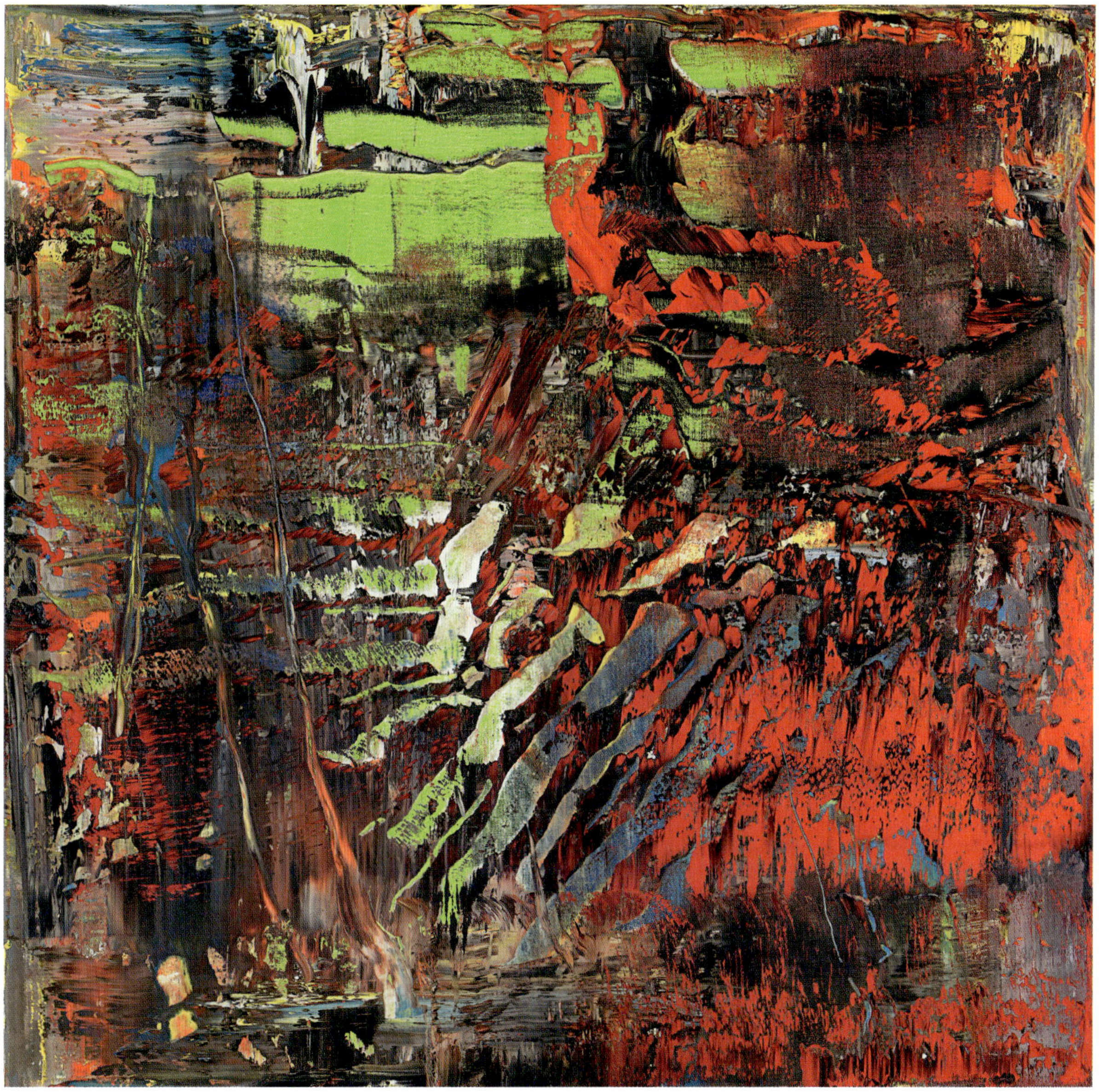

85 *Abstract Painting (Abstraktes Bild)* [952-2], 2017
Oil on canvas, 200 × 200 cm
Private collection

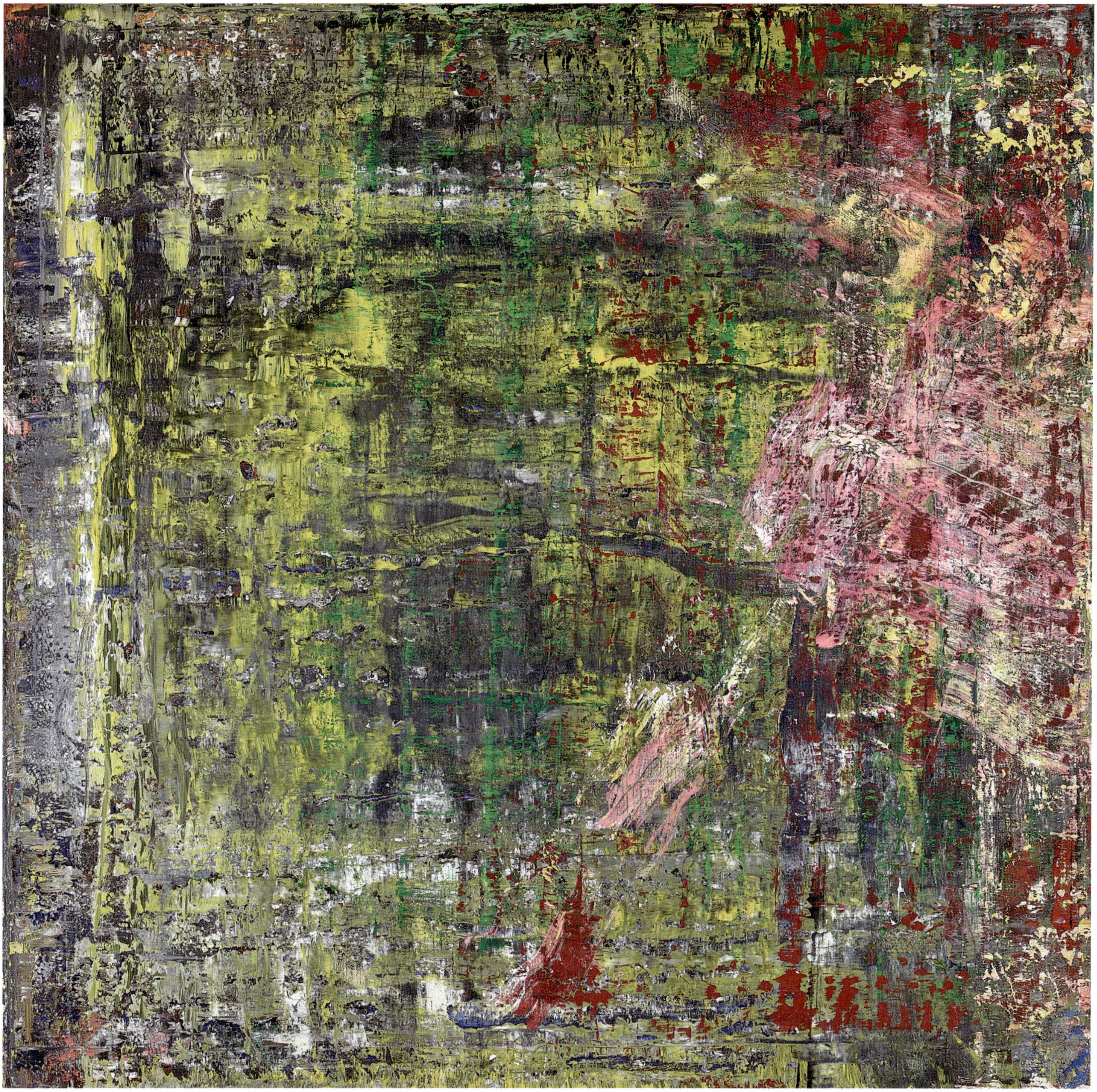

86 *Abstract Painting (Abstraktes Bild)* [952-3], 2017
Oil on canvas, 200 × 200 cm
Private collection

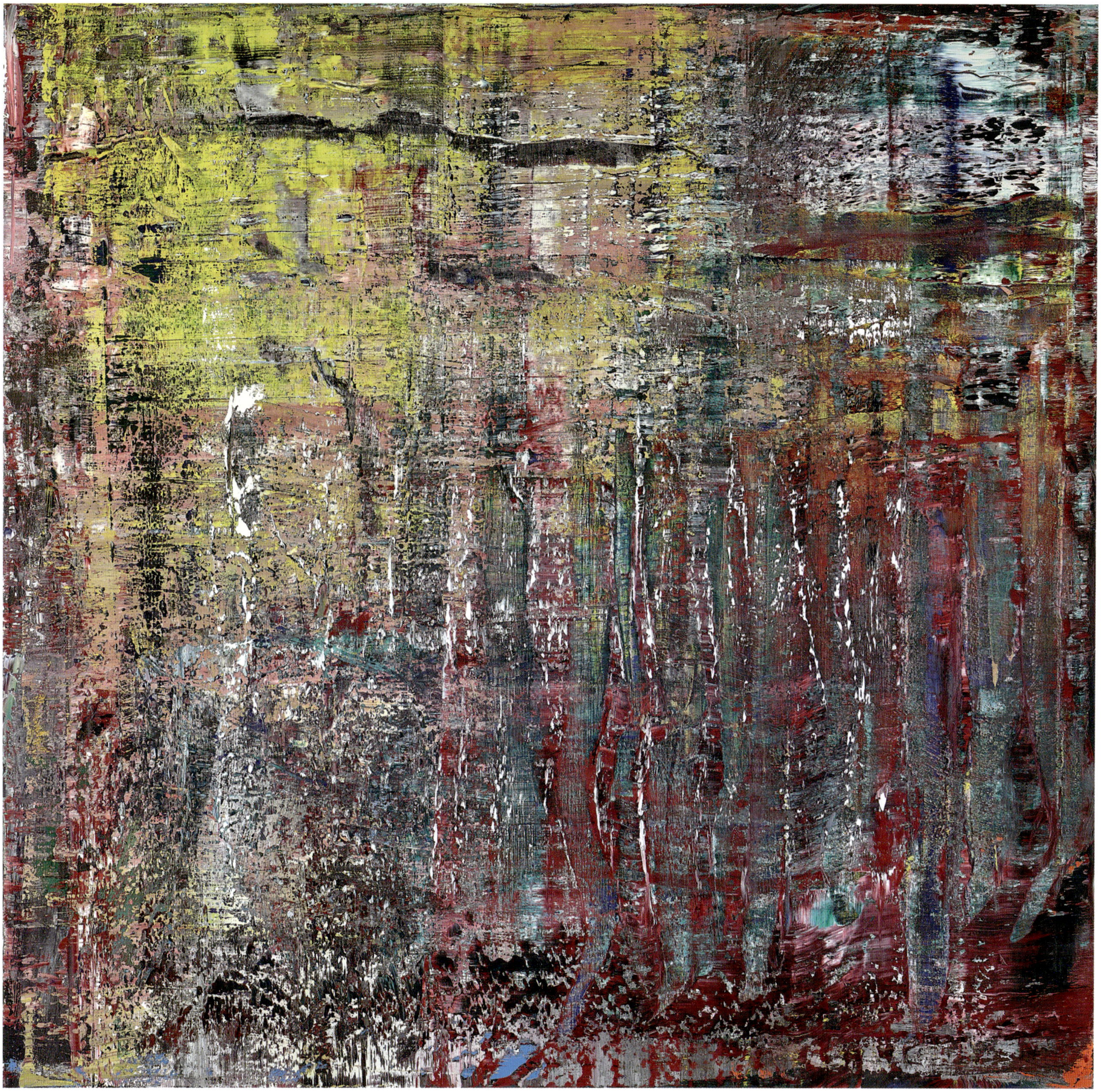

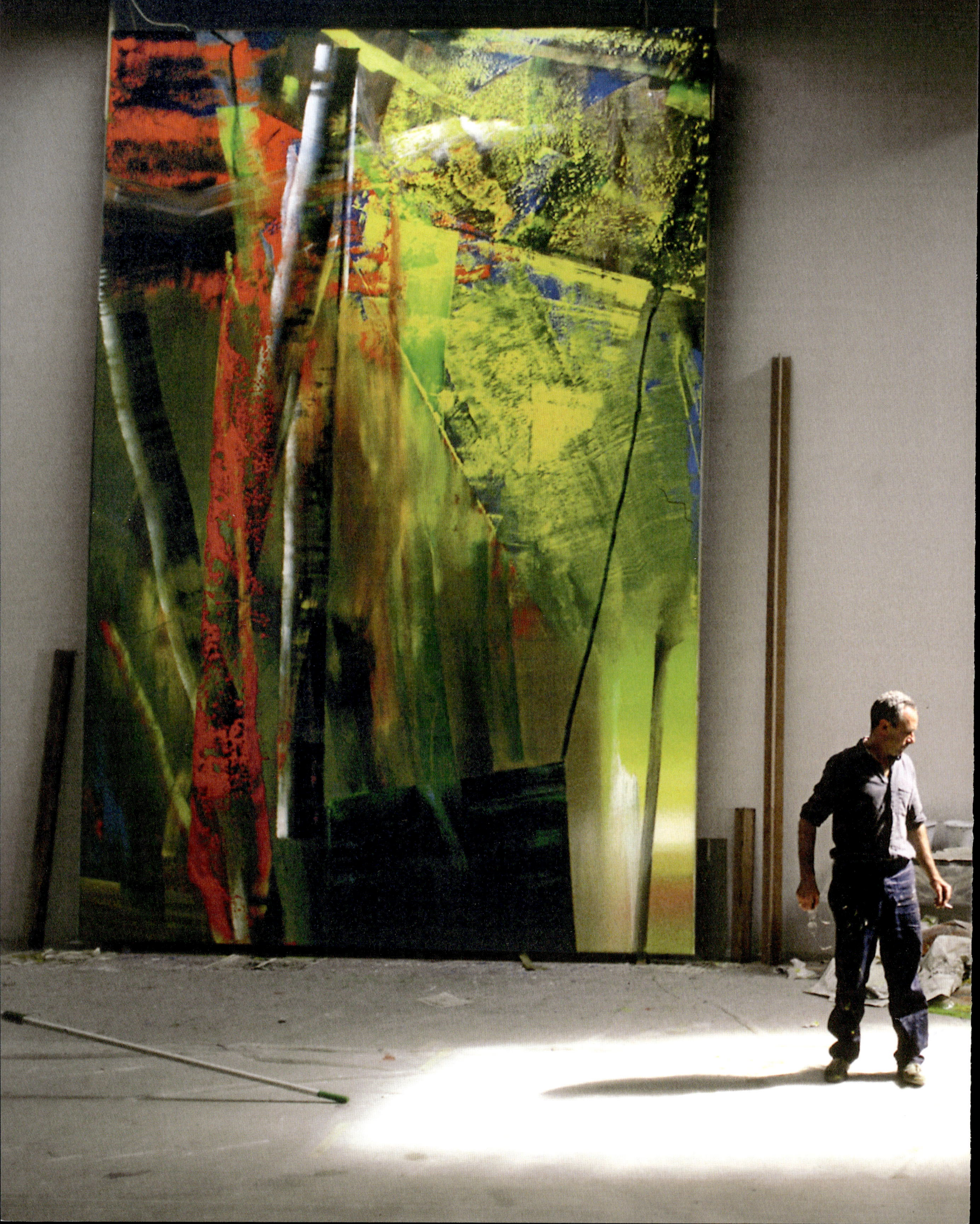

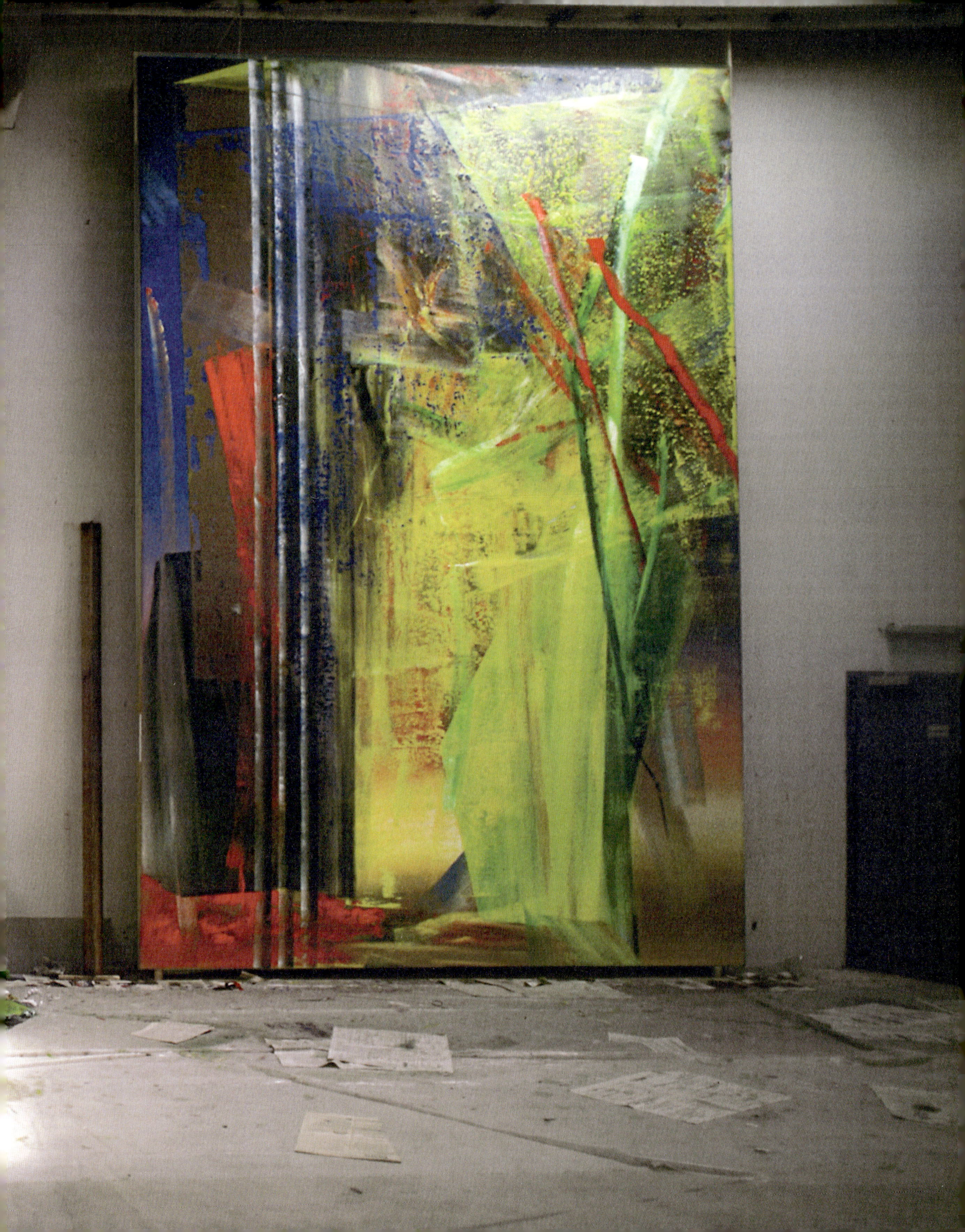

Biography of Gerhard Richter

Previous pages:
Timm Rautert: *Gerhard Richter, Düsseldorf 1986*
The artist working on his paintings *Victoria I* [601] and *Victoria II* [602]
Courtesy of Parrotta Contemporary Art, Cologne

1932 Gerhard Richter is born in Dresden on February 9.
He grows up in Reichenau (now Bogatynia, Poland) and Waltersdorf in Upper Lusatia, Saxony.

1939 His father Horst Richter is called up to the German army. After serving for years on both the Eastern and Western fronts, he is taken prisoner and later released in August 1945.

1944–45 Richter produces his first works of art, writes poetry, and takes photographs.

1946 For financial reasons, Richter has to leave his high school in Zittau, which would have prepared him for an advanced school certificate. He briefly attends a combined elementary/intermediate school in Waltersdorf and then a trade school in Zittau from September.

1948–49 He completes his schooling in Zittau with a basic high school certificate.
Richter paints signs for an advertising office in Zittau.

1950 Begins training as a set painter at Zittau's municipal theater.
Richter applies to the Dresden Academy of Fine Arts for admission to the winter semester of 1950–51 but is rejected.
Employed as a painter by DEWAG Werbung, a state-owned advertising company in Zittau.

1951 Richter applies to Dresden Academy of Fine Arts for the second time and is accepted. He begins his studies in the winter semester (fig. 1).
At the Academy he meets his first wife, Marianne (Ema) Eufinger, who is studying fashion.

1953 After completing the foundation course, Richter switches to the mural class taught by Professor Heinz Lohmar in the winter semester of 1953–54.

1955 Begins the two-semester diploma course.
Richter visits West Germany (Hamburg and Munich) for the first time and also travels to Paris.

1956 As his graduation piece he paints the mural *Joy of Life* at the German Hygiene Museum in Dresden. This has now been painted over.

1957 Richter begins a three-year postgraduate course, which comes with a studio at the Academy and a monthly stipend.
He receives various state commissions and takes part in his first exhibitions. Alongside this he produces independent works, such as the monotype series *Elbe* (cat. 47).
Marries Marianne (Ema) Eufinger in Lower Saxony (West Germany), where his in-laws live.

1958 Richter paints a mural for the Dresden district headquarters of the Socialist Unity Party (SED). The theme is the struggle of the working class.
Visits the World's Fair in Brussels.

1959 While visiting his in-laws on holiday, Richter travels to Kassel to see II. documenta. He is struck by the work of Jackson Pollock (fig. p. 61), Lucio Fontana, and Giorgio Morandi (fig. p. 15), and he produces his first informalist works, which he later destroys.

1961 Research trip to Moscow and Leningrad.
In late March, Richter leaves Dresden and moves to West Germany with his wife Ema. They make their home in Düsseldorf, where Richter is admitted to the class taught by Professor Ferdinand Macketanz at the Düsseldorf Art Academy.

1962 In Düsseldorf Richter meets the artists Manfred Kuttner, Konrad Lueg (who later became successful as a gallerist under his real surname, Fischer), and Sigmar Polke.
In the summer semester he transfers to the class taught by Karl Otto Götz (figs. pp. 10, 62).
Richter paints his first works based on photographs found in illustrated magazines. *Table* (figs. pp. 10, 24), later becomes the first piece in his personal catalogue raisonné.
In June he attends the "NEO-DADA in Music" concert performed by Nam June Paik at the Kammerspiele in Düsseldorf.
Galerie Junge Kunst in Fulda hosts Richter's first show of works produced in the West in a joint exhibition with Kuttner.
He visits the Venice Biennale.

1963 In February Richter visits the "Festum Fluxorum Fluxus" organized by Joseph Beuys at the Düsseldorf Art Academy.
He meets Blinky Palermo at the Art Academy.
His first self-staged exhibition, together with Kuttner, Lueg, and Polke, in an empty shop on Kaiserstraße 31A in Düsseldorf, where they coin the term "capitalist realism."
In summer Richter and Lueg travel to Paris and present themselves as German pop artists to leading gallery managers Ileana Sonnabend and Iris Clert.

In October Richter and Lueg stage the show *Living with Pop—A Demonstration for Capitalist Realism* (Leben mit Pop – eine Demonstration für den kapitalistischen Realismus) in the Berges furniture store in Düsseldorf, exhibiting themselves and their works.

1964 The first Curtain paintings (fig. 3, cat. 1, 2).
In February Richter, Kuttner, Lueg, and Polke show their work to Rudolf Jährling, who runs Galerie Parnass in Wuppertal, in what becomes known as the *Front Garden Exhibition* (Vorgartenausstellung) (fig. 2).
Richter visits documenta III in Kassel and has his first exhibitions at the Friedrich & Dahlem gallery in Munich and the Schmela gallery in Düsseldorf.

1965 Graduates from the Düsseldorf Art Academy.
Richter visits the Marcel Duchamp exhibition at Museum Haus Lange in Krefeld.

1966 The first nonrepresentational paintings (cat. 7) and Color Charts (cat. 13–15).
Birth of his daughter Babette (Betty).
During a series of events at Galerie Schmela called *Hommage à Schmela*, Richter presents his only art film, *Volker Bradke*.

1967 Richter paints his series of Corrugated Irons, Tubes, Grids, and Doors (cat. 5, fig. p. 15).
He also works with glass panes for the first time (fig. p. 15).
During the summer semester acts as a visiting professor at the University of Fine Arts (HfbK) in Hamburg.

1968 After a holiday in Corsica he paints his first romantic landscapes. Richter also paints Clouds, Mountains, and Lakes, as well as abstract Windows, Shadows (cat. 4), and Streaks (cat. 3).
Richter spends an academic year teaching art at the college preparatory high school in Gerresheim.
Together with Günther Uecker, Richter stages the exhibition and performance project *Living in the Museum* (Leben im Museum) at the Kunsthalle in Baden-Baden.

1969 The first Gray paintings (cat. 25–27) and the series of Star paintings (cat. 10–12).
Richter begins compiling the *Atlas* and his catalogue raisonné.
The Zentrum für aktuelle Kunst – Gegenverkehr, an art association in Aachen, is the first public institution to mount a solo exhibition by Richter.

1970 The first Detail paintings (cat. 28, 29).
With Palermo, Richter submits a proposal for artwork to accompany two sports facilities at the Olympic Games in Munich in 1972, but it is turned down.
In November he and Palermo travel to New York. They visit Robert Ryman and James Rosenquist.

1971 Richter returns to the Color Chart theme (fig. 4, cat. 16–18) and begins his series of Inpaintings (cat. 21–24).
At the start of the summer semester, Richter is appointed a professor of painting at the Düsseldorf Art Academy (a post he holds until 1994).

1972 Richter represents West Germany at the 36th Venice Biennale and participates in documenta 5 in Kassel.
In August he travels to Greenland via Copenhagen. The photographs he takes on the journey later serve as a basis for several landscape paintings, especially seascapes.

1973 The Munich-based automobile company BMW commissions three large-scale paintings, *Red, Yellow* and *Blue* (figs. p. 16), based on the same principle as the Detail paintings.

1976 The large-scale *Construction* [389] (cat. 30) initiates the series of Abstract paintings, Richter's largest group to date (cat. 31–41, 63–74, and 80–86).

1977 The newly inaugurated Musée National d'Art Moderne at the Centre Georges Pompidou in Paris devotes a retrospective to Gerhard Richter.
The night before documenta 6 opens in Kassel, Richter removes his works because he is dissatisfied with the way they have been exhibited.

1978 Richter accepts an appointment as a visiting professor at Nova Scotia College of Art and Design in Halifax, Canada (fig. 5). His key work of this period is *128 Photographs of a Painting* (fig. p. 54).
Richter publishes it as a book in 1980 and as an edition under the title *128 Details from a Picture (Halifax 1978) II* in 1998 (cat. 46).

1979 Separates from Ema. Richter begins a new partnership with the artist Isa Genzken, and they produce joint works.

1980 Richter first uses a squeegee in making his Abstract paintings.

1982 Marries Isa Genzken.
Richter begins an extended series of Candle and Skull motifs.
He takes part in documenta 7.

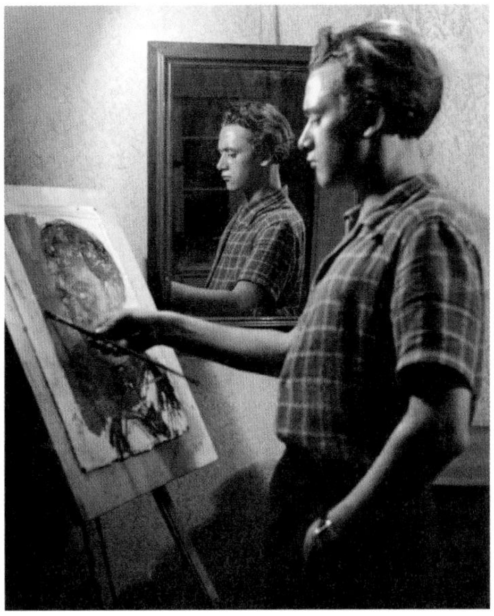

1 At his easel, Dresden, ca. 1951

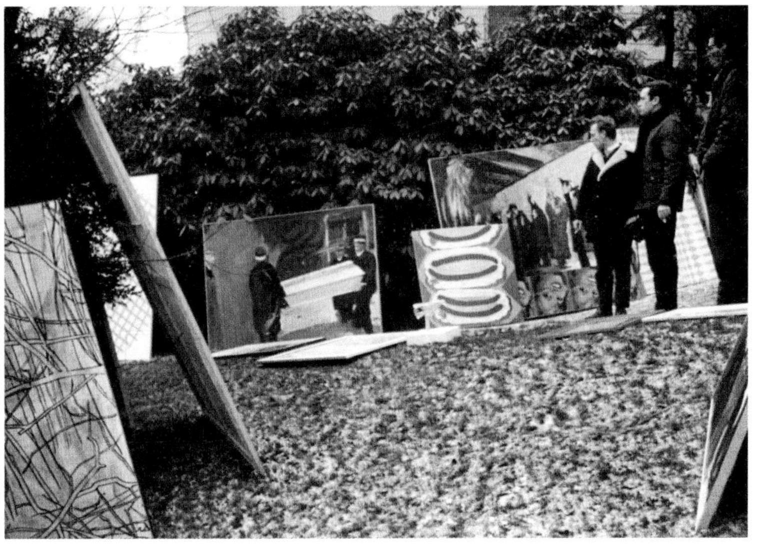

2 Manfred Kuttner, Gerhard Richter, and Konrad Lueg during the *Front Garden Exhibition*, Wuppertal, 1964

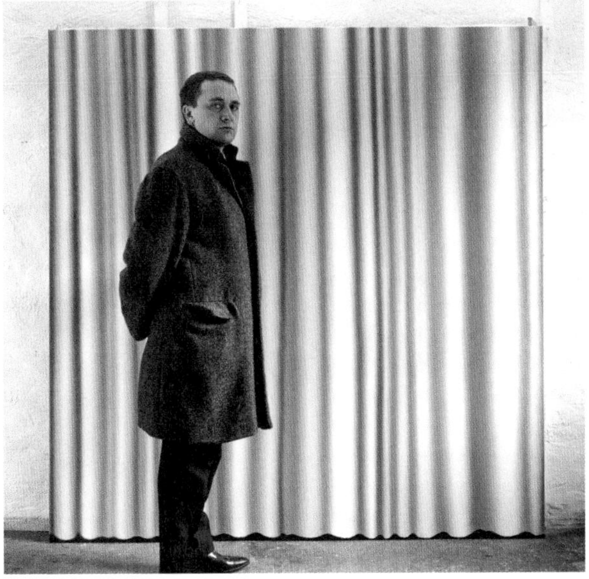

3 Standing in front of *Curtain III (Light)* [56] (cat. 2) in his studio, Düsseldorf, 1965

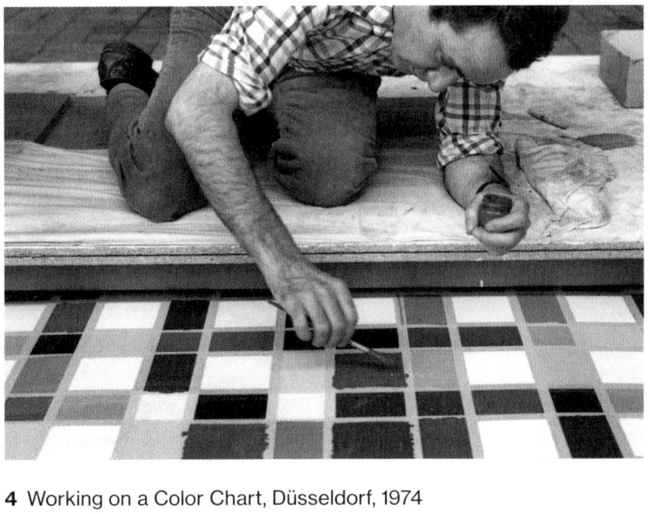

4 Working on a Color Chart, Düsseldorf, 1974

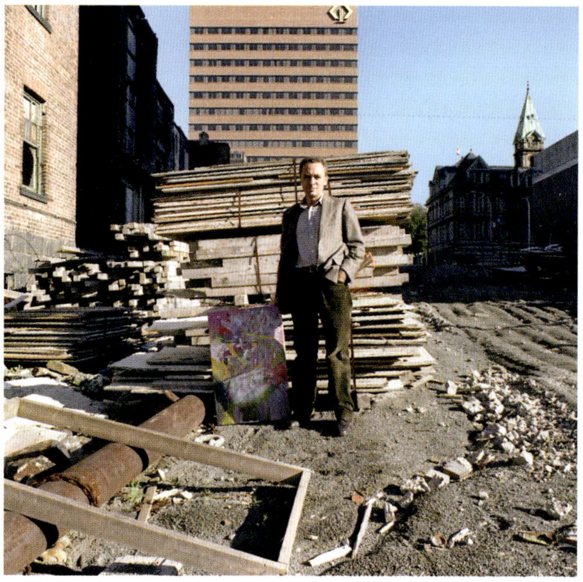

5 With *Abstract Painting (Halifax)* [432-5] (fig. p. 54), Halifax, 1978

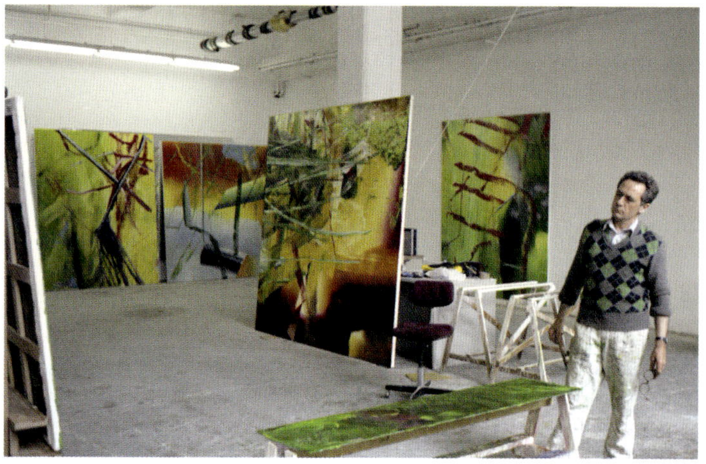

6 Working on his Abstract paintings in his studio, Cologne, 1983

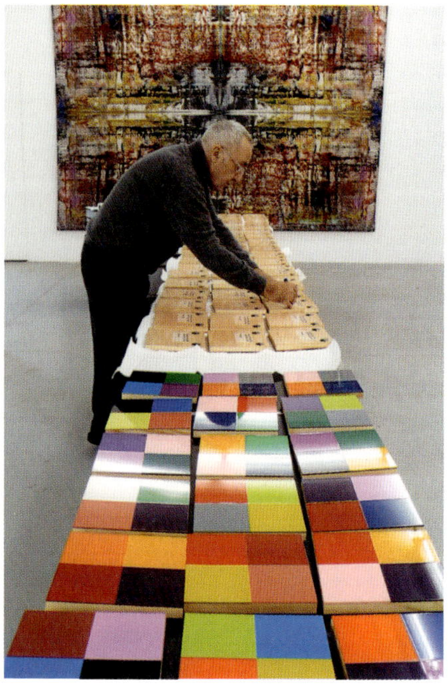

7 Signing *Quattro Colori* [Editions 138] in his studio, Cologne, 2008

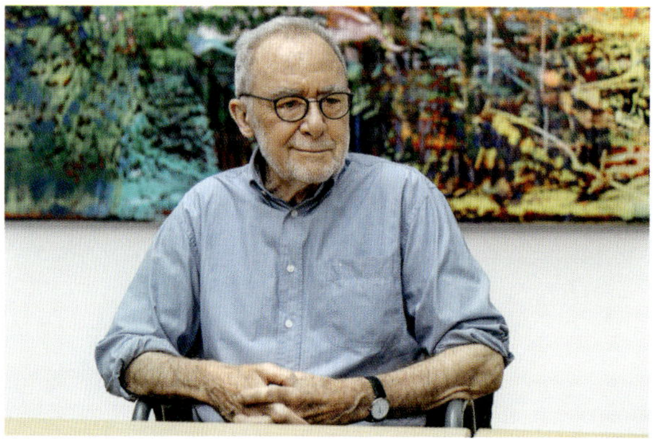

8 At the exhibition *Gerhard Richter: New Paintings* at the Albertinum, Dresden, 2017

1983 Moves from Düsseldorf to Cologne (fig. 6).

1986 Richter has a retrospective in Düsseldorf at the Städtische Kunsthalle and the Kunstverein für die Rheinlande und Westfalen, which later travels to the Neue Nationalgalerie in Berlin, the Kunsthalle in Bern, and the Museum of the 20th Century in Vienna. The first catalogue raisonné of his paintings and sculptures is published as part of the exhibition catalog.
Richter visits his birthplace, Dresden, for the first time in twenty-five years.

1988 Richter paints the fifteen-part cycle *October 18, 1977*, exploring the death of Red Army Faction members in prison at Stuttgart-Stammheim (Museum of Modern Art, New York).
He holds a visiting professorship at the Städelschule in Frankfurt am Main.

1991 Richter flies to Japan for a film project, but never completes it.

1993 A first publication of Richter's writings and a first catalogue raisonné of his editions.

1994 Richter stops teaching at the Staatliche Kunstakademie Düsseldorf.
Divorce from Isa Genzken.

1995 Birth of Richter's son Moritz.
Marries the artist Sabine Moritz.

1996 Richter begins painting on aluminum Dibond panels (cat. 20, 71).
Birth of his daughter Ella Maria.

1997 Richter is awarded the Golden Lion at the 47th Venice Biennale.
He shows his *Atlas* at documenta X.

1999 The twenty-meter-high *Black, Red, Gold* [856] is installed in the foyer of the Reichstag building in Berlin.

2002 The Museum of Modern Art in New York marks Richter's seventieth birthday with the retrospective *Gerhard Richter: Forty Years of Painting*. The show travels on to Chicago, San Francisco, and Washington, D. C.

2006 Birth of his son Theodor.
The Gerhard Richter Archive opens at the Staatliche Kunstsammlungen in Dresden.

2007 The *Cologne Cathedral Window* [900] (fig. p. 44) is completed in the south transept of Cologne Cathedral, based on the principle used in his Color Charts (cat. 13–20, fig. 7).

2008 Richter creates his first Reverse-Glass works (cat. 76, 77).
Retrospective at the National Art Museum of China, Beijing.

2011 The first works in the Strip series (cat. 78) with origins in the *Abstract Painting* [724-4] of 1990 (cat. 67).
The retrospective *Gerhard Richter: Panorama* is shown at Tate Modern in London, the Neue Nationalgalerie in Berlin, and the Musée National d'Art Moderne, Centre Pompidou in Paris.
Publication of the first volume in his six-volume catalogue raisonné.

2012 Richter shows drawings and watercolors at the Louvre in Paris.

2016 A pavilion with a permanent installation of fourteen panes of glass opens on the Japanese island of Toyoshima.

2017 The Museum Ludwig in Cologne and the Albertinum in Dresden mount the exhibition *Gerhard Richter: New Paintings* to mark the artist's eighty-fifth birthday (fig. 8).
Gerhard Richter lives and works in Cologne.

Compiled by Dietmar Elger and Valerie Hortolani

Translated from the German by Kate Vanovitch

List of Exhibited Works

Structures and Illusions: Abstract Works in the 1960s

1 *Curtain (Vorhang)* [58-1], 1964
Oil on canvas, 65 × 47 cm
Block Collection, Berlin

2 *Curtain III (Light) (Vorhang III [hell])* [56], 1965
Oil on canvas, 199.5 × 189.5 cm
Staatliche Museen zu Berlin, Nationalgalerie
Inv. no. B 1062

3 *Gray Streaks (Grauschlieren)* [192-1], 1968
Oil on canvas, 200 × 200 cm
Gerhard Richter Archive, Staatliche Kunstsammlungen Dresden, loan from a private collection

4 *Shadow Picture (Schattenbild)* [209-8], 1968
Oil on canvas, 67 × 87 cm
Collection Fundação de Serralves, Museu de Arte Contemporânea, Porto, acquired 1998
Inv. no. FS 0713

5 *Grid (Gitter)* [166], 1967
Oil on canvas, 155 × 130 cm
Vanmoerkerke Collection, Ostend

6 *Christmas Market (Weihnachtsmarkt)* [198], 1968
Oil on canvas, 67 × 87 cm
Private collection

7 *Untitled* [194-9], 1966
Oil on canvas, 80 × 40 cm
Hamburger Kunsthalle, permanent loan from the Elisabeth and Gerhard Sohst Collection
Inv. no. 300251

8 *Cloudy (Wolkig)* [194-11], 1968
Oil on canvas, 50 × 50 cm
Museum Wiesbaden
Inv. no. M 990

9 *Grid Streaks (Gitterschlieren)* [194-5], 1968
Oil on canvas, 65 × 50 cm
Museum Wiesbaden
Inv. no. M 945

10 *Star Picture (Sternbild)* [224-13], 1969
Oil on canvas, 70 × 70 cm
Private collection of Stefan Asbrand-Eickhoff, Hesse

11 *Star Picture (Sternbild)* [224-14], 1969
Oil on canvas, 70 × 70 cm
Private collection of Stefan Asbrand-Eickhoff, Hesse

12 *Star Picture (Sternbild)* [224-15], 1969
Oil on canvas, 70 × 70 cm
Private collection of Stefan Asbrand-Eickhoff, Hesse

Chance and Concept: Color Charts

13 *192 Colors (192 Farben)* [136], 1966
Oil on canvas, 200 × 150 cm
Hamburger Kunsthalle, permanent loan from the Elisabeth and Gerhard Sohst Collection
Inv. no. 300250

14 *Two Grays, One upon the Other (Zwei Grau übereinander)* [143-2], 1966
Lacquer on canvas, 200 × 130 cm
Olbricht Collection, Essen

15 *Six Colors (Sechs Farben)* [142], 1966
Lacquer on canvas, 200 × 170 cm
Neues Museum. Staatliches Museum für Kunst und Design, Nuremberg, permanent loan from a private collection

16 *1024 Colors (1024 Farben)* [351], 1973
Lacquer on canvas, 299 × 299 cm
Kunstmuseen Krefeld
Inv. no. GV 1977/583

17 *1025 Colors (1025 Farben)* [357-3], 1974
Lacquer on canvas, 120 × 123.5 cm
Private collection, Cologne

18 *1024 Colors (1024 Farben)* [356-2], 1974
Lacquer on canvas, 96 × 96 cm
Collezione Prada, Milan

19 *Abstract Painting (Abstraktes Bild)* [848-10], 1997
Oil on canvas, 36 × 51 cm
Anthony d'Offay

20 *Abstract Painting (Abstraktes Bild)* [848-11], 1997
Oil on Alucobond, 46 × 41 cm
Private collection

Gestures and Blendings: Inpaintings and Gray Paintings

21 *Untitled (Green) (Ohne Titel [grün])* [315-1 to 315-3], 1971
Oil on canvas, three parts, 200 × 150 cm each
Museum Küppersmühle für Moderne Kunst, Ströher Collection, Duisburg
Inv. no. G0938 a-b-c

22 *Inpainting (Vermalung)* [326-7], 1972
Oil on canvas, 70 × 55 cm
The "M" Art Foundation, Belgium

23 *Red-Blue-Yellow (Rot-Blau-Gelb)* [339-4], 1972
Oil on canvas, 98 × 92 cm
Private collection, Switzerland

24 *Red-Blue-Yellow (Rot-Blau-Gelb)* [333-2], 1972
Oil on canvas, 251 × 200 cm
Kunsthalle Bremen – Der Kunstverein in Bremen
Inv. no. 1142-1973/46

25 *Gray (Grau)* [334], 1972
Oil on canvas, 250 × 200 cm
Museum Küppersmühle für Moderne Kunst, Ströher Collection, Duisburg
Inv. no. G0944

26 *Gray (Grau)* [361-1], 1974
Oil on canvas, 250 × 200 cm
Museum Küppersmühle für Moderne Kunst, Ströher Collection, Duisburg
Inv. no. G0946

27 *Gray (Bark) (Grau [Borke])* [348-7], 1973
Oil on canvas, 90 × 65 cm
Private collection

Blurrings and Close-Ups: Details and Early Abstract Paintings

28 *Detail (Red-Blue) (Ausschnitt [rot-blau])* [273], 1970
Oil on canvas, 200 × 300 cm
Private collection

29 *Detail (Makart) (Ausschnitt [Makart])* [288], 1971
Oil on canvas, 200 × 200 cm
Museum Küppersmühle für Moderne Kunst, Ströher Collection, Duisburg
Inv. no. G0941

30 *Construction (Konstruktion)* [389], 1976
Oil on canvas, 250 × 300 cm
Neues Museum. Staatliches Museum für Kunst und Design, Nuremberg, permanent loan from a private collection

31 *Abstract Painting (Abstraktes Bild)* [421], 1977
Oil on canvas, 250 × 200 cm
Stedelijk van Abbemuseum, Eindhoven
Inv. no. 777

32 *Abstract Painting (Abstraktes Bild)* [436], 1978
Oil on canvas, 200 × 250 cm
Private collection, North Rhine-Westphalia

33 *Abstract Painting (Abstraktes Bild)* [449-3], 1979
Oil on canvas, 70 × 100 cm
Private collection, Switzerland

34 *Abstract Painting (Abstraktes Bild)* [479-1], 1981
Oil on canvas, 120 × 175 cm
Migros Museum für Gegenwartskunst, Zurich
Inv. no. 90578

35 *Abstract Painting (Abstraktes Bild)* [520-6], 1983
Oil on canvas, 70 × 50 cm
Sprengel Museum Hannover, permanent loan from a private collection

36 *Hedge (Hecke)* [504], 1982
Oil on canvas, 200 × 170 cm
Private collection, Hong Kong

37 *Abstract Painting (Abstraktes Bild)* [568-1], 1984
Oil on canvas, 200 × 180 cm
Private collection

38 *Pyramid (Pyramide)* [522-2], 1983
Oil on canvas, 100 × 70 cm
Würth Collection, Künzelsau
Inv. no. 10026

39 *Abstract Painting (Abstraktes Bild)* [563-1], 1984
Oil on canvas, 100 × 120 cm
Private collection, Hong Kong

40 *Abstract Painting (Abstraktes Bild)* [605-2], 1986
Oil on canvas, 62 × 72 cm
Private collection

41 *Abstract Painting (Abstraktes Bild)* [578-3], 1985
Oil on canvas, 120 × 85.5 cm
Private collection

Nature and Materials: Abstract Landscapes

42 *Abstract Painting (Abstraktes Bild)* [551-1], 1984
Oil on canvas, 43 × 60 cm
Private collection, Switzerland

43 *Abstract Painting (Abstraktes Bild)* [551-2], 1984
Oil on canvas, 43 × 60 cm
Private collection, Switzerland

44 *Abstract Painting (Abstraktes Bild)* [551-3], 1984
Oil on canvas, 43 × 60 cm
Private collection

45 *Abstract Painting (Abstraktes Bild)* [551-8], 1984
Oil on canvas, 65 × 80 cm
Private collection, Switzerland

46 *128 Details from a Picture (Halifax 1978) II (128 Photos von einem Bild [Halifax 1978] II)* [Editions 99], 1998
Eight offset prints in black and gray on cardboard, 64.2 × 100.6 cm each
Private collection

47 *Elbe* [Editions 155], 1957/2012
Thirty-one digital inkjet prints on cardboard, 29.5 × 21 cm each
Gerhard Richter Archive, Staatliche Kunstsammlungen Dresden

48 *Gray Forest (Grauwald) (10.1.08)*, 2008
Lacquer on photograph, 18.6 × 12.6 cm
Private collection

49 *Gray Forest (Grauwald) (11.1.08)*, 2008
Lacquer on photograph, 18.6 × 12.6 cm
Private collection

50 *Gray Forest (Grauwald) (12.1.08)*, 2008
Lacquer on photograph, 18.6 × 12.6 cm
Private collection

51 *Gray Forest (Grauwald) (22.1.08)*, 2008
Lacquer on photograph, 18.6 × 12.6 cm
Private collection

52 *Snow White (29.11.05)* [Editions 132], 2005
White acrylic and graphite on colored offset print, 22.5 × 32 cm
Private collection

53 *Snow White (13.12.05)* [Editions 132], 2005
White acrylic and graphite on colored offset print, 22.5 × 32 cm
Private collection

54 *Snow White (14.12.05)* [Editions 132], 2005
White acrylic and graphite on colored offset print, 22.5 × 32 cm
Private collection

55 *Snow White (1.1.06)* [Editions 132], 2006
White acrylic and graphite on colored offset print, 22.5 × 32 cm
Private collection

56 *MV. 72*, 2011
Lacquer on photograph, 10 × 15 cm
Private collection

57 *MV. 80*, 2011
Lacquer on photograph, 10 × 15 cm
Private collection

58 *MV. 12.9.11, 2011*
Lacquer on photograph, 10 × 15 cm
Private collection

59 *MV. 209*, 2011
Lacquer on photograph, 10 × 15 cm
Private collection

60 *MV. 229*, 2011
Lacquer on photograph, 10 × 15 cm
Private collection

61 *MV. 233*, 2011
Lacquer on photograph, 10 × 15 cm
Private collection

62 *40 Days (40 Tage)*, 2015
Colored offset print on paper, forty parts, thirty-five sheets 21 × 29.7 cm each, five sheets 30 × 40 cm each
Private collection

Paints and Layers: Abstract Paintings from 1986 to 2005

63 *A B, Quiet (A B, Still)* [612-4], 1986
Oil on canvas, 225 × 200 cm
Museum Barberini, Potsdam
Inv. no. S-2016-075

64 *Abstract Painting (Abstraktes Bild)* [666-2], 1988
Oil on canvas, 200 × 160 cm
Kunsthalle Emden – Stiftung Henri und Eske Nannen und Schenkung Otto van de Loo
Inv. no. 1994/29

65 *Position (Stand)* [660], 1988
Oil on canvas, 300 × 250 cm
Museum Frieder Burda, Baden-Baden
Inv. no. 185

66 *Abstract Painting (Abstraktes Bild)* [776-3], 1992
Oil on canvas, 92 × 82 cm
Private collection, Switzerland

67 *Abstract Painting (Abstraktes Bild)* [724-4], 1990
Oil on canvas, 92 × 126 cm
Private collection

68 *Abstract Painting (Abstraktes Bild)* [780-3], 1992
Oil on canvas, 260 × 200 cm
Private collection

69 *March (März)* [807], 1994
Oil on canvas, 250 × 200 cm
Gerhard Richter Archive, Staatliche Kunstsammlungen Dresden, loan from a private collection

70 *Wall (Mauer)* [808], 1994
Oil on canvas, 250 × 200 cm
Private collection

71 *Abstract Painting (Abstraktes Bild)* [860-7], 1997/1999
Oil on aluminum Dibond, 100 × 90 cm
Private collection

72 *Abstract Painting (Abstraktes Bild)* [891-4], 2005
Oil on canvas, 113.5 × 75 cm
Private collection

73 *Abstract Painting (Abstraktes Bild)* [865-2], 2000
Oil on canvas, 200 × 180 cm
Gerhard Richter Archive, Staatliche Kunstsammlungen Dresden, loan from a private collection

74 *Abstract Painting (Abstraktes Bild)* [889-10], 2004
Oil on canvas, 200 × 200 cm
Städtische Galerie im Lenbachhaus und Kunstbau, KiCo Collection, Munich
Inv. no. FH 464-2005-11

Transparent and Reflected: Mirrors, Glass, and Strips

75 *Mirror, Gray (Spiegel, grau)* [735-3], 1991
Pigment on glass, framed, 280 × 165 cm
Private collection

76 *Flow*, 2013/2016
Digital print on paper between glass and aluminum Dibond, 100 × 200 cm
Private collection

77 *Flow* [933-3], 2013
Lacquer on glass mounted on aluminum Dibond, 100 × 200 cm
Private collection

78 *Strip* [930-4], 2013/2016
Digital print on paper between aluminum Dibond and plexiglass, 200 × 1,000 cm (four panels at 200 × 250 cm each)
Private collection

79 *7 Panes of Glass (House of Cards) (7 Scheiben [Kartenhaus])* [932], 2013
Glass and steel construction, seven panes of glass, 270 × 180 cm each, 257 × 650 × 360 cm in total
Private collection

New Abstract Paintings from 2005 to 2017

80 *Abstract Painting (Abstraktes Bild)* [943-1], 2016
Oil on canvas, 144 × 220 cm
Private collection

81 *Abstract Painting (Abstraktes Bild)* [943-2], 2016
Oil on canvas, 144 × 220 cm
Gion Collection, Japan, Courtesy of Wako Works of Art

82 *Abstract Painting (Abstraktes Bild)* [946-3], 2016
Oil on canvas, 175 × 250 cm
Private collection

83 *Abstract Painting (Abstraktes Bild)* [950-3], 2017
Oil on canvas, 120 × 120 cm
Private collection

84 *Abstract Painting (Abstraktes Bild)* [950-4], 2017
Oil on canvas, 120 × 120 cm
Private collection

85 *Abstract Painting (Abstraktes Bild)* [952-2], 2017
Oil on canvas, 200 × 200 cm
Private collection

86 *Abstract Painting (Abstraktes Bild)* [952-3], 2017
Oil on canvas, 200 × 200 cm
Private collection

Without Plates

87 *Gray Forest (Grauwald) (13.1.08)*, 2008
Lacquer on photograph, 18.6 × 12.6 cm
Private collection

88 *Gray Forest (Grauwald) (14.1.08)*, 2008
Lacquer on photograph, 18.6 × 12.6 cm
Private collection

89 *Gray Forest (Grauwald) (21.1.08)*, 2008
Lacquer on photograph, 18.6 × 12.6 cm
Private collection

90 *Gray Forest (Grauwald) (14.2.08)*, 2008
Lacquer on photograph, 18.6 × 12.6 cm
Private collection

91 *Gray Forest (Grauwald) (25.2.08)*, 2008
Lacquer on photograph, 18.6 × 12.6 cm
Private collection

92 *Gray Forest (Grauwald) (7.3.08)*, 2008
Lacquer on photograph, 12.6 × 18.6 cm
Private collection

93 *Gray Forest (Grauwald) (10.3.08)*, 2008
Lacquer on photograph, 12.6 × 18.6 cm
Private collection

94 *Gray Forest (Grauwald) (14.3.08)*, 2008
Lacquer on photograph, 18.6 × 12.6 cm
Private collection

The number in square brackets following the title is a reference to Gerhard Richter's catalogue raisonné: see Elger 2011–2017.
The term 'Editions' in square brackets followed by a number is a reference to the catalogue raisonné of Richter's prints: see Butin et al. 2014.

Selected Bibliography

Amsterdam 1987
Gerhard Richter. Werken op papier 1983–1986. Amsterdam: Museum Overholland, 1987. Exhibition catalog.

Ansted 2017
Ansted, Darryn. *The Artwork of Gerhard Richter: Painting, Critical Theory and Cultural Transformation.* London, 2017.

Belz 2011
Belz, Corinna (writer and director). *Gerhard Richter Painting.* Documentary film, Germany 2011, 97 minutes.

Berlin 2002
Gerhard Richter: Acht Grau. Berlin: Deutsche Guggenheim, 2002. Exhibition catalog. English edition available.

Bielefeld 1982
Gerhard Richter. Abstrakte Bilder 1976–1981. Bielefeld: Kunsthalle, 1982. Exhibition catalog.

Bonn 2017
Gerhard Richter. Über Malen – Frühe Bilder. Bonn: Kunstmuseum, 2017. Exhibition catalog. English edition available.

Brisbane 2017
Gerhard Richter: The Life of Images. Brisbane: Queensland Art Gallery, 2017. Exhibition catalog.

Buchloh 2009
Buchloh, Benjamin H. D., ed. *Gerhard Richter*. Cambridge, MA, 2009.

Buchloh 2013
Buchloh, Benjamin H. D. *Scheiben und Strips von Gerhard Richter*. Cologne, 2013.

Buchloh 2016
Buchloh, Benjamin H. D. *Gerhard Richters Birkenau-Bilder*. Cologne, 2016.

Burgdorf 2005
Gerhard Richter. Ohne Farbe/Without Color. Burgdorf: Museum Franz Gertsch, 2005. Exhibition catalog.

Butin et al. 2014
Butin, Hubertus, Stefan Gronert, and Stefan Olbricht, eds. *Gerhard Richter. Editionen 1965–2013.* Ostfildern, 2014. English edition available.

Cologne 2007
Gerhard Richter – Zufall, das Kölner Domfenster und 4900 Farben. Cologne: Museum Ludwig, 2007. Exhibition catalog.

Cologne 2008
Gerhard Richter. Abstrakte Bilder. Cologne: Museum Ludwig, 2008. Exhibition catalog. English edition available.

Cologne 2017
Gerhard Richter. Neue Bilder. Cologne: Museum Ludwig, 2017. Exhibition catalog. English edition available.

Dresden 2013
Gerhard Richter. Streifen und Glas. Dresden: Staatliche Kunstsammlungen Dresden, Galerie Neue Meister, Albertinum, 2013. Exhibition catalog.

Düsseldorf 1986
Gerhard Richter. Bilder 1962–1985. Düsseldorf: Städtische Kunsthalle, 1986. Exhibition catalog.

Düsseldorf 2005
Gerhard Richter. Düsseldorf: K20 Kunstsammlung Nordrhein-Westfalen, 2005. Exhibition catalog. English edition available.

Elger 2008
Elger, Dietmar. *Gerhard Richter. Maler.* Cologne, 2008.

Elger 2009a
Elger, Dietmar. *Gerhard Richter: A Life in Painting*. Chicago, IL, 2009. German edition available.

Elger 2009b
Elger, Dietmar, ed. *Gerhard Richter. Texte zu 4900 Farben*. Ostfildern, 2009.

Elger 2011–2017
Elger, Dietmar. *Gerhard Richter. Catalogue Raisonné*, 4 vols. [6 vols. planned]. Ostfildern, 2011–17.

Elger 2018
Elger, Dietmar. *Gerhard Richter. Maler*, third updated and extended edition. Cologne, 2018.

Elger/Küster 2011
Elger, Dietmar and Kerstin Küster, eds. *Gerhard Richter. Fotografie als Malerei – Malerei als Fotografie. Acht Texte zu Gerhard Richters Medienstrategie*. Cologne, 2011.

Friedel 2011
Friedel, Helmut. *Gerhard Richter. Rot / Gelb / Blau. Die Gemälde für BMW*. Munich, 2011. English edition available.

Friedrich 2009
Friedrich, Julia. *Grau ohne Grund. Gerhard Richters Monochromien als Herausforderungen der künstlerischen Avantgarde*. Cologne, 2009.

Gelshorn 2012
Gelshorn, Julia. *Aneignung und Wiederholung. Bilddiskurse im Werk von Gerhard Richter und Sigmar Polke*. Munich, 2012.

Hamburg 2011
Gerhard Richter. Bilder einer Epoche. Hamburg: Bucerius Kunst Forum, 2011. Exhibition catalog. English edition available.

Honnef 1976
Honnef, Klaus. *Gerhard Richter*. Recklinghausen, 1976.

Kasper 2003
Kasper, Astrid. *Gerhard Richter. Malerei als Thema der Malerei*. Berlin, 2003.

Katz 2012
Katz, Benjamin. *Gerhard Richter at Work*. Munich, 2012.

Klinger 2013
Klinger, Florian. *Theorie der Form. Gerhard Richter und die Kunst des pragmatischen Zeitalters*. Munich, 2013.

Leverkusen 2008
Gerhard Richter. Übermalte Fotografien. Leverkusen: Museum Morsbroich, 2008. Exhibition catalog.

London 2008
Gerhard Richter. 4900 Colours: Version II. London: Serpentine Gallery, 2008. Exhibition catalog.

London 2011
Gerhard Richter. Panorama. London: Tate Modern, 2011. Exhibition catalog.

London 2015
Gerhard Richter. Colour Charts. London: Dominique Lévy Gallery, 2015. Exhibition catalog.

Mehring et al. 2010
Mehring, Christine, Jeanne Anne Nugent, and Jon L. Sedyll, eds. *Gerhard Richter: Early Work, 1951–1972*. Los Angeles, CA, 2010.

Mönchengladbach 1974
Gerhard Richter. Graue Bilder. Mönchengladbach: Städtisches Museum Abteiberg, 1974. Exhibition catalog.

New York 2002
Gerhard Richter. Forty Years of Painting. New York: The Museum of Modern Art, 2002. Exhibition catalog.

New York 2005
Gerhard Richter. New York: Marian Goodman Gallery, 2005. Exhibition catalog.

New York 2012
Gerhard Richter – Strip Paintings. New York: Marian Goodman Gallery, 2012. Exhibition catalog.

New York 2016
Gerhard Richter: Abstract Paintings and Drawings. New York: Marian Goodman Gallery, 2016. Exhibition catalog.

Nuremberg 2014
Gerhard Richter – Ausschnitt. Werke aus der Sammlung Böckmann/Detail: Paintings from the Böckmann Collection. Nuremberg: Neues Museum. Staatliches Museum für Kunst und Design, 2014. Exhibition catalog.

Obrist 1996
Obrist, Hans Ulrich, ed. *Gerhard Richter. 100 Bilder*. Ostfildern, 1996. English edition available.

Obrist/Schwarz 2013
Obrist, Hans Ulrich and Dieter Schwarz, eds. *Gerhard Richter. Bücher*. Cologne: Gerhard Richter Archive Dresden, 2013. English edition available.

Paris 2011
Gerhard Richter. Painting 2010–2011. Paris: Marian Goodman Gallery, 2011. Exhibition catalog.

Prague 2017
Gerhard Richter. Prague: National Gallery, 2017. Exhibition catalog.

Richter 1980
Richter, Gerhard. *128 Details from a Picture (Halifax 1978)*. Halifax, 1980.

Richter 1996
Richter, Gerhard. *Abstraktes Bild 825-11, 69 Details*. Frankfurt am Main, 1996. English edition available.

Richter 1998
Richter, Gerhard. *128 Fotos von einem Bild (WVZ 432-5), Halifax 1978*. Cologne, 1998.

Richter 2008
Richter, Gerhard. *Text 1961 bis 2007. Schriften, Interviews, Briefe*, edited by Dietmar Elger and Hans Ulrich Obrist. Cologne, 2008.

Richter 2009
Richter, Gerhard. *Text: Writings, Interviews and Letters 1961–2007*, edited by Dietmar Elger and Hans Ulrich Obrist. London, 2009.

Richter 2012
Richter, Gerhard. *Patterns*. Cologne, 2012.

Richter 2015a
Richter, Gerhard. *Atlas*, edited by Helmut Friedel. Cologne, 2015. English edition available.

Richter 2015b
Richter, Gerhard. *Birkenau*. Cologne, 2015.

Richter 2017
Richter, Gerhard. *40 Tage*. London, 2017.

Riehen 2014
Gerhard Richter. Bilder/Serien. Riehen/Basel: Fondation Beyeler, 2014. Exhibition catalog. English edition available.

Schwarz 2009
Schwarz, Dieter. *Gerhard Richter. Elbe 1957*, edited by the Gerhard Richter Archive Dresden, Cologne, 2009.

Storr 2009
Storr, Robert. *Gerhard Richter. Die Cage-Bilder*. Cologne, 2009.

Tokyo 2006
Gerhard Richter. Snow White. Tokyo: Wako Works of Art, 2006. Exhibition catalog.

Venice 1972
Gerhard Richter. Venice: German Pavilion, 36th Biennale, 1972. Exhibition catalog.

Wilmes 2009
Wilmes, Ulrich. *Gerhard Richter. Zur Entstehung der Abstrakten Bilder*. Dresden, 2009.

Winterthur 1999
Gerhard Richter. Aquarelle/Watercolors. Winterthur: Kunstmuseum, 1999. Exhibition catalog.

Authors

Janice Bretz has worked for the Gerhard Richter Archive at the Staatliche Kunstsammlungen Dresden since 2014. She studied art history, history, and architecture at the Technische Universität in Dresden, writing a master's thesis on the depiction of public figures in the work of Gerhard Richter and Andy Warhol.

Hubertus Butin is a writer and curator in Berlin. He studied art history in Bonn and Zurich. From 1996 to 1998, he worked at Gerhard Richter's studio in Cologne as an art history assistant before embarking on a career as a guest curator at museums in Germany and abroad. Since 1991, he has published numerous essays and books on contemporary art and art theory. He edited the catalogue raisonné of Richter's editions (2014) and the contemporary art dictionary *Begriffslexikon zur zeitgenössischen Kunst* (an updated, extended edition was published in 2014). He is currently working on a book about art forgeries and organizing a Richter exhibition in Vienna, to open in 2020.

Dietmar Elger has headed the Gerhard Richter Archive at the Staatliche Kunstsammlungen Dresden since 2006 and is curator of post-1945 art at the neighboring Galerie Neue Meister. He studied art history, history, and literature at the University of Hamburg, obtaining his doctorate in 1984 with a dissertation on Kurt Schwitters's *Merzbau*. From 1984 to 1985, he worked at Richter's studio as a secretary. From 1985 to 1988, he was deputy director at the Museum am Ostwall, Dortmund, then from 1989 to 2006 a curator of painting and sculpture at the Sprengel Museum, Hannover. He has authored numerous publications and exhibitions on Richter, including the biography *Gerhard Richter: A Life in Painting* (new, updated, German edition published in 2018), and is currently compiling the six-volume catalogue raisonné of Richter's paintings and sculptures.

Valerie Hortolani has been a curator at the Museum Barberini since 2016. She studied art history, musicology, and media studies in Marburg and at the Humboldt University in Berlin. From 2014 to 2016, she worked as an assistant curator at the Kunstsammlung Nordrhein-Westfalen in Düsseldorf, where she organized exhibitions on twentieth-century and contemporary art, including *Miró: Painting as Poetry* (2015, in collaboration with the Bucerius Kunst Forum, Hamburg) and *Alberto Burri: The Trauma of Painting* (2016, in collaboration with the Solomon R. Guggenheim Museum, New York), and developed several installations in the artists' room series. She recently curated the exhibition *Behind the Mask: Artists in the GDR* at the Museum Barberini (2017).

Matthias Krüger is an acting professor at the Ludwig Maximilians Universität in Munich, with a focus on twentieth-century and contemporary art. He studied art history, philosophy, and English in Hamburg, and in 2004 wrote a dissertation on the response of nineteenth-century art critics in France to applications of thick paint. Since 2005, he has been a research fellow, academic assistant, guest lecturer, and visiting professor at the universities of Hamburg, Munich, Bern, and Bamberg. He has written widely on modern art, with a focus on the materials, tools, and techniques used in painting, most recently for the exhibition *Manet: Painting the Gaze* at the Hamburger Kunsthalle (2016), and on Olafur Eliasson's *Weather Project* in the conference proceedings he coedited, titled *The Eighth Day: Images of Nature in 21st-Century Art* (2016).

Kerstin Küster has been working as a research associate for the Gerhard Richter Archive at the Staatliche Kunstsammlungen Dresden since 2008. She studied art history and modern German literature at the Technische Universität in Dresden, writing a graduate thesis in 2009 on the role of grisaille in the work of Pieter Bruegel the Elder. From 2009 to 2013, she was a researcher at the Technische Universität on the interdisciplinary DFG project "Transcendence and Public Spirit."

Ortrud Westheider was appointed director of the Museum Barberini in 2016. Her doctoral thesis treated the color black in the paintings of Max Beckmann. From 1998 to 2001, she worked at the Kunsthalle Bremen and the Westfälisches Landesmuseum in Münster. In 2002, she joined the Bucerius Kunst Forum in Hamburg as a curator, and served as its director from 2006 to 2016. Her exhibitions there included *Frida Kahlo* (2006), *Matisse: People, Masks, Models* (2009), *Gerhard Richter: Images of an Era* (2011), *New York Photography 1890–1950: From Stieglitz to Man Ray* (2012), *Rodchenko: A New Era* (2013), and *Picasso: Window to the World* (2016). At the Museum Barberini she was curator for the exhibitions *Impressionism: The Art of Landscape* (2017) and *Max Beckmann: The World as a Stage* (2018).

Armin Zweite is a Munich-based art historian and curator. He studied German, history, philosophy, and art history. In 1970, he was awarded his doctorate for a dissertation on Marten de Vos and art in sixteenth-century Antwerp. From 1970 to 1971, he was a visiting scholar at the University of California, Berkeley. From 1974 to 1990, he directed the Städtische Galerie im Lenbachhaus in Munich. He was appointed Federal Republic of Germany commissioner for the Bienal Internacional de São Paulo in 1983, 1985, and 1987. From 1990 to 2007, he was director of the Kunstsammlung Nordrhein-Westfalen in Düsseldorf, and from 2008 to 2013, he was director of the Brandhorst Collection in Munich. He has published numerous works and curated exhibitions on classical modernism and contemporary art, including on Der Blaue Reiter, Bernd and Hilla Becher, Joseph Beuys, Barnett Newman, Richard Serra, Mark Rothko, Katharina Sieverding, and Gerhard Richter.

Image Credits

Unless otherwise stated, all images are courtesy of the studio of Gerhard Richter, supplied by the Dr. Cantz'sche Druckerei, Esslingen.

Additional images have been provided by:
Ettore Products Company, Alameda, CA, USA: p. 64 middle left
akg-images, Berlin: p. 15 above (MONDADORI PORTFOLIO, Electa, photo: Sergio Anelli), p. 64 below (De Agostini Picture Library)
Archive of Hubertus Butin, Berlin: p. 39 above and below (photo: Dorothee Fischer), 40 below
Lutz Bertram, Berlin: pp. 168–69, 175
bpk, Berlin: National Portrait Gallery, Smithsonian Institution / Art Resource, NY: p. 61 above (photo: Hans Namuth): · RMN – Grand Palais: p. 67 above (photo: Hervé Lewandowski)
RECOM ART, Berlin: pp. 120–21, 141
zero one film, Berlin: p. 61 middle and below (director and screenwriter: Corinna Belz)
Gerhard Richter Archive, Staatliche Kunstsammlungen Dresden: pp. 24 below right, 27 above, 28 above, 31 above, 31 middle, 31 below, 36 below, 43 below, 54 above right, 54 below right, 154, 231 above, 231 middle left, 231 below, 232 above, 232 middle left, 232 middle right, 232 below (photo: David Pinzer)
SCALA, Florence: The Museum of Modern Art, New York 2018: p. 19 below
Hubert Becker, Cologne: pp. 162 below, 163 above, 163 below, 208–09
Ernst Wilhelm Nay Stiftung, Cologne: p. 36 above
Parrotta Contemporary Art, Cologne: pp. 226–27 (photo: Timm Rautert)
Hohe Domkirche Köln, Dombauhütte Köln: p. 44 (photo: Matz and Schenk)
Benjamin Katz, Cologne: p. 54 middle left
Zentralarchiv für deutsche und internationale Kunstmarktforschung (ZADIK), Cologne: p. 231 middle right (photo: Rolf Jährling, Galerie Parnass)
Archive of Ugo Mulas, Milan: p. 62 above (photo: Ugo Mulas)
Collezione Prada, Milan: pp. 88–89, 101 (photo: Roberto Marossi)
Collection of Rodchenko/Stepanova, Moscow: p. 16 below
K.O. Götz und Rissa-Stiftung, Niederbreibach-Wolfenacker: p. 62 below (photo: Willi Kemp)
Printmanagement Plitt, Oberhausen: pp. 193–94, 204–05
Saarlandmuseum Saarbrücken, Stiftung Saarländischer Kulturbesitz: p. 10 below (photo: Tom Gundelwein)
Salzburg Museum, Salzburg: p. 67 below
Private collection, Switzerland: pp. 104–05, 113
ARTOTHEK, Weilheim: p. 13 middle (Fine Art Images)

One image was taken from the following publication:
Anthea Callen, *The Art of Impressionism: Painting Technique and the Making of Modernity* (New Haven: Yale University Press, 2000), 138: p. 64 middle right

Colophon

This catalog was published in conjunction with the exhibition

Gerhard Richter: Abstraction
Museum Barberini, Potsdam
June 30 to October 21, 2018

Editors:
Ortrud Westheider and Michael Philipp

Exhibition:
Dietmar Elger and Ortrud Westheider
with Valerie Hortolani

in cooperation with the
Gerhard Richter Archive, Staatliche
Kunstsammlungen Dresden

Catalog Editor:
Valerie Hortolani

Picture Editors:
Anne Barz and Valerija Kuzema

Museum Barberini, Potsdam

Director:
Ortrud Westheider
Director Finance and Administration:
Claudia Thurow
Chief Curator:
Michael Philipp
Curator:
Daniel Zamani
Publications:
Sophie Reinhardt
Research Associates:
Linda Hacka, Julia Nagel
Registrar:
Anne Barz
Press and Communications:
Achim Klapp, Marte Kräher, Esther Knut
Information Management:
Remigiusz Plath
Personal Assistant to the Director:
Theresa Büning
Educational Service:
Dorothee Entrup, Andrea Schmidt
Events:
Marie-Christin Hupp, Julia Teller, Ines
Wenzel-Hirschfeld
Guest Management:
Jutta Bockhacker, Frauke Herlyn,
Vanessa Souli
Administration:
Sandra Spudy
Building Services:
Carsten Loeper, Frank Altmann,
Dennis Kokert

In collaboration with:
Conservation:
Felicitas Klein, Berlin
Friederike Beseler, Berlin
Exhibition Design:
Gunther Maria Kolck, Hamburg
BrücknerAping, Büro für Gestaltung,
Bremen
Museum Shop:
Museum Barberini. Der Shop,
Jörg Klambt

Catalog

Catalog front cover:
Gerhard Richter
Abstract Painting [952-2], 2017, cat. 85

2nd edition 2024

Editorial Direction, Prestel:
Markus Eisen
Graphic Design and Typesetting:
BrücknerAping, Büro für Gestaltung,
Bremen
Copyediting:
Sylee Gore, Only Today, Berlin
Proofreading:
Chris Murray, Nantwich
Translations from the German:
Steven Lindberg
Allison Moseley
Kate Vanovitch
Production Management:
Cilly Klotz
Separations:
Reproline Genceller, Munich
Printing and Binding:
Printer Trento, Trento
Typeface:
Neue Haas Grotesk
Paper:
150 g/m² Garda Matt Ultra

FSC www.fsc.org MIX Paper from responsible sources FSC® C015829

Penguin Random House Verlagsgruppe
FSC® N001967

Printed in Italy

A CIP catalog record for this book is available from the British Library.

ISBN 978-3-7913-7969-2
(German edition)

ISBN 978-3-7913-5992-2
(English edition)

www.prestel.de
www.prestel.com